THE GUIDE TO

The Handling of People

a systems approach

6th edition

hop 6

First published 1981
Second edition 1987
Third edition 1992
Reprinted January 1993 with amendments largely in Chapter 2
Fourth edition 1997
Reprinted February 1998 with revisions
Reprinted August 1998
Reprinted February 1999
Fifth edition 2005
Sixth edition 2011

Designed and produced by Pages Creative, Cheltenham

Illustrations by Gemma Hastilow and Kate Hitchen

Printed by Severnprint, Gloucester, on Purpose Offset 90gsm, Forest Stewardship Council certified

A catalogue record for this publication is available from the British Library
ISBN 978-0-9530528-1-3

Published by BackCare, the charity for healthier backs (registered as the National Back Pain Association).
16 Elmtree Road, Teddington, Middlesex, TW11 8ST

Tel: 020 8977 5474 Fax: 020 8943 5318 Website: www.backcare.org.uk

© BackCare

Forewords

BackCare

Moving and handling of people is, for many, a fact of everyday working life. Emergency and regular medical interventions frequently rely on it. Much of social care cannot be effective without similar assistance. Training staff how to do this is, of course, essential, but this alone is not enough. All too often, without appropriate work design, a clear understanding of the real issues and the monitoring and reinforcing of good practice, things go wrong. The service, the carer and cared for are put at risk both by direct practical mistakes and, more importantly, by the errors of understanding that allow or even encourage mistakes to be made before and after handling people.

It is self evident that mishandling of people could sometimes injure the back or trigger back pain. People with back pain will perhaps, understandably, avoid tasks for fear of aggravating an injury. But most instances of back pain at work are not caused by injury and not caused by work. Responding to them as if they were an injury when they are is, of course, correct. However, responding to them as if they were an injury when they are not is potentially very damaging, leading to care failures, unnecessary incapacity and reduced service performance. The latter is far more common than the former.

The Guide to The Handling of People, now in its 6th edition, provides the leading source of evidence based instruction and guidance.

HOP6 is for service managers, trainers and practitioners. The systems essential to introducing, maintaining, performing and reviewing safe, dignified and purposeful handling cannot be achieved by accident; the subject is far too complex for that and misunderstanding is still the norm. Good judgement is required. The expertise and experience captured in *HOP6* is without parallel. The lessons of research, best practice and professional judgement are combined in one resource.

BackCare is extremely grateful for the significant contribution of the National Back Exchange in the production of this book, and thanks all those who contributed to it as authors, peer reviewers and members of the production team.

Dr Andrew Auty
Chairman of the board of trustees

National Back Exchange

National Back Exchange is an international organisation that is passionate about reducing manual handling risks to both staff and the people they care for, and has been since it was founded in 1988. Then, as now, members have been carrying out research and gathering evidence to improve practice.

Since 2004, National Back Exchange has worked closely with BackCare and the editorial team in the production of *The Handling of People* series and we are again delighted to be involved with the latest edition. The series has been used as evidence of good practice in numerous court cases and has helped organisations, staff and manual handling practitioners across health, social care and education to develop robust training programmes and safer systems of work, based on sound evidence of best practice.

The Guide to The Handling of People, 6th edition, concentrates more on these systems and strategies, taking into account the important elements of manual handling; legal framework, risk assessment, ergonomics and biomechanics. In this edition, there are new chapters concentrating on organisation and policy, training, equipment and staff health and wellbeing to enhance our strategic planning.

As with the previous edition, the practical chapters and two chapters looking at bariatric management, and falls prevention and management, are supported by research and evidence collected by members of National Back Exchange. In order to develop further the field of people handling and to continue to safeguard both staff and those who are dependent on their care, National Back Exchange feels strongly that this research continues.

National Back Exchange has no doubt that this book will be a vital resource and will continue to have a significant impact.

Mike Betts
Chairman

Royal College of Nursing

Thirty years have elapsed since The Royal College of Nursing first collaborated with BackCare to launch the *Handling of Patients – a Guide for Nurse Managers*. Since its involvement in launching this pioneering work, the RCN has expended much effort through its professional and trade union work, in promoting change in healthcare safety culture in an effort to minimise the risk of injury to handlers, and people being handled, alike. In doing so, it benefited greatly from its relationships with BackCare, National Back Exchange and other stakeholders, not least through the RCN Back Pain Panel. Through its legal services, the RCN handled much of the early litigation in the field on behalf of injured members, relying in part on the accepted best practice of the time, set out in successive editions, and succeeded in many cases in persuading the courts that those practices represented what the reasonable employer was under a duty to ensure as a minimum standard to avoid legal liability. I relied on previous editions myself in acting as an expert witness.

The arrival of this 6th edition is a fitting way to celebrate this now seminal publication's 30th birthday, and, with the most helpful introduction by Jacqui Smith, gives us an opportunity to reflect on how far we have travelled during those 30 years. The healthcare workplace is now safer, at least to the extent that handling accidents and acute injury are less frequent, but, sadly, this has not substantially reduced the incidence of musculoskeletal injury, which, along with the physical and psychological injury caused by work related stress and violent assault, remain far too high.

Health and safety law and the Human Rights Act have had a bad press over the years, but sensibly interpreted, as by the authors of this new edition, underpin what is good professional and management practice. The adoption of the "systems" approach, and the provision of tools to inform the careful balancing of risk and benefits, combines good health and safety management and nursing professional practice. Handling assessments in individual cases are not always so easy in practice, and this is where the practical advice in this new edition is so invaluable.

On behalf of the RCN, I commend this new edition to the nursing and caring professions at all levels, as well as to those who manage and fund healthcare provision, and am confident that it will help to further advance standards of care, and of health and safety, for the benefit of all.

Dr Peter Carter
Chief executive and general secretary

CHARTERED
SOCIETY
OF
PHYSIOTHERAPY

Chartered Society of Physiotherapy

The Chartered Society of Physiotherapy (CSP) is delighted to welcome this latest edition of *The Guide to The Handling of People*, which provides the reader with current information relating to all aspects of moving and handling.

Moving and handling people is a core activity of many engaged in health and social care. Local and national organisations have policies in place in order to maintain the health and wellbeing of their workforce, while considering the needs of those to whom they provide care. *HOP6* provides information on current legislation, national policy, core handling skills and examples, alongside evidence based advice and recommendations on the process of assessing risk, planning, recording and implementing management activity. This is delivered in a clear format against which organisations may compare and revise local manual handling policies. It also articulates the competencies required by the workforce to meet the needs of individuals.

Musculoskeletal disorders in handlers continue to be a source of concern, both in lost productivity and in the impact on the handlers' lives. The responsibility for safer moving and handling sits at every level of an organisation, from regular policy review, through budget allocation, to implementation and training. The real value of this publication can be analysed, as the cost of lost productivity through sickness absence from injury is an area of potential cost savings to organisations.

The content of *HOP6* has been written and peer reviewed by acknowledged experts in the fields of moving and handling people and the associated legislation. Chartered physiotherapists use movement and activity in their work and many of the chapters in this resource have been written by members of the CSP. The CSP is campaigning for people to *Move for Health* and to increase their daily activity. Activity is acknowledged as essential for health, yet many adopt an increasingly sedentary lifestyle, poorly equipping them for the demands of manual work, or a healthier older age. This resource provides the detailed framework to help handlers, family and individuals move safely while facilitating movement in those less able to move independently.

I congratulate BackCare on its latest edition of *The Guide to The Handling of People*, which contributes to the health and safety of so many; in particular, to the additional section on moving and handling and enablement in bariatrics, and the prevention and management of falls.

Léonie Dawson
Professional adviser

College of Occupational Therapists

Occupational therapists, like other healthcare professionals, have been, and continue to be, predisposed to musculoskeletal disorders, which may be directly related to their involvement with people with both mental and physical disabilities. Having comprehensive guidance and information to assist the therapist to make a sound decision in what can, on occasions, be complex situations, can only assist in reducing risks to both the person being assisted and the person providing the assistance. Assisting and advising people with functional movement and mobility is an integral part of being an occupational therapist and during 2006 the College of Occupational Therapists published its own clinical guidance to manual handling, assisting clinicians to manage the many situations in which occupational therapists find themselves. The 5th edition of *The Guide to The Handling of People* (2005) was an important publication that was influential in developing the aforementioned guidance (COT 2006). The publication focused on both researched evidence and the importance of peer review and the use of assessment tools such as REBA, Mobility Gallery and the Functional Independence Measure, to assist people to make a "balanced decision" where the needs (and opinions) of the person requiring assistance were as important as the health and wellbeing of the person providing the assistance or treatment.

This new 6th edition demonstrates an evolution in the handling of people guidance, building on the extensive information and advice provided in the previous editions, while simultaneously reflecting on the current legislative climate and the most up to date research evidence. Notably a development of the previous editions, the 6th edition addresses key strategies that should be adopted to form the basis of effective management of manual handling risks, areas such as communication, training effectiveness and competencies, and enforces the need for involvement of management at all levels in protecting staff and people within our care from harm or injury.

The 6th edition continues to reinforce the importance of sound and balanced decision making by individual clinicians. It provides valuable and constructive guidance and evidence related to the core principles of safe handling of people and the core skills related to the use and prescription of manual handling equipment, the use of which will assist the therapist to make sound clinical decisions based on the needs of people (clients and handlers alike) within their care, rather than the mere prescriptive application of techniques.

Peggy Frost
Head of professional practice

Sara Thomas
Manual handling consultant
on behalf of The College of Occupational Therapists

Institute of Ergonomics & Human Factors

It is 30 years since the 1st edition of *The Handling of People* series was published and already six years since the 5th edition. There have been many changes in all aspects of this extensive and diverse subject over these 30 years so, as a key reference book for several professions, it is essential that the contents are frequently revised and kept up to date. New developments in technology, evidence, practice and procedures, legislation and even the characteristics of the people to be handled all need to be covered.

There is an increasing understanding of the importance of safe systems of work as recognised and advocated by the Health and Safety Executive and this is complemented by the growing body of knowledge in ergonomics, as systematically applied to health and social care provision and patient safety. *HOP6* has a number of new chapters not included in previous editions, including core hoisting skills, providing a useful insight into the promotion of safer systems or recognition of unsafe or risky systems/practices, together with a summary of the range of devices now available, their operating principles and how to use them. Chapter 3 describes the whole range of ergonomics involvement, especially from a systems perspective, from micro (individual) to macro (organisational) level applications, with the meso level in between. The importance of ergonomics towards influencing the culture of an organisation, as well as protecting health and social care workers, and those to whom they provide care, from harm, comes across convincingly. Ergonomics offers tools to understand problems and assess risks, methods to assist with the design of improved workplaces and working practices and, finally, procedures for effecting successful interventions. These apply at all levels of management and their adoption helps define the "corporate culture".

No book will ever be able to provide all the answers to situations that may confront back care practitioners and others regarding the handling of people. However, by presenting some basic theory together with relevant techniques, equipment and insight into the current legislation plus the encouragement to adopt a systems approach, this edition makes a further significant contribution towards evolving best practice. Personal experience is, arguably, the best form of on the job training. Nevertheless, I would contend that consulting this book to help analyse and reflect on professional judgements, in order to refine and review your professional performance, will enhance your continuing professional development and, thus, professional capabilities.

Dr Dave O'Neill
Chief executive

Health and Safety Executive

I am pleased to provide a foreword to support this latest edition of *The Guide to The Handling of People*, which has been produced by experts from the health and social care sectors who have first hand practical experience of the risks associated with their sectors.

Over the past 30 years, the series has helped a great deal in raising the profile of safer handling practice, providing guidance for practitioners, managers and health and safety professionals.

During this period, safer manual handling techniques have continued to evolve and the range, sophistication and availability of handling equipment has grown. Simultaneously, a wealth of competent advice has been developed and has been made available to NHS and private sector organisations.

Nonetheless, manual handling injury and musculoskeletal disorders continue to cause significant sickness absence. In the NHS alone, musculoskeletal disorders account for around 40 per cent of sickness absence. In social care, handling injuries accounted for over a quarter of all reported injuries to employees in 2009/10.

Moving and handling of people, who are often frail and incapacitated, continues to be an important part of care and nursing activities. Training, as well as access to sound, common sense advice on moving and handling techniques, will enable staff in these sectors to carry out their role more effectively, while minimising the risk of harm to them or those in their care.

This latest guidance builds on previous editions, reflecting the good practice expected in today's health and social care settings when assisting in the movement of patients and service users and offering practical help on how to implement. I am confident this guide will assist further those involved in the handling and moving of people to carry out their important role safely and effectively.

Judith Hackitt
HSE chair

Department of Health

Partnership for Occupational Safety and Health in Healthcare

The national Back in Work initiative, supported by the Partnership for Occupational Safety and Health in Healthcare (POSHH), a sub group of the NHS Staff Council, is pleased to support the publication of the 6th edition of *The Guide to The Handling of People*.

The Back in Work campaign is aimed at everyone who works in the NHS, whether in an acute hospital, the community or the local GP practice, and is more important than ever at a time when the NHS is about to move into a time of major change. This campaign, which is closely aligned to the wider staff health and wellbeing agenda, aims to show that it is to the benefit of everyone in the NHS, employers as well as staff, to address the problem of work related sickness and of the injuries that cause it. If the numbers of back injuries, musculoskeletal disorders and strains that are suffered by staff can be reduced wherever possible, then NHS users will, in turn, benefit from the healthier, happier staff who are fit for work.

In the NHS, manual handling accidents account for 40 per cent of all sickness absence. The cost to the NHS of manual handling accident related sickness, at a time when employers are looking to make major savings, is probably in excess of £400 million each year. As well as having to take time off because of injury, well motivated and productive people have to give up work because of pain and disability related to manual handling problems and often suffer pain for the rest of their lives.

Compensation claims for manual handling accidents to staff continue to rise and the largest payment to a member of staff in the NHS so far is £800,000. Every NHS employee who retires early because of a back injury costs the NHS at least an extra £60,000, money which could have been saved by effective training and, in the case of an unavoidable injury, fast, proper rehabilitation back into work.

This guide offers an important tool in the campaign by showing how the risks to those moving and handling people can be eliminated or minimised by safer handling practice. The new guide is essential reading for all those with a responsibility for handling people, whether directly or in training and managing others who do, to study BackCare's new guidance.

Julian Topping
Programme lead – health work and wellbeing

Contents

Section 1: Risk assessment and basis for control

CHAPTER 3

Ergonomics in health and social care   39
Sue Hignett

CHAPTER 4

Mechanics and human movement   53
Frances Polak

Section 2: Key strategies

CHAPTER 5

A systems approach to safer handling practice   63
Pat Alexander

CHAPTER 6

Training strategies   73
Pam Rose

CHAPTER 7

Equipment strategies 87
Jean Hutfield and Clive Tracey

CHAPTER 8

Health and wellbeing 107
Jacqui Smith

Section 3: Core skills

Section 4: Managing specific risks

CHAPTER 13

A systems approach to the prevention and management of falls   233
Melanie Sturman

Terminology

Throughout this text we have used the generic term "**handler**" to define the person encouraging, guiding, assisting or carrying out a handling task, and the term "**person**" to define the person who is being encouraged, guided, assisted or moved. The only exceptions are where a sentence is clearly referring to a patient, client, nurse or carer in the context of the sentence or where it is a quote from an earlier reference source.

Disclaimer

The risks associated with moving and handling tasks are complex and each situation must be judged on its own merits through a process of suitable and sufficient risk assessment carried out by a competent person(s). The guidance in this book is not intended to be in any way prescriptive and it is unreasonable for any reader simply to follow any aspect of the contents without undertaking an adequate risk assessment that takes full account of all relevant prevailing circumstances.

The authors, the editor, co-editors, collaborators and the publisher cannot accept responsibility for any consequences that might result from decisions made upon the basis of the advice given herein.

Contributors

Editorial team

Editor

Jacqui Smith MSc (Human Factors) MCSP Cert OH

Jacqui Smith is a consultant occupational health physiotherapist with a Master's degree in human factors. She has worked in the fields of occupational health physiotherapy, rehabilitation and ergonomics for more than 35 years. She is a founder member of the National Back Exchange and has been the editor of *column* since August 2000, a contributing author of *Guidance in Manual Handling for Chartered Physiotherapists* (2002 and 2008), and the editor of the 5th edition of *The Guide to The Handling of People* (2005).

Jacqui is a director of Work Fit, an occupational health physiotherapy, ergonomics and manual handling training company based in Leeds, delivering services nationally to diverse organisations, including DWP, the NHS and NHS Plus, local authorities and the private sector.

She has a particular interest and expertise in the systems approach to the prevention and management of work related musculoskeletal disorders in the health and social care sectors, including in the moving and handling of human loads. Since 1987, she has provided expert opinion in more than 1,500 personal injury and criminal cases for claimants, defendants and the HSE, and provided expert opinion to the CSP and HPC in professional practice hearings. Her interest in the relationship between work and health led her to the concept of "work instability", which has provided the platform for many years of research by the Academic Department of Rehabilitation Medicine of the University of Leeds, and to the development of validated clinical and occupation specific screening tools (Work Screens) designed to identify any mismatch between job demands and work ability at a very early stage, with the aim of limiting sickness absence and the risk of work loss (see chapter 8).

Jacqui is currently finalising a CSP guidance document *Guidelines in the carrying out and reporting of functional capacity evaluations* (in press, 2011) and, together with Dr Frances Polak (chapter 4), is working on a revised biopsychosocial model as a basis for further research into early intervention algorithms.

Co-editors

Mike Fray PhD BSc(Hons) BHSc MCSP

Dr Mike Fray is currently working as research fellow in the Healthcare Ergonomics and Patient Safety Unit in the new Loughborough Design School at Loughborough University.

He has worked in the fields of ergonomics, musculoskeletal injuries and rehabilitation, and patient handling for almost 20 years.

Between 1997 and 2010, he was the visiting fellow for the Back Care Management Programme at Loughborough University and he has supported many learning and research outcomes.

His recent PhD research has focused on the areas of measurement of outcomes from patient handling interventions and the improvement of patient handling strategies. Other projects have including using ergonomics methods to evaluate equipment formally for a number of commercial and governmental partners.

Dr Fray has had many peer reviewed journal and conference publications and he was a co-author of *Evidence-based Patient Handling* and the *Derbyshire Interagency Group Codes of Practice*.

He is a member of the European Panel on Patient Handling Ergonomics and is co-writing the ISO Technical Report on Patient Handling Ergonomics.

In 2010, he created a patient handling research forum for graduates of the Loughborough Back Care Management Master's Degree Programme to assist in the improvement of quality and the wider dissemination of patient handling research in the UK.

Julia Love RGN ONC Registered Member of National Back Exchange

Julia Love is an independent manual handling adviser providing support and training within a wide range of health, social care and educational settings. She is a director of LPS Training & Consultancy Ltd, a company based in the North of England, offering support and information to organisations involved in people handling, on risk management systems, equipment and training. Julia carries out risk assessments and bespoke training for the carers of adults and children with complex handling needs. She delivers facilitator training courses which have been adapted for a number of institutions and organisations, including for university lecturers, PCTs, acute NHS trusts, social services, special schools and private hospitals.

Julia has been a speaker at the Disabled Living Foundation and the National Back Exchange conferences and has a special interest in competency assessment. She is a consultant for Joerns Healthcare Ltd and, as part of a professional team, has developed training material and assessment tools.

Julia is a Registered Member of National Back Exchange and has been an active member for a number of years, having been chair of her local group (2004-2008). She is currently the secretary of the National Executive of National Back Exchange.

Contributing authors

Pat Alexander MSc PGDip PGCE MCSP CMIOSH MIfL

Pat Alexander has worked as a consultant manual handling practitioner for many years. She devises strategy, policies and courses at all levels in manual handling and also works as an expert witness in court, having written several reports for the HSE.

Her qualification, at a Master's level, is as a chartered physiotherapist but she also has a Postgraduate Diploma in Back Care and a Postgraduate Certificate in Education.

She has presented at many national conferences and seminars and has also spoken in Florida, Melbourne and Sydney.

Pat has contributed to the 4th and 5th editions of *The Guide to The Handling of People*, the 2nd and 3rd editions of *Manual Handling Guidance for Chartered Physiotherapists* for the CSP, the *IPC Framework and Evidence Based Patient Handling*. She is the co-author of the *Standards in Manual Handling* for National Back Exchange, having previously chaired the Professional Affairs Committee and produced standards for training and trainers.

Pat sits on many relevant committees, including that of the National Executive of National Back Exchange, of which she is a Registered Member, and steering committee for Skills for Care.

She also acts as an assessor, endorsing manual handling courses for the College of Occupational Therapy. She is a chartered member of the Institution of Occupational Safety and Health, a member of the Medico Legal Association of Chartered Physiotherapists, the Institute of Learning and is on the expert witness register for the RCN and CSP.

Ruth Boulton MSc RGN ONC

Ruth is a practising registered nurse with over 30 years' experience, largely in the National Health Service and the armed forces.

For the last 12 years, she has also worked as a health and safety inspector for the Health and Safety Executive. During this period, the majority of her work entailed inspection, investigation and enforcement in the healthcare sector. She is currently working as a specialist human factors inspector across a range of industries.

April Brooks MCSP PGDip Health Ergonomics

April is a chartered clinical physiotherapy specialist in the moving and handling of people. She holds a Postgraduate Diploma in Health Ergonomics and was runner-up in the CSP Physiotherapist of the Year Awards 2008 in the category "Achievement of Excellence in Improving Service Delivery".

April has conceived and developed Manual Handling Questions (MHQs), a tool for training, risk assessment and decision making in person handling (*column* 2008). In collaboration, she developed and delivered post registration Moving and Handling, Ergonomics, and Management of Change modules (5-7 days each) at the University of Southampton.

Ken Cookson RMN RGN Dip RSA

Ken is a health care professional (nursing) with 43 years' experience working within the NHS and industry sectors. He has been employed as the manual handling manager/adviser at University Hospital Aintree since 1996.

Ken has a special interest in developing safer systems of work and the risk management of morbidly obese people who may present with mobility problems. Ken is an international presenter and he has published articles in nursing, medical and government journals in the UK and USA, focusing on practical approaches to the management of morbidly obese patients and the complex admission and discharge scenarios that often occur.

Mike Fray PhD BSc(Hons) MCSP
See biography on page xx.

Sue Hignett PhD MSc MCSP MIEHF EurErg
Dr Sue Hignett has worked in the healthcare industry for more than 25 years, the last 15 in ergonomics. She is the director the Healthcare Ergonomics and Patient Safety Unit, Loughborough Design School, Loughborough University. She has carried out research for the Engineering and Physical Sciences Research Council, Health and Safety Executive, Department of Health and industrial sponsors. Dr Hignett is the past chair of the International Ergonomics Association Technical Committee on Hospital Ergonomics and co-chair of the European Panel on Patient Handling Ergonomics.

Jean Hutfield MIHM
Jean is chair of the National Association Equipment Providers (NAEP). She is a highly experienced NHS senior manager, with specific skills and experience in the provision of high quality facilities services to primary care trusts. Her role involves working strategically and operationally both nationally and locally in the commissioning of community equipment services and medical device training.

Jean holds a Certificate in Business Studies, a Diploma in Health Services Management, City and Guilds in Health and Safety, NLP Diploma in Advanced Communications, Prince 2 and IOSH. In addition to her role as NAEP chair, Jean is also chair of both Assist UK and the Assistive Technology Education and Training Partnership Board, and a member of the NHS Training For Innovation Steering Group.

Carole Johnson MCSP Cert Ed
Carole is a chartered physiotherapist in the UK working as a consultant manual handling adviser. She is a Registered Member of National Back Exchange, has been on the committee for a total of nine years and is currently the public relations officer. Carole's work spans 20 years. She specialises in analysis and resolution of simple and complex manual handling – showing there is often a win-win alternative. She speaks nationally and internationally and was one of the authors of *The Guide to The Handling of People* (5th edition) and the Chartered Society of Physiotherapists' publication *Guidance on Manual Handling Physiotherapy* (2008). She loves her work and making a positive difference.

Julia Love RGN ONC Registered Member of National Back Exchange
See biography on page xx.

Michael Mandelstam MSc DipLib
Michael Mandelstam worked at the Disabled Living Foundation and then at the Department of Health. He now works independently, providing legal training. He has written a number of books including *Manual handling: an A-Z of law and practice* (2002), *Community Care Practice and the Law* (2009, 4th edition), *Safeguarding vulnerable adults and the law* (2009), and he is a co-author of *The Guide to The Handling of People* (5th edition)

Sheenagh Orchard RGN RNT Cert Ed(FE) DipNurs(Lond)
Registered Member of National Back Exchange

Sheenagh is an independent trainer and moving and handling specialist. She works in all areas of the health care sector, developing the strategic managements of safe handling and undertaking complex risk assessments. She has worked with social services in projects considering the safe reduction of double handling situations in the community. Sheenagh was a contributing author for *The Guide to The Handling of People* (5th edition), having previously assisted in the development of the *Manual Handling Training and Trainer Guidelines* (NBE issue 1, 2001) and the production of *People Moving People* manual handling training pack (revised 2006).

Frances Polak PhD MSc MCSP HPC Reg

Frances Polak qualified in 1979 and has since worked within the occupational health arena and musculoskeletal outpatient setting, both as a clinician and a researcher. Her main interest is in clinical biomechanics, related to both injury prevention and treatment. Frances has a MSc in research methodology and a PhD from Nottingham University, where her thesis focused on muscle length changes derived from 3D motion analysis data, combined with force and power calculations. Frances currently works in the private sector with a specialist interest in movement and handling in the workplace. Her role includes training and the development of company policies to reduce the risk of musculoskeletal injury. Frances is a member of the Chartered Society of Physiotherapy Regulatory Board, and is immediate past chairman of the Association of Chartered Physiotherapists in Occupational Health and Ergonomics.

Pam Rose MCSP

Pam, a Registered Member of National Back Exchange, is a chartered physiotherapist. She has 25 years' experience as an independent moving and handling trainer and consultant, developing and delivering a vast variety of programmes and courses for many occupational groups across diverse settings and environments.

Pam is the commissioning editor of *column*, NBE's professional journal, and was an external reviewer of the CSP's Manual Handling Guidance in 2008. She has developed an international reputation, having presented papers and workshops in the USA and across Europe as well as the UK.

Pam also has a keen interest in moving and handling equipment design. She has worked with local and global manufacturers in product development and on developing sales teams through training in basic ergonomics, equipment use and best practice in order to understand and meet customer need.

Anita Rush MSc (Health Ergonomics) RGN Dip HCS

Anita is a registered nurse with a Diploma in Health Care Practice, incorporating ENB 298 Care of the Elderly, and a Master's Degree in Health Ergonomics.

She is the clinical lead for equipment provision within Berkshire and continues to undertake complex assessments to devise and implement manual handling and equipment solutions aimed at staff safety and customer enablement.

Anita has grown an international reputation for her work, focusing on bariatric care within the community. In 2008, Anita received the coveted Safety in Care award at the Health and Social Care Awards. She is a member of National Back Exchange, a tutor for the Disabled Living Foundation (DLF), chair of the NBE Bariatric Special Interest Group and is the educational representative on the Council for the National Association of Equipment Providers.

Jacqui Smith MSc (Human Factors) MCSP Cert OH

See biography on page xix.

Melanie Sturman MSc RGN

Melanie is a back care adviser for Norfolk County Council Adult Care Community Services. She has held the post for six years. Since graduating with a MSc in Back Care Management in 2008, Melanie has lectured on the manual handling back care and patient safety management courses run by Loughborough University. Melanie's MSc dissertation was titled *Are falls a problem for Local Authorities?* The dissertation identified falls were a problem and recommended organisations focus on falls management systems. In 2009, Melanie published a joint paper titled *Analysing falls management using failure and mode effect analysis*. Melanie is a regular speaker at National Back Exchange conferences.

Clive Tracey RGN DMS LLB(Hons)

Clive is currently head of tender and policy management at a community NHS trust and a visiting lecturer for Greenwich University covering moving and handling. He started his manual handling career in the late 1980s and became the founder of the Manual Handling Project Team within King's College Hospital. There he formulated a "five star" manual handling strategy and implemented the first UK facilities bed management contract. Clive is co-author of several text books and has written numerous articles related to manual handling.

Having completed a Bachelor of Law degree, he moved into risk management before becoming the clinical excellence director of a large global medical equipment company. He actively uses his clinical, risk management and commercial experience in the furtherance of improved healthcare solutions, assisting NHS trusts and managers in the development of risk based business cases.

External peer reviewers

Jane Bannon RGN PGCert (BackCare), moving and handling adviser.

Sue Barton MSc DipEd MCSP DipTP DipRG&RT Dip THRF, independent consultant in occupational kinetics and manual handling.

Elizabeth Hallows MCSP LPC (Back Care Management), independent manual handling adviser.

Heather Hetherington RGN, freelance manual handling consultant.

Emily Hobson MSc (Ergs) PGCert ED PGC Person Handling and Facilitation Dip COT.

Jo Holmes RM, manual handling adviser, Bedford Borough Council.

Sarah Iceton MA, Dip COT, HPC registered, Registered Member NBE, PGCHSCE, freelance manual handling consultant.

Simon Love BA(Hons) MCSP Registered Member NBE, manual handling consultant, LPS Training & Consultancy Ltd.

Mary Muir BA(Hons) Dip N (Lon) FAETC Person Handling Cert SRN, specialist therapy and regional contracts manager, ArjoHuntleigh.

June Pursey service manager, Bradford and Airedale Community Equipment Service

Cameron Raeburn MSc (Occupational Heath & Ergonomics), moving and handling service lead, NHS Greater Glasgow & Clyde.

Elizabeth Smith LLB, partner, Howard Kennedy Solicitors. Specialist in work related personal injury litigation.

Sara Thomas Dip COT PGD, independent occupational therapy consultant and back care adviser.

Sarah Tunstall BAOT, clinical lead OT and moving and handling adviser and trainer.

William Varnham PCCert Ed Advanced Certificate NMA Efficient Handling and Movement, PGDip Health Ergonomics MSc Back Care Management, back care manager Nottinghamshire Healthcare NHS Trust.

Margaret Ward MSc BSc(Hons) RGN SCM, moving and handling adviser.

Members of the National Back Exchange evidence review panel

Review panel chairman
Jo Holmes RM

Data analysis
Linda Curson RGN Cert Ed
Nicky Sharpe RGN MSc (Back Care Management)
Saintelia Douglas DMS LDP BA(Hons) Cert Ed RGN
Heather Hetherington RGN
Carole Johnson MCSP Cert Ed

Introduction

by Jacqui Smith

This definitive, peer reviewed text book is the sixth in a series first published in 1981. It is intended for all staff working in health, social care and the emergency services, and others who may be involved directly or indirectly with the moving and handling of people.

This includes board/cabinet members, policy makers, budget holders and senior managers responsible for strategic decisions essential for the implementation of prevention-focused safer systems of work, staff health and wellbeing and improved care in relation to manual handling practice.

It is also intended as a resource for back care practitioners, manual handling trainers, including trainers of vocational qualifications on the new Qualifications and Credit Framework (QCF), and the educators in universities of those working towards professional qualifications in health and social care. Person handling, and person handling decision making, are just as much core skills for health and social care professionals as any other area of their practice and, as such, the handling of people falls within professional practice standards and guidelines for competence and safety.

Importantly, this book builds on the 5th edition in recognising that staff health and safety must be balanced with meeting the needs of those of us with altered health status or disability. This includes adults, children, family members and informal carers, who may need advice or temporary/longer term assistance with care, mobility or movement that involves manual handling, and whose lives are affected by manual handling decisions.

No doubt this book will be relied on by the legal profession and expert witnesses involved in person handling related personal injury litigation and/or case management, as has each of the previous editions.

This edition is the sixth in the series of guides, the first four of which were produced in formal collaboration between BackCare (formerly the National Back Pain Association) and the Royal College of Nursing. In the 5th, and this new 6th, edition that collaboration is extended to include the National Back Exchange. We are delighted that this 6th edition is also commended by the Chartered Society of Physiotherapy, the College of Occupational Therapists, the Institute of Ergonomics & Human Factors, NHS Employers and the Health and Safety Executive.

The 1st edition in the series was rightly aimed at nurse managers who were seen as potential agents for change in response to growing concerns about the prevalence of low back pain, injury and work loss in the nursing profession. The thrust of the 1st edition related to key prevention strategies including ergonomics, safety training, pre-employment medical screening and the management of back pain at work through early access to occupational health services and physiotherapy treatment. The response to that publication by NHS employers was limited and involved mainly the provision of typically ad hoc training of limited duration and variable content. There is little evidence that training alone has been effective in reducing risks to staff, or enhancing person comfort, dignity or enablement and in this new edition we must therefore return to the systems approach to prevention first put forward in 1981.

The 2nd and 3rd editions each set updated standards in person handling practice. Each was considered in turn to be the gold standard text of its day and, on reflection, each provides a historical record of "where we were then" – and reminds us how far we have come. Since 1988, the Back Exchange (National Back Exchange from 1994), has provided a national multidisciplinary forum for the exchange of information and the development of consensus on evidence based core person handling practice to support all healthcare professionals seeking to reduce the prevalence of work related disorders and related sickness absence in the health and social care sectors, and to enhance care delivery and enablement.

On 1 January 1993, new legislation was implemented, including the Management of Health and Safety at Work Regulations (replaced in 1999), which required that formal risk assessments should be undertaken by employers as part of their risk management systems. The requirement, in the Manual Handling Operations Regulations 1992 (amended 2002), to avoid hazardous manual handling operations where reasonably practicable and assess those risks that could not reasonably practicably be avoided, did not immediately have a great impact on health and social care providers although they were welcomed by those working in the field of person handling and injury prevention at that time.

The RCN was a key stakeholder in launching the first in this series and it again took the professional lead in responding to the regulations and appended load guidance for the "lifting" of loads – and set down the benchmark that no two nurses should lift a person weighing more than eight stones, even in ideal conditions – the natural conclusion being that the lifting of people would have to cease altogether.

Initially, this led some individuals and organisations to implement increasingly prescriptive and proscriptive approaches to person handling practice and to the implementation of blanket "no lifting" policies and decisions that failed to take adequate account of the social, care and rehabilitation needs of disabled people, or of the full range of legislation impacting on manual handling decisions.

In 2002, the Chartered Society of Physiotherapy made its position clear and set clear guidance in its *Guidance in Manual Handling for Chartered Physiotherapists* by stating that "*it is not always reasonably practicable to avoid manual handling in physiotherapy without abandoning the goal of patient rehabilitation*". Insofar as I am aware, the now commonly utilised term "balanced-decision making" is first used in the CSP publication in respect of manual handling decisions. Similar ethics might be said to apply to the meeting of social, care and enablement needs in community/social settings.

At the beginning of 2003, the High Court attempted to reconcile health and safety legislation with human rights and community care legislation in the landmark *East Sussex* case by, in summary, enjoining the parties to adopt a "balanced approach" in which the family were to be fully involved in the risk assessment and decision making process.

Those working in the field of person handling will recognise that the continuing high prevalence of musculoskeletal disorders in health and social care workers arises not from situations in which effective manual handling risk management systems take account of both the person's and the handlers' needs but, rather, from the ongoing systematic failure in many organisations to implement safer systems of work that address adequate staffing, staff competence, staff health and wellbeing, access to appropriate equipment, supervision, risk assessment, care planning, monitoring and review.

What is new about this 6th edition?

It is now 30 years since the publication of the 1st edition of this guide. Over that period much has changed within health and social care with a paradigm shift in care delivery from the NHS to the community, and more recently towards the personalisation agenda. The relevant health and safety legislation has been variously updated, amended, extended and interpreted, and human rights legislation has refocused attention back on to the needs of the disabled person – which is why we joined the care professions in the first place.

Building on the structure of the 5th edition, Section 1, **Risk assessment and basis for control**, provides an overview of legislation influencing person handling decisions and practice, and provides a logical framework that can assist the process of risk assessment and control. Chapters on ergonomics and biomechanics offer tools and methods that can inform risk control processes.

Entirely new to this 6th edition, Section 2, **Key strategies**, addresses four essential underpinning strategies that must form the basis of any effective systems approach to the management of manual handling associated risk for handlers and people: policy and communications, training effectiveness and competence, accessing equipment and staff health and wellbeing. These key strategies resonate with the ambitions set out in the first of this series. There is good evidence that such approaches are effective and cost effective in not only reducing injury and sickness absence risk, but also through enhanced performance and improved care delivery. As stated at the end of the introduction to the 5th edition "*in the absence of a systems approach, safer handling practice will not flourish*".

The practical chapters of the 5th edition reflected the progress made in manual handling practice as manual handling/back care practitioners have come together to investigate, develop and agree evidence based core principles for safer handling practice. These principles are now well established and provide the focus for Section 3, **Core skills**, including a new chapter on core hoisting skills. These core principles form the basis for many bespoke handling techniques that are unique to specific and developing areas of practice so that it is now prohibitive to include all of these in a core publication. To that end, BackCare has initiated a new series of supplements, addressing specific aspects of manual handling that will be published two or three times a year – 2011 will see the publication of supplements covering Therapeutic Handling and Handling in the Ambulance Service. Longer term plans include Handling in Emergency Situations, Theatre Handling, Handling in the Community and other specialism/sector specific guidance.

Section 4 addresses **Managing specific risks** in two new chapters covering moving and handling/enablement in bariatrics, and the prevention and management of falls, since both subjects are now key areas of core practice.

As in the 5th edition, throughout all of the chapters herein the authors have quoted research evidence where it is available. Each chapter has been subject to extensive peer review by the editorial team, Registered Members of National Back Exchange and others with relevant expertise. In addition to the work of the individual authors, most of the tasks described in each practical chapter were analysed by an evidence review panel consisting of volunteer members of the National Back Exchange, and the results are set out in relation to each task/sub-task.

This guide is not intended to be in any way prescriptive. Review of the evidence recorded will support practitioners to develop their practice and support informed decisions relevant to a particular set of circumstances. There will inevitably be some differences in the approaches taken by trainers/practitioners/handlers to the core practice set out in these chapters. Some of these variations may be more, or less, hazardous to the handler or more, or less, comfortable for the person, or require more, or less, skill. It will, however, be relatively simple in future for evidence to be gathered in relation to these alternatives and compared to that in this book. It is also the case that the particular prevailing circumstances, and the nature and needs of the person, must be key influences on the handling intervention.

Readers must therefore be very clear that a review of a technique in this book, and consideration of the accompanying evidence, does not constitute a risk assessment, although certainly the information provided herein is aimed to develop practice and underpin person handling decisions. The authors hope that the content of this edition will encourage practitioners to appraise critically and develop their own practice within a safer systems framework.

Acknowledgements

I would like to express personal thanks to my co-editors, Dr Mike Fray and Julia Love, the design and publishing team at Pages Creative, the contributing authors, external reviewers and others for their contribution to the production of this 6th edition.

Manual handling: legal framework and balanced decision making

Michael Mandelstam MSc DipLib
Independent legal consultant and trainer

Introduction

This chapter focuses on law relevant to the moving and handling of people in health and social care.

The relevant legal framework is extensive. Health and safety at work legislation is about the taking of reasonably practicable steps to ensure the safety of employees. Welfare and human rights legislation is about the meeting of people's health and social care needs. Broadly, if there is a conflict between the two, a balanced approach is required in order to avoid undue detriment to either staff or the person being handled.

The legal framework includes social services (community care and children's legislation), the National Health Service (NHS), housing, human rights, disability discrimination, and health and safety at work legislation – not to mention the law of negligence, contract law and regulatory legislation.

In order to make this framework accessible to the reader, the chapter is divided into the various areas of law. Each area is broadly summarised and illustrated with everyday examples.

Note: Health and safety at work, human rights, disability discrimination and the law of negligence apply across the United Kingdom. However, the community care legislation referred to in the chapter covers England and, for the most part, Wales. The NHS Act 2006 applies to England only, but the NHS (Wales) Act 2006 is very similar. Otherwise, most of the principles and rules of social care and health legislation apply more or less in principle across the United Kingdom, but are to be found in different legislation in Scotland and Northern Ireland. Nevertheless, it should be noted that the policy of "personalisation", referred to on page 6, is further advanced in England than elsewhere.

Balanced decision making

The overall theme of the chapter is a legal requirement on local authorities and the NHS to achieve a measure of balanced decision making in the context of the moving and handling of people. Essentially, this means balancing the safety (and human rights) of paid staff with the assessed needs and human rights of service users.

At the beginning of 2003, the High Court attempted, in a lengthy and complex judgement, to reconcile health and safety at work legislation with community care legislation and human rights legislation. The judgement emphasised repeatedly the need to strike a balance, while recognising that this would not always be easy (*A&B, X&Y v East Sussex County Council*).

The *East Sussex* case involved a local authority. However, there is no indication that the principles of that case would not apply to the NHS as well; the Human Rights Act, which was central, applies to all public bodies.

Achieving the type of balance referred to in the *East Sussex* case can be elusive. In practice, it would appear that staff frequently either put themselves, or are placed by their employer, at excessive and unnecessary risk. Alternatively, they are directed to take such extreme precaution that the welfare of service users can suffer, their assessed needs may not be met – and sometimes their human rights may be breached.

One thing is plain though. Notwithstanding the recognition that a balance is required, there is nothing in any legislation or case law – human rights or otherwise – suggesting that staff should be put at unacceptable or undue levels of risk. Equally, nothing that those who require assistance with moving and handling should have their needs and human rights ignored or sidelined.

Conflicts of view

Sometimes local authority staff and managers feel that it is all very well for the courts to talk about balanced decision making, but that everyday reality gets in the way. Clearly, there will, from time to time, be tensions involving the needs and rights of service users, and the safety of staff.

Some of these tensions may be difficult, or on occasion, impossible to resolve fully.

Equally, manual handling practitioners frequently point out that with sufficient expertise devoted to assessment, the delivery of services and to negotiation, many apparently intractable problems can be overcome.

EXAMPLE: HOIST BREAKDOWN AND HUMAN RIGHTS

When hoists break down in people's homes, local authority staff are anxious because they feel there is a potential conflict between their own safety and the human rights and assessed needs of service users. Under current arrangements, the repair or replacement time for malfunctioning or broken hoists can sometimes be as long as 48 hours or more. An apparent dilemma arises as to whether service users – who pose a high manual handling risk to staff – should be left in bed during this period, even if this would be to their significant detriment. Alternatively, should staff get them out of bed manually, even at high risk? The local authority finds a simple solution; it places a new contract for the repair of hoists that guarantees, in case of urgency, a four hour response time.

EXAMPLE: IMPROVING PRACTICE

A local authority recognises that balanced decision making requires competent risk assessment and risk management. In order to achieve this, it employs two manual handling practitioners, puts in place enhanced basic training for its care staff, provides specialist training for its occupational therapists, and imposes more demanding contractual conditions on independent care providers to ensure the competence of their staff.

Local authorities: social services legislation

Logically, community care legislation is the place to start because it is here that assessment of people's needs by local authorities begins. It is the so called community care legislation that brings a local authority into contact with an individual.

There is plenty of it. This contrasts with comparable decision making in the NHS, which is more loosely governed by legislation.

Duty of assessment

Under section 47 of the NHS and Community Care Act 1990, which applies to England and Wales, a person is entitled to an assessment of his or her needs if it appears that he or she may be in need of community care services.

Section 47 is largely concerned with adults. The duty to assess is not absolute, in the sense that it depends on a person appearing to be in need of a community care service. However, it is a strong one and a lack of resources cannot excuse a lack of (adequate) assessment (*R v Bristol CC, ex p Penfold*).

In the case of a disabled person, the local authority must anyway make a decision about the person's needs under the terms of section 4 of the Disabled Persons (Services, Consultation and Representation) Act 1986. This decision may lead to a requirement for services under section 2 of the Chronically Sick and Disabled Persons Act 1970.

Having carried out an assessment, a local authority must then decide whether the person's assessed needs call for the provision of services by the authority. Not all needs will necessarily be judged to call for services; it is only assessed, so called "eligible", needs that will trigger service provision. An eligible need is a need that is assessed to come above, rather than below, a threshold that local authorities set in order to determine eligibility for service provision.

Views of the person being assessed

The Department of Health (DH) has issued "directions" about assessment. They amount to a duty. The local authority must consult the person being assessed; consider whether the person has any carers and, if appropriate, consult them; and take all reasonable steps to reach agreement, about community care services to be provided, with both the person being assessed and, if appropriate, any carer (DH 2004).

In the context of manual handling decisions, when there is a difference of views, these directions plainly mean the local authority has to make reasonable efforts to reach agreement – even if, in the end, it is not obliged actually to reach agreement.

Risks to independence

In England, guidance has been issued by the Department of Health stating that local authorities must assess need in terms of risk to people's independence. The guidance refers to "fair access to care" in its title (DH 2010).

The guidance states that local authorities should evaluate risks to a person's independence by focusing on:
● autonomy and freedom to make choices
● health and safety, including freedom from harm, abuse and neglect, housing and community safety
● ability to manage personal and other daily routines
● involvement in family and wider community life, including leisure, hobbies, unpaid and paid work, learning and volunteering.

All these aspects of people's lives may have manual handling ramifications, not just in respect of living in the home but also of accessing and participating in the community.

To assist with this evaluation, local authorities have been told that they should consider whether any such risks to a person's independence are critical, substantial, moderate or low.

The guidance then states that authorities should set a threshold, above which needs will be eligible for service provision, and below which they will not. Local authorities have not been told where to set the threshold. It appears that many have set it either between substantial and moderate or between moderate and low. The guidance applies only to social services provided for adults.

The guidance goes on to provide indicators to assist in the categorisation of these levels of risk to independence. A glance at the indicators makes it clear that assessment should be about far more than physical risk.

Certainly, under the critical category, reference is made to threat to life, significant health problems, little or no choice and control over vital aspects of the immediate environment, serious abuse or neglect, and vital personal care or domestic routines. But beyond such issues, reference in the critical category is made also to vital involvement in work or education or learning, vital social support systems and relationships, vital family and other social roles and responsibilities.

CRITICAL RISK TO INDEPENDENCE, HOME AND WORK

A local authority assesses a range of different needs that a disabled person may have. Of these, a number relate to how the person is going to transfer from place to place and thus they raise potential manual handling issues. These concern not just the home environment, but also the person's ability to go out to work each day. Therefore, among other things, the local authority assesses that there is a critical risk to the person's vital involvement in work.

Assessment of need: relevant factors and manual handling

Apart from the plentiful guidance issued by central government about assessment, the law courts have themselves identified, on a number of occasions, the factors that must be taken into account if community care assessments are to be lawful.

These factors have included, for instance, psychological issues (*R v Avon CC, ex p M*), cultural and language issues (*R (Khana) v Southwark LBC*), medical factors (*R v Birmingham CC, ex p*

Killigrew), people's preferences (*R v North Yorkshire CC, ex p Hargreaves*), social, recreational and leisure needs (*R v Haringey LBC, ex p Norton*). All of these different factors may bear on manual handling related issues.

In the following case, the medical condition of osteoporosis had apparently not been taken into account; at least nothing had been documented and there was no visible reasoning process. This meant the decision to hoist the person was unlawful and would have to be retaken by the local authority, this time looking at all the relevant issues:

CASE EXAMPLE: MEDICAL CONDITION UNLAWFULLY NOT TAKEN ACCOUNT OF IN A MANUAL HANDLING DECISION

A decision was taken about how a woman should be physically transferred at a day centre. She was diagnosed at the age of eight months as suffering from atrophy of the brain and there was evidence of brain damage. She had multiple learning difficulties and physical disabilities which were compounded by sensory disabilities. She was registered blind. She had been diagnosed as suffering from cerebral palsy, microcephalus and epilepsy. She was unable to walk and she suffered from a number of spinal problems. A decision was taken that she should be hoisted at a day centre rather than manually handled in a different way. There was no mention in the decision of the osteoporosis. This meant the decision was unlawful because it had not considered all relevant factors; the court held that the local authority would have to retake the decision (*R (SC) v Salford CC*).

In another case, specifically about manual handling, the court stated that the local authority would have to take account of the emotional, psychological and social impact on two women of the different methods, including hoisting, of effecting physical transfers. This would be in terms of their wishes, feelings, reluctance, fear, refusal, dignity, integrity and quality of life (*A&B, X&Y v East Sussex CC*).

A local authority, therefore, has to take into account all the factors relevant to an individual case when reaching its decision. But that final decision does, in law, rest with the local authority. For example, taking account of a person's preferences is one thing, following them in every case quite another. Neither community care legislation nor the Human Rights Act 1998 simply obliges a local authority to provide exactly what a person wants in every case.

Individual need and blanket policies

This very requirement to consider individual needs and situations underlays the judgement in the *East Sussex* case. The court stated that blanket "no lifting" policies would be likely to be unlawful; as would policies that necessarily prohibited lifting
● unless life and limb were at risk or
● if equipment could be used to effect a transfer.

Essentially, this was because such policies would prejudge the outcome of assessments. This point of view was nothing new; the Health and Safety Executive had already warned against such policies (HSE 2002).

The judge in the *East Sussex* case put it succinctly: "The assessment must be focused on the particular circumstances of the individual case. Just as context is everything, so the individual assessment is all" (*A&B, X&Y v East Sussex CC*).

Community care services

Community care assessments are conducted in order to decide whether a person has a need for community care services. Various services are referred to in the legislation covering local authority social services. They include care homes, a wide range of domiciliary care services, community activities, day services, respite care, adult placement schemes and so on – all with potential manual handling implications.

Residential accommodation

Local authorities place people in residential accommodation under the National Assistance Act 1948.

Non residential services

Under section 2 of the Chronically Sick and Disabled Persons Act 1970 (CSDPA), a local authority has a duty to provide various non residential services, in order to meet the assessed, eligible needs of disabled people.

Services that could involve manual handling issues include practical assistance in the home, recreational facilities, lectures, games, outings, taking advantage of educational facilities available to a person, works of adaptation to the home and additional facilities for greater safety, comfort or convenience, and holidays.

This means that manual handling decisions may involve diverse settings:

CASE EXAMPLE: MANUAL HANDLING AND ASSISTING PEOPLE IN THE COMMUNITY

In one protracted legal dispute, it was being argued on behalf of two service users with profound physical and learning disabilities that they must have access to swimming, horseriding and shopping trips. The local authority countered that the manual handling risks to paid carers were too great (*A&B, X&Y v East Sussex CC*).

Absolute duty to meet assessed, eligible needs

The courts have ruled that, at least under some community care legislation, an absolute duty is imposed on a local authority to meet assessed, eligible needs without undue delay. An eligible need means a need that has been assessed as coming over the threshold of eligibility that the local authority has set.

One piece of legislation to which this rule has been held to apply is section 2 of the Chronically Sick and Disabled Persons Act 1970, already referred to above (*R v Gloucestershire CC, ex p Barry*). Other legislation so governed, eg covering residential accommodation, includes section 21 of the National Assistance Act 1948 (*R v Sefton MBC, ex p Help the Aged; R v Royal Borough of Kensington and Chelsea, ex p Kujtim*).

Meeting a need cost effectively

Once a duty to meet a need has been incurred, the need must be met one way or another. If more than one way of meeting it exists, the local authority may offer the cheapest option, so long as that option does genuinely meet the need and is compliant with other relevant legislation such as the Human Rights Act 1998.

However, the eligible need must be met, even if the only way of doing so is relatively costly. A lack of resources would be no legal defence (*R v Gloucestershire CC, ex p Barry; A&B, X&Y v East Sussex CC, ex p Tandy; R v Royal Borough of Kensington & Chelsea, ex p Kujtim; R v Lancashire CC, ex p RADAR*).

EXAMPLE: DUTY TO PROVIDE PERSONAL ASSISTANCE RATHER THAN A HOIST

Following a serious car accident, a person is continuing a process of rehabilitation in his own home. He needs to build up strength over a period of time. Provision of a hoist and one assistant would be cheaper than providing two personal assistants each day to help transfer him.

However, hoist use has been assessed as not meeting the person's needs and indeed it would be a threat to his independence. He can reliably take some of his own weight on transfers. This is essential for the rehabilitation process. Hoist use is not necessitated by risk to staff, since the risk, if properly managed, has been assessed as low under the Manual Handling Operations Regulations 1992. In such circumstances, the hoist is unlikely to be a lawful way of meeting the man's assessed community care needs. The local authority would instead have to supply the two personal assistants, albeit at greater cost.

Thus, a local authority is not legally obliged to meet a need by means of an option that involves an unacceptable level of risk to staff; but it is obliged to seek to find an option that meets an assessed need without such a degree of risk, even if this means greater expenditure.

Withdrawing or changing services

Generally speaking, it is likely to be lawful for a local authority to change, reduce or withdraw services in the following circumstances.

First, a reassessment would have to take place (*R v Gloucestershire CC, ex p Mahfood*). Second, a reduction in service could only be justified if:
● the person's needs had likewise reduced or changed
● the same needs could be met in a different way
● the local authority's threshold of eligibility for services (see above) had risen
● there was explicit or implicit (eg through unreasonable behaviour) refusal of service by the person.

Absent these factors, and a reduction in service is generally likely to be unlawful even if, for instance, manual handling requirements have made a care package more expensive than hitherto.

CASE EXAMPLE: MANUAL HANDLING ASSESSMENT AND REDUCING A PERSON'S SERVICES

Following a manual handling assessment of a woman with multiple sclerosis, a local authority provides two personal assistants instead of one, but halves the amount of assistance provided. The local authority does not show that this reduction equated to a change in the woman's assessed, eligible needs, to a change in the eligibility criteria, or to meeting her needs in a different way. The judge is therefore concerned that the decision was totally resource led and strikes down the assessment decision as unlawful (*R v Birmingham CC, ex p Killigrew*).

Furthermore, even where a reduction may be legally justifiable, both the courts (*R v Gloucestershire CC, ex p RADAR*) and guidance have urged caution in deciding whether, or how, to withdraw services from people (DH 2010, p.36). The following is hopefully an exceptional case but nonetheless serves as a warning that such caution should be taken:

CASE EXAMPLE: WITHDRAWING MANUAL HANDLING SERVICES

A woman with Alzheimer's disease was doubly incontinent, completely immobile and required assistance from carers three times a day, seven days a week. She had received manual handling assistance in the past, but this now represented an increasing risk to staff. For this reason, the social services department then reportedly stated that unless her husband agreed to have a hoist installed, the carers would be withdrawn. This was after carers refused to lift her manually.

The husband then attempted to kill both himself and his wife by leading a hose from the exhaust of his car into the bedroom; however, a neighbour heard the car engine running, saw the hose and intervened. The husband had left a note blaming a social worker and the owner of a private care company, stating that those evil people had deemed that services should be withdrawn and his wife left unattended.

His wife died a month later in a care home from an unrelated chest infection; on release from hospital, he was arrested and charged with attempted murder. He pleaded guilty. The judge sentenced him to a year's probation but also criticised the Crown Prosecution Service for bringing the case at all, stating that it was not in the public interest to have done so (*R v Bouldstridge*).

Children

Disabled children's needs are, in large part, assessed under section 2 of the Chronically Sick and Disabled Persons Act (CSDPA) 1970 and section 17 of the Children Act 1989 (in England and Wales).

On request by a disabled child's informal carer (including parents), a local authority has a duty to decide whether the child's needs call for the provision of services under the CSDPA 1970. This duty is contained in section 4 of the Disabled Persons (Services, Consultation and Representation) Act 1986. This legislation applies to adults as well and has been covered above.

Under section 17 of the Children Act 1989, there is a general duty to safeguard and promote the welfare of children in need.

The duty is wide in scope, and provision of services in relation to manual handling issues could come under it. In addition, it covers not just disabled children but also other children whose health or development is at risk. It also allows for the provision of accommodation, something that cannot be provided under section 2 of the 1970 Act, and which might bear on manual handling issues.

Furthermore, services can be provided under section 17 not just to a child in need, but also to any member of his or her family.

Nevertheless, section 17 is a relatively weak duty; enforcement of it for an individual child is generally very difficult (*R (G) v Barnet LBC*). This compares with the relatively strong duty under section 2 of the CSDPA Act 1970 (eg *R v Bexley LBC, ex p B*).

Looked after children

Under section 22 of the Children Act 1989, local authorities also have a specific duty to safeguard and promote the welfare of any child they are looking after. A looked after child is a child in the local authority's care or provided with accommodation arranged by the local authority (including foster placements).

In the case of a disabled child for whom the local authority is providing accommodation under the Children Act 1989, the authority must, so far as is reasonably practicable, ensure that the accommodation is not unsuitable to the child's particular needs (section 23).

Further, in respect of local authority foster carers, regulations stipulate that the fostering service provider (local authority or independent agency) must ensure that each child is provided with the individual support, aids and equipment which he or she may require due to health needs or disability; and that the foster carers are provided with training, advice, information and support (Statutory Instrument (SI) 2002/57).

Self evidently, such obligations could bear on manual handling issues; a failure to heed could lead to manual handling related personal injury litigation (*Beasley v Buckinghamshire CC*).

Carers

In addition to assessing a disabled person, local authorities have various duties in respect of informal carers.

These duties are highly relevant, given the physical and mental stresses on informal carers involved in manual handling. There has been a perception that informal carers are not always supported and assisted in relation to manual handling by statutory bodies such as local authorities and the NHS.

This can compare unfavourably with those organisations' concern about their own staff (Marriott 2003) and lead to injury (Henwood 1998).

Generally, informal carers who are providing regular and substantial care, and who request it, are entitled to a local authority assessment of their ability to care. In addition, the local authority has a duty to decide whether the assessed needs of the carer call for services, and whether to provide those services.

EXAMPLE: ADVICE AND TRAINING FOR INFORMAL CARERS

By way of a carer's service, a local authority offers information, advice and training service for informal carers engaged on manual handling tasks.

Even if a carer refuses an assessment, the local authority still has a duty to "have regard" to his or her ability to care under section 8 of the Disabled Persons (Services, Consultation and Representation) Act 1986.

Personalisation

Local authorities in England are, at the time of writing, implementing a policy of what has been called personalisation or self directed support. The overall policy is not spelt out in legislation (DH 2007; LAC(DH) 2008 1; LAC(DH) 2009 1).

From a legal point of view, it has been introduced by the back door, although a key ingredient involves direct payments which are grounded in legislation.

Personalisation involves giving people a much greater degree of control and choice over how their needs are perceived and met. Elements of it include more self assessment, the allocation of a personal budget to people (in the form of a direct payment to the person, or managed by a third party) and much greater choice in how a need is met. For instance, going fishing instead of going to a day centre.

The greater choice and control envisaged may lead to more differences of view between users of services and professionals over what constitutes appropriate manual handling – as well as a wider variety of settings and activities in which manual handling assessments will be required.

The local government ombudsman investigated a case of two parents who, in the view of local authority professionals, were putting their mentally incapacitated adult son at undue risk through manual handling. The local authority ended up triggering the local authority's adult safeguarding procedures, which resulted in a referral of the matter to the police. The local ombudsman was scathing. The case illustrates the difficulties that may arise in trying to balance the views of service users and professionals:

CONFLICT OF VIEW ABOUT MANUAL HANDLING BETWEEN PROFESSIONALS AND PARENTS OF A MAN LACKING CAPACITY

A complaint was made by the parents of a 21 year old man. He could not walk, talk, stand or care for himself. His parents were lifting him out of bed. Local authority occupational therapists offered a portable hoist but insisted also, on safety grounds, that it be used with a hospital bed and not with the existing sofa bed. A hoist supplier agreed with the occupational therapists.

The parents wanted the hoist but refused the hospital bed because of what they considered to be insufficient space. The therapists maintained it was a question of both or neither. The parents then requested a direct payment so they could buy the hoist themselves. The local authority stated that it did not make direct payments for hoists. Concerned about the risk to the son (a risk he appeared to lack the capacity to consent to), the therapists triggered an adult protection/safeguarding referral that ended up with the police.

The ombudsman criticised the local authority for not taking a person centred approach, not involving a social worker and not acceding to the parents' wishes for the hoist sooner (the hoist was eventually provided). The adult protection referral was condemned as inappropriate, given the dedicated care the parents had always given their son; the ombudsman felt the matter was one of service provision and not adult protection. As to risk, the ombudsman understood the reservations of the occupational therapists about safety, "but it was ultimately for the family to make that choice" (Commission for Local Administration in England 2008).

Direct payments

A direct payment means that instead of itself arranging a service, the local authority gives service users a reasonable amount of money to enable them to purchase non residential services or equipment themselves. Some people might receive direct payments to purchase personal assistance and equipment that involves manual handling.

Direct payments are made under the Health and Social Care Act 2001 (section 57), the Children Act 1989 (section 17A) and regulations (SI 2009/1887).

The idea of direct payments is to give more choice and flexibility as to how a person's needs are met:

EXAMPLE: PURCHASING MANUAL HANDLING ASSISTANCE TO GET TO WORK

A person is assisted each day with getting out of, and going back to, bed. Manual handling with various items of assistive equipment is required. However, the local authority cannot provide the service before 9am, which is the time the person needs to be at work. She therefore suggests that the local authority provides her with a direct payment, so that she can purchase personal assistance on terms to suit her needs better.

Certain conditions must be satisfied. The person must consent to the direct payment; that is both have the ability to consent and also want the payment. He or she must also have the ability to manage the payment, with or without assistance. The service in question must meet the assessed need. There are a number of exclusions relating to some people who come under certain mental health and criminal justice legislation.

Since November 2009, it has also been possible for a local authority to make a direct payment, even when the disabled person lacks capacity to consent to it, to a suitable person.

Direct payments, health and safety, manual handling

The purpose of direct payments is to give people greater choice and control over their own lives. Nevertheless, local authorities still remain statutorily responsible in the sense that direct payments are made following assessment of need, and must then be used to meet that need. This situation may result in a degree of tension in some circumstances.

A dilemma may arise if a disabled person chooses to use the money in such a way as to give rise to serious health and safety concerns on the part of the local authority. If the local authority takes a "hands off" approach, it may be concerned about litigation in respect of any accident that occurs – even if the recipient has, as a condition of the direct payment, taken out insurance. Yet, an excessively "hands on" or interventionist approach would risk undermining the whole purpose of direct payments.

Guidance issued in England states that recipients should be given information about health and safety and also the results of any risk assessment carried out by competent staff on behalf of the local authority. In addition, recipients should be encouraged to develop strategies on lifting. However, the guidance clearly states that: "As a general principle, local councils should avoid laying down health and safety policies for individual direct payment recipients" (DH 2009).

This Department of Health policy appears to advocate what could be termed a "hands off" approach. However, in case of accident involving negligence, it is unclear whether the courts would necessarily approve such an approach, or would instead tend to hold a local authority liable for not intervening in situations of high risk.

From a legal (as distinct from a policy) point of view at least, the term "general principle" contained in the guidance might be better interpreted to mean that at least in some circumstances local authorities should consider intervening if serious health and safety risks are seen to arise. Not least, because separate guidance from the Department of Health contains what might be interpreted as a slightly more cautious approach: "The local authority remains accountable for the proper use of its public funds, and while the individual is entitled to live with a degree of risk, the local authority is not obliged to fund it" (DH 2007a).

EXAMPLE: EXCESSIVE RISK AND INTERVENTION

A local authority care manager visits to review a direct payments package. She finds that the personal assistant employed by the direct payment recipient is regularly carrying the latter up and down the garden path. They have fallen on more than one occasion. She suggests that this is, on any view, a high risk activity and therefore not acceptable. The direct payment recipient disagrees and maintains that it is up to her as employer to organise her assistance. The care manager ponders how to intervene, in order to try to find a compromise.

EXAMPLE: FINDING A DIRECT PAYMENT SOLUTION

A disabled person wishes to be transferred manually, rather than mechanically with equipment, in his own home and in the community. However, on the basis of an individual risk assessment, the manual handling protocols developed by the local authority rule this out. The man asks for a direct payment as a way around the problem. After much negotiation, the

local authority agrees not to impose directly its manual handling protocols as a condition of the direct payment. The disabled person in turn agrees to go to an independent living agency that specialises in setting up independent living packages for disabled people. This solution reassures the local authority because the agency is experienced in personal assistance and manual handling issues. The disabled person is likewise reassured because the agency has a good reputation in respect of independent living.

Community equipment services

Equipment plays a key role in manual handling. The ready availability of appropriate types of equipment is essential both to the meeting of people's needs and to staff safety. Indeed, sometimes the right type of equipment can resolve conflicts of view between local authority and service user.

Nevertheless, community equipment services have long been recognised as a confused area of provision. They have generally been characterised by poor organisation and funding, resulting in delay, non provision and considerable dispute between local authorities and the NHS about where responsibility for certain types of equipment lies (see, generally, Audit Commission 2000).

EXAMPLE: MANUAL HANDLING, HOISTS AND BEDS

Disputes sometimes arise about mobile hoists or special beds (eg profiling beds) to be used in people's homes. Local authorities may refuse to provide them, but the NHS provides them only if district nurses are in attendance. In such circumstances, the problem for the service user requiring such a hoist or bed without district nurse attendance is obvious. Even where there are jointly run community equipment stores, such a problem may still persist in terms of which staff can or can't authorise certain types of equipment – where such authorisation is linked to respective budget contributions from the local authority and the NHS.

The solution to such disputes is, of course, not to conduct endless arguments about what constitutes health, social care (or housing) equipment. Such arguments are often fruitless, since so much equipment falls into a grey area of being arguably either health or social care. Indeed, legally, it would almost certainly be a futile task attempting to get the courts to rule on such matters.

The answer would appear in part to be flexible joint working between local authorities and the NHS. To this end, Department of Health policy in England has been directed to improving these services (HSC 2001/008).

National Health Service (NHS)

NHS legislation does not spell out in detail administrative rules about assessment and eligibility for assistance.

Instead, the NHS Act 2006 imposes, on the Secretary of State for Health, rather general duties toward the population at large. These duties are (currently) cascaded down to primary care trusts, NHS trusts and NHS foundation trusts.

Duties include the promotion of a comprehensive health service designed to secure improvement in physical and mental health and to prevent, diagnose and treat illness. In addition, in order to meet all reasonable requirements, various services must be provided, including care and aftercare (NHS Act 2006, sections 1-3).

Nonetheless, the principle established in the *East Sussex* case (see page 3) about balanced decision making – setting off people's needs and human rights against the safety of staff – plainly applies to the NHS as well. In one Scottish NHS case, the judge ruled that of three options for the manual handling of a heavy, awkward patient with dementia, the middle one was appropriate. The first was not good for the patient but safest for staff; the third was perhaps best for the patient but too unsafe for staff. The middle way was a reasonable compromise between these extremes. The judge noted that patients were not sacks of cement:

CASE EXAMPLE: PATIENTS ARE PEOPLE, NOT SACKS OF CEMENT

"The 1992 Regulations clearly apply to the manual handling of hospital patients, as they apply to sacks of cement. Nevertheless, different considerations are relevant in the case of a patient (or, indeed, any person), on the one hand, and to a sack of cement, on the other. The comfort and safety of the patient are of importance… a nurse's job requires the manual handling of patients. Here, use of a hoist offered Mr G neither a comfortable nor a safe means of transfer to the commode whereas a swivel transfer was… reasonably safe for all concerned" (*Urquhart v Fife PCT*).

In 2010, the NHS began to pilot, in a few areas, direct payments for health services. The rules are set out in regulations (SI 2010/100). The principle of direct payments has been considered above.

Housing legislation: home adaptations

Adapting the environment is sometimes a way of solving mobility and manual handling issues in the home. Under the Housing Grants, Construction and Regeneration Act 1996, local housing authorities have a strong duty to award mandatory disabled facilities grants if certain conditions are met.

Grant applications must be approved if the adaptation is in respect of access to, and use of, various parts and facilities within the dwelling. In addition, the adaptation must be regarded as necessary and appropriate (eg in respect of meeting community care needs or of independence) and as reasonable and practicable in relation to the age and condition of the dwelling. A means test also applies, although not to children. Of course, if equipment could meet the relevant needs of a person, then an adaptation will not be "necessary and appropriate".

The Act itself, as well as guidance issued by central government, is clear that not only private sector owner occupiers and tenants are eligible to apply for grants, but so too are council tenants and tenants of registered social landlords. Unfortunately, some housing authorities neither recognise this eligibility across all these housing sectors, nor do they adhere to the timescales set in legislation for processing grant applications. The consequences of not carrying out adaptations in timely fashion can have drastic manual handling consequences for disabled people and their informal carers.

CASE EXAMPLE: MANUAL HANDLING IMPLICATIONS OF DELAY IN HOME ADAPTATIONS

An elderly man with chronic arthritis and Parkinson's disease requested help with adaptations. The request took several years to deal with. During this time, apart from distress, worry and inconvenience, the demands made on his wife were enormous. The husband was embarrassed and frustrated. Three years after the initial request, the wife was usually alone with her husband all day, having to get him up, dress him and help him on the stairs. His prostate problems meant that she needed to help him up and down more often – and when he fell, he often pulled her down with him. The local government ombudsman found maladministration (*Barking and Dagenham LBC*).

Sometimes an adaptation does not come within the remit of the disabled facilities grants legislation. Alternatively, the means test may affect some people unduly harshly because it can, by law, take no account of outgoings. In such circumstances, local social services authorities may have a duty to assist under section 2 of the Chronically Sick and Disabled Persons Act 1970.

Lastly, local housing authorities have a wide discretion to assist with adaptations outside the disabled facilities grants system, as well as to assist people to move house where this is the preferred solution. Such assistance can be given under the terms of the Regulatory Reform (Housing Assistance) (England and Wales) Order 2002.

Human rights legislation

In October 2000, the Human Rights Act 1998 came into force. It acted as the vehicle for bringing into United Kingdom law the European Convention on Human Rights. The Act and Convention apply to public bodies, such as local authorities, NHS trusts and central government departments – but not, on the whole, directly to independent care providers (except to care homes in some circumstances, namely, where the local authority has placed a resident in the home) (see section 145 of the Health and Social Care Act 2008).

This means that local authority decision making in respect of manual handling must comply not just with relevant domestic legislation, but also with the articles of the Convention.

A number of Convention articles are relevant to local social services authorities in general. In respect of manual handling issues, the courts have, to date, referred to three in particular. These concern the right to life (article 2), the right not to be subjected to inhuman or degrading treatment (article 3) and the right to respect for home, private and family life (article 8).

CASE EXAMPLE: BLANKET POLICIES ON MANUAL HANDLING

In relation to human rights, the courts have ruled that certain types of manual handling policy are likely to be unlawful in the context of community care. These were no lifting; no lifting unless life or limb were at risk; and no lifting if equipment could physically effect the transfer (*A&B, X&Y v East Sussex CC*).

CASE EXAMPLE: LEAVING PEOPLE TO PERISH FOR FEAR OF MANUAL HANDLING

Leaving disabled people as a matter of manual handling related policy or protocol to drown in the bath or perish in a fire could engage article 2 and the right to life (*A&B, X&Y v East Sussex CC*).

CASE EXAMPLE: LEAVING PEOPLE IN DEGRADING CIRCUMSTANCES FOR FEAR OF MANUAL HANDLING

If manual handling policies or protocols were to mean that care staff would leave disabled people for hours sitting in their own bodily waste or on the lavatory, article 3 might be engaged – ie the right not to be subjected to inhuman or degrading treatment (*A&B, X&Y v East Sussex CC*).

CASE EXAMPLE: DEGRADING TREATMENT OF A DISABLED PRISONER, INCLUDING MANUAL HANDLING OF DISABLED WOMAN BY MALE PRISON OFFICERS

A severely physically disabled person was sent to prison for contempt of court, for failing to disclose her assets in a debt case. In the police cell, she was unable to use the bed and had to sleep in her wheelchair where she became very cold. When she reached the prison hospital, she could not use the toilet herself, the female duty officer could not manage to move her alone, and male prison officers had to assist. The European Court found that to detain a severely disabled person in conditions where she is dangerously cold, risks developing pressure sores because her bed is too hard or unreachable, and is unable to go to the toilet or keep clean without the greatest difficulty, constituted degrading treatment contrary to article 3. Damages of £4,500 were awarded (*Price v United Kingdom*).

CASE EXAMPLE: PHYSICAL AND PSYCHOLOGICAL INTEGRITY OF A DISABLED PERSON; MANUAL HANDLING

Article 8 (right to respect for home, private and family life) has been held to include the physical and psychological integrity of disabled people, both within and without the home.

Thus, in a manual handling dispute involving two women with severe physical and learning disabilities, it applied both to issues such as the dignity surrounding hoisting and transfers within the home – and to their participation in the life of the community, including recreational and cultural activities.

However, the judge pointed out that paid carers, too, had rights relating to integrity and dignity under article 8. He also emphasised that hoisting was not inherently degrading, but that whether it was or not would depend on all the circumstances of the particular situation (*A&B, X&Y v East Sussex CC*).

Disability discrimination

Under the Disability Discrimination Act 1995 (DDA), which applies to the whole of the United Kingdom, providers of goods and services to the public must not discriminate against disabled people. NHS bodies and local authorities are providers of goods and services to the public. So, too, are independent care providers. (The Act also applies to the provision of education in schools, and in further and higher education.)

Discrimination occurs when such a provider treats a disabled person less favourably and unjustifiably for a reason relating to his or her disability. This would be in respect of not providing a service or of the terms or standards on which the service is provided.

In order to establish that treatment was less favourable, a comparison can be made between the disabled person and either a non disabled person or a disabled person with a different type of disability.

Alternatively, discrimination occurs when a provider fails to take reasonable steps, with the result that it is unreasonably difficult or impossible for a disabled person to use a service.

Nevertheless, even if less favourable treatment does occur, or reasonable steps are not taken, the Act allows for justification if certain grounds can be made out. One of those grounds relates to health and safety. This justification relies on the provider of services being of the opinion that the ground applies and that it is reasonable in all the circumstances for it to hold that opinion.

The lessons to be learnt from the following example, illustrating the importance of proper risk assessment, could easily be applied to a comparable situation involving manual handling.

CASE EXAMPLE: FAILURE TO CONDUCT A RISK ASSESSMENT

A school prevented a 14 year old boy with diabetes going on a water sports holiday with the school. This was on the basis of an episode of hypoglycaemia on a previous school trip, and his alleged irresponsible management of his own condition. A health and safety justification for this less favourable treatment was put forward.

The court rejected this on the basis that the "initial decision was fatally flawed in the manner in which it was taken and thereafter the school adopted a defensive stance and simply confirmed the decision. There was no involvement of [the boy] or his parents in the decision making process, the matters held against him were never put to him for an explanation and there was no serious attempt at a risk assessment taking into account the nature of the holiday and the medical realities. A climate of blame was used to justify a decision that would avoid a repeat of the earlier frightening incident. The belief that exclusion was justified could not be said to be based on a reasonably held opinion that it was necessary in order to not endanger [the pupil's] health or safety" (*White v Clitheroe Royal Grammar School*).

A second education case was directly about manual handling and alleged breach of the Disability Discrimination Act was argued. The reaction of the Court of Appeal in this case is highly instructive, indicating that the DDA is not about sweeping aside genuine, risk assessed health and safety matters.

It concerned a child who had been severely injured in a road accident. He was now paraplegic and incontinent of faeces. He could not change or clean himself. His intellect was unimpaired. He had a statement of special educational needs under the Education Act 1996. He was now attending a mainstream school. To start with, a learning support assistant, and then the special educational needs coordinator, had been cleaning and changing him by lifting the bottom half of his body. The facts of what occurred were as follows:

CASE EXAMPLE: ASSESSMENT OF RISK OF LIFTING FOLLOWED BY INJURY TO STAFF MEMBER

The principal of the school became concerned about the frequency of the bowel accidents and the inadequacy of appropriate facilities and staff to deal with them. The principal referred to the health and safety risks and the need for trained staff, hoists and standing frames, and suitable cleaning and changing facilities – including a sluice and private, properly equipped room. A health and safety consultant recommended that the placement in the school could not be sustained on health and safety grounds.

The principal instructed her staff not to lift the boy. But the special needs coordinator continued to do so, subsequently explaining that she had allowed her heart to rule her head. She was then seriously injured when lifting him. The principal consequently reiterated her instruction that he was not to be lifted, and sought the help of the local education authority (LEA). At the time, the LEA decided not to reassess and allocated no additional funding. On three subsequent dates, the boy had a bowel accident, no member of staff cleaned him up, and he was sent home in the care of an uncle (*K v X Grammar School Governors*).

The mother's argument was that the refusal to lift her son, and sending him home to be changed, was contrary to the education related provisions of the DDA. Neither the High Court nor the Court of Appeal was prepared to find discrimination. It transpired that a significant contributory factor to the whole problem was that the boy's statement of special educational needs, prepared under the Education Act 1996, had from the outset been flawed. This was for various reasons, including understatement by the mother about the frequency of, and difficulty in coping with, her son's incontinence; the glossing over of difficulties by the local education authority; and naivety on the part of the school.

What is notable is the Court of Appeal's view of health and safety in the context of the DDA. It held that, following the report of the health and safety consultant, the school's principal had no alternative but to instruct her staff not to change the boy.

CASE EXAMPLE: IMPORTANCE OF HEALTH AND SAFETY

"What other instruction could a responsible head teacher give? To have instructed a member of staff to lift and change [the boy] in the light of that report would have been... not only irresponsible: it would have been unlawful. Leaving on one side any criminal sanction for breaching health and safety regulations, continuing to lift [the boy] would certainly have laid the school open to an action for damages for personal injuries suffered by any member of staff involved in obeying an unreasonable, indeed unlawful, instruction.

The school, I accept, had a duty to take reasonable steps under DDA section 28C(1)... in my judgement it would have been quite unrealistic to expect the school to put in place the mechanisms properly required for changing and cleaning [the boy]. Such mechanisms are, in my judgement, well outwith any definition of a "reasonable adjustment" capable of being put in place by a school without an application to the LEA for further resources...

In my judgement... the school... has a cast iron defence to a charge of discrimination on two grounds. In the first place, the responsibility for providing the additional facilities required to change and clean [the boy] lay with the LEA... Secondly, the school was plainly justified in refusing to continue to change and clean [the boy] after the receipt of the health and safety report. In fact, of course, we know that [the special needs coordinator] disobeyed instructions and continued to do so. She has paid a heavy price for her humanity and altruism. But her accident simply adds weight to the obvious proposition that changing and cleaning [the boy] without the proper equipment, facilities and training was dangerous, and that the school's refusal to do so was manifestly justified" (*K v X Grammar School Governors*).

Health and safety at work legislation

Health and safety at work legislation is central to decisions about manual handling and applies across the health and social care sector, to local authorities and NHS bodies, and to independent care providers as well. The relevant provisions are not, however, limited to the Manual Handling Operations Regulations 1992 (SI 1992/2793).

In addition, the relevant legislation is not restricted in scope to employees alone. It applies as well, both explicitly and implicitly, to non employees, including service users and informal carers.

Reasonable practicability

Of pivotal importance to an understanding of the health and safety at work legislation, outlined below is the term "reasonably practicable". This term governs key duties relating to manual handling.

The traditional test of reasonable practicability used by the courts has arisen from cases involving risk to employees. The approach has been to weigh up the level of risk to employees against the cost of doing something about it in terms of resources, staff, time and effort. If the cost involved would be clearly disproportionate to the risk, then it might not be reasonably practicable to eliminate or reduce the risk.

CASE EXAMPLE: BALANCING RISK AGAINST RESOURCES

A local authority carpenter was carrying doors weighing 72 pounds up the stairs of a block of flats. He sustained an injury. The Court of Appeal accepted that the risk of manual handling injury appeared from the evidence to have been relatively low. However, providing him that day with an assistant would not have been a disproportionate drain on the resources of an employer the size of the local authority. The local authority was therefore found to be in breach of the MHOR 1992 (*Hawkes v Southwark LBC*).

Reasonable practicability: benefit or utility

In a number of cases involving public services, the courts have referred to another element that must be taken into account when deciding how far it is reasonably practicable to reduce risk to employees. This element is, namely, the benefit or utility of the activity in question to the relevant member(s) of the public. The courts are, in effect, pointing out that the test of reasonable practicability can be made sense of only if the relevant public service context is taken into account.

CASE EXAMPLE: MANUAL HANDLING IN THE COMMUNITY

A dispute arose between a local authority and the parents of two women with profound physical and learning disabilities. The parents were generally opposed to the use of hoists within the home and wished their daughters to be manually handled. They also wished their daughters to get out and participate in the community, particularly in respect of swimming, shopping and horseriding.

The local authority felt unable to agree to the wishes of the parents, because of what it perceived to be the high manual handling risks to staff.

The court held, in effect, that, when considering what was reasonably practicable to protect employees under the MHOR 1992, the local authority had also to consider the assessed community care needs of the women and their human rights. This would involve balanced decision making. It would not mean that the rights of disabled people should override those of paid carers; nor would it mean that those of paid carers should override those of disabled people. Nevertheless, it might mean that, in certain circumstances, paid carers might have to work at higher, but not unacceptable, levels of risk – depending on the needs, and threat to the human rights, of a disabled person.

On the other hand, staff – such as nurses and care assistants – "were not to be viewed as self sacrificing Mother Teresas; human rights did not mean a return to sending boys back up chimneys or women down coal mines" (*A&B, X&Y v East Sussex CC*).

CASE EXAMPLE: NHS CARE ASSISTANT: MAKING CHILDREN'S BEDS

A care assistant in an NHS residential home for disabled children allegedly sustained an injury through pulling out and making beds that were low and stood against the wall. The Court of Appeal accepted in principle that certain features of the beds, though potentially increasing the risk for staff, might be justifiable in relation to the needs of the children (*Koonjul v Thameslink NHS Health Care Trust*).

CASE EXAMPLE: AMBULANCE SERVICE: MANUAL HANDLING ON NARROW STAIRCASE IN RESPONSE TO URGENT CALL

The ambulance service was called to collect a man from his home and take him to hospital. It was an urgent call, requiring a response within an hour, but not an emergency. The man lived in a cottage, and was upstairs in a bedroom, reached by a steep, narrow staircase with a bend in it. The two ambulancemen started to carry the man down the stairs in a carry chair.

One of the ambulancemen momentarily relaxed his grip on the front of the chair; the other ambulance man briefly had to bear the whole weight, and suffered injuries to his thumb, back and knees.

The injured ambulanceman brought a personal injury case, arguing that he should have been trained to give serious consideration to the alternative of using the fire brigade to remove the man through a window with a crane – and that the ambulance service wrongly treated use of the fire brigade as an absolute last resort.

The Court of Appeal rejected the ambulanceman's argument, partly on the basis that public service workers sometimes have to work at higher, though not unacceptable, levels of risk. The court also pointed out that, in determining whether to call for the fire brigade to effect quite a drastic form of removal, various relevant factors had to be taken account of. These included distress to the patient and reaction of the carers (*King v Sussex Ambulance Service NHS Trust*).

The judicial approach illustrated in the above cases is consonant with Health and Safety Executive guidance, which points out that reasonable practicability does not necessarily entail that all risk be removed. Otherwise, there would, for instance, be no adequate fire brigade (HSE 2004).

In other words, risk assessment must be performed in context. The Health and Safety Commission has stated that within the health services, certain situations and activities will sometimes inevitably involve higher risk. One such activity would be rehabilitation (HSC 1998). This approach is further argued in guidance on manual handling issued by the Chartered Society of Physiotherapy (CSP 2008).

In the community care context, this benefit or utility as part of the reasonable practicability equation is, legally, supplied by people's assessed need and human rights under community care and human rights legislation respectively.

Duty to employees: Health and Safety at Work etc Act 1974

Under section 2 of the Health and Safety at Work etc Act 1974, employers have a duty to safeguard the health, safety and welfare of their employees at work, as far as is reasonably practicable.

The overall duty includes the provision and maintenance of safe systems of work, together with instruction, information, training and supervision. It also covers safe use, handling, transport and storage of equipment, as well as a safe working environment. All this has to be achieved insofar as it is reasonably practicable to do so. Clearly, these duties are generally relevant to manual handling, notwithstanding the more specific regulations outlined immediately below.

Duty to employees: Management of Health and Safety at Work Regulations 1999

Under the Management of Health and Safety at Work Regulations 1999 (MHSWR 1999), employers have various duties. These include the duty to assess risks to the health and safety of their employees at work, in order to identify risks relating to other, relevant health and safety at work legislation such as the Manual Handling Operations Regulations 1992 (MHOR 1992).

In addition, a range of other duties are contained in the 1999 regulations, including the provision of information and training to employees. Employers must also cooperate and coordinate activities in a workplace shared with other employers or self employed people in order to ensure compliance with relevant health and safety requirements. They are also obliged in a shared workplace to provide health and safety information to other employers or to self employed people working in the employer's undertaking. These duties could apply to manual handling situations.

EXAMPLE: SHARED WORKPLACE

A disabled person is receiving a complex care package in her own home. This includes various items of equipment for assisting with transfers and involves regular input from NHS district nurses, social services care staff, and care assistants from an independent care provider. The care package, therefore, involves three employers in a shared workplace (the person's home). Unnecessary risk may arise if communication is poor and relevant information is not shared about, for instance, changes in the service user's abilities. Likewise, if it is unclear, eg as to who is responsible for the maintenance of any manual handling equipment being used.

Duty to employees: Manual Handling Operations Regulations 1992

Under the MHOR 1992, employers must take various steps. As far as is reasonably practicable, they must avoid the need for their employees to undertake manual handling involving a risk of injury. The assessment that identifies such risk generally in the first place takes place under the 1999 regulations (see immediately above).

If it is not reasonably practicable for an employer to avoid the risk of injury to its employees, then it must carry out a suitable and sufficient assessment, and take appropriate steps to reduce the risk to the lowest level reasonably practicable. If reasonably practicable, it must also provide precise information on the weight, and heaviest side, of the "load".

The employer must have regard to the physical suitability of an employee to carry out the tasks together with clothing, footwear and other personal effects being carried. It must also have regard to any relevant risk assessment under regulation 3 of the 1999 regulations and whether an employee has been identified by that assessment as coming within a group of employees particularly at risk. It must have regard to the results of any health surveillance carried out under regulation 6 of the 1999 regulations.

EXAMPLE: MANAGING AND REDUCING A HIGHER RISK

A woman living in her own home is assessed as posing a higher risk to the local authority carers who will need to transfer her each day from bed to wheelchair, wheelchair to bath etc. Some of these transfers will need to be achieved by hoist and some by transfer board. The assessment also shows that failure to get the woman up and about by means of these transfers will have a detrimental effect on her physically, medically and psychologically.

It is therefore decided that she will be cared for by a named team of carers, who will be specially trained and supervised for the first two weeks of their involvement. A special sling is used. Some of the transfer activity involves kneeling. It is known that some carers working for the local authority have difficulty kneeling and so those carers are specifically excluded from the team.

Both the MHSWR 1999 and the MHOR 1992 impose a duty on employers to review the risk assessment if there is reason to believe that it is no longer valid or if there has been significant change in the situation. The employer must then make any changes required.

CASE EXAMPLE: MAINTAINING RISK ASSESSMENTS AND CARE PLANS

In one negligence case, the risks posed by a woman who was assisted to walk at a day hospital had increased. This had, correctly, been recorded in her notes. However, the physiotherapist had not taken correspondingly greater precautions, and this had resulted in injury to an occupational therapy assistant. The NHS Trust was held liable for the injury (*Stainton v Chorley and South Ribble NHS Trust*).

Employers should be in no doubt that the taking of shortcuts with matters such as suitable risk assessment, staff training, equipment and systems of work will lead to findings of liability under the MHOR 1992, other regulations or in negligence. Two cases involving high compensation payments illustrate the point.

They both involved nurses who provided care for highly dependent people in hospital. Serious injury was caused in the one case due to absent or defective hoists, and a system of work that tolerated routine use of a lifting technique (the "drag" lift) well known to be unsafe (*Knott v Newham Healthcare NHS Trust*). In the other case, the injury arose from an absence of adjustable height beds which brought about cumulative strain, and an ill maintained wheelchair, the straw that broke the nurse's back, as it were. The court found breaches of both the MHOR 1992 and The Provision and Use of Work Equipment Regulations 1998 (PUWER 1998) (*Commons v Queen's Medical Centre*).

Duties of employees

The Health and Safety at Work etc Act 1974 (section 7) imposes a duty on an employee to take reasonable care of his or her own health and safety and also that of other people who may be affected by the employee's acts or failure to act. Under the MHOR 1992, an employee must make full and proper use of any system of work provided in relation to the reduction of risk. And, under the MHSWR 1999, employees must use equipment in accordance with any training provided and with instructions provided by the employer.

Self employed people

Under section 3 of the Health and Safety at Work Act etc 1974, self employed people have a duty to conduct their undertaking in such a way as to ensure that, as far as reasonably practicable, other people who may be affected are not exposed to risk to their health and safety. In addition, the duties imposed on employers, as outlined above in both the MHSWR 1999 and the MHOR 1992, apply also to self employed people.

Duties of employers toward non employees

As already explained, employers must take account of non employees, such as service users, when deciding what is reasonably practicable in order to safeguard employees. However, there are, in addition, explicit duties owed toward non employees.

Under section 3 of the 1974 Act, an employer must conduct its undertaking in such a way as to ensure, so far as is reasonably practicable, that non employees who may be affected are not exposed to risks to their health and safety. In addition, under regulation 3 of the MHSWR 1999, there is a duty to carry out a suitable and sufficient assessment of the risks to the health and safety of non employees arising from, or connected with, the employer's undertaking.

The term non employee is wide in scope. Non employees of a local authority include, for example, community care service users, informal carers, NHS staff, employees of independent care providers, and self employed people providing a service to the local authority.

EXAMPLE: POOR CONTRACTING OUT OF A SERVICE INVOLVING MANUAL HANDLING

A local authority contracts out provision of its domiciliary community care services to a local independent care provider. However, the authority is in a financial crisis. It allocates inadequate funding to the contract. It also fails to check on the safety record of the contractor in question and to monitor the performance of the contract.

Poor practice and unsafe working flourish, leading to two serious accidents to the care provider's staff. The Health and Safety Executive considers whether to prosecute both the care provider and the local authority under, respectively, sections 2 and 3 of the Health and Safety at Work Act etc 1974. (For a comparable actual case, see *HSE v Barnet LBC*, which involved manual handling: the contractor provided a refuse collection service.)

Duties in respect of maintaining and reviewing manual handling equipment

Under the Lifting Operations and Lifting Equipment Regulations 1998, employers have various duties in respect of lifting equipment being used at work, including thorough examination. Under the PUWER 1998, employers have various duties in respect of all equipment used at work, including lifting equipment. These duties include a strict obligation to maintain work equipment in an efficient state, efficient working order and in good repair.

When equipment (for lifting or otherwise) is used only by service users or informal carers, these two sets of regulations do not apply, because it would not be classed as work equipment. However, a duty to maintain equipment to a comparable standard would still arise under section 3 of the Health and Safety at Work Act etc 1974 and regulation 3 of the MHSWR 1999 – both of which contain duties toward non employees (see above, and see HSE 2002).

Common law of negligence

The law of negligence is for the most part "common law" and is therefore to be found not in legislation but in the decisions of the law courts. It concerns harm (physical but sometimes psychological and, in some circumstances, financial) suffered. The claimant has to show that a duty of care was owed by the person who allegedly caused the harm, that the duty was breached by a careless action or omission, and that the breach directly caused the harm complained of.

In the manual handling context, the law of negligence is likely to be used in two main ways.

First, non employees who have suffered harm are not able to use health and safety at work legislation to bring a civil law claim for compensation. This is notwithstanding that they are in principle protected by section 3 of the Health and Safety at Work Act etc 1974 and by regulation 3 of the MHSWR 1999. Therefore, such claimants have to use the law of negligence.

Second, although employees can make use of some health and safety at work legislation (eg the MHOR 1992) to bring a civil compensation claim, they may nevertheless bring the claim in negligence as well. This would be just in case the claim were to fail under health and safety at work legislation. Although it is unlikely that a claim will succeed in negligence but fail under the MHOR 1992, this did occur in one Scottish case (*Fraser v Greater Glasgow Health Board*).

CASE EXAMPLE: INJURED SOCIAL WORKER

In 1989, a social worker aged 30 visited a service user at home who weighed 15 stone. She found him lying half out of bed, with a neighbour there (who happened to be a nurse). The nurse guided the social worker in moving him; the latter felt something give in her lower back. She had received no training in lifting techniques. The case succeeded in the County Court because it was reasonably foreseeable that she might be confronted with emergency situations. Although the situation was unusual, she should have been warned not to lift in such circumstances. Even if a long training course was not warranted, the risks of lifting should have been brought to her notice. There was no contributory negligence. She was eventually awarded over £200,000 damages (*Colclough v Staffordshire CC*; Zindani 1998).

Local authorities may owe a duty of care, too, to service users or to foster carers:

CASE EXAMPLE: DROPPING A SERVICE USER OR PROVIDING A DEFECTIVE BED

A woman with disseminated sclerosis sought damages for negligence against the local authority. Her claim relating to the adequacy of the home help provided failed because it related to a statutory duty (involving policy, priorities, resources etc). However, the court noted that a claim in negligence might have been possible if, for instance, the home help had dropped the woman and injured her, or if the bed provided by the local authority had been defective, collapsed and caused injury (*Wyatt v Hillingdon LBC*).

CASE EXAMPLE: SUPPORT AND EQUIPMENT FOR A LOCAL AUTHORITY FOSTER CARER

A woman had been acting as a paid foster carer to a disabled teenage boy, placed with her by the council. She claimed that she had suffered a back injury when trying to catch, lift, save or restrain him. She argued that she should have been provided with a hoist or other lifting equipment earlier than she was; that the local authority failed properly to assess the placement; and that, had it done so, it would not have placed such a heavy and disabled child with her. This was in the light of her complete lack of experience in caring for children with such a disability. She also claimed that she should have been trained in lifting techniques and should have been warned of the risks of the work. The local authority denied that it had a duty of care at all to her, let alone that it had acted without due care. The court found that it did owe a duty of care, and that a further hearing should take place to decide whether this duty had been breached through carelessness (*Beasley v Buckinghamshire CC*).

National regulatory legislation

Health and social care providers, public or independent, are now regulated by the Care Quality Commission (CQC). This takes place under the Health and Social Care Act 2008 and regulations. Among other things, the latter cover safety of users of services, dignity, and appropriate equipment – all directly relevant to manual handling (SI 2010/781).

If regulations are breached, the CQC can issue warning notices, impose or vary or remove registration conditions, issue

financial penalties, suspend or cancel registration, prosecute specified offences and issue simple cautions.

Discussion and conclusion

Discussion

This chapter has set out the legal underpinning for the taking of balanced decisions in health and social care, involving weighing up the safety of staff against the needs and rights of service users in the context of manual handling.

Nevertheless, concerns have been expressed that the courts' emphasis on such balanced decision making, in the light of human rights, could lead to a significant increase in manual handling injury to staff in health and social care (eg Griffith & Stevens 2004).

At first sight, there would appear to be some logic underpinning such concerns, insofar as the courts have confirmed that, in some circumstances, higher risks may have to be entertained in order that a public service be provided. A further, potentially unattractive, consequence is that if a higher risk has been properly assessed and managed, but injury still occurs, the employee may fail to win his or her personal injury litigation (eg *King v Sussex Ambulance Service NHS Trust*).

However, this view needs to be considered more carefully.

First, the courts have referred to the requirement to observe both the safety of paid staff, and the needs and rights of service users – and that neither set of rights overrides the other.

Second, the courts have not perversely demanded that paid staff must undertake higher risks and suffer injury merely for the sake of it. They have simply referred to the importance of not overlooking the assessed needs and human rights of service users. With sufficient thought, assessment and negotiation, those needs and rights can often be observed precisely without undue risk to staff of injury.

Third, the courts have referred to higher risks sometimes being taken by staff, but emphasised that this should not involve "unacceptable" risks. For instance, in the *East Sussex* case, the judge stated quite clearly that in the case of hazardous lifts in the home, manual handling would be the exception. Health and Safety Executive guidance likewise states that unsafe work practices are not acceptable (HSE 2002).

Fourth, it is arguable that much manual handling injury is not due to the taking of well managed, higher risk. It seems often to flow from the absence of proper risk management – in terms of adequate allocation of resources, expertise, assessments, care plans, staffing, training, information, supervision and equipment etc. The gulf between properly managed and unmanaged risk is vast; indeed, it is clearly arguable that higher risk, well managed, will ultimately pose a lower risk of injury than lower risk, poorly managed.

Fifth, there may be a temptation for some organisations (and individual professionals), which are failing to assess and to manage risk competently, irrationally to blame human rights for consequent injuries to staff. The temptation should be resisted; to blame such failure on human rights is seriously mistaken and a red herring.

Sixth, a balanced approach is likely to make it more difficult for local authorities (and care providers) to execute the short cuts that result in poor risk management (and all that it entails: see point four immediately above).

One such shortcut comes in the form of blanket policies that overlook the individual assessed needs of service users and sometimes breach their human rights. Driven typically by administrative convenience and financial constraint, these policies purport to protect staff that are poorly trained and supervised, and so are genuinely unable to assess and to manage even relatively straightforward and lower levels of risk. However, the policies are unacceptable, because they are operated and tolerated to the detriment of service users. In such circumstances, staff, too, may suffer detriment because, when confronted with risk (low or high, expected or unexpected), they are not equipped to identify, assess and manage it.

Last, the courts' concern that blanket policies should not be applied, and that the needs and human rights of service users must be weighed in the balance as well as staff safety, is no more than basic, good professional practice. Debate about human rights may have highlighted this, but good professional practice and existing law demanded such an approach even before the advent of the Human Rights Act.

A balanced approach based on individual assessment means those professionals carrying out manual handling assessments and drawing up care plans may sometimes have to make difficult decisions. Answers will not always be black and white and "served up on a plate". Instead, informed, professional judgement has to be exercised in individual cases and has to be justifiable in terms of documented evidence, reasoning and conclusions.

Conclusion

This chapter has shown the breadth of legislation applying to manual handling related decisions in health and social care. In order to comply with this legislation, the requirement of balanced decision making is inevitable. Tunnel vision, erring toward either only staff safety or only the rights of service users, simply will not do.

References

Cases

A&B, X&Y v East Sussex County Council, ex p Tandy [2003] EWHC 167 (Admin), High Court.

Barking and Dagenham London Borough Council (1998), Commission for Local Administration in England. Case 97/A/0337.

Beasley v Buckinghamshire County Council [1997] PIQR P473, High Court.

Colclough v Staffordshire County Council [1994] CL 94/2283, County Court, on liability; and (1997), High Court, unreported, see: Zindani 1998, p.189).

Commons v Queen's Medical Centre Nottingham University Hospital NHS Trust (2001, County Court, unreported).

Fraser v Greater Glasgow Health Board (1996) Rep LR 58, Court of Session, Scotland.

Hawkes v Southwark London Borough Council (1998), unreported, Court of Appeal.

HSE v Barnet London Borough Council (1997, unreported, Crown Court).

K v X Grammar School Governors [2007] EWCA Civ 165.

King v Sussex Ambulance Service NHS Trust [2002] EWCA Civ 935, Court of Appeal.

Knott v Newham Healthcare NHS Trust [2002] EWHC 2091, High Court.

Koonjul v Thameslink NHS Health Care Trust [2000] PIQR P123, Court of Appeal.

Price v United Kingdom (2001) 34 EHRR 1285, European Court of Human Rights.

R (G) v Barnet London Borough Council [2003] UKHL 57.

R (Khana) v Southwark London Borough Council [2001] EWCA Civ 999, Court of Appeal.

R (SC) v Salford City Council [2007] EWhC 3276 admin.

R v Avon County Council, ex p M [1999] 2 CCLR 185, High Court.

R v Bexley LBC, ex p B [1995] 1 CLYB 3225, High Court.

R v Birmingham City Council, ex p Killigrew [2000] 3 CCLR 109, High Court.

R v Bouldstridge (reported in Kelso P *(2000)*. "He only wanted to end his wife's pain. He ended up court, at 84", *The Guardian*, 7 June 2000, p1).

R v Bristol City Council, ex p Penfold [1998] 1 CCLR 315.

R v Gloucestershire County Council, ex p Barry [1997] 2 All ER 1, House of Lords.

R v Gloucestershire County Council, ex p Mahfood (1995) 160 LGRR 321, High Court.

R v Gloucestershire County Council, ex p RADAR [1996] COD 253, High Court.

R v Haringey London Borough Council, ex p Norton [1998] 1 CCLR 168, High Court.

R v Lancashire County Council, ex p RADAR [1996] 4 All ER 422, Court of Appeal.

R v North Yorkshire County Council, ex p Hargreaves [1994] 26 BMLR 121, High Court.

R v Royal Borough of Kensington and Chelsea, ex p Kujtim [1999] 2 CCLR 341, Court of Appeal.

R v Sefton Metropolitan Borough Council, ex p Help the Aged [1997] 3 FCR 573, Court of Appeal.

Stainton v Chorley and South Ribble NHS Trust (1998), unreported, High Court.

Urquhart v Fife Primary Care Trust [2007] CSOH 02.

White v Clitheroe Royal Grammar School (2002), Preston County Court.

Wyatt v Hillingdon London Borough Council [1978] 76 LGR 727, Court of Appeal.

Other references

Audit Commission (2000), *Fully equipped: the provision of equipment to older or disabled people by the NHS and social services in England and Wales*. London: Audit Commission.

Commission for Local Administration in England (2008), *Report on an investigation into complaint no 07/B/07665 against Luton Borough Council*. Coventry: CLAE.

CSP (2008), Chartered Society of Physiotherapy, *Guidance on manual handling in physiotherapy*, London: CSP, p.19.

DH (2004), Department of Health. *Community Care Assessment Directions*. London: DH.

DH (2007), Department of Health, *Putting people first: a shared commitment to the transformation of adult social care,* London: DH.

DH (2007a), Department of Health. *Independence, choice and risk*, London: DH, para 2.26.

DH (2009), Department of Health, *Guidance on direct payments for community care, services for carers and children's services.* London: DH, paras 132-34.

DH (2010), Department of Health, *Prioritising need in the context of Putting People First: A whole system approach to eligibility for social care: guidance on Eligibility Criteria for Adult Social Care, England,* London: DH.

Griffith, R & Stevens, M (2004), Manual handling and the lawfulness of no-lift policies. *Nursing Standard*; vol.**18**, no. 21, 4-10 February 2004.

Henwood, M (1998), *Ignored and invisible? Carers' experience of the NHS.* London: Carers National Association.

HSC (1998), Health and Safety Commission, *Manual handling in the health services*, Sudbury: HSC, p43.

HSC 2001/008; LAC (2001)13. Community equipment services, London: Department of Health.

HSE (2002), Health and Safety Executive, *Handling home care: achieving safe, efficient and positive outcomes for care workers and clients,* Sudbury: HSE, p3.

HSE (2004), Health and Safety Executive. *Manual handling: Manual Handling Operations Regulations 1992: guidance on regulations,* Sudbury: HSE, p8.

LAC(DH) (2008),1, *Transforming social care,* London: Department of Heath, 2008.

LAC(DH) (2009),1, *Transforming social care*, London: Department of Health, 2009.

Marriott, H (2003), *The selfish pig's guide to caring*, Clifton upon Teme: Polperro Heritage Press.

SI 1992/2793, *Manual Handling Operations Regulations 1992.*

SI 2002/2793, *Manual Handling Operations Regulations 1992 (as amended).*

SI 2002/57, *Fostering Services Regulations 2002, rr.15, 17.*

SI 2009/1887, *The Community Care, Services for Carers and Children's Services (Direct Payments) (England) Regulations 2009.*

SI 2010/100, *The National Health Service (Direct Payments) Regulations 2010.*

SI 2010/781, *Health and Social Care Act 2008 (Regulated Activities) Regulations 2010.*

Zindani, G (1998), *Manual handling: law and litigation*, London: CLT Professional Publishing.

Manual handling risk management

Carole Johnson MCSP Cert Ed

Registered member NBE, chartered physiotherapist, moving and handling consultant

Knowledge is knowing that a tomato is a fruit.
Wisdom is knowing not to put one in a fruit salad.

Miles Kington (as cited by Hammond 2008)

Introduction

Health and safety legislation places a duty on all employers to ensure the health, safety and welfare of their employees and others affected by their undertakings. Since the implementation of the Management of Health and Safety at Work Regulations (MHSWR) 1999, the method of compliance required is that the employer must have in place adequate systems for risk assessment and risk management. Risk assessment, on the face of it, should be easy and straightforward:

- identify the hazard
- decide who could be harmed and how
- evaluate the risk
- devise a plan aimed at reducing risk
- put the plan into action and review.

When applying these general principles provided by the Health and Safety Executive (HSE) to the moving and handling of people, often it can seem far more complicated and emotive than many envisage. Nevertheless, these general principles offer a robust foundation of a systems approach to safer moving and handling practice, whether in a person's own home or within large and complex health and social care organisations that may have multiple links and responsibilities.

This chapter will consider the relevant legislation, risk management processes, components of the risk assessment, principles for reducing risk, and suggest ways of improving the involvement of all the stakeholders. It will examine influencing factors that do not necessarily feature in a standard assessment protocol. Risk assessment is not an end in itself, but the first key element of a strategy that aims to reduce risk.

Risk management

© CartoonStock.com/S Harris

The employer must initially perform a general assessment of risk using MHSWR and the Health and Safety at Work etc Act 1974. If hazardous manual handling is then identified, the more detailed MHOR are applied.

The HSE (1999) summarises and gives further information on the general principles of risk assessment. These are:

- the purpose of the risk assessment is "to help the employer or self employed person to determine what measures should be taken to comply with *their* duties"
- identify the hazard
- identify *all* who can be harmed and the severity
- evaluate the risk
- include fire risks
- the assessment should be suitable and sufficient (in proportion to the level of risk)
- the assessment should be appropriate to the nature of the work and identify how long it is valid in order to encourage review and monitoring
- look at how the work is organised
- take account of routine and non routine activities, including interruptions
- employers (and self employed) take steps to help themselves identify risks by looking at good practice, other sources of information etc
- observe actual practice
- consider current preventative measures in place
- record – ensuring that it is retrievable (especially if recorded electronically) – including control measures, further action and proof (written evidence) that a suitable and sufficient assessment has been made
- review and revise as the work changes
- the employer is not expected to assess risks that are not foreseeable.

Risk management can be defined as:

"the culture, processes and structures that are directed towards realising potential opportunities, while managing adverse effects."

The risk management process can be defined as:

"the systematic application of management policies, procedures and practices to the tasks of communicating, establishing the context, identifying, analysing, evaluating, treating, monitoring and reviewing risk."

AS/NZS 4360:2004

Risk management principles should:
- create value
- be an integral part of organisational processes
- be part of decision making
- explicitly address uncertainty
- be systematic and structured
- be based on the best available information
- be tailored
- take into account human factors
- be transparent and inclusive
- be dynamic, iterative and responsive to change
- facilitate continual improvement and enhancement.

AS/NZS ISO 31000:2009

Applying these principles to the health and safety culture within health and social care, organisations would consider the following:

- Create value – recognition of the welfare of all those who are involved, including, but not limited to, the person being assisted, the handler, other staff and family. The increased value can be developed on several levels from better outcomes, cost improvements, feelings of worth, efficiency, for example.
- Part of organisational processes – in the field of health and safety culture, it is vital that the systems developed are part of the whole ethos of that organisation. This avoids knee jerk reactions to a crisis and allows "buy in" from all stakeholders.

EXAMPLE

A child who uses a wheelchair and is unable to weight bear is due to start a new school. The previous school has completed an assessment and has strategies in place to manage the moving and handling required. The child is likely to have a relatively smooth transition if the new school has a culture that recognises the issues and has processes for making the child's transition successful. Without a suitable system, the child and staff will feel unsupported and be at greater risk even if the plan was to undertake a risk assessment on the first day.

- Part of decision making – this is the opportunity for information collected as part of the risk management to contribute to the decisions that are being considered. For example, an annual audit on the number of hoists available and usage could form the basis of the decision on whether to change a supplier contract or maintenance programme.
- Address uncertainty – it may be possible to eliminate a risk completely, but often, especially where human beings are concerned, it is difficult to achieve. Accepting that there is uncertainty is the first step. However, tackling the effects of that uncertainty must also occur.

EXAMPLE

Overhead tracking is scheduled to be installed into a person's home as the handlers have found that turning a mobile hoist in the small bedroom has increased the incidence of back pain. However, due to some additional complications, there will be a six week delay. The tendency may be to do nothing for those six weeks as there is a known end date. It is not certain that anyone will be injured in those six weeks, but an interim plan is required, rather than ignoring the potential issue.

- Systematic and structured – the legal framework as detailed later in the chapter gives the clear structure for assessment of risk. Using the law, policies, audit and relevant assessment tools will mean that this aspect of risk management is achievable.
- Best available information – the employer will utilise published research, data collected by audit, including accident reporting such as collected under the Reporting of Injuries, Diseases and Dangerous Occurrences Regulations 1995 (RIDDOR) (HSE 1995) near miss information and complaints, for example.
- Be tailored – there may be generic information, assessment

or strategies that can form the starting point for risk management, but any strategy needs to meet the needs of the specific work organisation.

EXAMPLE

A manual handling training programme may use a general session to give an overview, but, for people handling, detailed training on the specific skills required is needed.

- Human factors – these can include such areas as psychology, equipment design, operations research and anthropometry.
- Transparent and inclusive – the processes and systems should be clear and include staff, self employed, visitors to the site.

EXAMPLE

An unassuming music therapist visited a residential home once a month. She had become responsible for setting up the room, including moving a heavy piano and now was starting to collect the residents. She had not been included in any of the assessment processes, had never had an assessment of the manual handling, until she reported back pain to her line manager.

- Dynamic, iterative and responsive to change – it can be very easy to set up a strategy and complete paperwork.
- Facilitates continual improvement and enhancement – regular review of the management structure and function will allow the management of risk to be flexible and develop.

Thomsett (2004) illustrates a possible risk management structure, but there are many variations. The process is continuous and relies heavily on good communication structures within an organisation.

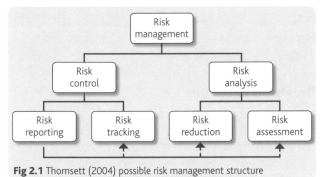

Fig 2.1 Thomsett (2004) possible risk management structure

Setting up a health and safety culture within the workplace

The HSE (2008) lists five steps to success in the management of health and safety:
- Set up the policy
  The health and safety policy should influence all your activities, including the selection of people, equipment and materials, the way work is done and how you design and provide goods and services. A written statement of your policy and the organisation and arrangements for implementing and monitoring it shows your staff, and anyone else, that hazards have been identified and risks assessed, eliminated or controlled.

- Organise the staff
  For an effective health and safety policy, the staff need to be committed, often referred to as a "positive health and safety culture".
  The four "Cs" of positive health and safety culture are:
  – Competence: recruitment, training and advisory support
  – Control: allocating responsibilities, securing commitment, instruction and supervision
  – Cooperation: between individuals and groups
  – Communication: spoken, written and visible.
  Competence in the field of manual handling, and in particular moving and handling people, is discussed by the Royal College of Nursing (RCN) (2003) and National Back Exchange (NBE) (2010). Competence will include the ability to assess the skills needed, supply the means for all employees to be adequately trained, to ensure that members of staff have all they need to function as safely as possible where they are working in more dangerous settings, be able to access suitable advice and able to carry out changes to ensure competency for those taking on new responsibilities within health and safety.
- Plan and set standards
- Measure performance
- Learn from experience – audit and review.

The risk assessor

The person carrying out the risk assessment will vary, depending on the type of assessment.

General assessment of all the health and safety risks will be carried out initially by a risk management group, managers or health and safety department. Once more specific risks are identified, eg for manual handling, the responsibility for completing the assessments may be passed to a ward manager, service manager or department manager. A manual handling practitioner may coordinate the assessments or undertake these personally. For very straightforward people handling assessments a Key Worker may be appointed (NBE 2010). Complex situations may require more expertise, utilising staff with specialist skills or external agents.

Legislative background

The Management of Health and Safety at Work Regulations 1999 (HSE 1999).
Manual Handling Operations Regulations 1992 (as amended 2004) (HSE 2004).
Lifting Operations and Lifting Equipment Regulations 1998 (HSE 1998a).

As discussed in chapter 1, the legislation forms the basis for risk assessment and how the law directs the employer to reduce the risk. For specific detail, it is important to read the relevant legislation and approved code of practice (ACoP) where available. The legislation is part of the risk management process and may be a significant driver for action. The employer not only has a duty to their employees, but, under the Health and Safety at Work etc Act 1974 (HSWA 1974), also has a duty (under section 3) towards people who are not their employees but are affected by their undertaking (eg patients, residents and visitors).

HSE advice

The HSE also summarises the additional steps required as well as the risk assessment in the leaflet *Five steps to risk assessment* (HSE 2008) as:

- make arrangements for implementing the health and safety measures identified as necessary by the risk assessment
- appoint competent people (often themselves or company colleagues) to help them to implement the arrangements
- set up emergency procedures
- provide clear information and training to employees
- work together with other employers sharing the same workplace.

Standards

A number of organisations such as National Back Exchange (NBE 2010), Royal College of Nursing (RCN 2003), Chartered Society of Physiotherapy (CSP 2008), and College of Occupational Therapists (COT 2006a, b, c), to name just a few, have written standards that will help anyone involved in devising and implementing the policy and risk assessment processes to apply the regulations to the moving and handling of people. This area is covered in more detail in chapter 5.

The Management of Health and Safety at Work Regulations 1999 (MHSWR)

(see Appendix 2 for more detailed information)

These regulations can be summarised as follows.

The general principles of prevention must be applied to the assessment of risk. A simple risk management model will help identify issues and actions. This is often simply summarised as:

- plan and set policy
- organise
- control the risks
- monitor and review
- complete a suitable and sufficient risk assessment
- consider workers who may be at greater risk such as young people, temporary workers and expectant mothers
- ensure that information and training is given to the workers
- ensure that a competent person is used for the risk assessment and analysis
- set up procedures for serious and imminent danger, eg planning emergency evacuation
- the need to cooperate and coordinate activities with other employers including, for example, those simply sharing premises, as well as organisations working in partnership to deliver care and other services.

Manual Handling Operations Regulations 1992 (as amended 2004) (MHOR)

(see Appendix 2 for more detailed information)

The MHOR apply the broad requirements of the MHSWR more specifically to manual handling risks. The regulations apply to a broad range of industries and sectors and are primarily focused on avoiding, or minimising, the risk of injury to employees from manual handling activities but compliance with these regulations should also ensure that the risks of injury to the person being assisted are minimised.

While still being risk based, the MHOR go further than MSHWR by introducing the duty for employers to avoid, as far as reasonably practicable, the need for employees to undertake manual handling operations which involve a risk of their being injured. Where this is not reasonably practicable, the regulations go on to detail how the risks shall be assessed and managed (as detailed later in the chapter). In applying the MHOR, the aim should be to "avoid the risk of injury so far as reasonably practicable".

EXAMPLE

A worker in a stores area asked for a manual handling assessment after experiencing a gradual increase in backache over a period of months. After a few questions, the assessor realised that the worker in any year was lifting 500,000 articles (some very light) from the full trolley to an empty but broken one, so that the working trolley could be taken away to be refilled. Immediately, the assessor suggested a way to avoid 250,000 lifts by arranging the repair of the wheels on the broken trolley.

It is reasonably practicable to repair the trolley wheels, whereas it is unlikely to be reasonably practicable to stop having deliveries made to the stores department.

In the field of people handling, the reader may be aware of stories or examples in their own work areas, where an activity has been stopped because of the risk of injury to the handler. However, stopping that activity may have a knock on effect on the person or may not be practical to continue in the long term. Therefore, as far as handling people is concerned, a balanced approach needs to be implemented.

Lifting Operations and Lifting Equipment Regulations 1998

These regulations and the Provision and Use of Work Equipment Regulations 1998 (HSE 1998b) are discussed in more detail in chapters 7 and 11.

Balanced decisions

A balanced decision is one that takes account of all relevant factors, balances the requirements of all legislation and the needs of the people involved. It aims to find a workable solution, rather than one party dictating an outcome to another.

Many staff trained before the easy access to specialised handling equipment so the expectation was to lift a person in their care manually. Any nurse or therapist would be able to recount stories of having to lift outside their capability, or in less than ideal circumstances. There were too many injuries, too many days off sick and too many professional staff being lost permanently.

The response was to follow the regulations to the letter and avoid manual handling wherever possible. This resulted in "no lift" policies in many larger institutions, banning full body lifting techniques and informing the person that they had to be lifted by equipment rather than the "nurse". See chapter 1 for more detail.

Some manual handling practitioners had predicted the clash that emerged in the public arena with the case of *A&B, X&Y v East Sussex County Council* (2003). What happens when the legal responsibilities to protect the workforce seem to conflict with the human rights of the person who needs assistance to move? The full judgement makes interesting reading. The principal paragraphs that are significant in the process for the employer in the first instance and handler (as the person carrying out the tasks) state that when assessing reasonable practicability (paragraph 128):

- the possible methods
- the context
- the risks to the employee
- the impact upon the disabled person

must be focused on the particular circumstances of the individual case. Just as context is everything, so the *individual* assessment is all. Thus, for example:

- the assessment must take into account the *particular* disabled person's personal physical and mental characteristics, be "user focused" and "user led" and should be part of the wider care planning process for that particular individual
- there must be an assessment of the particular disabled person's autonomy interests
- the assessment must be based on the particular workers involved (not workers in the abstract)
- the assessment must be based on the pattern of lifting in the particular case.

The result of the *individual* assessment would be to identify the risks, discuss and find the most appropriate system for handling and recognise that at times a manual lift may be required. The manual handling practitioner or person completing the assessment here needs to be the facilitator rather than the prescriber and balance the health and safety of the handler with the needs of the person being assisted.

A definition of commonly used terms may assist in understanding the process of risk assessment and are included as Appendix 1 to this chapter. The list is not meant to be exclusive or exhaustive.

Suitable and sufficient risk assessment
The risk assessment must:
- Identify the risks, with the level of detail being proportionate to the risk. A larger organisation or a complex task may need greater detail. The assessment should also consider all those who may be affected by the risks.
- Be appropriate to the nature of the work and a review period.
- Consider the broad range of risk where the nature of the work changes frequently.
- Be practical and include the views of the employees and safety advisers.
- Be collaborative if other employers visit or use the site.
- Consider making a "rough" assessment first to eliminate risks where no further action is required.
- Consider using "model" or generalised assessments where appropriate.
- Ensure that significant risk and hazards are addressed.
- Ensure that all aspects of the activity are reviewed and the assessment is systematic.

- Take account of non routine tasks.
- Take account of incidents, such as disruption to the activity.
- Consider how the work is organised.
- Take account of risks to the public.
- Take account of fire risks.
- Include observation the activity.
- Take account of existing measures.
- Be recorded.
- Monitored and reviewed.

The assessment should be completed by a competent person as described earlier. In the area of people handling, there are standards (NBE 2010; RCN 2003) that can be used as a measure of competency. Common sense will be insufficient without a background understanding of how the human body works, what the handler and person can safely manage and how the particular risks may influence each other and the long term health for that person.

The guidance for the MHOR suggests:
- the person should be familiar with the operation being assessed
- the assessor should be able to identify hazards and assess risks for the type of manual handling being completed
- using additional sources of information on risks
- making valid and reliable conclusions
- being able to identify solutions
- making a clear record of the assessment and communicating the findings to those involved
- recognising their personal limitations and when to ask for help.

Once the competent person has been identified, the assessment can begin, remembering that being able to avoid a task from the beginning can save a great deal of time and effort.

The requirements of Regulation 4 can be summarised as:

It is the duty of the employer as far as reasonably practicable to:
- **A** – avoid the need for his employees to undertake manual handling tasks where they may be injured
- **A** – assess the risk where it is not possible to avoid the task
- **R** – reduce the risk to the lowest reasonably practicable level
- **R** – review if the circumstances change.

The acronym AARR is often given to aid the memory. The components of the second bullet point, assess, will be considered in greater detail later in the chapter.

The employees' duties under Regulation 5 are:

"Each employee while at work shall make full and proper use of any system of work provided for his use by his employer in compliance with Regulation (1) (b) (ii) of these Regulations."

Employee responsibilities
The employee, while at work, shall make full and proper use of any system of work provided for his use by his employer and should cooperate with the employer in matters of health and safety.

The manual handling risk assessment

The manual handling risk assessment considers the task, individual capability, the load and the environment. This will be looked at in more detail.

It is much easier to assess the success of an assessment if the right management structure is in place at the outset. Many institutions have policies, equipment purchase programmes, training packages and monitoring processes in place. If this has not yet occurred, an audit of the current situation can avoid the feeling of being swamped at the start. The audit will be different in some details from place to place, but using the HSE model of risk assessment as detailed here can give the framework for a whole organisation as well as for a particular person or area.

> Avoid using single option solutions such as training or equipment purchase. Try starting with an audit to build a measurable picture of the current situation. Remember the bigger picture.

Before detailing the assessment itself, there are some additional questions that the HSE list as helpful for the employer when considering worker involvement in the risk assessment process:

- Have I asked them if their tasks are difficult to do safely?
- Do I ask them what health and safety needs improving and if they have all they need to do the job safely?

- Do I take account of employee views when there are changes in the workplace that might impact on health and safety and on arrangements for competent advice?
- And, when there are changes, how does this affect their information, instruction and training?
- Do I provide the necessary information and arrangements for the representative who could be elected by their colleagues or appointed by a trade union?
- Do I have suitable arrangements in place for consulting my employees, either directly or through their representatives?

The assessor's checklist

TILE(O) is a useful acronym to identify the main components of a manual handling risk assessment, standing for:

- **T** – task
- **I** – individual capability
- **L** – load
- **E** – environment
- **O** – other factors (see Appendix 2 on the Guidance on Regulations, Manual Handling Operations Regulations 1992)

Handling objects is very different from handling people and the way the assessment is completed and documented will necessarily be different, eg the MAC tool (HSE 2003a) cannot be used for people handling assessment.

Looking at each component in more detail:

Task

The tasks must be first identified. Often, a prepared list of the tasks that tend to occur in that establishment may be helpful, particularly when considering people handling. The assessor can show the list to staff or family as a starting point. Having a list ensures that a basic record is made of all the handling tasks that the person undertakes and will often spark discussion about additional activities or requests.

TABLE 2.1 TASK

Factor	Example
What is the task?	Object: Lifting a box of slings – a diagram or description may help explain/describe the task. Person: Verbal assistance through to a full manual lift. Types of task could include: personal care, standing transfers, off the floor, transfer onto a trolley, specialist procedure, transfer to equipment. Does it allow the dignity of the person to be preserved? Some tasks will be well understood and clear to the assessor, others may be more intricate or have interdependencies.
Does it involve:	
Holding or manipulating loads at a distance from trunk?	Object: Lifting a sack of rubbish into a bin. Person: Supporting a person's leg during a surgical procedure or treatment.
Twisting?	Object: Reaching for an object on the back seat of a car. Person: A nurse assisting a new mother to breastfeed by sitting on the bed.
Stooping?	Object: Lifting a large box from the floor. Person: Supporting a small child walking.
Reaching upwards?	Object: Reaching for files on a high shelf. Person: Lifting a child onto play equipment.
Excessive lifting or lowering distances?	Object: Lifting items from the floor to place on a high shelf. Person: Lifting a person from the floor.
Excessive carrying distances?	Object: Carrying equipment where no trolley is available. Person: Carrying a person downstairs.
Excessive pushing or pulling of loads?	Object: Pushing a hospital bed along a corridor Person: Pushing a person in a wheelchair up a hill.
Risk of sudden movement of loads?	Object: Carrying an object with insecure handles. Person: Person being assisted, slipping or falling.

TABLE 2.1 TASK (CONTINUED)

Factor	Example
Does it involve:	
Frequent or prolonged physical effort?	Object: Moving a large delivery of incontinence pads. Person: Supporting a person while walking.
Insufficient rest or recovery periods?	Object: Moving a delivery consignment. Person: Assisting a number of residents to get up in the morning in a short space of time.
A rate of work imposed by a process?	Object: Lifting to/from a conveyor belt. Person: Busy domiciliary care or institutional care settings – getting a number of people up in a certain timeframe/regular toileting regimes/put to bed routines, especially where there is a shortage of staff.
Exceptional circumstances to consider?	Object: Equipment failure. Person: Hoist or other equipment failure, evacuation of premises.

Individual capability (the handler)

This part of the assessment aims to identify the factors that influence the ability of the handler to do the task. Usually, the aim is to choose a method that everyone can complete safely, although this may not always be possible.

The health, safety and wellbeing of the handler is of paramount importance and is discussed further in chapter 8.

TABLE 2.2 INDIVIDUAL CAPABILITY (THE HANDLER)

Factor	Example
Does the job:	
Require unusual strength or height?	An expectation for the tallest and/or strongest members of staff to perform particular tasks, eg lifting people up from the floor, working around beds, matching of staff to particular patients/clients.
Create a hazard to those who might reasonably be considered to be pregnant or to have a health problem?	Are there aspects of the task that can be seen to constitute a risk to a pregnant woman, or, for example, to someone who already has a back problem or other health problem or recent operation?
Ever need to be undertaken by a person who does not usually take part in moving and handling or who is an occasional visitor?	A speech or music therapist, transferring the person from a wheelchair to another seat. The assessment should consider these specialists and ensure that they understand the risks and are included in the policy and action plan.
Require special information or training?	The person undertaking the task should have sufficient knowledge and skill to continue safely. Consideration should be given to the skill level required to do the task. The ability to communicate successfully with the person is vital; the handler's words, action and touch should facilitate the person to move successfully.
Involve additional requirements?	Consider the child protection policy, eg the Criminal Records Bureau (CRB) check.

Load (as an object)

On some objects, it may be possible to mark basic load information on the item itself, such as weight and whether there is a heavier side or if the contents are unstable. This is far more difficult in a community setting.

TABLE 2.3 LOAD (AS AN OBJECT)

Factor	Example
Is the object:	
Heavy?	Armchair or divan bed.
Bulky?	Printer or large boxes of incontinence pads.
Difficult to grasp?	Large piece of medical equipment.
Unstable or with contents likely to shift?	Bags of shopping, laundry or boxes with unsecured items.
Sharp, hot or otherwise potentially damaging?	Cooking pans, needles.

Load (a person)

The factors to consider are much more extensive when considering a person.

TABLE 2.4 LOAD (A PERSON)

Factor	Points of consideration
Does the method chosen encourage independence?	In the longer term, will the method of assistance encourage the person to be as independent as possible? Is it important to this person to be as independent? Is the physiotherapist and occupational therapist or any other professional involved? Does this handling plan need to be integrated with the therapy plan?
Able to weight bear?	Can the person stand and do so without the need for support or assistance? Does the person rely on standing to be able to transfer and move within their environment? Does the state of the person's feet affect weight bearing ability?
How much help does the person need?	Is the person able to perform all the tasks even without supervision? If the person needs help, how much help? Does he/she need equipment? Do you know what equipment is available? Do you know the benefits and dangers of the equipment or process you are using or recommending?
Person's expectations/wishes/concerns	Does the person have requests or wishes that will affect the moving and handling? Have these been discussed and considered? Is the person worried about the moving and handling task? Has that person given any indication of previous negative experiences?
Ability to communicate with others	Can the person explain their situation to you and follow requests?
Predictability	Is the person always the same or are there times when he/she is better than others? Does the person easily tire or have difficulty providing sustained effort? Does the variance mean that more than one action plan is needed?
Is the person a child or vulnerable adult?	For example, do there need to be considerations because the person has issues regarding his/her capacity to make decisions or may have been abused in the past and need extra care?
Pain/medication	Is the person in pain? Has the pain been diagnosed and a suitable system of pain relief established? Does the person need referral to his/her GP or a pain specialist? Does the person take any medication that affects his/her mobility? Does timing of drug administration need to be changed to ensure best effects occur during moving and handling tasks?
Tissue viability/infection	Does the person need any special considerations related to his/her skin or need disposable equipment such as slings because of infection?
Behaviour	Is the person likely to be anxious, passive, show inappropriate responses or be violent or aggressive? Are there any triggers to the behaviour? Is there a behaviour management plan?
Cultural issues	Have these issues been considered, eg possible differing expectations regarding gender of handlers, authority and acceptance, methods of managing personal hygiene?
Physical abilities/operations or interventions	Has the person a disability or health problem that affects how much he/she can help? Are there any special considerations that need to be included? Is there a health problem that may intermittently affect his/her ability (eg epileptic seizures)? Does the person have any problems with muscle tone, spasm, tremor, contractures, and/or stiffness? Has the person undergone surgery or had a recent heart attack? Can the person balance himself/herself in lying, sitting and standing? Does he/she have any muscle weakness?
Comfort	Is the method used comfortable and not causing any difficulties, eg skin damage, pain or undue stress on a part of the body?
Body shape	Does the person need specialist equipment because of his/her body shape, such as individually made hoist slings or postural equipment?
Height and weight of the person	How tall and heavy is the person? Will special equipment be needed to support him/her, such as beds, seats, hoists, commodes? Can that equipment support the combined weight of the person being assisted and the staff?
Falls	Does the person have a history of falls? Is there a falls assessment tool that should be completed?

Environment

TABLE 2.5 ENVIRONMENT

Factor	Points of consideration
Space constraints on posture	This could be due to extra equipment needed in a small space, storage difficulties or due to design of the equipment, layout of furniture in a person's home.
Uneven, slippery or unstable floors	Is there a leak or fluid/ice on the floor? Are there steps, thresholds or edges that make the moving and handling more difficult? Does the surface make pushing equipment over it difficult? Are you working outside?
Variations in levels of floors or work surfaces	Is the person or handler required to work on different levels or negotiate steps?
Extremes of temperature or humidity	Does the temperature or humidity need to be recorded and investigated? What temperatures are needed for the comfort of dependent individuals, compared with those handlers undertaking the work tasks?
Indoors/outdoors	Is the task being undertaken indoors or outdoors? Are there variable gradients, distances involved, weather conditions to consider, or the need to assist the person in public places?
Ventilation problems	Is there too little or too much ventilation?
Poor lighting	Can the person and handler see sufficiently to get the job done?
Equipment	Can the equipment assigned such as hoists, wheelchairs, standing frames be used easily in the space provided? Has the equipment been checked as part of a maintenance programme and does it comply with equipment regulations? Are there systems in place to obtain specialist equipment that may only be needed on an occasional basis?

Other factors

Often, this section is seen as a "catch all" where most aspects will have been covered in TILE. However, it is the author's experience that the "other factors" can be very significant where the manual handling of people is concerned.

TABLE 2.6 OTHER FACTORS

Factor	Example
Does clothing affect the task?	Is everyone wearing suitable clothing, including footwear? Has jewellery been removed? Does protective equipment affect the task (eg gloves, plastic overshoes at a swimming pool)?
Are there other personal factors that need to be considered?	Has the handler or the person being handled expressed concerns or views about any aspect of the task? Have that person's values been taken into consideration? Does the handler feel that the person is making an inappropriate handling choice? Does the person feel he/she must use methods he/she is not happy with?
Are there other legal factors that need to be considered?	Does the moving and handling task infringe the person's human rights or could it be considered discriminatory. Is the duty of care affected? Are there any issues over mental capacity?
Could a generic assessment save time and still meet the needs?	Some tasks may be the same for a ward or department, eg using a bath hoist to get into and out of the bath and anyone using that bath would follow the same procedure. Generic assessments can save time, but any variance must be documented and any form should have a question that leads the assessor to further assessment when required.
Is the handler the sole handler? Do they undertake frequent manual handling?	Sometimes one person ends up undertaking all the manual handling, such as a family member or one person who feels skilled enough. It is also possible that a skilled handler may may be asked repeatedly to complete difficult manual handling because other handlers do not feel as confident. This places an increased risk on that skilled handler.

Mobility assessments

The TILE(O) headings provide the assessor with a good structure on which to base an assessment, but an additional dimension is needed when considering humans and their mobility. A great deal of the assessment of the person's ability can be completed by a simple mobility assessment. It is much easier to teach the assessment face to face in a practical session.

Simply collecting the above data for a human load will not necessarily assist the assessor in understanding the risks relating to that person and their ability. Human beings are complex entities that require coordination of multiple systems in order to be able to move, change position. Unlike an object, people change their minds, feel well some days and poorly on others, like some activities and avoid others. The assessor has to piece a great deal of information together. The initial mobility assessment provides a benchmark against which the handler must check and measure each time the person is assisted.

A simple acronym can help the handler (BVS 2007):
- **L** – look
- **A** – ask
- **D** – demonstrate

Each aspect on its own will give insufficient information, but used together may provide the assessor or handler with valuable insight into the person's ability to help. Although each aspect is listed separately, very quickly all three aspects will be interacting. The ability of the assessor to concentrate and assimilate the information continuously can make the difference between a successful mobility assessment and a disaster.

Look

The assessor or handler starts to observe the person and surroundings well in advance of introducing himself/herself:

- Does the person show head control in the position he/she is currently in? Some head control is vital for all other movements.
- Does the person show trunk control in his/her current position? This may affect the person's ability to help.
- Are there any differences that you can see between the two sides of the person's body?
- Where is the person? Could this have a bearing on how he/she moves from here?
- If the person is sitting, do his/her feet reach the ground? If the person is in bed, can you estimate how tall he/she is?
- Can you estimate the person's weight? (Exercise caution here, many handlers have great difficulty estimating their own weight, never mind someone else's!)
- Are there any obvious signs of weakness?

The "look" continues throughout the rest of the mobility assessment.

Ask

Preferably, open questions should be used, eg the handler may ask "can you walk OK?" meaning "can you put one foot in front of the other more than once?" The person may interpret the question as "can you walk to the shops OK?" A better question may be "how far can you walk?" followed by "how comfortable is it to walk that distance?" And maybe "what help do you need to walk that distance?" The assessor has to develop the questioning skills to gain the maximum information and must always avoid using his/her own preconceived ideas, rather than listening and correctly analysing the information.

- Does the person respond verbally to your introduction? If not, can you ask another question to check that he/she has heard you and is able to respond?
- Can you ask the person to introduce himself/herself and give you some initial information? Useful information can be taken from the TILE(O) tables above, but need to include pain, person's view of his/her ability to help, additional questions that follow on from your observation under the "look" section. It is important at this point to understand that the answers the person gives are placed in context. You will need to verify the information by demonstration with your assessment of what is safe.

Demonstrate

Finally, you need evidence that helps you make a decision on whether to ask the person to assist with the task. If the person is unconscious, asleep or does not wish to comply, asking for a demonstration of his/her abilities is unlikely to be successful, but does contribute to the assessment.

Therefore, the activities you ask the person to demonstrate must be relevant to the task you want him/her to complete.

It is also important that the person does not feel patronised by the requests you are making or that you are taking too long to collect the information that to him/her seems obvious.

EXAMPLE

Look at the picture below. Use the "look" part of LAD to start your mobility assessment.

- What visual assessment would you make as you enter the room?
- What assumptions are you making looking at the picture?
- What questions would you ask the person regarding his/her mobility?
- Do you think that this person can stand unaided?
- Do you think this person needs help to stand? If so, how much?
- Do you think this person has any limitations on any activities? If so, what?
- How do you think this person may respond to your questions?

This person has a very arthritic left knee which is noticeable in the drawing. The person is sitting on a low surface, and may have difficulty getting up from this position. The questions that would be asked would at least partly depend on the relationship between the person sitting down and the person asking the questions. But at some point the assessor will need to ask questions and request demonstration of the range of movement and power of the left leg, and compare it to the right in order to make a decision on what help, if any, is needed.

Assessment tools

Often an assessment can be simple. If the organisation has a well established system for recording the risk factors, the options may be straightforward and easy to implement. However, at times, the assessor or handler may need to draw on other assessment tools to help identify issues or to clarify the potential impact of the risk factors. The following tools may be of help to the assessor and handler. It must be noted that not all tools can be used for person handling and that no tool can ever give the full picture. Further tools are also listed in *The Guide to The Handling of Patients* 5th edition (Smith (ed), HOP5 2005). Some of the tools are used in the data/evidence collection for the practical chapters (9, 10 and 11) and can easily be used in the workplace. Please also see Intervention Evaluation Tool section in chapter 3.

- Use the Manual Handling Assessment Charts (HSE 2003a) MAC tool to determine the level of risk related to handling objects by a person on his/her own, team handling or carrying an object. It is not suitable for assessment of people handling.
- Use the rapid entire body assessment (REBA) (Hignett & McAtamney 2000) to assess posture. It has been used within the practical chapters of this book to evaluate the posture of the handlers undertaking the moving and handling tasks.
- The rapid upper limb assessment (RULA) (McAtamney & Corlett 1993) is available on the internet. This works on a similar basis as REBA and looks more specifically at the upper limbs.
- Staff can use the Borg Scale of perceived exertion (Borg 1998). This may be helpful for staff to attempt to quantify the amount of effort required to undertake a task.
- The work ability index (FIOH 1998) has three uses. Firstly, to help the worker ascertain the subjective ability of that worker to perform his/her work. Secondly, to assist in the individual capability assessment and, thirdly, to "predict the threat of disability in the near future".
- Use Likert 10 point scales to gauge comfort and activity of the person being handled.
- Functional Independence Measure (Granger & Hamilton 1987).
- Risk indicators.
- Measurement of the time required to complete the task.

Clinical reasoning

"Clinical reasoning: students don't know it exists, therapists don't know that they're doing it. This seems to be such a battle." Lisa Mendez 2003

In simple handling situations, the reason for choosing a particular system of work may be obvious. Guides such as this book offer a supportive framework that explains the decision making process and the role of evidence.

However, there may be a number of conflicting issues and a number of possible options. It may be helpful to include the benefits and considerations of the options. The clinical reasoning gives the reader the opportunity to understand the thought processes of the assessor: how a decision was reached may then be clearer and available for others in the future. A decision made today may be obvious to the person making it but someone else looking back some time later may end up trialling equipment or methods that had already been excluded. The habit of evaluation by the assessor may be so automatic that the assessor forgets he/she has gone through a clinical reasoning process and therefore fails to communicate adequately with other members of the team. This can be frustrating for everyone involved, most of all for the person being assisted (Mendez & Neufeld 2003).

EXAMPLE

A person has trialled a number of different slings with a coathanger style spreader bar, all resulting in the person feeling discomfort under their legs. Eventually, a wishbone spreader bar is tried with great success, as the person feels that the bar can be tilted to ease the

pressure on his/her legs. The assessor simply documents that a wishbone type spreader bar was used but does not explain why, in this case potentially a very important piece of information.

This person then moves to another establishment that does not know that there is such a thing as a wishbone shaped spreader bar and starts the process again of trying to find something that works for the person with the new staff.

The person may be able to explain the reasoning process which originally solved the issue, but if he/she can't?

Documentation

There are many different ways of recording the assessment. Style may already be determined by the policy of the establishment: some institutes prefer to use tick lists as this gives the assessor a standard pattern. The most important point is that, where there are more than five employees, the assessment must be recorded.

An example initial assessment sheet has been included (see Appendix 3), but a full example assessment has not been completed. This is because the design of the form and the information included needs to be tailored to the particular organisation and circumstances. The initial assessment can help focus the assessor on the tasks that need to be assessed or trigger the handler's memory about other tasks that need to be considered at the next stage. However, the list below gives the minimum information that should be included on the assessment record.

The balance must be struck between being easy to read and to access and giving sufficient useful information to make a decision. The use of colour and tables can make the information much more accessible.

In order for the documentation to be useful for people handling, the assessment should include the following information as a minimum:
- Name of the person being assisted (date of birth/NHS number or other identifier may be helpful in large organisations).
- Date of the assessment.
- Address/ward where assessment has taken place.
- Name of the assessor and space to sign and date and contact details.
- Presenting issue/reason for starting the assessment.
- Weight of the person.
- Build of the person.
- If the person is independent (if this is the case, then the assessment need go no further).
- Physical abilities and disabilities using plain English (eg "weakness in right arm unable to support weight through that arm or hold objects" rather than "left sided cerebrovascular accident with resulting right hemipareisis"). This can also include information on tissue viability or falls for example (see Load table for additional useful information).
- Person's ability to communicate and how this occurs.
- Person's wishes and concerns and how they are expressed.

2 Manual handling risk management

- The tasks that person undertakes and the risks identified (see Task table).
- Issues related to the environment.
- The number of staff required.
- The method to be used.
- The equipment required.
- Any residual issues that will need ongoing monitoring.
- A review process.

Some organisations also have space for all members of staff to sign that may be working with the person. This can be helpful to ensure that everyone has read the assessment and safe system of work but does not negate or reduce the responsibility of the employer to monitor and be accountable for the manual handling.

Risk assessment forms

There are many examples of forms and documentation that are already available such as All Wales Passport Scheme (All Wales 2010) and Derbyshire Interagency Group protocols (DIAG 2001), as well as work undertaken by groups such as the London Group of National Back Exchange (currently in development) that can provide useful information, including possible forms. A trawl on the internet will also produce a myriad of local examples.

Designing a safe system of work

What if...

Your planned intervention reduces the risks from lack of space and decreases the loading on the handler's spine but... it means the handler is now more likely to adopt poor posture and repeat that poor posture more often...

Have you really reduced the risk?

Sometimes, assessing the risks is the easy part, especially if your documentation encourages easy readability of the risks (eg by using colour, easy to read tables). Some common issues that occur when trying to reduce risk are:

- decreasing the risk in one area may just create a problem in another area
- different people may have different views on the best solution and may be insistent that his/her way is right
- there may be limitations on equipment or strategies that can be used in a particular area
- there may be training issues that take time to filter through the organisation
- one or more of the stakeholders may have issues with the recommendations
- the intervention may change the day to day life of the person or handler
- multiple agencies need to be aware of the change and all implement the same change
- equipment may take a while to arrive
- the assessor is not aware of all the options or is not up to date with current practice.

In simple situations, there may be an obvious answer to the assessor. Follow the example in Table 2.7 of a handler experiencing backache:

Another assessor may come up with a different option. This should be viewed positively and an opportunity to discuss the benefits and considerations and the reasoning behind the suggestions. Personal experience can be really helpful, but must be kept in context.

The importance of encouraging continuing professional development (CPD) cannot be overemphasised. This will help the assessor keep abreast of current developments, new equipment and changes to legislation or standards.

TABLE 2.7

Presenting issue	Handler experiencing backache
Current practice	Transferring a person using a pivot transfer between bed and chair with the person on a turning disc, clasping his/her hands around the handler's neck.
Person	The person can hold on with one hand, stand but not step. The person is receiving therapy with the aim to return home.
Individual capability	Handler has been experiencing back pain and reported this to her line manager.
Environment	Space is limited, no other issues.
Other factors	The person feels they prefer to trust a handler rather than equipment.
Options	Stand and turn device that can be used with one handler with practice and encouragement to overcome fear of equipment.
Clinical reasoning	This option will be very similar to the transfer the person has already used, but significantly decreases the risk of injury to the handler, as he/she is no longer being used as a piece of equipment.

Of course, the same scenario could become more complex:

TABLE 2.8

Presenting issue	Handler experiencing backache
Current practice	Transferring a person using a pivot transfer with the person on a stiff turning disc, clasping his/her hands around the handler's neck between bed and chair with a second handler guiding the person's hips round onto the bed.
Person	The person can hold on with one hand, stand but not step. The person is disillusioned with therapy and is becoming depressed, thinking he/she may never return home. The person is starting to become unreliable on his/her feet.
Individual capability	Handler has been experiencing back pain and reported this to her line manager. She is not up to date with training and questioning reveals she has childcare issues so does not attend sessions.
Environment	Space is limited, no other issues.
Other factors	The person feels he/she prefers to trust the handlers rather than equipment.
Options	<ul><li>Discussion with person on reasons for slower improvement than hoped.</li><li>Standing aid with transport sling.</li><li>Walking harness with overhead tracking.</li><li>Transfer board.</li><li>Adaptation of the therapy programme to encourage strengthening.</li><li>Support from medical team or suitable person regarding the depression.</li><li>A visit home or change of scene.</li></ul>
Clinical reasoning	It is still important to encourage standing to encourage improvement of muscle power, protect bones, aid digestion and breathing. The order in which methods are tried will depend on the reaction of the person, but must be carefully considered in order to be successful. Changing or adding to the therapy programme may give new vision and encouragement.

As the situation becomes more complex, finding out whether there is a central issue may be the key to setting up the safe system of work. In the above scenario, just trying a list of methods or equipment may not help without planning for success and dealing with the underlying issue that the person feels he/she is not progressing fast enough.

How much does the risk have to be reduced?

It is often believed that it should be the target of the assessment to eliminate ALL risk. Realistically, this is not possible. In the past, the introduction of "no lift" policies sought to achieve just that but human beings are far too complex; there are far too many factors and too many variables for no risk ever to be possible.

The legal requirement is that the risk is reduced; the assessor will need to demonstrate that this has occurred by using assessment tools, available studies or information, consultation with others and current best practice.

> Measure, measure, measure...
>
> Using qualitative and quantitative tools to demonstrate the reduction in the risk (REBA, RULA Borg etc) and hopefully the rise in quality of life for the person and the handler.

If, after implementation, the safe system of work does not appear to be successful, this will trigger a review. (See later section.)

Tips to setting up successful safe systems of work:

You (the assessor)
- Know your subject, options and limitations
- Facilitate rather than dictate wherever possible regarding the solutions
- Know current best practice
- Consult peers
- Admit it if the solution isn't working

The person
- Know the person you are trying to help
- Keep flexible in your options, avoid emotive phrases such as "We are not allowed..."
- Use your experiences to guide, but don't be trapped by the same experiences.

The handling team
- Know the availability of handlers and equipment
- Know the skill level and capability of the handlers being expected to undertake the safe system of work.

The process
- Identify any key issues that have a wider effect
- Measure and remeasure using appropriate tools
- Record
- Review and reflect.

The role of training, equipment interventions, organisational decisions

There are multiple factors as to whether a safe system of work is successful and these are dealt with in greater detail in chapters 5 to 8. An important point to recognise is that an intervention will always affect other practices, be influenced by opinion and need to be supported by those carrying out that intervention.

Complex handling

The issue of complex handling has been alluded to in the last section. The principles already mentioned should still be used in order to aim for positive outcomes, but the skill and ability of the assessor to communicate positively may need to increase. The issues may have to be referred back to a line manager of a different assessor invited to join the team. At times, it is more important to recognise that a complex situation cannot be solved, but can be managed. The example below can be used for discussion.

EXAMPLE

Miss A has severe rheumatoid arthritis that is still very active after 40 years, mainly affecting hips and knees. In addition, she has osteoarthritis in the left knee. She suffers extreme pain that limits her ability to move and is very exhausting. She has had a number of falls and hospital admissions and respite admissions. She often manages only a few hours back at home before she is re-admitted.

She refuses to transfer to a residential or nursing home as she had been dropped by staff and she has lived in the same home for 70 years. She has no issues with her ability to make decisions, but, at times, is so racked by pain she is forgetful.

She has multiple health problems such as diabetes, investigations for weight loss, low blood pressure. On a bad day, she needs to use a hoist, on a good day she can perform a 90 degree or 180 degree transfer just holding onto equipment to steady and with a person nearby. She loves to get out and about on her mobility scooter and is an accomplished artist.

Pain control in hospital is improving, making this much easier and improvement is steady. Miss A has not had any falls in hospital on this last admission (lasting four months).

Issues:
- Everyone except Miss A believes she should be hoisted all the time to avoid the falls and fractures that have occurred in the past.
- The pain control used in hospital is not available in the community, due to the remoteness of Miss A's home.
- Miss A has been assessed as needing two people to be available for transfers due to the unpredictability and no one is prepared to fund two live in carers. When she goes home she is alone except for twice daily visits by the care agency.
- There are no family members nearby.
- Her environment could support an H frame

tracking system at home, there is space for her to live in one room which she is prepared to do. Unfortunately, the system is to undertake an assessment at home once the person is discharged and Miss A has already had a fall and returned to hospital before the assessment is arranged.

How would you approach this situation as the hospital manager? How would you approach this as the handler?

In a simple assessment, it can be easy to identify the issue and the solution. However, often there are interacting issues and making a decision in this type of situation is more complex. Weighing up cause and effect can be difficult. A common example could be:

Two handlers have to hold a stooped position for eight minutes without a break to place a sling on a person sitting in a tight fitting wheelchair. The staff are struggling, become tired and believe that a two handler lift, one person at the top, the other lifting the person's legs is quicker, safer and means that the handlers are not holding a prolonged stooped position. It may or may not be easy to choose between the two methods. There may be other options that could be included, but have not yet been considered.

In complex situations, the assessor may need to move towards being a facilitator and collect information and opinions from everyone involved and guide all the stakeholders towards a joint solution. This can be a difficult and time consuming process and the temptation may be to dictate the action plan. While presenting a firm stance it may help in some situations, generally, reaching consensus and compromise will have a better long term outcome.

EXAMPLE

A 13 year old student uses a standing harness and overhead tracking hoist (H frame) to transfer from his powered wheelchair to his prone standing frame and for toilet transfers. He uses a universal sling to transfer to the therapy bench, which is in a room next to the hygiene room.

The physiotherapist has noticed deterioration in his posture because he uses the standing frame only once a day for 15 minutes. He is rarely transferred to the therapy bench for stretches and his therapy programme as staff have indicated there is insufficient time in the school day.

The student uses the toilet 6-8 times a day, each visit takes 15-20 minutes because of the distance he has to travel to the hygiene room and because he is afraid that he may not get to the toilet in time. This takes a range of 1.5-2.75 hours out of a 6.5 hour school day.

The teachers have noticed a deterioration in his school work and feel this is because he has to leave the classroom so many times a day for personal care, appointments with a number of professionals (physiotherapist, occupational therapist, speech and language therapist, music therapist, visual impairment nurse, continence adviser etc).

The family is unhappy because the student has become so afraid of not making it to the toilet his continence has worsened, resulting in the need to change his clothes. This increases handling time and the washing required at home.

Each professional has presented a case for how much time he/she feels should be allocated in the school day for his/her particular activity. In order to achieve everyone's aims, the student would need to remain in school for 10 hours per day. This is not feasible.

After much discussion a solution was found:

A case was made for a powered wheelchair that could bring the student into an upright standing position. This meant he could:

- use several toilet areas around the school, bringing the chair to the standing position and using a urine bottle
- increase his independence as, with just a little help from staff, he could bring himself into a standing position and use the urine bottle himself
- significantly decrease the amount of time spent on personal care and, therefore, more time for learning and therapy
- reduce the amount of washing/change of clothes needed
- have standing practice for short bursts throughout the day
- stand for tasks in some lessons (previously not possible as the standing frame could not be easily moved around the school).

The new wheelchair did not solve everything, but made an important contribution to dealing with some of the core issues.

Funding for additional equipment may be difficult, especially where multiple agencies are involved. The assessor will need to present a business case to the fundholders and encourage interagency communication.

Using a combination of the tools listed on page 27 can help the assessor focus on the main issues. For example, a high REBA and Borg score combined with a low FIM, comfort and workability score for tasks that are taking a long time, can be used by the assessor to focus the stakeholders on the issues. Once the issues are brought to the fore, the range of options may be clearer.

Often in complex situations, a nub or core issue can be found and addressing this is key to working towards resolution.

Some common core issues that should not be glossed over by the assessor and professionals are:

- previous bad handling experience by the person being handled
- mechanical aids being too cumbersome, invasive and time consuming
- equipment being ugly or utilitarian in style
- over emphasis on the needs of the handlers without consideration of the wishes of the person being handled
- the person's perception that his/her dignity is being compromised

- the lack of understanding that handling of people is as much a skill as many other medical procedures
- the feeling by the person that he/she is losing control.

Reviewing the manual handling risk assessment

The law requires that the assessment is reviewed if circumstances change. When attempting to decide whether a review is required, routinely reading the assessment and safe system of work will help identify if anything has changed. The following tips may help and can be applied at local and individual level and the principles should always be applied at management/employer level:

- set up a system so that the assessors and handlers know where the assessment is kept
- routinely and frequently read the assessment
- develop suitable systems for monitoring and supervision
- have good communication systems between the handlers, assessors and line managers
- ensure that there is a recognised system for reporting changes or issues
- regular use of audits
- make sure that everyone is aware of situations that alter quickly, or where the person is unpredictable
- where there are unresolved issues, escalate via line management
- use the systems already in place for reporting of accidents or near misses
- consult with other professional organisations, eg Patient Advice Liaison Service (PALS), Patient Safety, Patient Complaints, who may be able to add valuable feedback from the people receiving the care.

Conclusion

This chapter has shown that government regulations provide a basic framework to tackle risk assessment. Key regulations include The Management of Health and Safety at Work Regulations 1999 and The Manual Handling Operations Regulations 1992. However, they are insufficient by themselves. People need systems that are known and used by others in their environment. They need systems so that they can understand both their role and responsibilities and those of the people around them. They need systems that acknowledge and anticipate human error and insight. A system can facilitate a mutual definition of success.

In order for this system to work, there must be good communication built in. Whether you are part of risk management, staff or the person (or the person's advocate), you need to take responsibility for communication and inform the appropriate authority of the unique information you access. The assessor, in particular, needs to communicate information and assimilate extremely diverse data efficiently. Necessarily, then, the assessor must practise and develop a wide skill range and it is vitally important he/she is able to say when he/she needs assistance.

Of course, this process is complex and you cannot learn the necessary skills from a book – and no book can address the intricate web of personalities, issues and limitations that you face. However, I hope that you can use the ideas in this chapter to develop a well rounded view of risk assessment and to facilitate ongoing wisdom in the workplace. Risk assessment should not be dry bureaucracy; it should be a system of communication and skill that makes life easier and safer for everyone involved.

References

A&B, X&Y v East Sussex County Council, ex p Tandy [2003] EWHC 167 (Admin), High Court.

All Wales (2010), *All Wales NHS Manual Handling Training, Passport and Information Scheme*, 2nd edition, 2010 Wales: All Wales Trust Manual Handling Advisers Group.

AS/NZS 4360:2004 Risk Management, 2004, – Australian and New Zealand Standard 4360, 2nd edition, Australia, Standards Australia International.

AS/NZS ISO 31000:2009 Risk Management – Principles and guidelines, 2009, Standards Australia/Standards New Zealand: Australia/New Zealand.

Borg, G (1998), Perceived exertion and painscales,1998, Human Kinetics: USA.

BVS Training Ltd (2007), *Moving and Handling Assessments, Care Home Series* (DVD).

COT (2006a), *Manual Handling, 2006*, College of Occupational Therapists Guidance 3 2006, London: COT.

COT (2006b), *Record Keeping, 2006*, College of Occupational Therapists Guidance 2, London: COT.

COT (2006c), *Risk Management, 2006*, College of Occupational Therapists Guidance 1 2006, London: COT.

CSP (2008), *Guidance on Manual Handling in Physiotherapy 2008* (3rd edition) London: Chartered Society of Physiotherapy.

DIAG (2001), *Care Handling of Adults in Hospitals and Community Settings – A code of practice*, UK, Derbyshire Interagency Group.

FIOH (1998), *Work Ability Index, 2006*, Finland.

Granger, C & Hamilton, B (1987), The Functional Independence Measure. In: McDowell, I & Newell, C, eds. *Measuring Health: A Guide to Rating Scales and Questionnaires*, 2nd edition. New York: Oxford University Press, 115-121.

Hammond, P (2008), *Trust me I'm (still) a Doctor, 2008*, Edinburgh: Black and White Publishing Ltd.

Hignett, S & McAtamney, L (2000), Rapid Entire Body Assessment, *Applied Ergonomics* **31** (2000) 201-205.

HSE (1995), *Reporting of Injuries, Diseases and Dangerous Occurrences Regulations 1995*.

HSE (1998a), *Lifting Operations and Lifting Equipment Regulations 1998*, Norwich, HMSO.

HSE (1998b), *Provision and Use of Work Equipment Regulations 1998*, Norwich, HMSO.

HSE (1998c), *Evaluation of the Six Pack Regulations 1992*, Sudbury, HSE Books.

HSE (1999), *Management of Health and Safety at Work Regulations 1999*, (2nd edition) Norwich: HMSO.

HSE (2003a), *Manual Handling Assessment Charts, 2003*, Health and Safety Executive, London: HSE.

HSE (2003b), *The principles of good manual handling: Achieving a consensus*, Sudbury, HSE Books.

HSE (2004), *Manual Handling Operations Regulations 1992 (as amended)* (3rd edition), Norwich: HMSO.

HSE (2008) *Managing Health and Safety: five steps to success*.

HSWA (1974), Health and Safety at Work etc Act 1974.

McAtamney, L & Corlett, N (1993), RULA: A survey method for investigation of work-related upper limb disorders. *Applied Ergonomics 1993*, **24**(2), 91-99.

Mendez, L & Neufeld, J (2003), *Clinical Reasoning…What is it and why should I care?* CAOT Publications ACE Ottawa, Canada.

NBE (2010), *Standards in Manual Handling 2010* (3rd edition), Towcester: NBE.

Oxford (2002), *Oxford English Dictionary 2002*, 2nd edition, Oxford: Oxford University Press.

RCN (2003), *Safer Staff, Better Care – RCN Manual Handling Training Guidance and Competencies, 2003*, London: RCN.

Smith, J (ed), *The Guide to The Handling of People*, 5th edition 2005, BackCare.

Thomsett, R (2004), Risk in Projects: The Total Tool Set.

www.hse.gov.uk

www.investorwords.com

Appendix 2.1

Definition of terms

Term	Definition
Risk	The possibility that something unpleasant or unwelcome will happen.
Hazard	A potential source of danger.
Likelihood	The state of being likely, words used range from unlikely to almost certain.
Consequences	A result or effect. The range can be from a negligible effect to severe/catastrophic.
Audit	An appraisal of the current situation, usually completed to identify current issues, prioritise the assessment process and to use as a measure for future comparison.
Risk management	The process of analysing exposure to risk and determining how to handle such exposure best.
Risk analysis	Scrutiny of the assessment information to reach a conclusion or action plan.
Risk control	If a risk cannot be eliminated, consider ways of containing that risk and the introduction of contingency plans.
Risk assessment	Identification of the risk factors. In manual handling, this would include task, individual capability, load, environment and other factors. Generally, the greater the number of factors the greater the risk. However, the interaction in human factors can, at times, be very difficult to quantify.
Risk reduction	The methods of reducing the risk or controlling the risk using the information from the assessment.
Risk tracking	If a risk has not been removed, set up a pathway for monitoring.
Risk reporting	A system for any person to identify (preferably in writing) a new risk or continuing risk that has not been addressed.
The load	Discrete moveable object, which includes, for example, a human patient.
Mobility assessment	Assessment of the person's ability to move, not normally required for an object but an integral part of the manual handling assessment for people.
Action plan	A list (usually in written form) of tasks that need to be completed as a result of the assessment.
Safe system of work	A detailed (usually in written form) set of information that allows the employee to undertake a manual handling task more safely than before the assessment.
Review	A re-examination of the original assessment, usually in the light of new information or changes.

Sources: Oxford Dictionary of English (Oxford 2002); www.investorwords.com; www.hse.gov.uk

Appendix 2.2

This appendix précis the MHSWR 1999 and MHOR 1992 but it is helpful to read the regulations in full to understand how they piece together. Please refer to the HSE website for more detailed information on any publication by the HSE.

The 1999 regulations, the principal legislation in this area, emphasises the *employer* as the leading driver to reduce risks. Organisations need good communication and rapport to make the whole system work, but the responsibility to implement the process is squarely with the employer. Fig 2.2 shows how the regulations fit into a risk management model.

> MHSWR 1999 supplies a legal framework for the employer to reduce the risk of injury to the workforce. The responsibility is always with the employer to initiate and monitor this requirement.

Fig 2.2 summarises the MHSWR 1999 into a risk management model as described in Fig 2.1 (page 19) for easy reading.

Please remember to refer to the regulations and guidance notes published by the HSE for more information.

Regulation 3 considers the purpose of risk assessment. Paragraphs 1-5 are summarised below:
> "Every employer shall make a suitable and sufficient assessment of:
> (a) the risks to the health and safety of his employees while they are at work; and
> (b) the risks to the health and safety of persons not in his employment arising out of, or in connection with, the conduct by him of his undertaking."

The self employed must follow the same requirements (paragraph 2) with additional duties for those who employ young people (paragraphs 4 and 5).

Paragraph 3 explains when to update a risk assessment:
> "Any assessment such as is referred to in paragraph (1) or (2) shall be reviewed by the employer or self employed person who made it if:
> (c) there is a reason to suspect that it is no longer valid; or
> (d) there has been a significant change in the matters to which it relates; and where, as a result of any such review, changes to an assessment are required, the employer or self employed person concerned shall make them."

Paragraph 4 emphasises additional considerations before employing a young person:
- inexperience, lack of awareness and of risk and immaturity
- outfitting the workplace and workstation.
- type, degree and duration of exposure to physical, biological or chemical agents
- equipment and its use
- organisation of processes and activities
- extent of training to be provided.

Regulation 4 – Schedule 1 in the code of practice gives a helpful summary. General principles of prevention:

- avoid risks
- evaluate the risks which cannot be avoided
- combat the risks at source
- adapt the work to the individual, especially as regards choosing: the design of workplaces; work equipment; and working and production methods. These choices should reduce adverse health effects, alleviate monotonous work and work at a predetermined workrate
- adapt to technical progress
- replace the dangerous by the non dangerous or the less dangerous
- develop a coherent overall prevention policy which covers technology, organisation of work, working conditions, social relationships and the influence of factors relating to the work environment
- give collective protective measures priority over individual protective measures
- give appropriate instructions to employees.

Regulation 5 considers the principles of prevention.

A summary of Regulation 5 highlights that every employer must have arrangements in place appropriate to the organisation size to cover health and safety, considering the "effective planning, control, monitoring and review of the preventative and protective measures". If there are more than five employees, the arrangements must be recorded.

Regulation 6 deals with health surveillance. It states:

> "Every employer shall ensure that his employees are provided with such health surveillance as is appropriate having regard to the risks to their health and safety which are identified by the assessment."

Health surveillance could be introduced where:
- there is an identifiable disease or adverse health condition related to the work concerned
- valid techniques are available to detect indications of the disease or condition
- there is a reasonable likelihood that the disease or condition may occur under the particular conditions of work
- surveillance is likely to further the protection of the health and safety of the employees to be covered.

Regulation 7 identifies the need for the employer to appoint people who are competent to assist with health and safety. The employer carries the responsibility for ensuring that they are competent to help.

EXAMPLE

In the field of manual handling, a manual handling practitioner or occupational health nurse who uses the rapid entire body assessment (REBA) could give detailed recommendations for someone's posture.

Regulation 8 deals with procedures for serious and imminent danger. Most importantly, you must first establish those procedures, then nominate sufficient numbers of competent people to implement them. Employees should not have access to potential risk areas without adequate health and safety instruction. If someone is exposed to imminent danger, you should inform them and enable them to withdraw until the situation is safe.

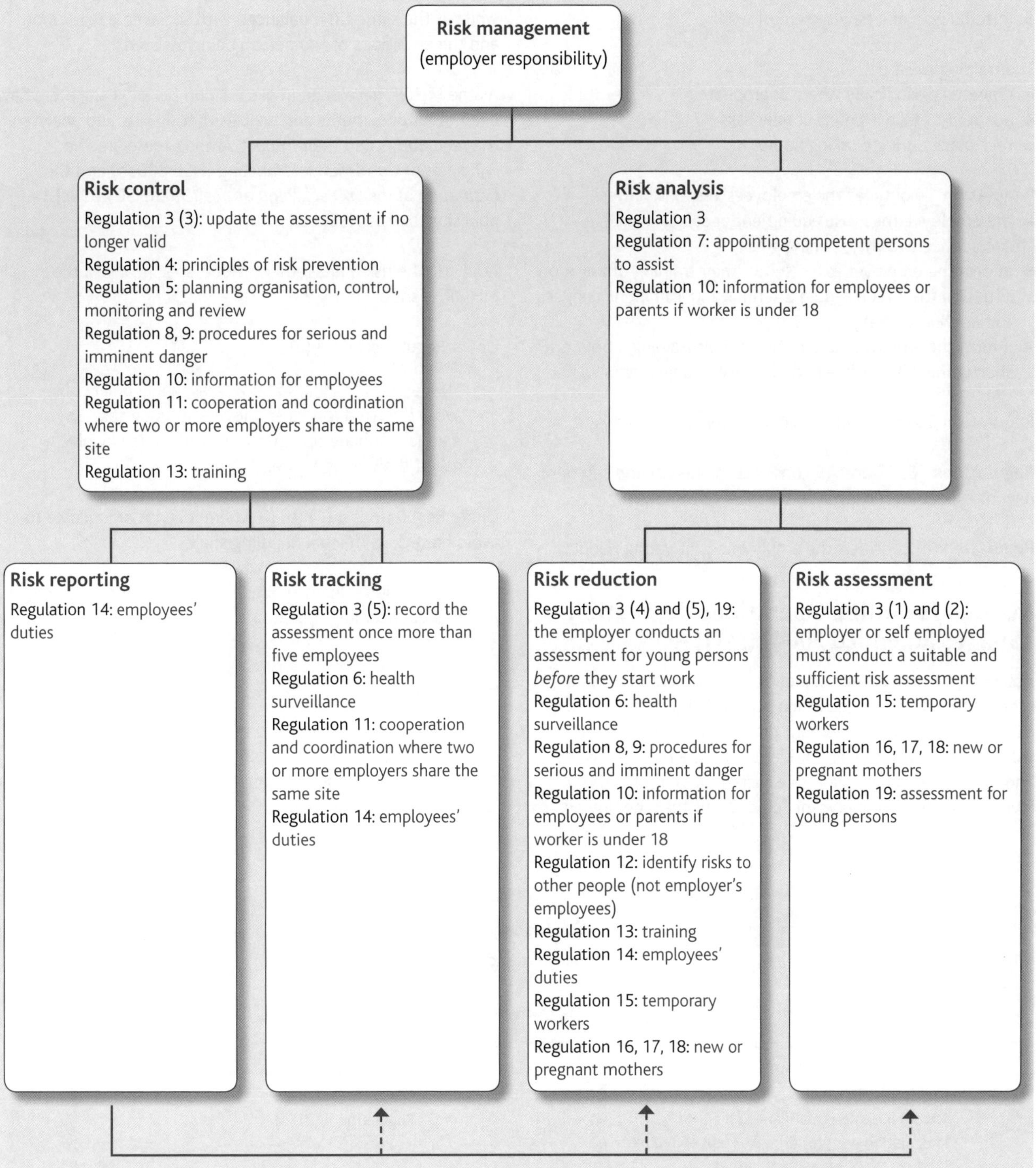

Risk management
(employer responsibility)

Risk control

Regulation 3 (3): update the assessment if no longer valid
Regulation 4: principles of risk prevention
Regulation 5: planning organisation, control, monitoring and review
Regulation 8, 9: procedures for serious and imminent danger
Regulation 10: information for employees
Regulation 11: cooperation and coordination where two or more employers share the same site
Regulation 13: training

Risk analysis

Regulation 3
Regulation 7: appointing competent persons to assist
Regulation 10: information for employees or parents if worker is under 18

Risk reporting

Regulation 14: employees' duties

Risk tracking

Regulation 3 (5): record the assessment once more than five employees
Regulation 6: health surveillance
Regulation 11: cooperation and coordination where two or more employers share the same site
Regulation 14: employees' duties

Risk reduction

Regulation 3 (4) and (5), 19: the employer conducts an assessment for young persons *before* they start work
Regulation 6: health surveillance
Regulation 8, 9: procedures for serious and imminent danger
Regulation 10: information for employees or parents if worker is under 18
Regulation 12: identify risks to other people (not employer's employees)
Regulation 13: training
Regulation 14: employees' duties
Regulation 15: temporary workers
Regulation 16, 17, 18: new or pregnant mothers

Risk assessment

Regulation 3 (1) and (2): employer or self employed must conduct a suitable and sufficient risk assessment
Regulation 15: temporary workers
Regulation 16, 17, 18: new or pregnant mothers
Regulation 19: assessment for young persons

Fig 2.2 Management of Health and Safety at Work Regulations 1999 – applied to the risk management model (Thomsett 2004)

Regulation 9 requires the employer to have contacts with services such as the emergency services.

Regulation 10 identifies the information that employees need, such as:
● risk assessment officers
● risks to their health and safety identified in the assessment
● preventive measures put in place
● fire precautions
● risks where two or more employers share the same workplace.

If employing a child, this information should be provided to the parent of a child before the child is employed.

Regulation 11 identifies the particular issues where two or more employers share a workplace and the need to cooperate on issues of health and safety and to take all reasonable steps to inform regarding the risks.

Regulation 12 considers the importance of other people who may be in the workplace and the need to protect their health and safety.

Regulation 13 deals with capabilities and training. Adequate health and safety training must be provided on:
● induction
● exposure to new risks
● introduction to new equipment

- introduction to new technology
- introduction of a new system of work.

The training must be:
- repeated periodically where appropriate
- adapted to take account of new risks
- take place during working hours.

Regulation 14 outlines the employees' responsibilities:
- the employee must use equipment or safety device in accordance with the training given
- inform the employer as a result of their training of any work situation that "represented a serious and imminent danger to health and safety"
- inform the employer, as a result of their training, about any shortcoming in the health and safety arrangements.

Regulation 15 considers the safety of temporary workers.

Regulations 16, 17 and 18 considers the health and safety of new or expectant mothers.

Regulation 19 considers the employment of young people.

Manual Handling Operations Regulations 1992 (as amended 2004) (MHOR)

Assessing risk in a manual handling environment requires a more detailed framework, which is provided by the MHOR. It allows a systematic assessment process of all the relevant subject areas, with the aim of identifying the main areas of risk and then developing a plan (safe system of work) for those involved. Again, it is important to point out that the driving force behind implementing these regulations is the employer, while at the same time balanced with social care legislation and the ambitions of the person being assisted.

As the MHOR have been in place a number of years, there have been other documents and articles that discuss and analyse the regulations and their impact. Among these are *The Principles of Good Manual Handling* (HSE 2003b) and the *Evaluation of the Six Pack Regulations 1992* (HSE 1998c), both published by the HSE.

Applying the risk management model specifically to the MHOR, is shown in Fig 2.3:

Under Regulation 4 (1) (a):

> "The employer shall, so far as reasonably practicable, avoid the need for his employees to undertake any manual handling operations at work which involve a risk of their being injured."

Under Regulations 4 (1) (b) (i) where it is not practicable to avoid hazardous manual handling shall:

> "make a suitable and sufficient assessment of all such manual handling operations to be undertaken by them..."

And 4 (1) (b) (ii):

> "take appropriate steps to reduce the risk of injury to those employees arising out of their undertaking any such manual handling operations to the lowest level reasonably practicable..."

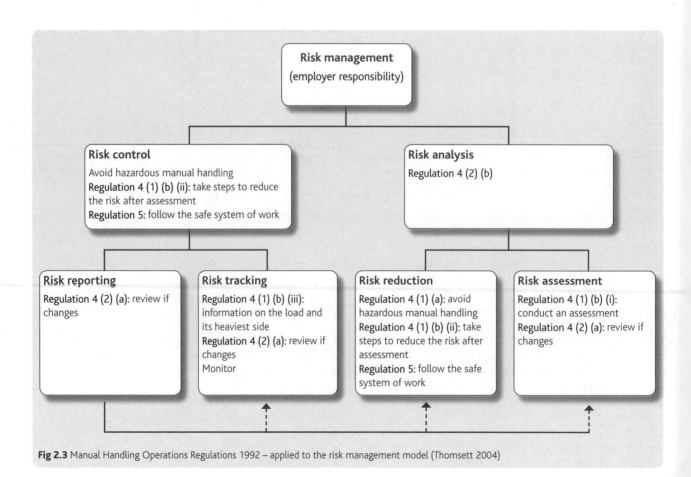

Fig 2.3 Manual Handling Operations Regulations 1992 – applied to the risk management model (Thomsett 2004)

And 4 (1) (b) (iii):

"take appropriate steps to provide any of those employees who are undertaking any such manual handling operations with general indications and, where it is reasonably practicable to do so, precise information on –

(aa) the weight of the load, and

(bb) the heaviest side of any load whose centre of gravity is not positioned centrally."

Applying these regulations to people handling will need more detailed information than just the weight of the person and his/her heaviest side. There is a great difference between assessing the manual handling needs of people and inanimate loads.

Appendix 2.3

Moving and handling initial assessment

Person details				Assessor details	
Name				Name	
Height		Weight	Age	Designation	
Address/location seen				Signature	
				Assessment date	
				Review date	

Checklist of handling tasks

Task	Is the person fully independent?*			
	Yes	No	Variable	Comments
Turning in bed				
Rolling in bed				
Lying to sitting in bed				
Repositioning up the bed				
Getting into bed				
Getting out of bed				
On toilet/commode				
Off toilet/commode				
In bath/shower				
Out bath/shower				
Sitting to standing				
Standing to sitting				
Standing				
Walking				
In/out walk frame				
Into wheelchair				
Out of wheelchair				
In armchair				
Out armchair				
To floor				
Up from floor				
In/out car				
On/off transport				
In/out swimming pool				
Other				

Is the person fully independent for all tasks?   If **yes** – end of assessment   If **no** – complete detailed assessment

* *Fully independent means that the person needs no manual assistance*

Ergonomics in health and social care

Sue Hignett PhD MSc MCSP MIEHF EurErg
Director, HEPSU, Loughborough University

Introduction

This chapter presents an overview of ergonomics in health and social care. It gives examples of a wide range of person handling activities and shows how ergonomics can be used to reduce the risk of musculoskeletal disorders (MSDs).

A broad outline of ergonomics is given to identify the two central principles of:
● design, for products, systems and interventions
● change, relating to organisational systems and interventions.

There are sections giving information about epidemiology, task analysis, postural analysis, participatory ergonomics and case studies to illustrate how ergonomic methods have been applied in health and social care.

Ergonomics

Ergonomics is the "*scientific discipline concerned with the understanding of interactions among humans and other elements of a system, and the profession that applies theoretical principles, data and methods to design in order to optimise human wellbeing and overall system performance*" (International Ergonomics Association 2000).

There are various models which have been used to illustrate the theory and practice of ergonomics. Fig 3.1a gives a model

which is commonly used to show the theoretical background, drawing on physical dimensions (eg anthropometry, biomechanics, engineering and physiology), cognitive dimensions (psychology) and organisational dimensions (management studies, sociology). In contrast, Fig 3.1b proposes a model to represent the interactions at an individual level (micro), group level (meso) and organisational level (macro). These three levels can be clearly seen in the example for office design in Fig 3.2.

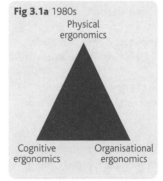
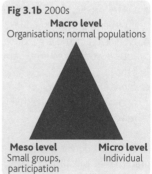

Fig 3.1 Models of Ergonomics (Hignett & Wilson 2004)

In practice, there are two key elements that define ergonomics. These are design (Helander 1997) and change (Caccamise

At the **micro** level, intervention is represented by modifications to a single physical workstation or working pattern for one person to address an individual problem.

At the **meso** level, all the employees in the office might be involved in a group intervention looking at the workflow and interactions between individuals as well as other groups of workers (physical work movements in the office).

At the **macro** level, the systems of the organisation impinging on the office design would be considered, including working patterns (hot desking, flexible working) as well as communication channels for introducing change. There may be issues relating to product design, specifying products from preferred or single suppliers, and resources.

Fig 3.2 Example of multilevel application of ergonomics (Hignett 2001a)

1995). The design element is used in all projects to a greater or lesser extent whereby a product design may be evaluated and recommendations made, or an organisational system (eg risk management) may be designed. The change element is more applicable at a systems level when an intervention programme is being implemented. The aim is to achieve a change in the working practices, attitudes, behaviours etc. There are ergonomic methods that can be used operationally to assist with the implementation of new systems as well as for evaluation, eg participatory ergonomics.

Dul & Neumann (2009) discuss the value of ergonomics beyond health and safety. They argue for ergonomics to be an integral part of the organisational systems rather than just for protecting the workers. This is set out at three levels – business function strategies, eg product design, operations; operational strategies, eg quality management; and corporate strategy, eg cost benefit analyses. If ergonomics is seen as separate from the main strategic objectives of an organisation (eg as part of health and safety or occupational health), the benefits are likely to lag behind the operational decisions.

Hendrick (2008) sets out his view of ergonomics as an escalating definition of system from a single person with a tool to a multinational corporation. Drawing on more than 40 years of experience and application of macro (systems) ergonomics, he summarises five key areas for the future:
- all ergonomics projects should include a cost benefit analysis set out in a "*comprehensive and concise manner to management*"
- translation of ergonomics research into practical guidelines for design use
- better prediction of outcomes from ergonomics interventions (see section 2.10)
- expansion of the ergonomics knowledge base to include future working environments, eg working from home, virtual offices
- more understanding of the role of ergonomics at the organisational level with involvement in strategic decision making.

In order to address a range of dimensions, the ergonomics practitioner will almost always use multiple methods, often mixing qualitative and quantitative, in order to get as much information as possible about the complex systems of human interactions.

Patient safety

Vincent (2006) defined patient safety as "*the avoidance, prevention and amelioration of adverse outcomes or injuries stemming from the process of healthcare*". The process of healthcare includes all areas of activity, with direct patient care being supported by, among others, information technology, equipment and consumable supplies, design of buildings and technology.

Since the two pivotal publications – *To Err is Human* (Kohn *et al* 1999) and *An Organisation with a Memory* (Department of Health 2000) – summarised the level of harm experienced by users of healthcare systems, there have been many patient safety initiatives, often drawing on the experience of other industries (eg aviation, nuclear). However, healthcare presents additional levels of complexity, scale and potential impact on a wide range of stakeholders (Buckle *et al* 2006; Carayon & Buckle 2010). Vincent (2010) suggests that many of the accidents in healthcare need to be viewed from a broad systems perspective if they are to be fully understood.

Reason's model of organisational accidents (Reason 1997) shows how the micro, meso and macro factors can interact to result in an accident trajectory ("Swiss cheese model"). This allows a series of decisions, actions, contributory factors and failure of barriers (defence mechanisms) to culminate in an adverse event (incident).

Once an incident has occurred, a detailed investigation is required to both understand it and prevent recurrence. Root cause analysis (RCA) is an investigatory approach that has been widely advocated and used. RCA is defined as "*a process for identifying the basic or causal factors that underlie variation in performance, including the occurrence or possible occurrence of a sentinel event [unanticipated occurrence involving death or major permanent loss of function unrelated to the natural course of the patient's illness or underlying condition]*" (Croteau 2010). It is an amalgam of methods, with origins in Total Quality Management (Vincent 2010). Data is gathered from documents (eg case notes, incident reports) and interviews with key staff to develop a timeline, perceived care delivery problems and possible contributory factors. Some healthcare providers are using other tools (eg the Six Sigma approach is widely used in the USA), as it has been suggested that RCA can be misleading by implying a single (or small number) of causes when there is usually a chain of events with many contributory factors (Vincent 2010).

Epidemiology of back problems in nursing

Pheasant summarised epidemiological issues about back problems in nurses in the 1998 edition of *The Guide to The Handling of Patients*. He defined epidemiology as the branch of medical science which deals with the statistics of disease by identifying the risk factors which are statistically associated with the onset and development of diseases. He suggested that back problems were difficult to study epidemiologically for a number of reasons:
- Back problems have a diverse pathophysiology; the back can go wrong in a number of different ways.
- Back problems have multifactorial aetiology: a person may be at risk for a number of different reasons. Some of these risk factors are external to the individual concerned – most

importantly the nature of their work. Others are specific to an individual – eg relating to the person's lifestyle, physical make up and genetic endowment.

- Back problems have a diverse natural history. Many episodes are short lived but they may be precursors of something worse to come. There is a danger that the results of surveys based on the self reporting of symptoms may be swamped by these relatively trivial episodes – and the risk factors which are associated with more serious problems may be hidden.

There have been various epidemiological studies studying back pain in nurses (Stubbs et al 1983; Seccombe & Ball 1992; Smedley et al 1995). These have all found that the incidence and prevalence are significantly higher than in comparison with the general population.

Musculoskeletal disorders (MSDs) have been one of the most commonly self reported work related injuries for many years. The estimated prevalence (three year average) of MSDs was over 538,000 for a 12 month period in 2008/09 (Health and Safety Executive (HSE) 2010). Health and social care work continues to be the highest reporting industrial sector for work related illness, with health and social welfare associate professionals having a statistically significant higher than average three year prevalence of work related MSDs mainly affecting the back (HSE 2010).

The National Audit Office (NAO) (2003) compared the level of accidents and sickness absence in the NHS with a previous report in 1996. It found that the overall proportion of accidents due to moving and handling had increased from 17 per cent to 18 per cent, whereas a decrease was reported for needle stick/sharps incidents and for slips and trips. The major reason for staff absence in the NHS is sickness, at an average rate of 4.9 per cent, compared with an average of 3.7 per cent for other public sector organisations. When looking at the implementation of risk management policies, the NAO found that only 12 per cent of trusts included risk assessment in induction training and that there were often different reporting routes to the trust board for clinical and nonclinical risks.

More recently, Eriksen et al (2004) looked at the predictors of low back pain in a group of 4,266 Norwegian nurses' aides in a prospective study over 15 months. They found that, after a wide range of adjustments, low back pain symptoms were predicted by:
- frequent positioning of patients in bed
- perceived lack of support from immediate superior
- perceived lack of pleasant and relaxing culture in the work unit.

These findings agree with Smedley et al (1995) where a significant association was found between back pain and the frequency of manually moving patients around the bed, manually transferring patients between bed and chair, and manually lifting patients from the floor.

Engkvist (2004) also attempted to identify predicting factors with a prospective (13 month) study with 127 nurses in Australia. Cluster analysis revealed five well defined clusters but the majority of accidents occurred during patient transfer in the bed or to/from the bed. Engkvist found a number of contributing factors, including a lack of transfer devices and a reluctance to use transfer devices. Kneafsey (2000) explored

occupational socialisation in relation to patient handling activities, suggesting that manual handling could be viewed "as an area of ritualistic practice". By this, she means that the methods of transferring patients have been developed over time and that manual techniques (rather than the use of equipment) may be the established norm of behaviour. So, students and new staff may be socialised into a culture where patient handling is badly managed and change can be introduced only if the implementation strategy is aimed at the staff members who set the norms of behaviour. This may be the ward managers and senior nursing staff but may also be health care assistants who carry out many of the care handling activities.

Ergonomics methods

A number of methods are described in this chapter that can be used as part of a wider ergonomic assessment. These include task analysis, postural analysis, physiological assessment, participatory ergonomics and user trials.

Task analysis

Task analysis is the study of what an operator (or team of operators) is required to do in terms of actions and/or cognitive processes to achieve a system goal (Kirwan & Ainsworth 1992). It includes many methods which can be used to document and display information. This provides a blueprint of human involvements in a system which is used to build a clear and detailed picture of the system. Kirwan & Ainsworth (1992) describe task analysis in terms of five steps with associated methods as shown in Table 3.1. More detail about the individual methods can be found in Kirwan & Ainsworth (1992) and Wilson & Corlett (2005). As with most ergonomics analyses, it would be rare to use only one method. Generally, a combination of data is used which have been collected from interviews, observations, document analysis and experiments.

TABLE 3.1 TASK ANALYSIS STAGES AND METHODS

Data collection	Critical incident technique, questionnaires, structured interviews, verbal protocol analysis (VPA), activity sampling
Task description	Hierarchical task analysis (HTA), link analysis, timeline analysis, charting and networks, operational sequence diagrams
Simulation	Walkthroughs, mockups, computer modelling, tabletop analysis
Behaviour assessment	Event trees, fault trees, hazard and operability analysis (HAZOP), failure mode and effects analysis (FMEA)
Evaluation	Checklists, interface surveys

The outputs from a task analysis can include information about the allocation of function (between human and machine), person specification (knowledge and skills required to perform the task), job organisation (and staff needed to achieve the task goals), the interface design and finally a quality assurance of the performance of the task by providing a benchmark against which the task can be evaluated.

Postural analysis

Postural analysis provides a description of the posture with respect to the spatial arrangement of individual body sections and an assessment of the posture tolerability (Colombini & Occhipinti 1985). Postures are considered to be tolerable when they do not involve feelings of short term discomfort or cause long term MSDs. There are many ways to collect information on posture but the assessor should always report findings in the context of a full ergonomic assessment as posture is only one component of human interactions.

There are a number of postural analysis tools and more information about the range can be found in Wilson & Corlett (2005). The methods described below are all used mostly for field data collection.

RULA

Rapid upper limb assessment (RULA) was developed by Lynn McAtamney and Nigel Corlett at the Institute for Occupational Ergonomics, University of Nottingham (McAtamney & Corlett 1993). It is a quick survey method which can be used as part of an ergonomic workplace assessment where MSDs involving the upper limbs are reported. RULA assesses biomechanical and postural loading on the neck, shoulders and upper limbs and was designed to assess predominantly sedentary work. It allocates scores based on the position of groups of body parts with additional scores for force/load and muscle activity. The final RULA score is a relative rather than an absolute score and gives an indication of the risk level on a four point action category scale from action category (AC) 1, where the posture is acceptable, through to AC4 where investigation and changes are needed immediately.

REBA

Rapid entire body assessment (REBA) is a whole body assessment tool. It was initially designed to provide a pen and paper postural analysis tool to be used in the field by direct observations or with photographic stills/video (Hignett & McAtamney 2000). A full version of REBA is included at the end of this chapter (see Appendix 3.1).

REBA was developed to assess the type of unpredictable working postures found in healthcare and other service industries and was validated using examples from the electricity, healthcare and manufacturing industries. Data is collected about the body posture, forces used, type of movement or action, repetition and coupling. A final REBA score is generated, giving an indication of the level of musculoskeletal risk and urgency with which action should be taken on a five point action category scale of 0-4 from no action required (AC0) through to action necessary now (AC4). The AC reflects the magnitude and severity of exposure and recommends the priority for the control measures. The method was designed to evaluate tasks where postures are dynamic, static or where gross changes in position occur. In particular, REBA was designed to:
- provide a postural analysis system sensitive to musculoskeletal risks in a variety of occupational tasks
- divide the body into segments which are coded individually with reference to movement planes
- provide a scoring system for muscle activity caused by static, dynamic, rapid changing or unstable postures
- reflect that coupling is important in the handling of loads but may not always be via the hands
- give an action level with an indication of urgency
- require minimal equipment.

Physiological method (Borg Scale)

The Borg Scale or scale of rated perceived exertion (RPE) provides a linear scale to reflect the curvilinear relationship between the intensity of a physical stimuli and human perception of the intensity (Borg 1985; Kilbom 1990). The scale steps (6-20) are adjusted so that they relate to the heart rate divided by 10 (Fig 3.3). The scale is presented to participants with the endpoints (6 and 20) defined and they are asked to rate their activity. Kilbom (1990) recommends that RPE scales should be used cautiously for industrial applications as there have been suggestions that the ratings are not only influenced by the overall perception of exertion but also by previous experience and the motivation of subjects, whereby highly motivated subjects tend to underestimate their exertion.

Fig 3.3 Borg's RPE Scale

6	No exertion at all
7	Extremely light
8	
9	Very light
10	
11	Light
12	
13	Somewhat hard
14	
15	Hard (heavy)
16	
17	Very hard
18	
19	Extremely hard
20	Maximal exertion

Participatory ergonomics

Participatory ergonomics can be very simply described as a concept involving the use of participative techniques and various forms of participation in the workplace (Vink & Wilson 2003). The degree of employee participation can range from a top down approach with information flowing from management to workers on plans for action; gathering of information and experience from workers; consultation where workers can make suggestions and present points of view; negotiations in formalised committees; through to joint decision making in agreement between involved parties (Dachler & Wilpert 1978; Haines et al 2002).

The participative techniques can include (Haines & Wilson 1998):
- problem analysis, eg link analysis, activity analysis
- creativity stimulation and idea generation, eg round robin questionnaire, world map
- idea generation and concept development, eg design decision group, focus groups
- concept evaluation, eg layout modelling and mockups, checklists
- preparation and support, eg team formation and building.

The practicality of tools is important as the educational background of the participants may vary, so it may be useful to start with a hands on exercise, eg simulations or mockups, and then progress into problem solving, from idea generation and concept evaluation, ending in an action proposal with a recommendation for implementation (Kuorinka 1997).

Hignett (2003a) reported on a systematic review looking at the range of interventions used to reduce musculoskeletal injuries associated with patient handling tasks. It was found that, although a number of intervention strategies were successful, the best results were obtained when multifactor intervention strategies included worker participation. The most successful strategies involved changes in work organisation, working practices and the design of the working environment. One example of a participatory ergonomics intervention programme in a UK hospital was evaluated by the HSE. The intervention used a range of ergonomics methods to tackle MSD problems in all staff groups (Hignett 2001b) and was evaluated to have made a saving in excess of £3.6 million over three years (www.hse.gov.uk/healthservices/casestudies/nottingham.htm).

User trials

Many of us will have made comments about both domestic products as well as the equipment we use in the workplace and often feel that we can suggest design improvements. User trials provide a systematic framework to collect data from a range of user populations about different aspects of a product so that the design can be reviewed and improved. They are used to answer one or more specific questions about the effectiveness of a product (Wilson & Corlett 2005). It is useful for designers to test their ideas and prototypes to find out how future users might operate them, whether they will understand the intended way of operation and if they are likely to perform the manipulations required for correct functioning (Roozenburg & Eekels 1995). There are more examples of comparative testing, eg the Consumers Association (www.which.co.uk), than prototype and developmental testing due to commercial confidentiality.

The NHS is the largest purchaser of medical equipment in the UK. Although Buying Solutions Health (www.buyingsolutions.gov.uk/healthcms/) does include as one of its aims the "development and improvement of the provision of comparative information on the purchasing and supply performance of the NHS", its advice seems to be directed more towards comparative cost than functionality or usability. The Medical and Healthcare products Regulatory Agency (MHRA) publishes product evaluations on a wide range of topics. These include mobile hoists and slings (A3 1993: A10 1994; MH2 2000), moving and transferring equipment (A19 1996), handling equipment for moving dependent people in bed (A23 1997), portable bath lifts (MH1 1998) and electrically powered profiling beds (MH4/MHRA 03038 2003). Information about these publications, together with descriptions of how to plan and carry out user trials for moving and handling equipment, can be found at www.mhra.gov.uk/index.htm. See also chapter 7.

Systematic reviews in patient handling

There have been at least four systematic reviews of patient handling interventions. Three used a Cochrane approach (Amick et al 2006; Dawson et al 2007; Martimo et al 2008). Although they only reviewed a small number of studies, they concluded that there is:
- a moderate level of evidence for the effect of OHS interventions on musculoskeletal conditions in healthcare settings (Amick et al 2006)

- a moderate level of evidence for multicomponent patient handling interventions and physical exercise interventions (Amick et al 2006)
- moderate evidence that training in isolation was not successful and that multidimensional interventions were effective (Dawson et al 2007)
- no evidence that training, with or without lifting equipment, was effective in the prevention of back pain or consequent disability. They suggested that either the advocated techniques did not reduce the risk of back injury or that training did not lead to adequate change in moving and handling technique (Martimo et al 2008).

The fourth (Hignett et al 2003) used a more modern mixed methods approach (Pluye et al 2009) to systematic review methodology by including all study types (quantitative and qualitative). To achieve this heterogeneity, each study was defined within a study type hierarchy. A quality score was then allocated by using an appraisal/extraction tool within each category rather than comparatively between categories. Interventions were grouped as multifactorial, single factor and technique training based. The results were reported as summary statements with the associated evidence level (strong, moderate, limited or poor). The findings are summarised as:
- strong evidence that interventions predominantly based on technique training have no impact on working practices or injury rates
- multifactor interventions, based on a risk assessment programme, are most likely to be successful in reducing musculoskeletal injuries related to handling activities.

The seven most commonly used strategies were identified (Table 3.2). It is suggested that these seven factors could form the basis of a generic programme, although it is likely that an intervention strategy and programme will need to be developed further and extended in order to be responsive to local organisational and cultural factors. The risk assessment process could facilitate the detailed design of the programme, and identification of additional appropriate strategies, with the allocation of priorities based on local negotiation with managers and staff.

TABLE 3.2 INTERVENTION STRATEGIES FOR MULTIFACTOR INTERVENTIONS (HIGNETT 2003a)

Intervention strategy	Number of occurrences	Average quality rating of studies
Equipment provision/purchase	18	50%
Education and training (range of topics)	18	54%
Risk assessment	13	55%
Policies and procedures	10	50%
Patient assessment system	8	43%
Work environment redesign	7	58%
Work organisation/practices changed	7	63%

Based on the findings of the systematic review, Hignett (2003b) recommended the provision of a minimum set of equipment for all clinical environments where patient handling occurs on a regular basis: lifts (mobile and ceiling), stand aids (standing lifts), sliding sheets, lateral transfer boards, walking belts, adjustable height beds and baths.

Intervention evaluation tool

For many years, the evaluation of patient handling interventions has been difficult. A new evaluation tool – intervention evaluation tool (IET) – has been developed to try to address the complexity of these multifactorial interventions and allow the comparison of interventions across different types of outcomes (Fray 2010). The IET has 12 targeted and detailed outcome evaluations. It can be used to compare the performance of patient handling management systems before and after interventions, between organisations and can also be used to guide future interventions in any healthcare location.

The development and evaluation of the IET had two phases. In phase one (Fig 3.4), focus groups were held in four European countries (Finland, Italy, Portugal and the UK) to explore the intervention outcomes that were both currently being used and would, in the future, be the preferred outcomes. The groups were coordinated by a member of the European Panel on Patient Handling Ergonomics (EPPHE) with real time whispering interpretation and subsequent translation/cross translation of the recorded focus group and written data. This resulted in a priority list of the 12 most important outcomes for patient handling interventions. Also in phase one, an extensive literature review systematically reviewed previously used and published patient handling intervention measurement tools.

Measurement tools for the 12 outcomes were selected from the literature (where possible) and included if they had previously been used in a published (peer reviewed) patient handling study; had been used to score an intervention trial; and were assessed to have a quality rating over 50 per cent (Hignett et al 2003). It was found that tools to evaluate patient outcomes were poorly represented in the literature, so new measurement tools were developed (but not validated).

Safety culture. Safety culture is a measure of organisational behaviour and how the organisational systems manage the patient handling risks. The data for safety culture in the IET is from interviews with the ward/unit manager, with additional questions about management commitment to managers, advisers and staff. This section is based on the Patient Handling Organisational Question Set (PHOQS) (Hignett & Crumpton 2005). It gives an audit of procedures rather than behaviours, eg policy, risk assessment, records of training etc and should measure support for the prevention programme both financially and organisationally.

Musculoskeletal Health Measure. The MSD Health Measure uses a shortened and validated version of the Nordic Questionnaire (Dickinson et al 1992) as a self completion questionnaire. It provides a measurement of the level of MSDs in the working population including injuries, chronic conditions, fitness for work, etc.

Competence compliance. This section uses the DiNO score system designed and evaluated by Johnsson et al (2004). This observational checklist looks at individual staff behaviour when carrying out patient transfers, including competence, skill, compliance with safe methods and equipment use.

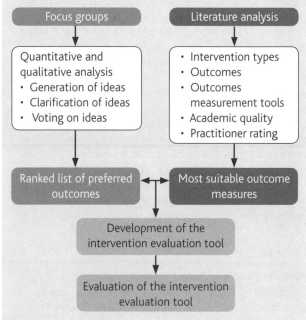

Fig 3.4 Development of intervention evaluation tool (Fray 2010)

Absence or staff health. Sickness absence data is collected in the organisation with a standardised form to record the time away from work or lost productivity due to patient handling related MSD, days/shifts lost, staff on reduced work capacity, staff turnover. It does not record data from self reported systems. The IET calculation is standardised for exposure per work hour per individual to allow comparisons between work areas and different size samples.

Quality of care. The quantification and assessment of quality of care has challenged researchers and there are many suggestions for calculations. Nelson et al (2008) reported measures of quality of care to patient handling to give a complex observational tool of all aspects of care delivery (with more than 30 different measures). The IET evaluates whether patient needs are being considered for dignity, respect, safety, and security when they are moved or handled during a hospital stay.

Accident numbers. The inclusion of incident numbers that have patient handling factors is unclear and complex. The IET scoring system includes an under reporting ratio from the unit manager and self reports of unsafe practice by the staff as well as accidents or near misses from patient handling where staff could have been injured.

Psychological wellbeing. The measurement of the staff mental health status, psychological stress, strain and job satisfaction etc is based on using a three section assessment tool used by Evanoff et al (1999) as a single page staff questionnaire.

Patient condition. As with quality of care, there were few precedents of measuring patient condition (length of stay, treatment progression, level of independence) in patient handling studies. The concept of being able to improve the patient's condition due to high standards of patient handling management is unproven, but has a high level of intent among practitioners. Meeting the clinical needs of the patient and improving care delivery is evaluated using a questionnaire given to staff and management, as it was suggested that patients may not have enough understanding of what should happen to them in a care situation.

Patient perception. The subjective assessment of a patient when being moved in a single transfer or mobility situation, fear, comfort etc is recorded as a direct assessment (comfort, security, fear) of the transfer or task using a nine point scale (Kjellberg *et al* 2004).

MSD exposure measures. This section evaluates the physical workload factors that place the staff under strain, eg forces, postures, frequency of tasks and workload measures. The question set used in the IET was developed from three studies: self reported workload measure (Knibbe & Friele 1996), patient parameters and workload (Cohen *et al* 2004) and the Arjo Resident Gallery (Arjo Ab 2006).

Patient injuries. Accident reporting systems were examined for patient harm accidents (bruises, lacerations, tissue damage, falls, etc) and pressure ulcer prevalence scores related to the movement and positioning of patients.

Financial. The financial impact of MSD in an organisation is due to lost staff time, lost productivity costs, compensation claims, litigation and all direct and indirect costs against the costs of any prevention programme. These organisational outcomes are recorded as part of the management interview for the cost of days lost, reduced capacity days, MSD claims, treatments for the MSD (internal or external) and interventions extra to the organisational set up. The data is standardised using the OSHA formula (Charney 1997; Charney *et al* 2006; Collins *et al* 2004) and the calculation can then be used as a cost benefit model (eg Siddarthan *et al* 2005).

In phase two, a preliminary evaluation of the IET was carried out at hospitals in the UK, Finland, Italy and Portugal to complete an IET assessment on two separate ward areas (a well managed unit and a poorly performing unit) to give eight datasets. The data collection tools and instructions for data collection were translated and sent to the EU facilitators to check for typographical and interpretation differences. The trials were coordinated by the EU facilitators (EPPHE member) with the assistance of the managers and patient handling practitioners in each hospital. Where appropriate, the local permissions and ethical approval were obtained.

The final evaluation process was an expert panel, with members from EPPHE, to review the IET. The facilitators from the EU trials reported good success with the data collection, with no parts of the documents requiring further clarification during the trials. The growing body of knowledge about patient movement has resulted in a series of recommended methods that are becoming acceptable worldwide, and there is now much less variation in recommended practice across many countries.

| Organisational behaviour measures (1) | Measures of safe or quality behaviour (3,5,6) | Measures of effects on individuals (patients and staff) (2,4,7,8,9,10,11) | Financial outcomes (12) |

Fig 3.5 Strength of outcome by level of interaction (Fray 2010)

Some outcomes may have effects on other outcomes (Fig 3.5), which raises the level of their contribution to the overall score. Safety culture (1) interacts with all other groups, while financial analysis interacts with no other outcomes which may explain the order of the priority rating in phase one. Other high priority outcomes showed higher levels of interaction; competence and compliance (3), quality of care (5), and accident numbers (6), all had effects on eight or more other outcomes. Several outcomes interacted with four to six others; MS health measures (2), psychological wellbeing (7), patient condition (8), MSD exposure and patient injuries (11). Placing a high priority on financial outcomes will probably only be achieved with good performance in all the other outcomes, and interventions aimed at 1, 3, 5, 6 will probably give the best return. The effect of these interactions may influence the selection of interventions to improve the IET performance.

In its present form, the IET analysis delivers two sets of scores, 12 individual section scores and a total IET score. The patient handling experts and facilitators involved in the evaluation indicated as much interest in the section scores as the total. It may create opportunities for the future use of the IET by focusing on specific improvements in individual sections, while maintaining the scores in other sections. This should result in an improvement in the total IET score.

Examples of ergonomics in health and social care

Social care
Alexander (2003) evaluated a risk management programme for community nurses with respect to the nursing managers' ability to implement the recommendations for risk reduction. The risk reduction recommendations included provision of hoists, increasing staffing levels, addressing space constraints, tackling difficulties identified with both patients and carers (including sudden changes in clinical condition). She found that the managers perceived that an increased awareness through education would be the main factor in reducing sickness absence for back and neck pain, whereas the staff believed that provision of equipment would be the main factor. A significant relationship was found with respect to the implementation of risk reduction recommendations. There was also a reduction in sickness absence from 28 per cent to nine per cent in the implementation group over 12 months.

Home care
Sitzman & Bloswick (2002) referred to the repealed OSHA Ergonomics Program Standard (www.osha.gov/SLTC/ergonomics/index.html) suggesting that ergonomics could be applied to a range of risk activities associated with the provision of home care, eg moving clients, carrying nursing bags and driving. This included basic screening tools and detailed ergonomics guidelines and information.

Owen & Skalitsky Staehler (2003) looked at nursing activities in persons' homes to identify the tasks perceived to be the most physically stressful. They found that the nurses rated lifting a person up in bed as the most stressful (user rated perceived exertion) with body mechanics listed as the most frequent contributor due to bending, reaching, twisting, lifting and enduring static postures. They also collected stress reduction ideas from the nursing aides, including environmental factors (eg adjustable beds, assistive devices for lifting and transferring patients), policy changes (eg permit more than one aide for visits with heavy and difficult persons) and person factors (eg encourage the person to help more).

Disability services

Ore (2003) reported on an analysis of approximately 2,700 manual handling injuries among disability services workers in an Australian state government agency between 1997 and 2000. These workers support people living in small group homes (about five in a house) who require varying levels of support. The client group included people with an intellectual disability, autism, neurological disability and acquired brain injury and most are involved in rehabilitation programmes. Nearly half of the workers' injuries were associated with providing support, eg assisting unsteady clients into the bath and shower; dressing clients; assisting clients into and out of bed; holding clients during epileptic seizures and preventing clients from falling out of bed. He suggests that ergonomics interventions could include providing sufficient space in the bathing areas to minimise awkward postures, redesigning the client rooms, toilets, beds, wheelchairs and recommending appropriate transfer devices.

Space to care

Health Building Notes were developed by NHS Estates in the 1980s to assist architects to plan sufficient space for clinical activities, but there were limitations identified in the process by Stanton (1983) with respect to the inclusion of user data. Hignett & Lu have carried out a number of Functional Space Experiments (FSEs) to determine the average spatial requirements for specified clinical activities as a complex spatial representation to incorporate multiple activities, participants and interfaces (Hignett & Lu 2008). The resultant dimensions support the design process through the provision of information about the incompressible spatial requirements for functional activities rather than prescribing specific layouts. A five step protocol was used to determine the dimensions (Fig 3.6).

Step 1: Define an example to test from "real life".

Step 2: Observe task activities using hierarchical task analysis (HTA) and link analysis (LA) to develop a test scenario.

Step 3: Conduct FSEs with the test scenario to determine the average spatial requirements.

Step 4: Take additional information into account, eg storage, family space and circulation, regulations, standards etc for a specified (generic) room dimension. This step is usually carried out by the building designer in consultation with the ergonomics adviser.

Step 5: Use steps 1-4 to test spatial requirements following changes in working practices and the introduction of new equipment/technology.

Fig 3.6 Five step protocol to determine spatial requirements

The observations for step two are carried out for frequently conducted and safety critical nursing tasks. HTA (Kirwan & Ainsworth 1992) was used to identify individual variance and generic task components to develop the simulation scenarios. An LA is also completed for each task. The simulations in step three are designed to test the different layouts and dimensions using patient scenarios. Bed space mockups are built using

- Intensive care unit bed space average spatial requirement was 22.89m^2 (average width of 4.86m, length of 4.71m).
- Ward bed space average spatial requirement was 10.84m^2 (average width of 3.18m, length of 3.41m).
- Toilet/shower average spatial requirement was 5.04m^2 (average width 2.01m, length of 2.52m).
- Bariatric bed space average spatial requirement was 16.61m^2 (average width 3.93m, length of 4.23m).

Fig 3.7 Average spatial requirements (Hignett & Lu 2008)

different coloured floor tape at 10-20cm intervals for measurement. Moveable walls facilitate the nurses' experience of the physical space and can be "pushed out" if more space is needed during the task. Multidirectional videotaping is used to record the participant's movements between equipment, furniture and the simulation mannequin (patient) and the video data is analysed frame by frame to plot the movement of each nurse.

FSEs were carried out for ICU bed spaces, medical/surgical ward bed spaces, toilet/shower spaces and bariatric bed spaces (Fig 3.7).

Ultrasonography

Ultrasonography is used for general investigations of soft tissues as well as specific diagnostic tests in a range of clinical specialities, eg gynaecology, obstetrics, cardiology, vascular and paediatrics. Sonography has been available as a diagnostic tool since 1942 and was recognised as a separate profession in 1974 (Ransom 2002). Sonographers use a hand held transducer which is applied to the area needing investigation, linked to a scanning machine, which relays the images collected by the transducer. It typically involves a static posture to maintain the arm in a fixed position (unsupported abduction) while pressing the transducer against the patient (Fig 3.8). The layout of the workplace may vary according to the preferences of the person and sonographer. In the case of obstetrics, the mother may wish to view the monitor during the scan and the sonographer may prefer to use his/her dominant hand for either the transducer or the scanning machine controls.

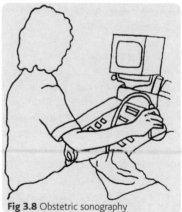

Fig 3.8 Obstetric sonography

Russo *et al* (2002) reported on a survey in British Columbia, finding that the majority of sonographers (91 per cent) had work related musculoskeletal problems. They collected data about the work environment and corporate culture, schedule, tasks and equipment to look for associations with physical symptoms. Factors included the number of hours scanning, static and awkward postures, and psychosocial factors, including social support (co-worker, supervisor and senior management) and decision making with respect to planning the workload and taking breaks.

Summary

A range of examples has been given to illustrate how ergonomics methods and tools have been used to assist in the design and evaluation and the investigation and modification of health and social care tasks. Most are related to musculoskeletal risks, but ergonomics methods are also used in a wide range of other areas, eg military, manufacturing, consumer product design, human computer interaction, process and transport control, health and safety, human error analysis, pollution and waste management. There is a growing body of ergonomics research in health and social care in the area of person safety and it is important that the interaction between person and handler safety is made clear. Both need to be addressed to improve the system rather than changing one element at the cost of the other.

References

Alexander, P (2003), Community Care nurses. In Hignett, S et al (2003). Evidence-based patient handling, Tasks, equipment and interventions, London: Routledge.

Amick, B, Tullar, J, Brewer, S, Irvin, E, Mahood, Q, Pompeii, L, Wang, A, Van Erd, D, Gimeno, D & Evanoff, B (2006), Interventions in healthcare settings to protect musculoskeletal health: a systematic review, Institute for Work and Health, Toronto.

Arjo Ab d (2006), The Residents Gallery, www.arjo.com/uk/Page.asp?PageNumber=817 (accessed 7 July 2010).

Borg, G (1985), An Introduction to Borg's RPE-Scale, Ithaca, NY: Movement Publications.

Buckle, P, Clarkson, PJ, Coleman, R, Ward, J & Anderson, J (2006), Patient Safety, Systems Design and Ergonomics. Applied Ergonomics, 37, 491-500.

Caccamise, DJ (1995), Implementation of a team approach to nuclear criticality safety: The use of participatory methods in macro-ergonomics, International Journal of Industrial Ergonomics, 15, 397-409.

Carayon, P & Buckle, P (2010), Editorial for special issues of applied ergonomics on patient safety, Applied Ergonomics, 41, 5, 643-644.

Charney, W (1997), The lift team method for reducing back injuries: A 10 hospital study, AAOHN Journal, 45, 6, 300-304.

Charney, W, Simmons, B, Lary, M & Metz, S (2006), Zero Lift Programs in Small Rural Hospitals in Washington State: Reducing Back Injuries Among Health Care Workers. AAOHN Journal, 54, 8, 355-8.

Cohen, M, Village, J, Ostry, A, Ratner, P, Cvitkovich, Y & Yassi, A (2004), Workload as a Determinant of Staff Injury in Intermediate Care. International Journal of Occupational and Environmental Health, 10, 4, 375-83.

Collins, JW, Wolf, L, Bell, J & Evanoff, B (2004), An evaluation of 'best practices' musculoskeletal injury prevention program in nursing homes, Injury Prevention, 10, 206-211.

Colombini, D & Occhipinti, E (1985), Posture Analysis, Ergonomics, 28, 1, 275-285.

Croteau, RJ (2010), Root Cause Analysis in Healthcare: Tools and Techniques. Joint Commission on Accreditation of Healthcare Organizations, Oakbrook Terrace, Illinois.

Dachler, HP & Wilpert, B (1978), Conceptual dimensions and boundaries of participation in organisations: a critical evaluation, Administrative Science Quarterly, 23, 1-39.

Dawson, AP, McLennan, SN, Schiller, SD, Jull, GA, Hodges, PW & Stewart, S (2007), Interventions to prevent back pain and back injury in nurses: a systematic review, Occupational and Environmental Medicine, 64, 642-650.

Department of Health (2000), An Organisation with a Memory: Report of an Expert Group on Learning from Adverse Events in the NHS, The Stationery Office, London, UK.

Dickinson, C, Campion, K, Foster, A, Newman, S, O'Rourke, A & Thomas, P (1992), Questionnaire development: an examination of the Nordic Musculoskeletal Questionnaire, Applied Ergonomics, 23, 3, 197-201.

Dul, J & Neumann, WP (2009), Ergonomics contributions to company strategies, Applied Ergonomics, 40, 745–752.

Engkvist, I-L (2004), The accident process preceding back injuries among Australian nurses, Safety Science, 42, 221-235.

Eriksen, W, Bruusgaard, D & Knardahl, S (2004), Work factors as predictors of intense or disabling low back pain; a prospective study of nurses' aides, Occupational and Environmental Medicine, 61, 398-404.

Evanoff, BA, Bohr, PC & Wolf, LD (1999), Effects of a participatory ergonomics team among hospital orderlies, American Journal of Industrial Medicine, 35, 4, 358-365.

Fray, M (2010), A Comprehensive Evaluation of Outcomes from Patient Handling Interventions. PhD Thesis, Loughborough University.

Haines, HM & Wilson, JR (1998), Development of a framework for participatory ergonomics, Contract Research Report 174/1998, Health and Safety Executive, London: HSE Books.

Haines, HM, Wilson, JR, Vink, P & Koningsveld, E (2002), Validating a framework for participatory ergonomics, Ergonomics, 45, 4, 309-327.

Hasselhorn, H-M, Tackenberg, P & Müller, BH (2003), Working conditions and intent to leave the profession among nursing staff in Europe, National Institute for Working Life, Stockholm, Sweden.

Health and Safety Executive (2003), Health and Safety Statistics Highlights. www.hse.gov.uk/statistics/overall/hssh0203.pdf. Accessed 8 June 2004.

HSE (2010), Health and Safety Executive, Health and Safety Statistics 2008/09, Sudbury, Suffolk: HSE Books.

Helander, MH (1997), The Human Factors Profession, Chapter 1. In Salvendy, G (Ed), Handbook of Human Factors and Ergonomics (2nd Ed), New York: John Wiley & Sons.

Hendrick, HW (2008), Applying ergonomics to systems: Some documented 'lessons learned', Applied Ergonomics, 39, 418-426.

Hignett, S (1998), Ergonomics: Chapter 13 in Pitt-Brooke, J, Reid, H, Lockwood, J & Kerr, K, Rehabilitation of Movement, Theoretical Basis of Clinical Practice, London: WB Saunders Co Ltd, 458-494.

Hignett, S (2001a), Using Qualitative Methodology in Ergonomics: theoretical background and practical examples, PhD thesis, University of Nottingham.

Hignett, S (2001b), Embedding ergonomics in hospital culture: top-down and bottom-up strategies, Applied Ergonomics, 32, 61-69.

Hignett, S (2003a), Intervention strategies to reduce musculoskeletal injuries associated with handling patients: A systematic review, Occupational and Environmental Medicine, Vol 60, no 9, e6 (electronic paper), www.occenvmed.com/cgi/content/full/60/9/e6.

Hignett, S (2003b), Systematic review of patient handling activities starting in lying, sitting and standing positions,

Journal of Advanced Nursing, **41**, 6, 545-552.

Hignett, S (2004), Physical Ergonomics in Healthcare, Chapter 20. In Carayon, P (Ed), *Handbook of Human Factors and Ergonomics in Health Care and Patient Safety*, Mahwah, NJ: Lawrence Erlbaum Associates, Inc 309-321.

Hignett, S & McAtamney, L (2000), Rapid Entire Body Assessment (REBA), *Applied Ergonomics*, **31**, 201-205.

Hignett, S, Crumpton, E, Alexander, P, Ruszala, S, Fray, M & Fletcher, B (2003), *Evidence-Based Patient Handling: Tasks, Equipment and Interventions*, Routledge, London.

Hignett, S & Wilson, JR (2004), The role for qualitative methodology in ergonomics: A case study to explore theoretical issues, *Theoretical Issues in Ergonomics Science*, **5**, 6, 473-493.

Hignett, S & Crumpton, E (2005), Development of a patient handling assessment tool, *International Journal of Therapy and Rehabilitation*, **12**, 4, 178-81.

Hignett, S & McAtamney, L (2006), REBA and RULA: Whole Body and Upper Limb Rapid Assessment Tools. In Karwowski, W & Marras, WS (Eds), *The Occupational Ergonomics Handbook* (2nd Ed), Boca Raton, Fl: CRC Press. 42-1 – 42-12.

Hignett, S, Fray, M, Rossi, MA, Tamminen-Peter, L, Hermann, S, Lomi, C, Dockrell, S, Cotrim, T, Cantineau, JB & Johnsson, C (2007), Implementation of the Manual Handing Directive in the Healthcare Industry in the European Union for Patient Handling tasks, *International Journal of Industrial Ergonomics*, **37**, 415-423.

Hignett, S & Lu, J (2008), Ensuring bed space is right first time *Health Estate Journal*, February www.healthestatejournal.com/Story.aspx?Story=3395 (accessed 10 April 2008).

International Ergonomics Association (2000), *Triennial Report*, Santa Monica, CA: IEA Press, 5.

Johnsson, C, Kjellberg, K, Kjellberg, A & Lagerstrom, M (2004), A direct observation instrument for assessment of nurses' patient transfer technique (DINO), *Applied Ergonomics*, **35**, 591-601.

Kilbom, Å (1990), Measurement and assessment of dynamic work. In Wilson, JR & Corlett, EN (Eds), *Evaluation of Human Work, A practical ergonomics methodology*, (1st Ed), London: Taylor and Francis.

Kirwan, B & Ainsworth, LK (1992), *A Guide to Task Analysis*, London: Taylor and Francis.

Kjellberg, K, Lagerström, M & Hagberg, M (2004), Patient safety and comfort during transfers in relation to nurses work technique, *Journal of Advanced Nursing*, **47**, 3, 251-259.

Kneafsey, R (2000), The effect of occupational socialization on nurses' patient handling practices, *Journal of Clinical Nursing*, **9**, 585-593.

Knibbe, JJ & Friele, RD (1996), Prevalence of back pain and characteristics of the physical workload of community nurses, *Ergonomics*, **39**, 2: 186-198.

Kohn, LT, Corrigan, JM & Donaldson, MS (Eds) (1999), *To Err Is Human: Building a Safer Health System*, National Academy Press, Washington, DC.

Kuorinka, I (1997), Tools and means of implementing participatory ergonomics, *International Journal of Industrial Ergonomics*, **19**, 267-270.

McAtamney, L & Corlett, EN (1993), RULA: a survey method for the investigation of WRULD, *Applied Ergonomics*, **24**, 2, 91-99.

Martimo, KP, Verbeek, J, Karppinen, J, Furlan, A, Takala, E, Kuijer, P, Jauhiainen, M & Viikari-Juntura, E (2008), Effect of training and lifting equipment for preventing back pain in lifting and handling: systematic review, *BMJ* doi: 10.1136/bmj.39463.418380.BE.

National Audit Office (2003), *A Safer Place to Work, Improving the management of health and safety risks to staff in NHS Trusts*, London: National Audit Office, ISBN: 0102921431.

Nelson, A, Collins, J, Siddharthan, K, Matz, M & Waters, T (2008), Link Between Safe Patient Handling and Patient Outcomes in Long-Term Care, *Rehabilitation Nursing*, **33**, 1, 33-43.

Ore, T (2003), Manual handling injury in a disability services setting, *Applied Ergonomics*, **34**, 89-94.

Owen, BD & Skalitsky Staehler, K (2003), Decreasing Back Stress in Home Care, *Home Healthcare Nurse*, **21**, 3, 180-186.

Pheasant, S (1998), Back Injury in Nurses – Ergonomics and Epidemiology. In Lloyd, P, Fletcher, B, Holmes, D, Tarling, C & Tracy, M (1998, revised) *The Guide to the Handling of Patients*, (4th edition), National Back Pain Association/Royal College of Nursing.

Pluye, P, Gagnon, M, Griffiths, F & Johnson-Lafleur, J (2009), A scoring system for appraising mixed methods research, and concomitantly appraising qualitative, quantitative and mixed methods primary studies in Mixed Studies Reviews, *International Journal of Nursing Studies*, **46**, 4, 529-546.

Ransom, E (2002), *The causes of musculoskeletal injury among sonographers in the UK*, Society of Radiographers, 207 Providence Square, Mill Street, London SE1 2EW.

Reason, JT (1997), Managing the risks of organisational accidents, Ashgate, Aldershot.

Roozenburg, NFM & Eekels, J (1995), *Product Design: Fundamentals and Methods*, Chichester: John Wiley & Sons Ltd.

Russo, A, Murphy, C, Lessoway, V & Berkowitz, J (2002), The prevalence of musculoskeletal symptoms among British Columbia sonographers, *Applied Ergonomics*, **33**, 385-393.

Seccombe, I & Ball, J (1992), *Back injured nurses: a profile, A discussion paper for the Royal College of Nursing*, London: Institute of Manpower Studies.

Siddarthan, K, Nelson, A & Weisenborn, G (2005), A business case for patient care ergonomic interventions, *Nursing Administration Quarterly*, **29**, 1, 63-71.

Sitzman, K & Bloswick, D (2002), Creative Use of Ergonomics Principles in Home Care, *Home Healthcare Nurse*, **20**, 2, 98-103.

Smedley, J, Egger, P, Cooper, C & Coggon, D (1995), Manual handling activities and the risk of low back pain in nurses, *Occupational and Environmental Medicine*, **52**, 160-163.

Stanton, G (1983), The development of ergonomics data for health building design guidance, *Ergonomics*, **30**, 2, 359-366.

Stubbs, DA, Buckle, PW, Hudson, MP, Rivers, PM & Worringham, CJ (1983), Back pain in nursing profession: Epidemiology and pilot methodology, *Ergonomics*, **26**, 8, 755-765.

Troup, D, Lloyd, P, Osborne, C & Tarling, C (1981), *The Handling of Patients. A Guide for Nurse Managers*, Back Pain Association/Royal College of Nursing, Teddington, Middlesex.

Vincent, C (2006), *Patient Safety*, Edinburgh: Elsevier Churchill Livingstone.

Vincent, C (2010), *Patient Safety* (2nd Ed), Chichester: John Wiley & Sons Ltd.

Vink, P & Wilson, JR (2003), Participatory Ergonomics. *Ergonomics in the Digital Age. Proceedings of the XVth Triennial Congress of the International Ergonomics Association and The 7th Joint conference of the Ergonomics Society of Korea/Japan Ergonomics Society,* August 24-29, 2003, Seoul, Korea.

Wilson, JR & Corlett, EN (2005), *Evaluation of Human Work, A practical ergonomics methodology* (3rd Ed), Boca Raton, FL: CRC Press.

Appendix 3.1

Using REBA (Hignett & McAtamney 2006)

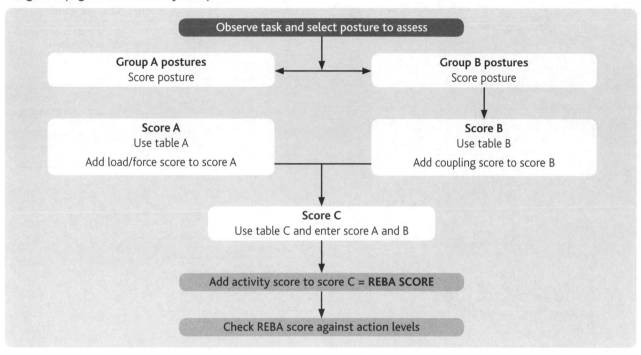

Group A postures (Hignett 1998)

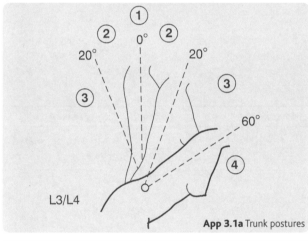

App 3.1a Trunk postures

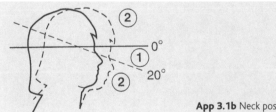

App 3.1b Neck postures

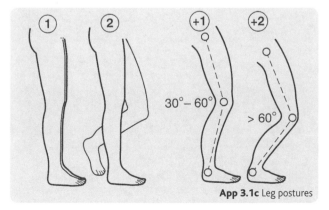

App 3.1c Leg postures

Group A definitions

TRUNK POSTURES

Movement	Score	Change score
Upright	1	
0°-20° flexion 0°-20° extension	2	+1 if twisting or side flexed
20°-60° flexion >20° extension	3	
>60° extension	4	

NECK POSTURES

Movement	Score	Change score
0°-20° flexion	1	+1 if twisting or side flexed
>20° flexion or extension	2	

LEG POSTURES

Movement	Score	Change score
Bilateral weight bearing, walking or sitting	1	+1 if knee(s) between 30° and 60° flexion
Unilateral weight bearing, feather weight bearing or an unstable posture	2	+2 if knee(s) >60° flexion (NB not for sitting)

Group B postures (Hignett 1998)

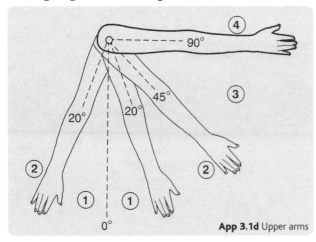

App 3.1d Upper arms

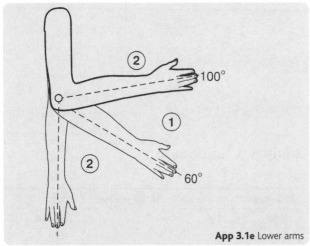

App 3.1e Lower arms

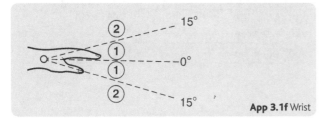

App 3.1f Wrist

Group B definitions

UPPER ARMS

Position	Score	Change score
20° extension to 20° flexion	1	+1 if arm is abducted and/or rotated
>20° extension 20°-45° flexion	2	+1 if shoulder is raised
45°-90° flexion	3	-1 if leaning, supporting weight of arm or if posture is gravity assisted
>90° extension	4	

LOWER ARMS

Movement	Score
60°-100° flexion	1
<60° flexion >100° flexion	2

WRIST

Movement	Score	Change score
0°-15° flexion/extension	1	+1 if wrist is deviated or twisted
>15° flexion/extension	2	

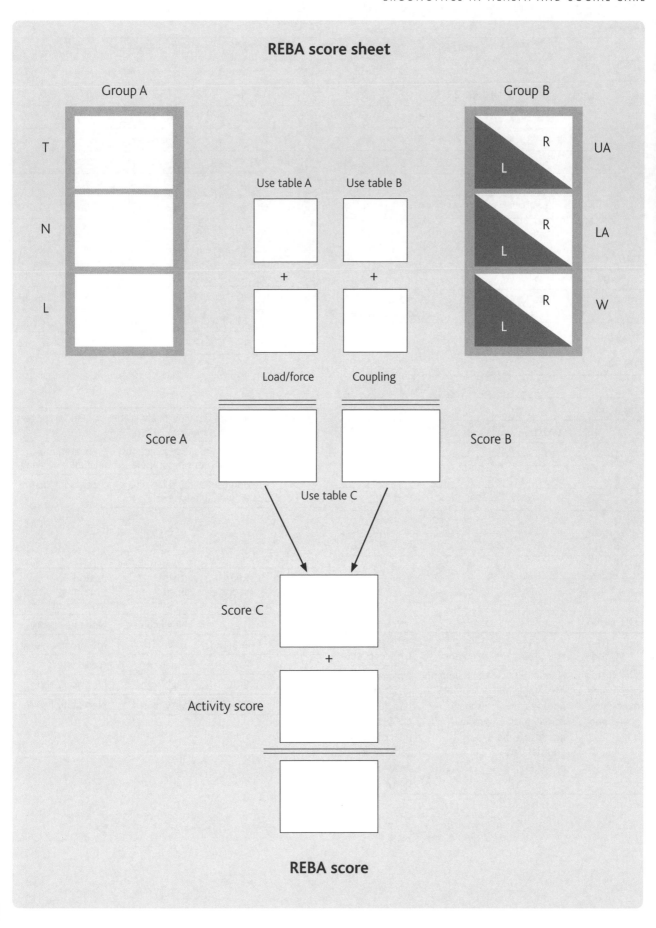

TABLE A

Trunk		Neck											
		1				**2**				**3**			
	Legs	1	2	3	4	1	2	3	4	1	2	3	4
1		1	2	3	4	1	2	3	4	3	3	5	6
2		2	3	4	5	3	4	5	6	4	5	6	7
3		2	4	5	6	4	5	6	7	5	6	7	8
4		3	5	6	7	5	6	7	8	6	7	8	9
5		4	6	7	8	6	7	8	9	7	8	9	9

LOAD/FORCE

0	1	2	+1
<5 kg	5-10 kg	>10 kg	Shock or rapid build up of force

TABLE B

Upper arm		Lower arm					
		1			**2**		
	Wrist	1	2	3	1	2	3
1		1	2	2	1	2	3
2		1	2	3	2	3	4
3		3	4	5	4	5	5
4		4	5	5	5	6	7
5		6	7	8	7	8	8
6		7	8	8	8	9	9

COUPLING

0 Good	1 Fair	2 Poor	+3 Unacceptable
Well fitting handle and a midrange power grip	Hand hold acceptable but not ideal or coupling is acceptable via another part of the body	Hand hold not acceptable although possible	Awkward, unsafe trip, no handles. Coupling is unacceptable using other parts of the body

TABLE C

Score A	Score B											
	1	2	3	4	5	6	7	8	9	10	11	12
1	1	1	1	2	3	3	4	5	6	7	7	7
2	1	2	2	3	4	4	5	6	6	7	7	8
3	2	3	3	3	4	5	6	7	7	8	8	8
4	3	4	4	4	5	6	7	8	8	9	9	9
5	4	4	4	5	6	7	8	8	9	9	9	9
6	6	6	6	7	8	8	9	9	10	10	10	10
7	7	7	7	8	9	9	9	10	10	11	11	11
8	8	8	8	9	10	10	10	10	10	11	11	11
9	9	9	9	10	10	10	11	11	11	12	12	12
10	10	10	10	11	11	11	11	12	12	12	12	12
11	11	11	11	11	12	12	12	12	12	12	12	12
12	12	12	12	12	12	12	12	12	12	12	12	12

ACTIVITY SCORE

+1	1 or more body parts are static, eg held for longer than one minute
+1	Repeated small range actions, eg repeated more than four times per minute (not including walking)
+1	Action causes rapid large range changes in posture or an unstable base

ACTION LEVELS

Action level	REBA score	Risk level	Action (including further assessment)
0	1	Negligible	None necessary
1	2-3	Low	May be necessary
2	4-7	Medium	Necessary
3	8-10	High	Necessary soon
4	11-15	Very high	Necessary NOW

4

Mechanics and human movement

Frances Polak PhD MSc MCSP HPC Reg
Consultant occupational health physiotherapist

Introduction

Improving health and work: changing lives (Department for Work and Pensions 2008) is the Government's response to *Working for a healthier tomorrow* (2008), Dame Carol Black's review of the health of Britain's working age population. The publication of the Government's response has placed great emphasis on the health and wellbeing of working age people. There is a growing base of evidence that working is good for health and the Government is keen to show the positive link between work and wellbeing while facilitating schemes for people with health conditions to find and remain in employment. While the aspiration is for everyone to achieve a healthy and fulfilling working life, the reality can be quite different. Some workers can be exposed to occupational hazards within their workplace, often as a result of poor practice. Approaches to identify, control and prevent poor practices which can result in musculoskeletal injury is a high priority for most employers and workers. An understanding of the biomechanical mechanisms of the causation of many injuries, and the mechanical principles which underpin good practice, should help in the design and implementation of effective strategies to enable tasks including handling to be undertaken safely and with confidence.

Injury, by definition, means mechanical disruption of tissues (Kumar 1999) and is a traumatic event in which the integrity of the tissue is damaged and the mechanical properties of the tissue altered. However, tissues can also be damaged by mechanical stresses over time, with no single traumatic event, often these stresses being prolonged and frequent in the workplace. While there is no definitive study which demonstrates an undisputed causal link between risk factors, such as repetition and exposure with tissue injury, there are several studies reporting a strong association between exposure to mechanical risk factors and the precipitation of injury. An understanding of the biomechanical risk factors associated with human movement is, therefore, needed to help control these risks and the development of musculoskeletal disorders. This understanding will help in the elimination of poor practice and inform good practice, not only during the handling of people, but also when helping them move independently as we promote functional gain and independence.

Biomechanical principles affecting movement

The understanding of movement is based upon mechanical principles, and applying the physical laws of mechanics to the body is known as biomechanics. Mechanics is often studied in two approaches – kinetics and kinematics – the former being the study of force and their effects, the latter being the study of motion in terms of angles, ranges, accelerations and velocities. In order to reduce the risk of injury and facilitate the moving and handling of people and the use of assistive devices, a firm grasp of mechanical principles is required.

Force

Force is a concept that cannot be seen, although its effect can be felt. Force can be designated as an applied force (contact), inertial force (motion) and gravitational force (weight or load). The unit of force is the Newton (N). Forces can produce movement, prevent movement and change both the direction and velocity of movement.

In the seventeenth century, Newton formulated three basic laws of motion.

1. An object will remain at rest or continue to move with constant velocity as long as the net forces equal zero.
The propensity of an object to remain in its present state is termed inertia, and this law is often referred to as Newton's Law of Inertia. All objects with a mass have inertia, and the larger the mass the more difficult it is to change the object's state of motion. For example, an object with a large mass has large inertia, and thus it is more difficult to slow down, speed up or change direction.

PRACTICAL APPLICATION

Imagine two people sitting in identical beds both waiting to go to the X-ray department. One person weighs 80kg and the other 40kg, both beds will remain stationary until you commence pushing them. The force required to overcome inertia and start to move the bed will be greater for the 80kg person than the person half his/her mass.

2. The acceleration of an object is proportional to the net force acting on it and inversely proportional to the mass of the object. Force = mass x acceleration.
If we want to change the state of motion of an object, we need to apply a force. This law tells us that the lighter the object the faster it will accelerate under a given force.

PRACTICAL APPLICATION

For our two people in their hospital beds, the larger person would have less acceleration if the same force were applied to both. To push the beds at the same rate, a greater force would need to be applied to the heavier person's bed.

3. For every action, there is an equal and opposite reaction.
This means that if we apply a force against something, and we do not apply enough to overcome the inertial properties of the object, the object will exert an equal and opposite reaction force against us. The net or resultant force is zero and the object will not move until some force alters this equilibrium. This state of zero force is often referred to as equilibrium and is expressed as $\Sigma F = 0$.

PRACTICAL APPLICATION

For the people in the beds, enough force has to be applied to overcome the mass of the person, the bed mass and the frictional force between the wheels and the floor to enable you to push the bed along the corridor.

When calculating forces acting upon an object, we can use force diagrams, eg the forces on the body are readily visualised by the use of simplified drawing, usually of a stick man. The forces are represented by arrows and show the magnitude of the force (greater force indicated by a longer arrow), the direction of force and the point of application of the force (see Fig 4.1). All these components play a part in relation to human movement and potential injury.

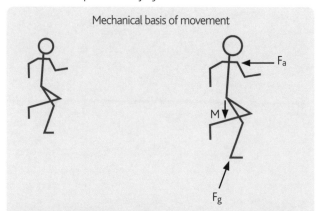

Mechanical basis of movement

Fig 4.1 Free body diagram to analyse forces (F_a, force of air resistance; M, mass; F_g, ground reaction force)

Gravity and equilibrium

Gravity is an invisible force that attracts all objects to the centre of the earth. Gravity is constant due to the curvature of the earth's surface and, from Newton's calculation, is 9.81 m/s². The centre of gravity of an object is an imaginary point in the centre of its mass. If the object is uniform in shape and density, eg a cube, the centre of gravity will be the geometric centre. However, in relation to humans, it is important to remember that the centre of gravity will alter depending on the posture adopted. In upright standing, it is generally accepted that the centre of gravity lies anterior (in front of) the second sacral vertebra. However, this depends on many factors, including body size, muscle mass, fat distribution, gender differences, etc. In the human, it is not necessary for the centre of gravity to remain within the body to remain in balance as long as there is sufficient muscle strength and normal neurology to control the body posture. The centre of gravity moves with the position of the body (see Fig 4.2).

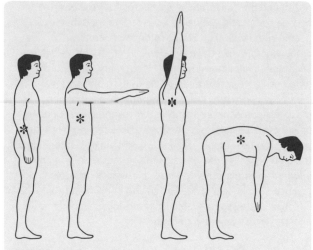

Fig 4.2 The centre of gravity moves with the position of the body.
✳ centre of gravity

The centre of gravity is important in determining the stability of an object. The object is most stable when its centre of mass is low and the line of gravity falls at the centre of its base of support, ie stable equilibrium.

Thus, a body is in equilibrium when all the forces acting on it equal zero. Equilibrium can be stable, unstable or neutral. A body is in equilibrium when its potential energy (the amount of energy a body has by virtue of its position) is at a minimum, and a force must be applied to cause a change in position of the body. In the human, the body is in stable equilibrium when lying flat on a horizontal surface that supports the entire body and the centre of gravity is very low, keeping the body very stable.

Unstable equilibrium occurs when the potential energy is at maximum and the base of support is small, so that very little force need be applied to move the line of gravity outside the base of support.

Neutral equilibrium occurs when the body comes to rest in a new position with no change in the level of the centre of gravity when it is displaced, eg a rolling ball (see Fig 4.3).

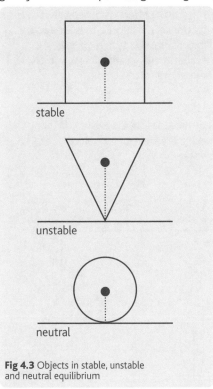

stable

unstable

neutral

Fig 4.3 Objects in stable, unstable and neutral equilibrium

Friction
Friction is the force that resists movement between two surfaces. It is measured in the unit called the coefficient of friction (μ) and is the level of resistance a material offers to horizontal movement or sliding. A low coefficient of friction indicates that materials will slide easily against each other. Friction adds to the inertial force of an object to overcome before movement can occur, and friction is often responsible for the object's deceleration.

PRACTICAL APPLICATION

The use of transfer boards and slide sheets when transferring a person returning from the operating theatre will help reduce friction and thus make the procedure easier and more comfortable. The transfer

allows a friction reducing surface to be utilised and the material from which the sheets are made usually has a lower coefficient of friction, helping to reduce the force needed to complete the horizontal/sliding technique (see Figs 4.4 and 4.5). Injury risk to the handler can still remain high and best practice advice should be followed.

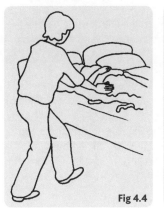

Fig 4.4

Fig 4.5

Stress and strain
Having considered what constitutes a force and the effect it may have on an object, in addition to moving the object, we need to consider the effects of forces within the object or internally – known as stress and strain (Lockwood 1999). Stress is the force within a material and the effect of stress is strain. Hooke's Law states that when a force (stress) is applied to an elastic object, the amount of deformation of the elastic object is proportional to the force applied to deform it. Most biological tissues obey Hooke's Law over a small or limited range of stresses and strains, provided that the stress is for a brief period. If the load is applied for a long period, then elongation of the tissue continues to increase. Materials in which stress and strain are time dependent are said to be viscoelastic. Eventually, stress may exceed the material's elastic limit, and the material will assume new dimensions, becoming plastic before finally failing completely. The tensile strength of a material is the maximum stress that it can absorb before it enters the plastic state.

Pressure
Pressure is the force acting perpendicularly, per unit area. The unit of pressure being the Pascal (Pa). Pressure is defined as the total force per area of application or P = F/A.

PRACTICAL APPLICATION

When considering tissue viability issues for people with limited mobility, the area of force application needs to be maximised to help combat high pressure areas, which can result in poor circulation and finally tissue breakdown and ulceration. Pressure cushions and mattresses that offer greater contact area with the person's body and help distribute pressure applied to the skin, can be beneficial in this regard.

Levers
A lever is a device for transmitting force over its distance. Usually a rigid structure, of which one point acts as a fixed fulcrum or axis, another is connected to the force being applied or effort, and the third is connected with the resistance force or load. To calculate the effort and load, we need to take into account the distance between each and the fulcrum. The load arm is the distance from the load/resistance force and the

fulcrum, and the effort arm being the distance between the applied effort and the fulcrum. When effort is equal to the load, the lever is in equilibrium. If the effort required to turn the lever is less than the load, mechanical advantage occurs.

Mechanical advantage = Resistance force/load in Newtons
                         Effort/applied force

Levers are categorised according to the relationship between the fulcrum, the effort and the resistance.

First class levers
The first class lever has the fulcrum located between the applied force (effort) and the resistance force/load (see Fig 4.6).

Depending on the relative distances of the applied force and the resistance force from the fulcrum/axis, the amount required to move the load may be large or small.

EXAMPLE
A common cited example of first class lever is the posterior cervical muscles extending the head across the atlanto-occipital joint.

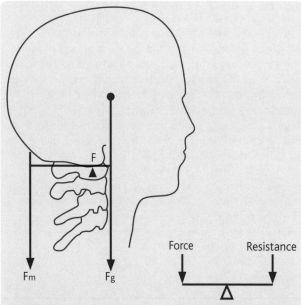

Fig 4.6 First class lever (F, fulcrum = atlanto-occipital joint; Fm, force of posterior cervical muscles; Fg, weight due to gravitational force tending to flex

Second class levers
A second class lever has the resistance located between the fulcrum and the applied force. Consequently, the effort arm will always be greater than that of the resistance.

EXAMPLE
An example of second class lever is a man pushing a wheelbarrow. The weight to be moved is nearer to the fulcrum than the effort, therefore less force is required (as the effort arm is long) and mechanical advantage is gained (see Fig 4.7).

Both first and second class levers confer mechanical advantage, meaning the magnitude of the applied force will move a force greater than itself, especially if the resistance is closer to the axis or fulcrum.

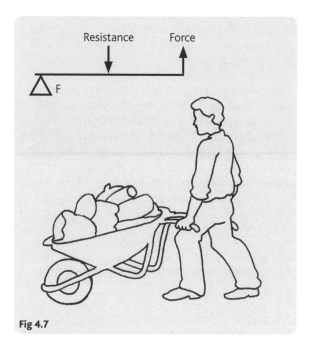

Fig 4.7

Third class levers
In a third class lever system, the effort is applied between the axis and the resistance. Hence, the effort arm is always less than that of the resistance arm. This system of levers is, therefore, less powerful but there are advantages in the speed and range of movement afforded.

EXAMPLES
Many examples of third class levers exist in the body, eg hamstrings flexing the knee joint or biceps brachii flexing the elbow (see Fig 4.8).

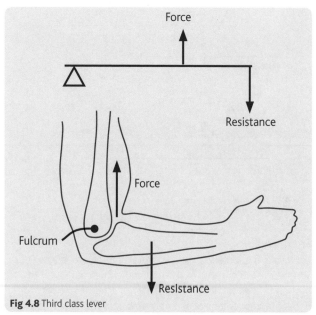

Fig 4.8 Third class lever

Moment of force or turning force
A moment of force is the force that creates the turning movement of a lever around the fulcrum or axis. In the body, this is usually the movement of a bone around a joint. The unit of moment of force is the Newton metre (Nm) and is calculated as:

moment = force x distance

To calculate the effort required to resist the moment at a joint, we need to know:
- the position of the axis (joint)
- the point of application and line of application of the effort
- the point of application of the load and its line of action
- the magnitude of the load.

In the human body, most muscular moment arms are short relative to the lever that they move, eg the biceps flexing the elbow joint. The disadvantage is that the force generated to move the forearm is greater than the weight of the forearm. The advantage, however, is that relatively small movement at the attachment of biceps produces a large range of motion at the distal forearm, and the wrist and hand are brought upwards at a greater velocity than the proximal elbow.

Although we often use free body diagrams to calculate the forces associated with manual handling and with the adoption of different postures, it is important to acknowledge the limitations of these simplistic calculations of external moments (moments applied to the body). True human movement occurs in 3D, with each segment having different mass and inertial properties, moving through the three planes with changing accelerations.

A simple diagram showing one joint in 2D is, of course, a simplification, although we do use these calculations to provide a guide to the amount of load the human tissue may be experiencing. This information has contributed to our understanding of safer handling practices and the use of mechanical principles to our advantage when handling people. These simplified calculations are often considered when carrying out risk assessments and reviewed to calculate how we can avoid or minimise risk, and are often integral to the risk assessment process and subsequent elimination or control strategy. For example, the REBA tool (see chapter 3) looks at total body postures, their frequency, load to be lifted and the coupling employed to calculate the risk level of musculoskeletal injury and the action level required (Hignett & McAtamney 2000).

When moving and handling a load/person, it is best to keep levers short and this often means keeping close to the centre of mass of our patients. The position of the centre of mass will vary, depending upon many factors, including posture both for the handler and the subject. A person's posture is often affected both by his/her condition and pain.

Stability and equilibrium
The mechanical stability of a person is measured by how easily his/her balance can be displaced by a force. We inherently know that a person in lying is more stable than one sitting, and a seated person is more stable than one standing. There are several key factors that affect his/her stability:
- size of base of support
- location of centre of gravity within the body (a person is more unstable with arms raised and centre of gravity raised)
- position of line of gravity within the base (more unstable as line of gravity moves towards edge of base)
- mass of the body.

A larger base allows for greater displacement of the body without the body falling. Standing with our feet close together is a relatively unstable position for the service user and

handler; while walk standing or stride standing is much more stable as the feet move apart and the size of base and our stability increases. Both the elderly and young toddlers readily adopt a wider based gait for this very reason. The young child progresses from lying, to lying with head and some arm control, before total body rolling, and then to supported and independent long sitting. Once the child has mastered some head, trunk and pelvic control, he/she often commences crawling. The child gains further motion control and will start to stand with a wide base before walking while holding onto support, before walking independently, starting to run, finally achieving hopping and skipping at about age four. Of course, not all children follow this progression, but we often use this sequence from lying to walking during rehabilitation as we try to promote independent ambulation. Walking aid devices, often used to enable someone to walk, provide the mechanical effect of increasing base of support and these are covered in more detail on page 59. Conversely, stability is reduced by close standing or even standing on one leg and, therefore, foot placement and base of support plays an important function in safe handling. Consideration should always be given to the base of support size, the height of the centre of gravity and the position of the centre of gravity within the base when planning to handle people. Lowering the centre of gravity and increasing the base size will increase the stability of the handler or person.

Human movement

Human movement and function depends on a complex interaction between five main systems. Impairment to any of these systems affects how a person functions and his/her dependence and independence. Rehabilitation aims to restore normal function and, as handlers, we aim to provide the right assistance, often mechanical, to enable the person to become independent. The five main systems which enable human movement to take place are all complex and interdependent and comprise of:
- skeletal or bony system
- joint or articular system
- muscular system
- cardiorespiratory system
- nervous system.

Skeletal system
Humans have an endoskeleton (internal support structure) and are vertebrate (have a backbone). The vertebral column, along with other bones, forms the framework of the human body and has many functions, including the mechanical function of support for functional activities and protection of underlying organs, and the skeleton provides sites for muscle attachments. The muscle attachment to the bones facilitates human movement by mechanical leverage. The skeletal framework also has physiological functions, including storage of calcium and the production of blood cells within the bone marrow.

The skeletal framework provides many functions and there are variations in the composition and shape of the bones to meet the different functional requirements. The long bones in the limbs consist of compact bone and act as rigid levers between the joints to produce movement, whereas the primary function of the flat bones of the skull is protection of the brain. The short bones in the foot are constructed of a thin outer layer of compact bone, and internal spongy or cancellous bone, which plays an important role in absorbing the compressive forces applied to the body during weight bearing, walking and running. The long bones in the lower limb experience compressive forces during standing, while the upper limb long bones experience tension when carrying a load in the hand (Abernethy *et al* 2005).

Articular system

During weight bearing movement, forces are transmitted through the long bones from one to the next via joints and a larger contact area helps spread the load and results in less pressure on the joint surface. The joints provide flexibility within the skeletal system, such that we can functionally alter the length of our limbs by joint motion. The spinal column and intervertebral joints offer both protection to the spinal cord and, due to the "S" shaped curves within our backs, act as shock absorbers. In addition, the spinal column provides attachment for the spinal muscles, enabling us to maintain an upright posture.

Muscular system

Skeletal muscles cross the joints and thus initiate and control movement, while muscles' other important function is stabilisation of the joint, often combined with ligamentous control. Muscle force is transmitted to bony attachment via tendons, and muscles themselves are made up of contractile elements which can shorten and lengthen. Adequate muscle strength is essential for normal function and joint protection, and, when handling or assisting a person, it is vital to ensure he/she has adequate control and strength to complete the task. One important component to consider is that most muscles develop maximum tension in their middle range of motion, and in this position greater force is generated by the muscle (see Fig 4.9).

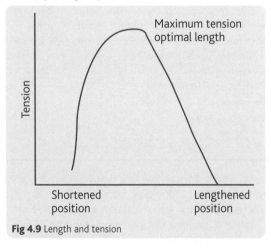

Fig 4.9 Length and tension

To minimise muscular work, keep joints within their midrange (or middle third) of movement but also consider the effect of fatigue. Repetitive muscular action leads to fatigue and this is particularly notable when the muscle is working statically, ie no change in dynamic length. When muscles fatigue, they lose their ability to control joint motion and shock absorb. Forces are then transmitted to the bones or joints which can lead to pathological changes.

The cardiorespiratory system

The cardiorespiratory system includes the heart, lungs, veins and arteries. The cardiorespiratory system is responsible for the uptake of oxygen, for the transportation of oxygenated blood around the body, and the removal of carbon dioxide and other waste products from the muscles and vital organs. Impaired

movement function can have a large effect on the cardiorespiratory system as inefficient movement can be very energy demanding. It can be the cardiorespiratory system which limits movement and function, eg the active movement is so strenuous or energy demanding. Impairment of the cardiovascular system itself can limit movement or function as the body cannot receive sufficient oxygenated blood to meet demands, or there is failure in the removal of waste products that alters muscle function.

Nervous system

The nervous system plays a vital role in the control, speed and range of human movement. The central nervous system (brain and spinal cord) generates impulses which travel along nerves to the rest of the body (peripheral nervous system). These impulses direct the muscular system for movement and then transmit sensory feedback to allow the brain to modify and respond to static and dynamic movement.

For people to move and function independently, all these five systems need to interact and work in an efficient manner. Many health issues can adversely affect the function and effectiveness of movement and the person may then need assistance from handlers or may self-use mechanical aids.

Promoting independence

Maintaining mobility and functional independence is important for a person's self esteem as well as avoiding the physical and psychosocial consequences of immobility and dependency. Promoting and supporting independence can be challenging due to his/her health needs, cultures, values and differing social and environmental circumstances. It is a careful balance between provision of adequate support and equipment to enhance independence, while avoiding over or under provision, both of which can be detrimental.

Maximising independence often involves the provision of aids working to the person's mechanical advantage but should also include a review of the wider environment in which that person participates and undertakes activities (see chapter 3). Examples of types of mechanical aids are plentiful in the hospital environment, eg a long handled reacher, hoists, sliding sheets or longer levers on basin taps. Poles with grab handles over the bed or handle blocks can assist a person achieve an independent change of position/posture within his/her bed, and, wherever possible and practicable, enablement aids should be utilised in preference to manual handling.

Seating is important and can sometimes be overlooked when, often, independent movement within the bed and ambulation are the primary concerns. Yet, the importance of appropriate seating in the maintenance of independence, people interaction and comfort should not be underestimated. A chair seat pan of inappropriate height will not allow the person to transfer his/her centre of mass optimally horizontally over his/her feet (base of support) to enable him/her to stand. There are many mechanical factors which need to be taken into consideration when reviewing the seat itself (and beyond the scope of this chapter) but will include the height, width, depth of the seat pan, the seat back and armrests, the seat pan cushion's construction and shape and its ability to distribute load, the safety and stability of the chair, and the castors and floor covering on which the chair may be placed.

The tasks of transferring from sitting to sitting and to standing are covered in the practical chapters.

When looking to maximise independence and participation, we should also consider the wider environment, ensuring we facilitate access and egress into rooms and buildings, eg with the appropriate provision of ramps, handrails, automatic door openings. While we strive to maximise independence, this is always balanced against safety and avoidance of placing the person or handler in danger, eg due to trips and falls (see chapter 13). Risk assessment will help identify where mechanics may be of assistance for the person and identify risk levels associated with the activity/task with and without mechanical assistance.

Assistive devices

In this section, assistive devices refer to walking aids, probably the most commonly used mechanical assistance for someone with movement difficulties. This section focuses on the mechanical advantages gained by the use of these aids. People use walking aids to help them stand and walk for a variety of reasons. The use of the walking aid can, for example, reduce pain in a joint, help accommodate muscular weakness, assist with walking when a person has poor or limited active joint range of motion, if he/she experiences proprioceptive difficulties (loss of feeling of joint position), or loss of confidence. A walking aid can help improve posture or increase the base of support, making balancing easier, aiding confidence in mobility. Many different walking aids exist but, basically, they all fall within three categories – walking stick, crutches and frames, each working under the same principles of supporting part of the body weight through the upper limb or increasing the size of the base of support.

Walking stick
The simplest form of walking aid – the walking stick – allows a force to be transmitted to the ground through the upper limb. The applied force is along the axis of the walking stick. Often used by persons with an impairment to assist their mobility, the simple walking cane has also been used through history as a sign of status (the mace, doctor's gold topped stick etc). The amount of force applied through the stick is limited by the strength in the hand and the shape of the handle can affect this significantly. Some sticks have a specific, shaped handle to allow the force to be spread more evenly through the palm, reducing pressure and increasing comfort. Other modifications are a broad base to the stick, such as a tripod or quadripod. These types of devices stand up on their own and will tolerate a small amount of lateral force being applied as long as the force vector remains within the base of support. These devices are often useful and can offer greater stability between standing and sitting, but they are more cumbersome and can be heavier than the single stick. Tripods are often used by a person who has experienced a hemiplegic cerebral vascular accident, who may be experiencing some balance or postural sway in addition to weakness or change in tone on the affected side.

Three main factors for the use of walking sticks, which can be combined, are:

1 Improve stability
Increasing the size of the area of support from the relatively small area of the person's two feet, makes it easier to position the centre of gravity within the base of support. If one walking stick is used, it is advanced at the same time as the "better" lower limb. Two sticks offer a triangular base of support and are usually advanced independently, with opposite limb advancement to maximise stability.

2 Generate a moment of force
The person applies a vertical force through the stick in the ipsilateral hand (same side) as the "good" leg, creating a counter clockwise moment at the shoulder girdle and pelvis, reducing the moment which needs to be generated by the hip abductors on the stance "bad" leg to keep the pelvis level.

3 Reduce the load through the lower limb
A walking stick can be used in the same hand as the "bad" leg, and placed on the ground close to the foot. The person often tends to lurch laterally over the stick during stance, thus load sharing is achieved by the leg and the walking stick. More often, the stick is used in the opposite hand as this avoids the lateral trunk bend. However, the degree of off loading may be less (Whittle 1996).

Crutches
The main mechanical difference between the crutch and the walking stick is that crutches are able to transmit significant forces in the horizontal plane. The crutch has two points of attachment, one at the hand and the other further up the arm, which provide a lever arm for the transmission of forces (Whittle 1996). There are two basic types of crutches, axillary crutches and elbow crutches. For the axillary crutches, the lever arm between the axilla and wrist is long, and enough horizontal force can be generated to allow walking with two poorly functioning lower limbs. The elbow crutches have a lower point of contact to the arm, usually the lower arm, and thus the lever arm is shorter than the axillary crutches. These types of crutches are often chosen as they are aesthetically more acceptable, less cumbersome, lighter in weight and, depending on the injury, requiring support can be more efficient and less energy draining. Gutter crutches allow the forearm to transmit the force applied to the crutch and have their uses for persons with hand impairments (see Fig 4.10).

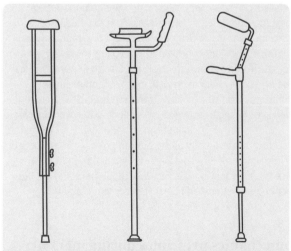

Fig 4.10 Types of crutch: axillary (left), gutter (centre), elbow (right)

Walking frames
The walking frame is the most stable of walking aids and allows the person to stand and walk within the area of support provided by its base. The frame is usually lifted forwards (or rolled in the case of a rollator frame) and the person steps

forward with each leg towards the frame, thus a slow "walk to" type pattern is often adopted. Considerable force can be applied vertically through the frame, and moderate horizontal forces provided the overall force vector remains within the base of support.

Age related gait changes

Sutherland *et al* (1988) provide a detailed study of the development of gait by children. The main ways in which gait of small children differs from adults are:
- wider base
- stride length and speed are lower and the cycle time (known as cadence) shorter
- children have no heelstrike, initial ground contact is made with a flat foot
- minimal stance phase flexion at the knee
- increased external rotation at the hip during the swing phase
- absence of reciprocal arm swing.

The time by which children achieve their characteristic walking pattern (or gait pattern) varies, with a child developing heelstrike, stance phase flexion and reduction in external leg rotation relatively early, and the development of stride length, cadence and walking velocity, which are related to growth, strength and coordination, later. It is generally accepted that mature gait has developed around 15 years of age (Whittle 1996).

Gait in the elderly is subject to two major factors, the effects of ageing itself and any pathological conditions which co-exist. Physical factors, such as osteoarthritis and motor control or neurological conditions such as Parkinson's Disease, can affect the same person, both of which will alter his/her gait by different means. Typically, the onset of age related changes in gait commences in the decade between 60 and 70 years of age (Whittle 1996). There is a decreased stride length, an increase in the size of the walking base and increased cycle time (decreased cadence). Both the decreased stride length and the wider base make it easier to balance, as does limiting the amount of time spent in swing phase, as this allows a greater percentage of the gait cycle to be spent with two feet on the ground (double support stance phase). Independent gait in the elderly can become increasingly difficult due to co-existing pathologies which impact not only on the physical ability to walk, their motor control to perform the task, but also their psychological wellbeing and confidence to walk independently. Failing eyesight may lead to a "shuffly" gait pattern and the fear and incidence of falling becomes more evident with advancing years.

The correct selection of walking aid can greatly assist a person with impaired mobility to achieve independent ambulation. Choice is dependent on the person's impairment and should reflect his/her activity and participation needs, and the environment in which he/she will walk.

Biomechanics principles during manual handling

Epidemiological studies have shown that mechanical factors do have a role in the development of disc degeneration and low back pain (Goel *et al* 1999). It is now widely acknowledged that it is beneficial to reduce the effects of loads on the spine by reducing the magnitude of force on the discs, and limiting the

duration of exposure. Significant changes in clinical practice have developed to reduce these risks, both by a greater understanding and awareness of biomechanical principles, and also by the increased use of mechanical aids for handling people. Detailed advice on practical people handling is provided throughout this book, but this chapter should provide the reader with an understanding of the biomechanical principles underpinning good handling practice, policies and procedures. The principles outlined here should augment the summary of recommendations from manual handling training materials produced by the Health and Safety Executive (HSE 2003).

- The handler should be as close as possible to the person (reduce moment arm), and undertake a reasonably wide base of support. A base that is too small makes balance difficult, and a step stand or wide base is usually better. If the base becomes too wide, this can be disadvantageous and friction may play a larger role in maintaining contact between the floor and the feet (Jones & Barker 1998). A stooped posture is poor practice as this introduces longer levers for the spinal muscles as often the load is further away from the body. This scenario worsens when a person's limbs are passively lifted (eg when washing a leg, applying a dressing), as the load/weight being lifted by the handler's spinal muscles increases. Over reaching also increases the lever arm and should be avoided.
- Keep the load near to the handler's body by the appropriate height adjustment of equipment, beds etc and the close positioning of the handler. These principles apply when the handler is standing, sitting or kneeling. The safe lifting zone is between shoulder and knee height.
- A squatting type posture is preferred to a stooped posture, especially when lifting a load from the floor. By adopting a squatting posture, the load is transferred to the larger leg muscles which are stronger than the back, and the load is closer to the body/lumbar spine region (provided the dimensions of the load allow), resulting in a smaller moment arm (White & Panjabi 1990).
- The handler's lower back should be moderately flexed, but not too flexed, so that maximal bending stresses are placed on the intervertebral discs and ligaments (Adams & Dolan 2002).
- Load should be carried close to the body and lifted in a slow, controlled method. Do not rush and do not pull quickly. By keeping the load close to the body, you reduce the moment arm and help keep the centre of gravity close to or within the base of support.
- Prolonged effort is to be avoided, especially in a stooped position and cyclical, repetitive loading is often associated with musculoskeletal disorders. Take rest breaks and consider your posture during rest periods.
- Friction reducing devices can make handling practices more efficient, especially for lateral transfers combined with optimally located handles (Lloyd & Baptiste 2006).
- Anthropometry (body sizes) can play a large role in the shear forces placed on the spine (Granata & Marras 1999) and should be considered when planning handling. Restrictive workspaces, such as reduced headroom, forces handlers to stand with their trunks more flexed and increases the compressive forces on the spine (Elfeituri 2001). Consider spatial restraints and ensure there is sufficient space for the handling or facilitation task to be completed.
- Asymmetrical lifting which involves lateral bending of the trunk produces larger trunk motion and is predicted the

most hazardous type of loading with regard to damage to the spinal disc (Natarajan *et al* 2008). Asymmetrical lifting may also cause the centre of gravity to move towards the edge of the base of support and can make the lift increasingly unstable.

- The greater the twisting or rotation angle, the higher the predictive compression and shear forces experienced by the spine (Elfeituri 2001).

Conclusion

A thorough understanding of biomechanical principles underpins good handling practices and the development of safe policies and procedures. Mechanical principles apply equally to the handling of people and tasks undertaken to enable people to maximise their independence. Increasing use of mechanical aids is commonplace in the hospital and social environment, and their safe use remains of paramount importance to both the users and the handlers. While increasing use of mechanical aids to promote human movement and interaction is welcome, their usage still requires the handler to undertake formal risk assessments and adhere to sound mechanical principles.

References

Abernethy, B, Hanrahan, SJ, Kippers, V, Mackinnon, LT & Pandy, MG (2005), Basic concepts of the musculoskeletal system, Chapter 2 in *Biophysical Foundations of Human Movement*, Second edition, Human Kinetics.

Adams, M & Dolan, P (2002), Biomechanics of low back pain, in Smith, J (ed) *The Guide to The Handling of People*, 5th edition 2005, BackCare.

Black, C (2008), Review of the health of Britain's working age population, *Working for a Healthier tomorrow*. Department for Work and Pensions, www.dwp.gov.uk/docs/hwwb-working-for-a-healthier-tomorrow.pdf.

Department for Work and Pensions (2008), *Improving health and work: changing lives*. www.dwp.gov.uk/docs/hwwb-improving-health-and-work-changing-lives.pdf.

Elfeituri, FE (2001), A biomechanical analysis of manual lifting tasks performed in restricted workspaces. *International Journal of Occupational Safety and Ergonomics*, Vol **7** (3) pages 333-346.

Goel, VK, Montgomery, RE, Grosland, NM, Pope, M & Kumar, S (1999), Ergonomic factors in the workplace contribute to disc degeneration. Chapter 14 in *Biomechanics in Ergonomics*, Taylor & Francis, London.

Granata, KP & Marras, WS (1999), Relationship between spinal load factors and high risk probability of occupational low back disorder, *Ergonomics*, Vol **42** Sep (9), p1187-1199.

Hignett, S & McAtamney, L (2000), Rapid Entire Body Assessment (REBA), *Applied Ergonomics*, Vol **31**, Issue 2 p201-205.

HSE Research Report (2003), Research Report 097, *The principles of good manual handling: Achieving a consensus*, prepared by the Institute of Occupational Medicine. www.hse.gov.uk/research/rrpdf/rr097.pdf.

Jones, K & Barker, K (1998), Mechanical basis of movement, chapter 1 in *Human Movement Explained*, Butterworth-Heinemann, Oxford.

Kumar, S (1999), Selected theories of musculoskeletal injury causation, chapter 1 in *Biomechanics in Ergonomics*, Taylor & Francis, London.

Lloyd, JD & Baptiste, A (2006), Friction-reducing devices for lateral patient transfers: a biomechanical evaluation, *American Association of Occupational Health Nurses*, March: Vol **54** (3) p113-118.

Lockwood, J (1999), Classification and terminology Chapter 1 in *Rehabilitation of Movement: Theoretical basis of clinical practice*, (Eds) Pitt-Brooke, Reid, Lockwood & Kerr, Saunders, London.

Natarajan, RN, Lavender, SA, An, HA & Andersson, GB (2008), Biomechanical response of a lumbar intervertebral disc to manual lifting activities: a poroeleastic finite element model study, *Spine*, Aug 15; Vol **33** (18) p1958-1965.

Sutherland, DH, Olshen, RA, Biden, EN & Wyatt, MP (1988), *The Development of Mature Walking*, Mac Keith Press, London.

White, AA & Panjabi, MM (1990), *Clinical Biomechanics of the Spine*, JB, Lippincott.

Whittle, M (1996), Pathological gait, Chapter 3 in *Gait Analysis An Introduction*, 2nd edition, Butterworth-Heinemann.

A systems approach to safer handling practice

Pat Alexander MSc PGDip PGCE MCSP CMIOSH MIfL
Consultant manual handling practitioner

Introduction

This chapter demonstrates how an organisation, with a flexible and integrated systems approach in the assistance of mobility impaired people, can ensure the health and wellbeing of staff, as well as service users. Setting up or consulting a Back Care Advisory Service (BCAS) will support an organisation's claim to possessing, or intending to institute, a safer system of work in manual handling matters. An employer is not obliged to follow this approach but, if this or a similar system is not followed, he may be obliged to justify his own methods of achieving safer handling and the accompanying outcomes required by law. Previous editions of this book have been referred to in litigation as a gold standard of best practice in health and social care. However, person handling is now an integral task in many other walks of life, such as education and community transport, in fact, in any situation where a mobility impaired person may be employed, cared for or follow his or her leisure pursuits.

Therefore, this chapter will be of relevance to a large number of organisations, including health, social care, private healthcare providers, departments of children, school and families and associated agencies, as well as service providers and users in work and leisure pursuits.

Previously, the emphasis of safety in manual handling has been seen mainly as a concern for nursing staff – either their own or

their patient's wellbeing may be threatened by poor practice – but perhaps more thought should be directed as to why unsafe practices persist. For many years, it has been seen that nurses' apparent reluctance to use equipment has been a potential cause of injury (Moody *et al* 1996). Peer pressure has previously been seen as a factor influencing the behaviour of student nurses (Kane 1994). Other factors may also be seen as relevant in this area; there should be management commitment, sufficient time, space and peer support to allow safer practices to occur. The first *Guide to The Handling of Patients* was, in fact, addressed to nurse managers, although later editions increased their readership to those working with mobility impaired people (Royal College of Nursing (RCN) 1981,1983). The RCN and National Back Pain Association had recommended a manual handling standing committee under the RCN in several publications, starting with *The Guide to the Handling of Patients*, 1st edition (1981), and an ergonomics and patient handling research unit be set up under the NHS Supply Council.

Health and safety systems

Many authorities see the ethos of an organisation as having a strong influence on safety practice. Health and safety must come from the top down as well as bottom up (Hignett 2001). Unsafe practices may become more common if this is not the case, and accident recording will probably decrease, as staff see no response to their concerns. This may lead to an insidious downward spiral in safety behaviour, resulting in lack of awareness of any existing problems. Health and safety in general, and manual handling practice in particular, may be seen as indicators of the commitment of an organisation to the safety and wellbeing of both staff and clients.

> The safety culture of an organisation is the product of individual and group values, attitudes, perceptions, competencies and patterns of behaviour that determine the commitment to, and the style and proficiency of, an organisation's health and safety management. Organisations with a positive safety culture are characterised by communications founded on mutual trust, by shared perceptions of the importance of safety and by confidence in the efficacy of preventive measures (Advisory Committee on the Safety of Nuclear Installations study group on Human Factors 1993).

Health and safety policy

Many an organisation has come to grief at court, even though it had clear and well written health and safety policies, because these policies were not widely available to staff. It is a management responsibility to ensure the dissemination of these policies throughout the organisation, and the responsibility of the staff to be familiar with them.

A systems approach would ensure that clear responsibilities are laid out in the policy, from the chief executive downward, to ensure that all understand their own role in promoting/sustaining health and safety. The importance accorded to this subject will be reflected in the resources, including time, allocated to it. The Health and Safety Executive (HSE) has identified that successful organisations include this subject in forward planning (Institute of Directors and Health and Safety Executive accessed 2010). An organisation should have management commitment to ensure the health and safety culture comes from the top.

Once sufficient funds have been allocated for health and safety functions, adequate protocols should ensure that this investment is used to produce best value. The HSE has long advised that health and safety should be built in to the business plan (HSE 1993), allowing for staff consultation to inform on prioritisation of need.

In *Management of health and safety in the health services* (Health and Safety Commission (HSC) 1994), there is an important clarification on accident causation. It recognises "that accidents, ill health and incidents result from failings in management control, and are not necessarily the fault of individual employees". This admission of systems failure puts the onus on management to reduce risks and implement safe systems to protect staff and clients. Many accidents that occur do not happen in isolation, but may be the tip of an iceberg of management problems (Pidgeon 1991). Adequate accident and incident investigation should allow management to identify any systemic failures. Regular reporting of accident investigation should occur at health and safety committee meetings, and reported by the board member with responsibility for health and safety.

The law requires that a health and safety policy is recorded and disseminated by all employers of more than five employees. Employers of staff working in the field of health and social care would be expected to have a policy on all relevant risks in this field, including manual handling. For many years, it has been known that nursing staff are at a serious risk of work related injuries from the assistance given to mobility impaired people (Cust *et al* 1972; Magora 1970; Dehlin *et al* 1976). More recently (*HSE v Birmingham PCT* 2008), the HSE has identified a risk to patient safety from poor management commitment.

> An elderly patient fell through a wrongly sized sling and sustained a fatal injury. The hospital was successfully prosecuted under a breach of section 3 (1) of the Health and Safety at Work etc Act 1974. The HSE commented that "it is also vital that professional carers and nursing staff receive adequate information, instruction and training in the correct selection and safe use of that equipment" (National Back Exchange (NBE) *column* Winter 2008).

Setting up and running a BCAS to facilitate safer systems in manual handling matters

For some 30 years in healthcare, and some years in other settings, the developing role of a health professional specialising in techniques and the use of equipment has been in existence, known as a manual handling or back care practitioner. This role has developed with the introduction of postgraduate qualifications, and an acceptance of the importance of ergonomics to manual handling safety (HSE in foreword to *Essential Back-up II* (NBE 2002)). It is now felt by many practitioners that this work could become a profession in its own right, with its own body of knowledge and code of practice. To include all those in similar roles covered by those working in back care, the name of manual handling practitioner (MHP) has been suggested as an umbrella term (NBE, *Standards in Manual Handling*, 3rd edition 2010).

This advice is not aimed solely at healthcare. The NBE standards also refer to other organisations, such as those providing social care and including those who handle inanimate loads.

According to *Essential Back-up II*, the aims of setting up a BCAS should enable an employer to:
● comply with legal requirements
● develop a comprehensive and ongoing programme for the prevention of work related back disorders in healthcare staff
● improve standards/quality of patient care.

Advice from a competent person is required to enable risks to be assessed and managed. Not only must a sufficient number of advisers/trainers be appointed, but they must have support to enable them to fulfil their role (NBE 1993, 2004). This BCAS may be inhouse or a contracted service provider. In either case, the credentials required for the lead adviser should be similar.

Previously, it had been felt (Inter-professional Advisory Group 1995, 1997) that the person in this lead role should have a healthcare qualification as well as specialised knowledge in manual handling, ergonomics and teaching. Later thinking concluded that if this postholder had a postgraduate qualification in back care, teaching and relevant experience, they may be able to fit the selection criteria. NBE set up its register of members in 2006 with approved qualifications and experience, and included the opportunity for those without the full criteria to work towards registered membership by the Accreditation of Prior Learning and Experience process.

The person in this lead role may need to be supported by trainers, who would also help implement the training strategy, depending on the size of the organisation. The ratio of advisers/trainers to employees has been recommended at one per 1,000, derived from the ratio recommended for occupational health nurses in an organisation (NBE, *Essential Back-up II* 2002). It is now apparent that the lead in such a department will require management skills, those of negotiation, and the ability to work at a strategic level (NBE, *Standards in Manual Handling* 2010). Under the knowledge and skills framework (*ibid*) this post is suggested to be at the higher end of the levels available. This level will not only attract those manual handling practitioners aspiring to reach their potential (and the top of their profession), but will also allow them to interact with, and directly advise, senior management in their own organisation.

An MHP cannot work in isolation. Organisational culture is as important as the safety policies; it determines how these are resourced, implemented and relayed to all staff.

> Access to a competent manual handling or back care advisory service can play a primary role in providing health and safety assistance and, where there is good communication with senior management, can help the organisation be assured it is doing the right things the right way (James in NBE, *Standards in Manual Handling* 2010).

A sub-committee of those with a special interest in manual handling could be devolved from the health and safety committee, with the remit to report back on a regular basis.

The HSE (2010) states that manual handling practitioners can enable an organisation to meet its legal requirements under the Manual Handling Operations Regulations (as amended) 2002. However, it is important that an overemphasis is not placed on the provision of training on its own. It has long been known that training alone is not an effective tool in ensuring safer practice (Hignett *et al* 2003) – see chapter 6. Research has shown (Alexander 1998) that, when asked what would improve safer handling, managers believed that provision of hoists was the solution, while operational staff believed that an increase in staff numbers would improve safety.

The specialist knowledge available in a BCAS could be used to advise on new building plans and alterations, contributing to policies, as relevant, and devising and managing the manual handling strategy for the employer. This may involve advising on more complex risk assessments, investigating accidents and troubleshooting, as well as delivering or supervising training. A relevant training in safer working behaviour will be complemented by sufficient personnel, occupational health advice and problem solving skills, provision of equipment, plus the space, time and motivation to use it (Crumpton 2001).

NBE recommends that training should not only involve, but commence with, management (NBE, *Standards in Manual Handling* 2010). In this way, the need for providing relevant training for the manager's own staff could be clarified.

Manual handling policy

There should be a method of direct communication from the BCAS to the employer, in order to allow the "responsible person" to allocate resources appropriately. This budget should be reviewed regularly, in line with the annual health and safety report, the risk register and the requirements of governance and quality assurance. Those service providers outside the NHS would do well to liaise with a BCAS if manual handling of people is within their remit. A strategy encouraging safer systems of work should be part of their business plan, showing that sufficient resources are available to facilitate safer manual handling.

A manual handling policy should commence with a statement accepting the responsibilities owed by the employer to employees, and those affected by their work. Hignett (2001), as part of an ergonomic intervention programme, found that organisational policy played an important part in reducing musculoskeletal problems. The risks to staff will include potential manual handling injuries, identification of which should act as a trigger for the implementation of the Manual Handling Operations Regulations 1992 (as amended). These insist that, where reasonably practicable, hazardous tasks should be avoided. Where unavoidable, they should be assessed and steps taken to reduce the risks. This assessment, of course, will include patients/clients and family members visiting or assisting at home (Management of Health and Safety at Work Regulations (MHSWR) 1999). Strategies should be devised that promote health and safety of staff and service users, while ensuring the dignity, and allowing participation, of service users.

Roles and responsibilities as set out in the manual handling policy

The chief executive of an organisation is legally responsible for the health and safety of staff and those affected by their actions. However, supervision of this task may have been delegated to another member of the board. The accountable person has duties that are clearly set out under Section 37 of the Health and Safety at Work etc Act 1974 (HASAW). In theory, if it can be proved that the law has been broken through his/her action or inaction, then he/she could face personal prosecution (HSC 1994). It is essential that sufficient funding and importance is given to allow this aspect of work to progress successfully. This will include the provision of information, instruction, training and supervision to ensure safe working practices ensue (HASAW 1974). Both generic and specific risk assessments are required (MHSWR 1999) to inform staff of strategies to manage risks at work.

It is important that leadership in this aspect of business is strong and visible, and that decisions in health and safety and manual handling are integrated with business decisions (Institute of Directors and Health and Safety Executive accessed 2010). As well as obtaining competent advice in such matters, employers are required to ensure that their arrangements for manual handling strategies are robust, and disseminated to all staff, who should also be consulted about these matters. Training, review, audit and monitoring can demonstrate that adequate risk assessments and control measures are producing the expected results.

The board ensures that health and safety/manual handling matters are regularly discussed as agenda items, and achievable targets set to encourage proactive initiatives and targets. The role of safety representatives should be acknowledged in the policy, as should the need to consult with employees on matters concerning manual handling; this should be embedded into the process.

Departmental managers are given specific responsibilities for their area, and set up systems to implement the board's strategies on manual handling. At this level, management would be expected to monitor and review the efficacy of these plans, and report back to the board on their success or otherwise. If managers liaise with the BCAS department, outcomes could be set that could be audited. In this way, the efficacy of the delivered programme can be measured and amended, as required.

Research has shown that if managers are able to implement their recommendations for managing risk in people handling, sickness absence is reduced (Alexander 1998). They must ensure that all their staff are familiar with the manual handling policy, and that all related accidents and incidents are reported and investigated. Adequate staffing levels, resources and supervision must be given to staff to ensure that best practice is used.

Managers are responsible for identifying the training needs of their staff, and ensuring they are freed up to attend relevant training. There should be departmental records of staff attendance at training in manual handling. Many organisations will have a risk register, and managers are responsible for ensuring risk assessments and solutions are recorded in the relevant organisational documentation. These may be generic or situation specific. It is expected that most people handling assessments will be person specific. Complex person handling may require them to consult the organisation's MHP or adviser.

The MHP – current best practice guidelines recommend that the MHP will be directly responsible to the board or head of the organisation in devising the organisation's manual handling strategy, reporting the results/effectiveness of the policy and devising manual handling protocols. This role could be fulfilled by inhouse staff or a subcontractor. They will be expected to keep abreast of new developments in the field, and inform the board, or head of the organisation, of these, as appropriate. They will be able to provide competent advice to the employer, thus their own knowledge and skills must be at a level suitable for the responsibility of their role. This standard is clearly identified in *Standards for Manual Handling* (NBE 2010), and the expertise required is set out in the section on Knowledge and Skills Framework for the NHS, and in the Dreyfus model of acquisition of skill (*ibid*). This section details the levels of expertise required for a key worker role, right up to that of an acknowledged expert in the field.

The MHP should devise the manual handling strategy as well as a training programme, and, depending on the size of the organisation, may be involved in delivering training. He/she may supervise other manual handling trainers in larger organisations and, in addition, may train and supervise link

workers, if this system is to be set up. Problem solving in complex situations will be integral to the role, as will offering advice and consultancy to managers when required.

The role may include disseminating relevant health and safety information throughout the workplace, as well as working in health promotion initiatives, possibly alongside staff from occupational health. He/she may be required to assist in manual handling accident investigations and prepare reports in the event of litigation.

Key worker/link worker – if a key worker system is put in place, this will involve the MHP in the training and monitoring of these staff. Alternative names for such workers, who provide local, inhouse expertise to their colleagues, include ergo coach or link worker. These workers have a continuing role in their own department, but have undergone extra training to enable them to monitor local practice, carry out risk assessments, problem solve and know when the expertise of the MHP is required.

Employees have a legal duty to comply with the policy and report any shortcomings in health and safety arrangements affecting themselves or at their workplace. Any unexpected tasks at work, where they are unsure of the correct procedure to follow, must be reported to their manager for further guidance. Accidents and health factors that may affect work must also be reported.

Persons requiring mobility assistance – service users, or people requiring assistance to move, must also be included in the policy, to ensure that their needs and rights as individuals are respected. The need for enablement and participation are an important part of the manual handling risk assessment and must be considered alongside health and safety concerns. They will need to be aware of the requirement to agree to an assessment of their individual handling needs before commencement of service, and the protocols that will be initiated should they refuse this.

Agency staff, family carers, students and volunteers – the needs of staff, other than direct employees of the organisation, and family carers may also need to be included in the policy, if relevant. The organisation is legally obliged to accept its responsibilities for those affected by its work, but not necessarily in its employment – eg students, agency staff, volunteers and family carers – and devise strategies to ensure their competency and capability in manual handling, if this work is seen to be within their remit (MHSWR 1999). If not, then organisational protocols could ensure that this group of people does not get involved in manual handling involving persons, as, should an accident occur, the employer may be liable for injuries to the person assisting and the person.

Need for extra appendices or sub-policies

This policy is usually an overview of the whole organisation, and each department may require a local code of practice, reflecting the specific needs of its own service. Any special handling situations, eg accident and emergency, handling of the unconscious, deceased or obese person, must be covered in this policy if relevant.

Policy for handling the very obese (bariatric) client

Most organisations providing care will be aware of the rising trend in obesity. Either included in this policy, or as a separate issue, a policy for the manual handling of the very obese person (bariatric) is essential. This should include definitions, risks and the strategies to reduce these (see chapter 13). There must be clear paths of responsibility, allowing staff to obtain help at any time as necessary. Necessary equipment must be provided, and the ability to obtain this speedily out of hours must be delegated to a designated role that is always available for consultation and authorisation.

- Those departments that specialise in persons known to have obesity problems, such as diabetic clinics and those supplying surgery for gastric banding and similar procedures, must be properly equipped to deal with their needs. Managers must ensure their equipment is sufficiently robust and that an adequate staffing level is on duty at the appropriate time.
- The MHP will be expected to advise on equipment and facilities required, and facilitate the person journey throughout his/her need for the provision of services, including discharge planning or in case of his/her demise. A list of suitable equipment and its source/location should be appended to the policy, as this information may be required on a 24 hour basis.
- Should a domiciliary bariatric referral be received by social care staff, or in a discharge plan, outside experts may need to be consulted. Structural surveys as to the loading of floors, width of doors and elevator safe working load may also be required. Staff experienced in these matters should be consulted. Access to family dwellings may be restricted and delivery staff require a full risk assessment to be made.

Treatment handling in rehabilitation

- There should also be a reference to handling as part of a rehabilitation programme in the policy, as its accompanying risk of work related musculoskeletal disorders is well known (Chartered Society of Physiotherapy (CSP) 2005). This should include those working in rehabilitation, whether in hospital or as part of an intermediate care team in the community, with acknowledgement of the accompanying risks involved in their work, and suggestions of risk reducing strategies (Department of Health 2002). These could include extra equipment, extra personnel, training and the need for management commitment to enable rehabilitation to occur and reduce risks to both patients and staff. Healthcare professionals already owe a duty of care to their patients, staff from their own or other agencies and the families, insofar as their work or its delegation may include manual handling (CSP 2008; College of Occupational Therapists 2006).
- Those staff involved in delegating therapy programmes need to be guided by assessing the required competence to carry them out. This could be achieved by consulting the Dreyfus levels of competency (Dreyfus & Dreyfus 1986). The Dreyfus model clarifies the steps by which a novice acquires expertise. The therapist, having identified the skills required for the task, could then ensure that these skills are possessed by the appropriate staff. The employer of these staff must be aware of, and responsible for, their health and safety.

Emergency handling procedures

- Protocols must be included for situations such as emergency evacuation as in a fire or bomb threat scenario. Although hospitals are usually able to use horizontal evacuation strategies, many schools, nursing homes, respite units and workplaces will need to devise personal emergency evacuation plans for mobility impaired persons and staff (HSE 2005). These plans must be achievable by the organisation and should not rely on the fire and rescue services intervening. "Refuges" are to be used only as resting stages, people with mobility and other impairments should not be left in a refuge awaiting the arrival of fire service personnel.
- Paramedics and accident and emergency departments will need tailored protocols, such as handling the critically injured, the violent or those brought in unconscious in a car etc.
- Undertakers will also require specific manual handling procedures for dealing with extremely large bodies.

All these policies and protocols are required to be easily available, as hard or electronic copies and also, possibly, on the organisation's intranet. Many employers require staff to sign and date that they have read the policy during induction, but managers must also be aware of any changes made to the policy, and ensure that existing staff are given the opportunity to familiarise themselves with additional information. New equipment may require new protocols. This policy should be reviewed and updated on a regular basis (NBE, *Manual Handling Standard* 2004).

> Radiotherapists have been asked to reposition persons for treatment using innovative equipment. This sometimes involves them working at shoulder level attempting to replicate the exact treatment position as before. They are concerned about work related musculoskeletal disorders and a MHP is asked to devise a solution. Some persons are positioned in a precast shell to ensure the replication of position on the previous day. Manoeuvring a person in such a close fitting mould adds to these difficulties. Slide sheets and use of an "octopus" (a many tailed turning device designed for use in endoscopy) may be among the solutions trialed. Some persons are treated on their own bed, and their position ensured by synchronising tattoos on their trunk with marked points in the room.

Use of algorithms to aid staff in problem solving

Guidance needs to be provided to enable inexperienced staff to formulate safer ways of working in set conditions. When faced with alternative solutions, algorithms can provide staff with a logical method of choosing the correct one (Nelson 2006). Experienced staff may be able to internalise the relevant factors and appear to select the correct solution "off the top of their heads". However, in reality, their decision is reached after using their experience of similar situations to inform their choice. Less experienced staff may require more guidance in deciding, and may find that following an algorithm may help them justify their clinical decision making.

5 A systems approach to safer handling practice

Fig 5.1 Sit to stand – algorithm to identify a strategy © Alexander in *British Journal of Community Nursing* 2008

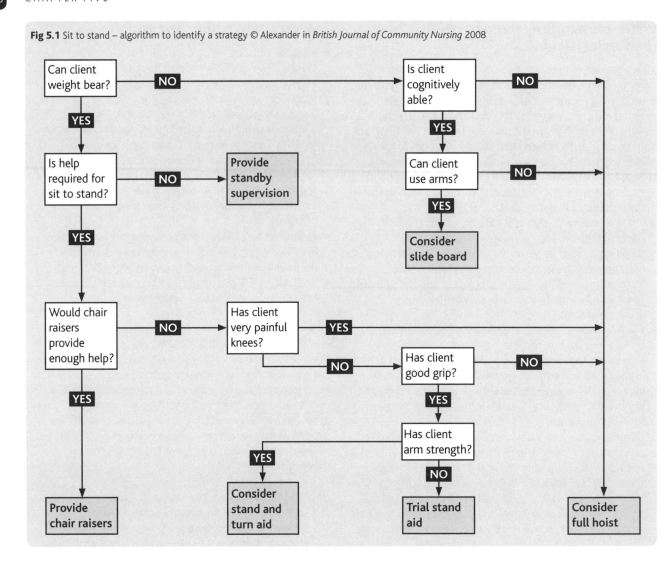

Commonly encountered situations should be prepared for, as they are reasonably foreseeable. A selection of algorithms could be produced by the MHP and team, enabling staff to rationalise the choice of strategy. An example of this could be one detailing the pathway for deciding which standing aid a person requires to assist in mobilisation. First, the criteria for the use of each piece of equipment should be listed, then arranged into alternative pathways. This should enable staff to match the appropriate equipment to the abilities of the person (see Fig 5.1).

Change management

Any new system of work introduced may face resistance from existing staff. This may be due to a defensive reaction from staff who feel that present work practices are threatened, or a natural reluctance to accept new ways of working. MHPs must be familiar with theories of change and devise strategies to encourage smooth transitions.

Many theories identify the stages through which people must pass to move on. These are known by a variety of names, but usually involve "unfreezing" the present beliefs or practices, introducing different ones and "refreezing" these new ideas into accepted behaviour. Changes in health and social care are frequently imposed by government and may change as politicians dictate. Such top down policies may result in only partial success, as staff may be aware of the possibility of successive revision at a later date (Hignett 2001). Reasons for

failure may also include poor leadership or perceived lack of ownership from staff (Scott *et al* 2003).

Consultation will allow staff the opportunity to express fears and investigate the possible consequences of continuing present behaviour. The MHP occupies the enviable position of

Fig 5.2 Links between the MHP and other significant contacts

being consulted by staff in complex situations, allowing him/her the opportunity to facilitate change (see Fig 5.2). Opening up the discussion to participants who will be directly affected by change may enable them to work through their misgivings and identify the advantages of the desired behaviours. A good facilitator will encourage discussion and problem solving exercises, while introducing possible alternative strategies. Skilled leadership and the ability to maintain the impetus for acceptance of change, once instituted, are essential to achieve any change in behaviour. Once the advantages of the change are demonstrated to staff and person, a self-perpetuating "conversion" may occur.

Liaison with other departments and agencies
There should be liaison with many other departments in the health or social care setting. These could include health and safety, risk management, legal and insurance advisers, procurement or supplies, portering, infection control, tissue viability, fire safety, medical and hospital regulatory agency, education and training, maintenance and, not least, the client safeguarding and advocacy professionals.

Interagency working proliferates in social care and many problems may occur through differing perceptions of risk. Considerable negotiating skills are required by the MHP obliged to cross these minefields.

Providing/delivering a training strategy
A training needs analysis should inform the organisation of the content, duration and frequency of training required for each staff group (see chapter 6). Training must be linked to the local policy; this should be a two way process. The policy will be informed and amended by staff experience and training, and the training should reflect changes in legislation and policy. An experienced MHP should facilitate this process.

Training may be delivered in formal sessions or onsite as local guidance. It may be direct, or cascaded, or complemented by key workers, acting as a local resource. This subject will be covered in more detail in the following chapter. Training will also be required for those making risk assessments at work.

Training records should be kept for the time suggested by the employer's insurer. This will allow for litigation to be commenced within the time allowed by the legal limitations period (Limitation Act 1980). An electronic version of these records will allow for their economical storage, eliminating the need for vast archives. The RCN suggests that even onsite advice should be recorded in that individual staff member's file (RCN 2002).

These records demonstrate compliance with legal requirements, provide legal proof of training and allow for the arrangement of updated training as required. This administrative role requires allocation of clerical support for the MHP or trainer.

Assisting workers to return to/stay in work
Consulting an occupational health department may allow for fast track rehabilitation of injured staff. It will also be able to advise both staff and employer of the worker's ability to participate in his normal work. This may include the length of sick leave and/or whether it is to be a phased return to work.

Some MHPs contribute to back in work schemes in conjunction with the Occupational Health Service (see chapter 8). They may be able to check that a person returning from sickness leave is able to participate in people handling, and some MHPs may even devise work hardening schemes, if they have the relevant knowledge and skills. Many MHPs will be able to suggest amended ways of working or simple changes to the environment to enable a worker to return to work, demonstrating compliance with the Disability Discrimination Act 1995.

In line with the Black Report (Black 2008), employers should encourage staff to return to work as soon as possible. They need not wait until the employee is pain free. In fact, the Royal College of General Practitioners states (1996) that the approved method of managing patients with back pain is an early return to work, with adaptations to working as required.

Equipment advice, evaluation and audit
MHPs are ideally situated to arrange equipment trials at the workplace (see chapter 7). They should have a wide knowledge of equipment available for mechanising handling, and arrange for user trials to take place in the relevant departments. Involving staff in these evaluation exercises will give them ownership of the selection of equipment decided on by the group.

The choice ratified by the user trial may then require that a business plan is devised, to put before the head of the organisation or board. This must identify the needs of staff and persons, the advantages of the chosen items, and a cost benefit analysis. It must also include the cost of regular maintenance, as this is required by law (Lifting Operations Lifting Equipment Regulations 1998 (HSE 1998a); Provision and Use of Workplace Equipment Regulations 1998 (HSE 1998b)).

An inventory of equipment available, and its safe working load (SWL) should be compiled, and contracts arranged for regular inspection and maintenance. An annual audit should identify any gaps in provision of lifting aids, both for materials handling and aiding persons with impaired mobility. There must be suitable systems in place for cleaning and disinfection as required by infection control guidance, or best practice in hygiene standards.

Training in the use of equipment must be arranged before it is used, information provided concerning its SWL and everyday checks made. Staff must check the safety of equipment each time it is used, and put in place protocols to ensure any batteries are recharged as required.

Accident investigation and report writing
Accident investigation will be an important part of managing manual handling, if handling is involved in the mechanism of injury (see chapter 1). A report should be submitted to management, bearing in mind that this may be used as evidence in litigation. Some health and safety professionals may find this situation difficult to resolve; their duty is clearly to investigate an adverse incident and prevent its recurrence. However, apportioning blame in an admissible report may put the employer at a disadvantage in any ensuing legal case. The aim of the report should be made clear; is it to allow the employer to provide a safer system of working or to provide criminal evidence? The report commissioner may wish to seek

legal protection from disclosure (Cameron & Stocker 2010). Many organisations now have a whistle blowing policy, allowing staff to report concerns on health and safety in a no blame culture.

Such reports may also be requested by the organisation's own insurance provider; this report may obviously be used in legal liability issues and will require the MHP to give a balanced view of the factors involved. This may also inform the employer whether to seek to settle the case and pay any compensation in an out of court agreement.

Balanced decision making and arbitration

As Mandelstam (2002) states, the MHP may be required to arbitrate in contentious manual handling situations (see chapter 1). The safety and welfare of both staff and person must be considered in such a case. Indeed, the HSE publication *Handling Home Care* (2001) states that any decision that does not take both into account will not succeed. Clearly, under client centred legislation such as the Human Rights Act 1998, Disability Discrimination Act 1995 and the Mental Capacity Act 2005, consideration must be given to the rights and needs of persons. Equally, staff have a duty not to put themselves or others at risk under HASAW 1974.

When issues involving conflicting views exist, a communication problem has usually arisen between all parties. The MHP may be called in to negotiate a settlement by their joint employer, or as an unbiased outside expert. In either case, the approach must be in the best interests of both parties. Although the use of direct payments is sometimes used in the community to settle such a conflict, there are still the safety issues of the person and staff to be considered in the ensuing solution. Many authorities issuing such payment schemes offer a service of risk assessment and staff training; indeed, there is often a specific amount set aside for this. These community cases are often complex, with staff safety sometimes being perceived as being in opposition to person wellbeing. As Mandelstam states in NBE *column* (Mandelstam 2002) that is why qualified staff are asked to make such decisions, as their professional background and clinical expertise should help in the decision making process.

In the judicial review of the *East Sussex* case (*A&B, X&Y v East Sussex County Council 2003*), the need for balanced decision making was clarified. Simply because a person manual handling operation could be mechanised, Justice Munby confirmed that this was not an imperative that it must be. A decision, taking into account the health and welfare of both person and carer, must be evidenced in any contentious situation. This case should remind staff that there is not always a clear solution to problems. Not only must the problem and its solution be documented, but the clinical reasoning leading to it must also be recorded (CSP 2003). This decision will be informed by client centred and health and safety legislation; civil and common law as well as criminal. The MHP will need to be aware of recent legal cases and judicial reviews on this subject and may need to seek advice from the employer's legal and insurance advisers.

> In a recent case brought before the Medical Ombudsman, the healthcare staff had apparently acted in the client's best interests in a safeguarding issue. However, they were reprimanded for taking the action they did. (Mandelstam, in NBE *column* Nov 2009).

Need for continuing professional development of back care staff to ensure the currency of their advice

Such instances of public and official opinion on health and safety actions evidence the need for continuing professional development (CPD) for staff expected to make such decisions. Attendance at seminars and conferences will provide them with the knowledge and skills required to enable them to offer the correct guidance to the employer. Authoritative sources, such as this book, may well be used in court as a gold standard, and employers must ensure that their staff are given the freedom to act as advised in their own professional guidance.

The Skills for Care standards recommend the number of guided learning hours for staff requiring manual handling training, and set minimum training standards for staff working in social care settings (see chapter 6). Those MHPs teaching in the NHS are more vulnerable to the political situation, sometimes facing pressure from employers to reduce content and frequency of training in this important aspect of their work. However, in times of financial constraint, all employers must beware of allowing financial pressure to put persons or staff at risk, bearing in mind their duties under HASAW 1974. This will be discussed further in the following chapter. MHPs must record their concerns to management when asked to shorten mandatory training, or reduce its frequency. Lack of management support must be recorded and taken to relevant meetings such as health and safety committees, where it should be minuted. However, the training needs analysis must assist in focusing training where it is most required, and where further development of problem solving skills will enhance safer behaviour. Clearly, employers will demand value for money from MHPs, who must ensure they meet the goals they have been set, within the resources made available.

Development of the MHP

To ensure that the lead MHP is qualified to give competent advice, consideration must be given by the employer to the quality of his/her CPD. This may involve research, attending relevant seminars, conferences and meetings, and publishing in relevant journals etc. Opportunities for research should be available and staff encouraged to present findings. Whether staff are employed by the NHS, social services, private organisation or are self employed, this aspect of their role is essential to ensure professional credibility.

The Dreyfus model of skill acquisition has been used in the manual handling field by several authors. Both *The Guide to the Handling of People*, 5th edition (2005) and the CSP *Guidance in Manual Handling in Physiotherapy* (2008) use this model when discussing the expertise required to assist in or teach particular techniques. NBE continued on this pathway in *Standards of Manual Handling* (NBE 2010) and equated levels of achievement of MHPs with Dreyfus' work (Dreyfus & Dreyfus 1986).

In order to progress their careers, MHPs must be able to demonstrate increased knowledge and experience in the field. Evidence of update must be kept in their CPD portfolio, with reflective journals alongside attendance certificates. Healthcare professionals are already responsible for evidencing their CPD in order to retain their registration with the Healthcare

Professions Council, and MHPs without a healthcare qualification should, of course, also be required to justify remaining or advancing in post.

Expected benefits of a BCAS supporting the systems instituted

An important part of the BCAS' work is to ensure it is working effectively. This could be achieved by setting a baseline in reported accidents and incidents, then measuring any changes following implementation of the strategy. However, other confounding factors must also be taken into account. These could include the introduction of a total equipment management policy, changes in staff uniform, cuts in staffing levels, changes in person group or dependency levels, job satisfaction and an ability to make decisions affecting its own work. Some human resources departments store sickness absence in a system allowing those due to work related musculoskeletal conditions to be identified. However, this may produce difficulties in establishing those cumulative problems due to work or pursuits and home life away from work.

Audits of risk assessments may allow perceptions of risk to be reviewed. In any organisation, there will be some staff who are risk aware, some who are risk averse and some who may have very poor perception of any risk at all. One method of "levelling" these mixed perceptions is peer review of each other's work (Fink *et al* 1984). Adams (1995) states that many decisions on risk are taken by those far away from where risks are taken. Walk through audits and consultation with staff involved can allow MHPs to be aware of the problems in the local workplace.

The HSE, in *Guidance on Regulations L23* (HSE 2004), advises that the staff actually involved in the manual handling operation must always be consulted during a formal risk assessment process. Those MHPs involved in writing standard operating procedures (SOPs) must be aware of equipment currently used in the workplace, other equipment that could be used, staffing levels required, as opposed to commonly available, and any specific problems associated with the person group involved, as well as organisational pressures.

Any alternative SOP offered may not be complied with by staff unless these pressures are understood and dealt with, eg operating theatre staff may feel obliged to compromise their own safety to ensure that of the person, and may also feel under pressure when there is a long list of procedures that session. The theatre manager must be made aware of the issues of stress and peer pressure among staff. In the community, if a number of staff is specified in an SOP then this should be adhered to. Staff must be aware that if they deviate from the SOP then they may be liable for injuries so caused. The MHP must ensure that any alternative strategies devised must be at least as safe for the person as those used currently, and acceptable in a time pressured environment. Without this understanding, the suggested strategies may not be used or useful. However, those employers able to demonstrate use of a safe system of work will be complying with the HASAW 1974, and this may be reflected by reduced insurance premiums (HSC 1994).

NHS employers able to provide evidence of risk reduction, safe systems of work and a reduction in reported accidents/incidents and sick leave may well benefit from reduced insurance liability from the NHS insurance scheme. Any employer with a bad record on the health and safety front may have additional financial constraints placed on its budget by raised insurance premiums. Compliance with the All Wales Manual Handling Passport and Information Scheme (2003) has shown such benefits for the NHS trusts involved.

Summary

The management of manual handling in an organisation must be seen to be important at all levels. A sound strategy must be in place, familiar to all staff and carried out as directed and monitored by the "responsible person". In order to ensure that staff are working safely, they must be given the resources and encouragement to enable them to do so, whether this be time, equipment or personnel. Attention given to the health and wellbeing of staff will be reflected in their work with the mobility impaired, and can only be beneficial to both parties.

Training in the use of equipment and problem solving should be delivered by competent trainers and sufficient time allowed for this to be effective. Advice on ergonomic practice should be available as required, and especially when designing or adapting an environment for people handling. Proper regard for the needs of all who will use the workspace should ensure comfort and safety of all.

- A process is only as good as those who operate it.
- If the strategy for safer manual handling is included with the business plan, it will become an essential element of "the way we do things here".
- The benefits of this scheme should result in better person care, delivered by healthier staff and managed by successful executives.

References

A&B, X&Y v East Sussex County Council (2003), EWHC 167 (Admin) High Court.

Advisory Committee on the Safety of Nuclear Installations (1993), study group on human factors (3rd report), *Organising for Safety*, HSE Books, Sudbury.

Adams, J (1995), *Risk,* UCL Press, London.

Alexander, P (1998), Risk management in manual handling for community nurses. In *Contemporary Ergonomics* ed Hanson, M, Taylor & Francis, Padstow.

All Wales NHS Manual Handling Training Passport and Information Scheme (2003), www.wales.nhs.uk/documents/NHS_manual_handling_passpor.pdf.

Black, C (2008), *Working for a healthier tomorrow*, Crown Copyright, Norwich.

Cameron, L & Stocker, T (2010), Keep Calm and Carry On *Safety and Health Practitioner,* March 2010.

CSP (2003), Chartered Society of Physiotherapy, *Guidance in Manual handling for Chartered Physiotherapists*, CSP, London.

CSP (2005), Chartered Society of Physiotherapy, *Work related musculoskeletal disorders affecting members of the Chartered Society of physiotherapy*, CSP, London.

CSP (2008), Chartered Society of Physiotherapy, *Guidance in Manual Handling in Physiotherapy*, Ch 4, CSP, London.

College of Occupational Therapists (2006), *Manual Handling – College of Occupational Therapists Guidance 3*, College of Occupational Therapists, London.

Crumpton, E (2001), *Changing practice – improving health*, RCN, London.

Cust, G, Pearson, J & Mair, E (1972), The prevalence of low back pain in nurses, *International Nursing Review*, **19**, 169-179.

Dehlin, O, Hedenrud, B & Horal, J (1976), Back symptoms in nursing aides in a geriatric hospital: an interview study with special reference to the incidence of back symptoms. *Scandinavian Journal of Rehabilitation Medicine*, **8**, p47-53.

Department of Health (2002), *The manager's guide*, Back in Work Campaign, Crown copyright.

Disability Discrimination Act 1995, www.legislation.gov.uk/ukpga/1995/50/contents.

Dreyfus, L & Dreyfus, SE (1986), *Mind over Machine: the power of human intuition and expertise in the era of the computer*, Blackwell, Oxford.

Fink, A, Kosecoff, J, Chassin, M & Brook, R (1984), Consensus methods: characteristics and guidelines for use, in *American Journal of Public Health*, Vol **74**, No 9.

Health and Safety at Work etc Act 1974, HMSO.

HSC (1994), Health and Safety Commission, *Management of health and safety in the health services*, p8, HSE Books, Sudbury.

HSE (1993), Health and Safety Executive, *Successful health and safety management*, p5-13, HSE Books, Sudbury.

HSE (1998a), *Lifting Operations Lifting Equipment Regulations 1998*. HSE Books, Sudbury.

HSE (1998b), *Provision and Use of Workplace Equipment Regulations 1998*, HSE Books, Sudbury.

HSE (2000), *Management of health and safety at work regulations 1999*, Approved code of practice and guidance (2nd edition), HSE Books, Sudbury.

HSE (2001), *Handling Home Care*, HMSO, Sudbury.

HSE (2002), *Guidance on Manual Handling Operations Regulations*, HSE Books, Sudbury.

HSE (2004), Manual Handling Operations Regulations 1992 (as amended), *Guidance on Regulations L23* (3rd edition) HSE Books, Sudbury.

HSE (2005), *Regulatory Reform (Fire Safety) Order 2005*, HSE Books, Sudbury.

HSE v Birmingham PCT 2008, www.hse.gov.uk/press/2008/coiwm33408.htm

HSE (2010), in *Standards in Manual Handling* (3rd edition) NBE, Towcester.

Hignett, S (2001), Embedding ergonomics in hospital culture: top down and bottom up strategies, *Applied Ergonomics*, **32**, 61-9.

Hignett, S, Crumpton, E, Ruszala, S, Alexander, P, Fray, M & Fletcher, B (2003), *Evidence-based patient handling*, p5-7, Routledge, London.

Hollis (1985), *Safer Lifting for Patient Care* (2nd edition), Blackwell Scientific Publications Oxford.

Human Rights Act 1998, www.legislation.gov.uk/ukpga/1998/42/contents.

Institute of Directors and Health and Safety Executive, *Leading health and safety at work*, p1-3, accessed at www.hse.gov.uk/pubns/indg417.pdf on 14 July 2010.

Inter-professional Advisory Group (1995), *The Inter-professional Curriculum a course for Back Care Advisers*, NBE, Harrow.

Inter-professional Advisory Group (1997), *The Inter-professional Curriculum Framework for Back Care Advisers*, edition II College of Occupational Therapists.

James, A (2010), in foreword to *Standards in Manual Handling*, National Back Exchange, Towcester.

Kane, M (1994), Lifting: why nurses follow bad practice *Nursing Standard*, **8**, (25) 34-38.

Limitation Act (1980), www.legislation.gov.uk/ukpga/1980/58.

Magora, A (1970), Investigation of the relation between low back pain and occupation, Part I *Industrial Medicine Journal*, **39**, 465-471.

Management of Health and Safety at Work Regulations 1999.

Mandelstam, M (2002), Manual handling and balanced decision making, *column*, February 2002.

Mandelstam, M (2009), in National Back Exchange 2009, *column*, **21.2** Summer 2009, p12, NBE, Towcester.

Mental Capacity Act 2005, www.legislation.gov.uk/ukpga/2005/9/contents.

Moody, J, McGuire, T, Hanson, M & Tigar, F (1996), A study of nurses attitudes towards mechanical aids, *Nursing Standard*, **11**, 4, 37-42.

NBE (1993), National Back Exchange, *Essential Back-up*, NBE, Towcester.

NBE (2002), National Back Exchange, *Essential Back-up II,* NBE, Towcester.

NBE (2004), National Back Exchange, *Manual Handling Standard*, p3-6, NBE, Towcester.

NBE (2010), National Back Exchange, *Standards in Manual Handling* (3rd edition), NBE, Towcester.

Nelson, A (Ed) (2006), *Safe Patient Handling and Movement*, chapter 5, Springer, New York.

Pidgeon, N (1991), Safety Culture and risk management in organisations. *Journal of cross-cultural psychology* 22 (**1**) 129-140.

Royal College of General Practitioners (1996), *Clinical guidelines for the management of acute low back pain*, RCGP, London.

RCN (1995), Royal College of Nursing, *Patient handling standards*, RCN, London.

RCN (1981), Royal College of Nursing, *A Guide to the Handling of Patients*.

RCN (2002), Royal College of Nursing, *RCN Manual Handling Training Guidance*, RCN, London. Funded by a research grant from Liko (UK) Ltd www.rcn.org.uk www.anaesthesiaconference.kiev.ua/Downloads/Safer%20staff,%20better%20care_2004.pdf.

National Back Pain Association (1987), *A Guide to the Handling of Patients* (2nd edition).

Smith, J (ed) (2005), *The Guide to The Handling of People* 5th edition 2005, BackCare.

Scott, T, Mannion, R, Davies, H & Marshall, M (2003), Does organisational culture influence health care performance? A review of the evidence, *International* Journal for *Quality in Health Care*, **15**(2):111-118 (2003).

The Regulatory Reform (Fire Safety) Order 2005, www.legislation.gov.uk.

6

Training strategies

Pam Rose MCSP

Registered member NBE, chartered physiotherapist, moving and handling consultant and trainer

Introduction

The previous chapter addresses an organisational systems approach to developing and implementing an effective moving and handling policy and considers how the different roles and responsibilities of relevant stakeholders involved in this policy ought to collaborate to achieve common goals. Training is one key strategic element of this approach, and an integral thread of a manual handling policy based in legislative compliance; aimed at safer systems of work; focused on improved care and rehabilitation; and underpinning balanced decision making.

A training strategy is the long term plan developed with agreed goals and measurable objectives to be aimed for within a defined time period. The responsibility for developing a training strategy can be held by a variety of departments within different organisations. These departments might include human resources, health and safety or a dedicated workforce development unit; and may be audited through clinical governance protocols. Policy and training strategy must also be consistent with systems for equipment selection, procurement and provision.

Some organisations employ back care practitioners (BCPs) who may work alone or lead a training team, and some organisations subcontract to external training and ergonomics providers with proven experience in assisting in the policy development process.

Where training is contracted to external providers, it is important that these organisations can demonstrate the experience and expertise to be able to influence change and have the opportunity to contribute to ongoing policy development.

Definition of training

The term training has been defined as the acquisition of knowledge and competencies as a result of the teaching of vocational or practical skills (Reece & Walker 2007). In addition to the basic training required on induction to a new job or work area, it is recognised that there is a need for continued training beyond initial qualifications, both formal and informal, in order to maintain, upgrade and update skills and competencies throughout a working life. People within many professions and occupations may refer to this sort of training as continual professional development (CPD).

It has already been acknowledged in chapter 1 that there is a legal requirement for an employer to provide a safe system of work and also to provide adequate information, instruction, training and supervision so as to ensure the health, safety and welfare of employees. Within the area of moving and handling people, safer systems of work have been created by concentrating on the areas of risk assessment, equipment provision and training. Fray (in Smith 2005) discusses these interventions and argues that without behavioural change the training intervention is unlikely to be successful. He also points out that all the interventions are interlinked and unlikely to result in safer practice without management commitment and support.

Training approaches

Training is typically delivered in two approaches; onsite, on the job training and offsite, classroom based training.

● On the job training takes place in a usual working situation, using the actual equipment, documents or procedures that trainees use on a daily basis. This is considered by many to be the more successful type of training.
● Off the job training takes place away from normal work situations, usually in a classroom. This has the advantage of allowing people to get away from work and concentrate more thoroughly on the training itself. It is generally

considered to be difficult to transfer these skills back into the workplace effectively.

This chapter will examine a number of training strategies and methods of training development in the area(s) of the moving and handling of people in order to address the following basic questions:

● What should a training strategy achieve?
● What is the legal basis for training provision?
● What are the published standards for training or course accreditation?
● What are the recognised qualifications for trainers?
● What type of training is most effective?
● Who needs to be trained and what training do they need?
● How is this training carried out in order to be the most effective?
● What training documents are required?
● How is the success of the training evaluated?
● How can the evaluation results influence the continued development of safety policies?

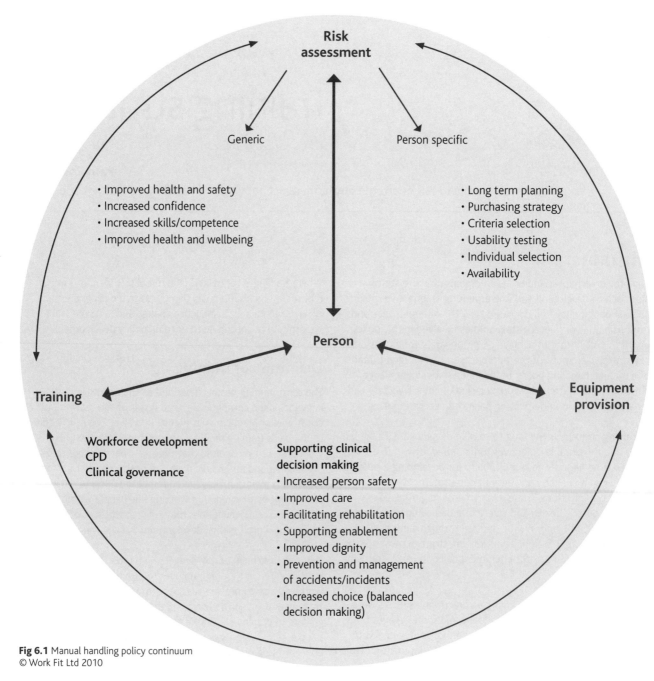

Fig 6.1 Manual handling policy continuum
© Work Fit Ltd 2010

What should a training strategy achieve?

In the light of legislation and case law, it might be argued that an effective manual handling policy is one that balances all strategic policy elements, achieving person and handler safety through good practice insofar as this can be achieved. The essential elements to be addressed in any adequate manual handling policy include risk assessment systems, equipment provision and prescription and training strategies. The link between these three elements is shown in Fig 6.1.

The risk assessment element is addressed in chapter 2 of this publication. Manual handling risk assessments can either be generic or person specific, aimed at acknowledging where risks exist and then taking measures to reduce those risks to a level reasonably practicable. As these assessments are required to be carried out by a "competent" person, then specific training in manual handling risk assessment skills is paramount in any organisation.

The element of equipment provision is also covered in detail in other chapters, but the continuum shown in Fig 6.1 demonstrates the need for a coherent link between equipment provision and person choice as well as safety, both for the handler and the person being moved/assisted to move. In order to prescribe appropriate equipment, training and updated training in the selection and use of this equipment is essential.

The training element, with competent delivery and effective implementation, should result in the following outcomes:

For the person being moved:
● increased safety
● improved care
● extended options for rehabilitation and enablement
● improved dignity
● personal choice
all within a culture of balanced decision making

For the handlers:
● increased skills and competence
● increased confidence in problem solving
● increased staff health and safety
● improved staff wellbeing and morale
● improved staff retention.

Human rights law, disability discrimination legislation and more recently Mental Capacity Act considerations have impacted greatly on manual handling decision making. Appropriate and sufficient training, therefore, needs to be provided for decision takers.

An effective training strategy should be person centred, both for the person being moved and for each trainee. Training should, ideally, include the importance of detailed person assessment, and be tailored to the individual abilities and learning styles of the trainees. Training sessions should also aim to be enjoyable and a valued part of any job role, rather than a chore in order merely to fulfil a duty of employment.

Historically, as detailed in the very early editions of this publication, many training courses have had the emphasis on staff safety, with underpinning health and safety law being the focus. But, more recently, the need for balanced decision making in the carrying out of risk assessments has been recognised and has led to a slightly different training approach. There has been a move towards a more person centred approach. The choices of the person being moved/assisted to move in manual handling decisions must now be considered as an essential part of training content for all trainees.

The issue of staff safety remains an important consideration and the aims of training must be to increase safety through improved skills, competence and confidence. In addition to basic safety, an effective training programme would aim to reduce incidents and injuries to staff and have the potential of reducing sickness benefits, increasing staff wellbeing and improving employee retention. The reporting of injury and incident is to be, as is the communication of these reports, to the training department to enable the development of training content in order to address, and suggest solutions to, any potential issues that emerge as risk factors.

What is the legal basis for training provision?

There are many legal considerations and best practice manual handling guidelines that affect an employer's moving and handling training strategy and form the basis for decisions about frequency, duration and content of training as well as methods of delivery and selection of training provider.

The Health Services Advisory Committee (HSAC 1984) produced a guidance document that highlighted the extent of the risk of musculoskeletal injury to employees in the health and social care services associated with the moving and handling of people, and made a number of recommendations aimed at managing risk. These recommendations included conducting training to heighten awareness of manual handling problems, the development of safer handling techniques and the use of equipment where it can lessen the risk of injury. It is specifically suggested that moving and handling training be provided on induction, and also refresher training should be provided at a minimum of two year intervals.

This guidance was updated in 1992 (HSAC 1992), at which time it was suggested that the duration of induction training in person handling should be between 3-5 days for those with no previous training or experience. It went on to say that "at the very least it ought to be long enough to provide sufficient time for explanation, demonstration and practice in the classroom, and preferably also in the workplace".

From January 1993, the requirement for employers to identify, assess and manage risk, was formalised with the implementation of a raft of new health and safety regulations, including the Management of Health and Safety at Work Regulations (MHSWR) 1992 and the Manual Handling Operations Regulations (MHOR) 1992.

In the MHSWR (1992 and 1999), it is stated that training should be both adequate and appropriate and take place:
● on induction
● on being given new responsibilities
● where any new work equipment or system is introduced
● thereafter at "regular intervals".

© BackCare

It was recommended in the Common Induction Standards published by the Commission for Social Care Inspection (now the Care Quality Commission), following the Care Standards Act 2000, that induction training should take place in some work areas over at least one or two full days of classroom based training followed by work based reinforcement. It is important that training programmes designed for any particular area of work are specific to that type of work and have enough time allocated to meet an agreed set of competencies. Having agreed and established the training need in any work area and developed an appropriate programme, manual handling trainers should not be influenced to cut corners by shortening any agreed training programme, and any agreement to do so must be documented and agreed by the manager or purchaser of the training.

It is now generally accepted that refresher training in health and social care for people handlers should be an annual requirement (Ruszala *et al* 2010). However, this is not to say that more frequent training could not be identified for individuals where this is deemed to be needed or appropriate. The emphasis is on the fact that training ought to be "suitable and sufficient" for the work area, the level of responsibility and the capability of the handlers. All training should be followed by on the job supervision and evaluation (Ruszala *et al* 2010).

There are many interpretations of the Health and Safety at Work etc Act (HASAW) 1974, which could be applied to the area of the moving and handling of people. Employers in the health and social care sectors have statutory responsibilities aimed at person safety (see chapter 1), as well as a duty of care in common law to staff and patients/service users, and duties towards their employees under health and safety legislation.

There is a duty under the MHSWR to provide competent employees who have the skills to conduct relevant risk assessments, some of which may be complex. These assessments would ideally lead to balanced and reasoned moving and handling decisions, taking account of staff safety but also the care, dignity, safety and enablement needs and choices of the people being moved/assisted to move. In addition, under MHOR, employees also have a duty to put the training they have received into practice and use whatever safe systems of work have been demonstrated.

The Health and Safety Executive (HSE 2007) recommends that the content of moving and handling training should be risk assessment based, and also include the incidence and potential causes of injuries and safer systems of work, including practical sessions in equipment use and handling techniques.

What are the published standards for training or course accreditation?

There is no single national institute or body that publishes or accredits manual handling courses. There are organisations, professional bodies and other groups who publish standards and guidelines to inform health and social care organisations and for trainers to follow, or refer to, to assist with establishing a policy or training programme, and against which trainers can measure their practice. There are educational institutes and organisations able to accredit the educational merit of a particular course or training programme. The important point is

that within a proposed training programme there should be a standard which is agreed by the parties involved as a baseline from which to start, and a method of monitoring the learning of the trainee.

Here are some examples of different standards and professional guidance.

National Back Exchange (NBE)

NBE has produced a guidance document *Standards in Manual Handling* 3rd edition (Ruszala *et al* 2010) which

> "provides the minimum standards and performance criteria to enable organisations and individuals to benchmark their progress in manual handling in care and materials handling environments".

Why do we need standards?
- Ensure compliance with the law
- Reduce the risks to carers and people being moved from poor practice
- Provide protection for employers
- Meet best practice requirements
- Meet the trainers' own professional requirements
- Promote national consistency
- Promote national recognition of the role of the back care practitioner or manual handling trainer.

© National Back Exchange

This document also sets out the development pathway for a manual handling practitioner (MHP) and details a standard of training content to reflect best practice. This document replaces the second edition published in 2004 that clearly set out the skills and experience required for manual handling trainers of all levels from key workers to expert consultants. It also sets out a prescription for course content, numbers of trainees and duration of courses. The 2010 edition also states that all training should be based on the specific needs of the workplace and the knowledge and ability level of the trainees. This guidance also specifies that:

> "A principles based approach to training and skills should be adopted, with sufficient practice to allow the trainee to demonstrate practical handling skills relevant to their work area by the end of the session."

Royal College of Nursing (RCN)

The RCN sets out manual handling training guidance and competencies in *Safer staff, better care* (Crumpton 2003). This provides a set of competencies for nurses to work towards and sets a framework against which to measure training success. For trainers delivering courses in the NHS, these competencies should be considered when developing their programmes. Manual handling training is also undertaken as part of nursing undergraduate courses.

National Health Service Litigation Authority (NHSLA)

A key function for the NHSLA, is to:

> "contribute to the incentives for reducing the number of negligent or preventable incidents".

It aims to achieve this through an extensive risk management programme that includes setting standards for moving and handling, against which healthcare organisations can be audited.

The Chartered Society of Physiotherapy (CSP)

In the CSP's updated *Guidance on Manual Handling in Physiotherapy* (2008), it is stated that:

> "All chartered physiotherapists require education and training in manual handling throughout their careers"

and that they should continue

> "to develop skills, knowledge and experience within manual handling situations as an integral part of their CPD".

It also recommends that all levels of staff should receive regular updates on manual handling from a competent person. This guidance also cites the NBE as the reference for trainer and training content standards.

The College of Occupational Therapists (COT)

In its guidance document (2006) the COT states:

> "It should not be assumed that a qualified occupational therapist will possess all of the skills and knowledge to undertake complex manual handling assessments, or have complex manual handling skills. It is advised that manual handling forms part of continuing professional development for all occupational therapy personnel."

Once again, this guidance refers the reader to the 2004 NBE guidance as the standard for both content and trainer standard.

All practising physiotherapists and occupational therapists are required to be registered with the Health Professionals Council (HPC). The HPC requires evidence of appropriate CPD to support practitioners' scope of practice. The CPD of experienced therapists working within the field of manual handling would include attending national conferences and reading recognised journals in order to remain current and be able to teach and advise based on the most up to date gold standard guidance and evidence based research.

Skills for Care

Skills for Care is part of an alliance of six organisations, which together form the Sector Skills Council for social care, children and young people's services called Skills for Care & Development.
- Care Council for Wales
- Children's Workforce Development Council
- General Social Care Council
- Northern Ireland Social Care Council
- Scottish Social Services Council
- Skills for Care.

Skills for Care is a government funded, independent, registered charity working with 35,000 adult social care employers to set the standards and qualifications to equip 1.5 million social care workers with the skills and knowledge needed to deliver high quality care to people who use services and carers. This is a very large number of employees, all of whom require basic skills in the moving and handling of people.

A range of new qualifications is being developed by Skills for Care in partnership with awarding organisations. It is intended that there will be many different units (or parts of qualifications) that reflect what workers should "know" and "do", so that some units are based on knowledge and some units are based on competency, and these will be elements of a number of different qualifications. The current Health and Social Care (HSC) NVQs level 2 and 3 will be replaced by Health and Social Care (HSC) Diplomas at level 2 and 3. These were launched in January 2011.

There are several core moving and handling units required for these qualifications, and therefore moving and handling training directed at trainees who work in these areas, and are completing these qualifications, will need to meet these standards. These units will give a clear direction as to the number of guided learning hours that each trainee is expected to need in order to complete each unit, thus setting a considerable time aside for manual handling training.

All Wales NHS Manual Handling Training Passport and Information Scheme (AWP)

The aim of the AWP scheme (currently in its version 2.1 dated January 2010) is to set a minimum standard aimed at ensuring consistency in manual handling training within the NHS trusts of Wales, so that staff can change jobs and roles across employment areas in Wales and give new employers confidence in their training achievement and skills if they have already completed "the passport". Other healthcare providers within the local authorities, private and voluntary sectors are also encouraged to participate in the passport scheme to extend the consistency of manual handling skills and knowledge.

The training element of the passport is modular in nature and sets a framework for trainers across the sectors to work towards. There is also standardised, recommended documentation for both risk assessments and for training records. This training system is somewhat prescriptive in nature but aims to raise basic standards in manual handling training across the country.

The passport states that it uses the NBE trainer standards in full as part of its standards on training delivery and gives direction as to expected frequency and duration of courses.

There are currently no plans to develop a passport for England but plans for a scheme across Scotland are expected to be published in 2011.

Derbyshire Interagency Group (DIAG) code of practice

This is one example of a locally agreed standard developed by an interagency group and supported and implemented in a specific locality. Training providers in this area would be expected to meet this standard. The code of practice (DIAG 2001) sets three specific levels of training within its structure, and guidance is also included in relation to the content of training that is expected. The three levels are introduction, basic handling skills and specific handling skills, and each has its own standards and aims to be work specific.

This code of practice is specific to Derbyshire and under copyright. Therefore, it is not a model that can be adopted elsewhere but is an excellent example of what can be achieved to reach consensus in a particular area or within a group of different authorities.

The important point to note is that there is no one specific standard but a series of standards which can be used as reference tools when developing a training strategy for any organisation, large or small.

Educational accreditation

After developing a programme for any organisation, it is possible to register as a training centre with one of a number of accreditation organisations to be able to offer a "qualification" that can be endorsed and quality assured. The larger awarding organisations currently include Edexcel, City & Guilds and the Open College Network.

In order to achieve this accreditation, the training provider needs to demonstrate high quality training processes, including the development of learning outcomes and policies and procedures that meet the standards of the awarding organisation. The accreditation process involves the awarding organisation examining a course against how it intends to meet its learning outcomes and how these are to be measured. A training provider would need robust internal and external verification systems to measure the outcomes. If the training provider meets the criteria of the awarding organisation, an inhouse training programme can then hold the status "accredited". For training providers working in the area of social care and attempting to win funding for their training, this may become more important in the future.

What are the recognised qualifications for trainers?

National Back Exchange (Ruszala *et al* 2010) publishes trainer guidelines that have been referred to in much of the guidance detailed above. The title "manual handling trainer" can apply to many different roles, each of which would require different experience or qualification. These roles may include:

- a key worker in a ward or department who has attended key worker training and has responsibility for cascading training to a designated group of workers in his/her own area
- a back care practitioner or lead trainer in a larger organisation employed to deliver all the programmes within a trust
- a self employed or freelance trainer selling training provision into the public or private sectors
- a trainer employed by an ergonomics/training company delivering services to health and social care organisations.

Within the NBE standards, the criteria for these types of job role are described, and these same standards are also used as reference for the CSP, the COT and within the All Wales Passport.

Manual handling may also be taught by teachers/lecturers employed within a college of further education and delivering the units within the social care environment (see Skills for Care 2009, page 5) or within university undergraduate or postgraduate courses.

Within all standards of training delivery, there is a requirement for the trainer to have a teaching qualification in addition to attending manual handling courses or being an experienced professional in their own field of nursing, physiotherapy, occupational therapy or care management (this list is not necessarily exclusive).

Different areas will require different teaching qualifications and these range from the older Certificate in Education or Adults

Teaching Certificate to the more recent PTLLS qualification, the "award in preparing to teach in the lifelong learning sector", which is required if the training delivered qualifies for funding from Skills for Care. There may also be a requirement to register with the Institute for Learning, which is a new body representing all trainers working in the field of adult education.

NBE also has a registered members' section, which was designed to assist organisations in selecting manual handling trainers/practitioners of verified competence. In order to become registered, applicants must meet specific criteria and achievements that include, as detailed above, recognised qualifications in teaching and "hands on" experience in the moving and handling of people.

> **Benefits of registered membership to an organisation or an individual:**
> - Confers professional status
> - Recognises the member as a competent practitioner and offers a quality assurance logo to be used on his/her individual training materials and certificates
> - Demonstrates professional accountability and adherence to a code of practice
> - Establishes a criterion for employment and/or career development linked with a knowledge and skills framework
> - Reinforces the role and status of the manual handling practitioner
> - Enables peer and external credibility and status
> - Recognises expertise which has undergone peer review
> - Increases business potential and may have insurance benefits.
>
> NBE

Trainers must keep CPD portfolios up to date to demonstrate relevant CPD and that sufficient effort is being made to understand current thinking and demonstrate an awareness of all new publications, professional guidance or case law. This can be done by attending national conferences, joining professional or membership organisations and receiving/reading relevant journals. The category of registered member of NBE was established so that BCPs and trainers could demonstrate that they have this expertise and ongoing development and so that employers and purchasers could use this as a benchmark.

What type of training is the most effective?

Training in manual handling principles, techniques and equipment selection is one very important area of a safe system of work but there is considerable evidence that, if undertaken in isolation and not as an integral part of a system or strategy, it will be ineffective and will not produce change or improvement in practice.

The HSE (2007) conducted a literature review that concluded that training alone is ineffective in reducing the rate of back injuries associated with manual handling (Hignett *et al* 2003; Hignett & Crumpton 2007; Maher 2000; Straker 2000).

Hignett, in her most recent in depth review of person handling published in 2003, stated that manual handling training alone was insufficient to produce a reduction in back injury rates in nurses and that a more cohesive and integrated approach, combining risk assessments and environment redesign together with problem solving and equipment and technique training, would be a better strategy. She also comments that any strategy needs to be tailored to the needs of an individual organisation and be work specific.

The lack of effectiveness of technique and educational based training is a conclusion made by many authors listed in the literature review of the HSE (2007).

Kroemer (1992) suggests reasons for this may include:
- trainees tend to revert to previous habits if new ways of working are not reinforced or regularly refreshed
- the job requirements are inherently too stressful and high risk
- there are emergency situations which cannot always have a planned strategy to manage.

Kroemer concludes that it is better to design a safe job than try to train people to behave safely.

Snook (1988) states:

> "the problem is not in training the employee, but with the employee's compliance with the training".

In any effective policy, it would be the employer's responsibility to ensure that any training provided in the workplace is work specific, relevant and produces attitude change through regular supervision.

Graveling (1991) states when evaluating manual handling training:

> "... training is seen by many as the easy option. It is easy for an employer to buy a training package off the shelf and to feel that by showing the video and other material to the workforce he had met his obligations. Any continuation of injuries subsequently is deemed as the intransigence of the workforce in "not doing what they have been told". Small wonder, therefore, that training is regarded by many as totally ineffective!"

Hignett *et al* (2003) in their systematic review of evidence based patient handling found that, in their examination of the evidence available to support the use of training as the main factor in an intervention programme, patient handling interventions that are predominantly based on training and education have no impact on working practices or injury rates.

The main outcomes of the HSE (2007) effectiveness review of training strategies, are as follows:

Training strategies that in summary are less effective:
- There is strong evidence that training in lifting techniques is ineffective in reducing injuries from manual handling.
- There is also strong evidence that educational based training alone is ineffective.
- There is strong evidence that principles learnt during training are not transferred into the working environment.
- There are differing views on what constitutes appropriate handling techniques.

Training strategies that in summary are effective:
- Training that is tailored to the trainee's knowledge and awareness of risks is likely to be more effective. This is supported by recent research carried out by Haslam *et al* (2007) and Whysall *et al* (2006, 2007). There is evidence that training employees and managers to assess and report risks in the workplace is effective in reducing manual handling injuries.
- There is strong evidence that ergonomics interventions, including the tailoring of training to suit the person and specific task requirements along with effective and appropriate equipment selection, are effective in reducing manual handling injuries.
- The most successful ergonomics interventions are those that have included the observation of employees in their working environment prior to the development and implementation of a training strategy.

A prudent employer would take all these factors into consideration when deciding on a new training strategy or modifying an existing one.

Who needs to be trained and what training do they need?

When planning a training strategy, one of the most important considerations is the desire to make it work specific. Quite simply, the existing gap between skills presently held and those required in any given task determines the training need. In the professional guidelines already detailed, some previous very prescriptive training programmes have been replaced by those that are modular in nature, allowing for flexibility to cater for existing needs while including core competencies applicable to all person handlers. Evidence suggests that standardised lesson plans that are generic and repeated for large numbers of employees within one organisation may not be the most effective. A detailed training needs analysis would highlight who would need what training and where that training should take place, ie in a training room or in a specific work area.

CASE STUDY

It would not be applicable to teach the use of hoisting equipment to support workers employed in an environment with people who were independently mobile and did not use a hoist at all and, in fact, did not have a hoist available. If that staff member then changed work role some months later and did require hoisting skills, then that would be the time for the line manager to highlight this as a training need and then source hoist specific training. This training would then be relevant and more likely to be transferred directly to the workplace. Skills taught in a classroom and then not used for some months will not be remembered accurately and could lead to unsafe practice, particularly if management identified the worker as "trained" according to a dated certificate of attendance, allocated work accordingly.

Whether the training strategy is designed for very large organisations, such as an NHS trust with several thousand employees, or designed for smaller organisations such as a residential care home or domiciliary care agency, or even for one single employer with direct payments employing their own small team of carers, the principles of the development of that training are the same.

A training needs analysis should be carried out to identify the training needs and any specific work areas requiring specialist attention.

Fig 6.2 shows a flow chart to explain the development of the process.

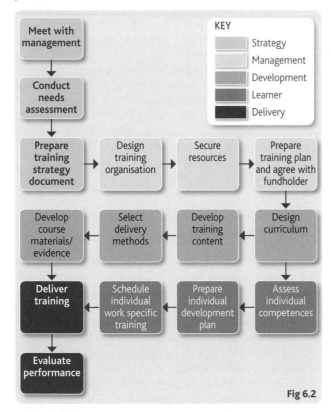

KEY
- Strategy
- Management
- Development
- Learner
- Delivery

Fig 6.2

The initial groundwork should start with detailed discussions with the manager or the purchaser of training as to what he/she expects from the training delivery. These discussions ought to begin with the manual handling policy of the organisation and a clear picture of what the policy says about training so that all sessions can be designed around this policy. Other issues that could be discussed at the outset would be knowledge of how the equipment provision and prescription procedures are carried out, and what risk assessment reporting measures are in place, so that correct advice can be given to course trainees.

The development of training programmes can be broadly divided into five phases.
- Analysis
- Design
- Development
- Implementation
- Evaluation.

Analysis

The analytical phase is sometimes referred to as a needs analysis or a needs assessment. An effective needs analysis answers the following questions:
- What is the problem?
- Is training the answer to the problem?

- What knowledge and skills should be included in the training course?
- Who needs to be trained?

This information could be hard to find for a large organisation and it may be necessary to rely on the workforce development department to provide the information. However, because of the complex nature of some manual handling activities and especially person handling, suitably qualified and experienced practitioners should be involved in the process. Within a smaller organisation, the manager may not have thought about training in this way as often the training section of a policy is treated in isolation and not as part of a collective strategy. The training provider would need to request the policy and explain the importance of developing training content to reflect the content of this policy.

In respect of ongoing training delivery, it is important that the policy is kept under review and updated to maintain consistency with evolving best practice and training content.

There would also need to be protocols and feedback mechanisms in place to manage non attendance and non achievement of agreed standards appropriately, to include:
- action
- feedback mechanisms
- remedial action.

Design

On completion of a robust training needs analysis and identification of course outcomes, it is time to begin the design phase. During this phase, a training blueprint is developed that includes:
- learning outcomes
- content outlines
- course structure
- training methods, course tools and materials
- assessment/evaluation.

Development

The next phase is the development of the training course. The steps of this phase are:
- develop a draft set of training tools and materials
- pilot test these materials with a target audience and make the necessary revisions
- finalise and publish these tools and materials.

Implementation

The implementation phase involves conducting the training programme and completing any related follow up activities to ensure the transfer of learning to the job setting. If the training is carried out over a long period of time, or in the case of an employed back care practitioner, as part of a continuous rolling programme, it is important to adapt training regularly to reflect change in practices, work structures, changing roles and responsibilities etc. Regular meetings to analyse direct feedback from the training and also from managers, who may record behavioural and cultural change in the workplace, would be critical to ongoing training development.

Evaluation

The final phase is to determine whether the training was successful. There are various methods of evaluating training and which method is selected depends upon what results are being sought and who needs these results. The trainer needs one type of feedback, for example, and the manager or purchaser may need another. Training evaluation is a feedback tool that promotes continuous quality improvements to training programmes and may be used to:

- determine how well the training met the trainees' needs
- determine to what extent the trainees mastered the training content
- identify whether the training methods, materials and tools helped trainees achieve the learning objectives
- assess how much of the training content, including newly acquired knowledge and skills, transferred on to the job behaviours.

How is this training carried out in order to be the most effective?

It has already been highlighted that successful training should aim to be trainee centered where possible. This approach should aim to cater for individual training needs in two areas:

- training should be tailored to meet the individual learning needs of the trainee
- training should be work specific and relevant to job roles and responsibilities.

To tailor training to meet the needs of a variety of trainees, good preparation and lesson planning is vital. For each session to be delivered, a structured lesson plan needs to detail timings, content of each session, the activity required by the trainer and the trainee and the resources to be used. This is often presented in a simple table as illustrated here.

TABLE 6.1

Content	Time	Trainer activity	Trainee activity	Resources
This would indicate the precise content of each session	The time allocated for each session/ part of session	This may include activity, eg lecture, demonstration or supervised practice	This may include activity, eg listening, participating and small group working	This would identify any resources used, eg flip chart, PowerPoint, DVD and then also practical requirements such as a bed, a chair, a hoist and all accessories

Recording lesson plans in this way will also help with formal documentation of completed training, which will be discussed later in this chapter.

The type of training, length of sessions and amount of student participation will be determined by the designed and agreed training strategy. Training may be delivered by the same trainer or team of trainers throughout an organisation or there may be a key worker system aimed at disseminating training across an organisation by the key workers who themselves attend a suggested minimum five day trainers' course (NBE Standards 2004) and are tested on their competence, both in their knowledge of moving and handling principles, techniques and problem solving skills, but also in their ability to pass this knowledge on to others successfully.

Training programmes may be designed which have some of their initial modules taught in classroom situations and then followed up by work based mentoring and observation to develop practical skills. There are other programmes where the theory part of the required content is completed electronically. This is a recent development in the training for the moving and handling of people and there is no evidence, yet published, as to how successful this is. The advantages would be that individuals can complete the electronic learning package in their own time and the computer programme will monitor their progress. It must, however, be supported by suitable and sufficient practical training in the workplace or the classroom where the trainee must be able to transfer the learnt principles into good practice techniques.

Within the classroom environment, there are many teaching strategies to consider when developing lesson plans and associated material and tools. There are teaching strategies which are trainer led and, at the other end of the scale, some strategies which are very much trainee controlled. The following table summarises some of these:

Teaching strategy	Level of student participation
Lecture	Low
Demonstration	Low
Discussion	Medium
Question/answer	Medium
Video	Medium
Workshop	Medium
Quiz	Medium
Practical following demonstration	High
Role play	High
Case study	High
Assignment	High
Distance learning	High

It is suggested by Reece & Walker (2007) that, when choosing a teaching strategy, consideration ought to be given to the attention span and ability of the students. It is also suggested that more mature students have a longer period of concentration while the less mature benefit from more regular changes in teaching style and that the less able will have an attention span of no more than 10 minutes. It is also known that trainees with lower cognitive skills learn by memory and recall and not necessarily by needing to understand fully, and that the more developed a trainee's cognitive skills are the more they are able to analyse situations and find solutions. This can be demonstrated by Bloom's taxonomy (Bloom 1956), Fig 6.3, as related to moving and handling skills by Brichard in *column 22.2*.

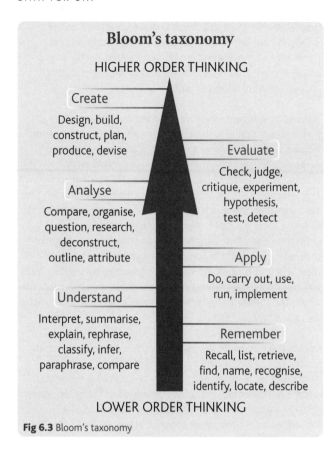

Bloom's taxonomy

HIGHER ORDER THINKING

Create
Design, build, construct, plan, produce, devise

Evaluate
Check, judge, critique, experiment, hypothesis, test, detect

Analyse
Compare, organise, question, research, deconstruct, outline, attribute

Apply
Do, carry out, use, run, implement

Understand
Interpret, summarise, explain, rephrase, classify, infer, paraphrase, compare

Remember
Recall, list, retrieve, find, name, recognise, identify, locate, describe

LOWER ORDER THINKING

Fig 6.3 Bloom's taxonomy

In addition to understanding the learning abilities of the trainees, consideration must also be given to their learning styles when designing effective lesson plans. As the aim of any training session is for learning to take place, it needs to be understood by the trainer that trainees will have different preferred learning styles. They can be broadly divided into three distinct types of style:

- the visual learner
- the auditory learner
- the kinaesthetic learner.

The visual learner responds best when information is presented in picture format, so using diagrams, charts, colours and handouts of plans and text will be the most effective. These trainees will create plans and charts to find possible solutions to problems.

The auditory learner benefits most from taking part in discussions or listening to lectures and will often be able to reason through solutions to problems by talking out loud to colleagues.

The kinaesthetic learner will benefit from being physically engaged in hands on activity. They will find practical, demonstration and role play effective and be keen to take part in these sessions.

For both effective teaching and learning to take place, there does need to be a balance of activity to meet the needs of all trainees, both for a range of cognitive abilities and a variety of learning styles.

Work specific training

There is vast variety of different working environments in which people work and where people handling training is

required. Some trainers will need to adapt their training regularly and some who work in one small given area hardly at all. The healthcare areas requiring training, designed with a specific role in mind, would be, eg:

- domiciliary carers
- intermediate care teams or enablement teams
- bariatric care workers
- workers in intensive care
- workers in operating theatres
- workers in X-ray departments
- physiotherapists in outpatient clinics
- therapists who work with children
- district nurses
- school support workers and school nurses
- workers in residential care homes
- workers caring for people with dementia or challenging behaviours
- workers in child or adult mental health settings
- workers in the specialist fields of dentistry and podiatry
- nursing and care workers in prisons
- workers in maternity departments
- accident and emergency workers
- ambulance workers and paramedics
- workers in mortuaries.

(This list is not exhaustive.)

In order to personalise training to meet the needs of these groups, an occupational and task analysis needs to be carried out. For example, the trainer may wish to observe the work area, eg X-ray department, and list the activities observed, including the working postures, the type of person being assisted to move, the design of the furniture, the layout of the department, the type and amount of moving and handling equipment used etc. The staff from this department would then attend a basic introduction module to moving and handling training and then a module specifically designed to cover the risk factors within their own work area and possible solutions that could be implemented.

Each of the work areas above has its own inherent moving and handling issues. Those working in the community may need help with decision making regarding risk assessments and environmental controls. Clinic based dental workers and podiatrists may assist people to move at times and also work in very difficult postures.

Emergency handling and resuscitation handling training with ambulance and accident and emergency workers will require a different module altogether.

Trainers should be familiar with the policy of the organisation with regards to the falling and the fallen person, and their training programme should address these issues where appropriate (see chapter 13).

Workers in the field of bariatric care need to understand the environmental and equipment demands, as well as the issues of assisted handling and emergency evacuation (see chapter 12).

Trainers must have the skills to be able to observe these different areas and transfer this information into changes in the content and emphasis of training. Some of the more specialist areas would highlight a potential need for more experienced and skilled trainers with hands on experience in those areas. This would be one argument to support the key worker and dissemination system of training.

It is clear that any system with a standard content of training will not meet the needs of all staff groups within a large organisation, although it may be more appropriate for a small, specialist group, eg a nursing home. The more specialised the training requirement is, the more skills the trainer should demonstrate, ideally in both work observation and course development. One of the most common feedback comments after moving and handling training is reported to be:

> "That was okay, we've done it all before every year, but it doesn't really apply to what I do."

Certificates of attendance should be issued to all attendees on completion of modules, detailing the training content. During the sessions, the trainer should constantly try to assess whether learning has taken place by conducting workshops with feedback from trainees, question and answer sessions and by observing all practical sessions. All trainers have a duty to report to the manager or purchaser of the training if any individual did not, or was unable to, participate in the practical sessions or failed to show any understanding of the theoretical part of the session. Although certificates awarded are usually of attendance, there would need to be an agreement at the outset about what action would be taken by the trainer if a trainee was noncompliant or unable to demonstrate the willingness or ability to achieve a practical standard.

In some instances, an experienced trainer may issue certificates of competence after training. Each trainee would have to demonstrate some personal development in the area of his/her work and, for example, present a case study which was individually assessed and deemed to have met a pre-agreed standard of competence at the time of assessment for such a certificate to be awarded.

Training for the "competent person" to conduct risk assessments

There is a duty under the MHSWR (1992, 1999) for a "competent person" to conduct risk assessments. In many organisations, the people carrying out moving and handling assessments receive no further training beyond their statutory moving and handling training. It is sometimes assumed that these skills will be an inherent part of their professional qualification of nurse, physiotherapist or occupational therapist. Chapter 2 deals with the subject of risk assessment in detail, highlighting the need for these to be conducted by people with sufficient skills and relevant competencies. Training people to acquire these advanced skills is a more specialised form of training than already mentioned. It would also necessitate the trainer being able to deem the trainee competent in order for the organisation to fulfil its legal duty.

Defining and measuring competency is fraught with problems and certainly difficult to achieve in a classroom environment. Perhaps the definition from The Training Agency (1988) in their guidance on National Vocational Qualifications (NVQs) is one of the most useful in this situation.

> "Competency is a wide concept which embodies the ability to transfer skills and knowledge to new situations within the occupational area. It encompasses organisation and planning of work, innovation and coping with non routine activities."

Competency in moving and handling decision making certainly requires indepth understanding of all the issues involved and an intuitive ability to solve problems. It also involves the passing on of information accurately and appropriately. In order for a trainer to award a certificate of competence to a trainee, then some individual assessment process would be required. It would be almost impossible to observe every trainee his/her own workplace to assess competence during real activity, so a written assignment or a verbal and practical presentation may be the most cost effective way to measure competence. Discussions would have taken place prior to the commencement of the course about any extra training or one to one help for trainees who do not meet the desired competency.

One example of an assessment method may be:

EXAMPLE
- Conduct a two day course in risk assessment skills with course content to include those risk assessment skills required for the area of work or occupational group of the trainees.
- Day one would include the legal background and all risk assessment tools with some practical problem solving.
- Prior to day two, the trainees would prepare a case study using the tools learnt on day one, plus clinical reasoning.
- On day two, each trainee would present his/her case study to the group for discussion, comments and feedback.
- The trainer would complete the matrix shown in Fig 6.4 during the presentation and after examining any completed documents.

Although this is a measurement in a matrix style to record that the content of assignments includes definite areas of clinical reasoning and problem solving, this could be followed with questionnaires within the workplace and discussion with management to ensure that training received had resulted in behavioural adjustment and a positive change in working practices. All feedback from the assessment of the case studies would be reported back to management and then, in turn, influence future training and risk assessment protocols.

Name	%
Person profile	
Clinical reasoning	
Risk assessment criteria	
Staff safety/REBA	
FIM scores/capability	
Environmental considerations	
Individual capability/Benner	
Conclusion of assessment	
Solutions suggested	
Review date	
Total score %	

Fig 6.4 Matrix © Work Fit 2010

What training documents are required?

A trainer may be asked at any time about the training he/she has delivered and who attended. Management has a duty, as has been explained in the previous chapter 5, to keep robust training records. The trainer is expected to complete several levels of documentation.

- A prepared lesson plan giving details of content, references, timing etc and any deviation from the prepared plan with reasoning.
- A signed attendance sheet of all trainees, including the consent of all trainees to take part in practical sessions and a declaration that they are fit to do so. The attendance sheet should also note any late arrivals, early finishers with explanations.
- A record of what was demonstrated and practised and if any trainee failed to participate in practical activity.
- Copies of any exercises or scenarios given, including any handouts or workbooks, references etc used.
- A training record, signed by trainer and the trainee, to agree theoretical and practical content of the course.
- An evaluation or feedback sheet completed by each trainee and collected by the trainer.

Where records are kept in a central register it is good practice for the trainer to keep his/her own copies of attendance sheets and lesson plans.

Accurate record keeping is essential for many reasons. When delivering update or refresher training, it is important to have records of what was included in previous sessions in order to progress training content appropriately. It may be required if there is a legal case when training is one of the issues raised by the claimant. It would not be sufficient to provide, as evidence, verbal descriptions of training content. Some written proof would be required. In the case of an employed BCP or key worker, the organisation would assist with collecting and formulating evidence. This would not be the case if the trainer was self employed.

Insurance

For the self employed trainer, insurance ought to be a consideration. Most professionals are members of their professional body, eg CSP, COT, or RCN and receive legal support as part of their subscription. The trainer must be able to demonstrate good practice by having his/her documentation backed up by sufficient CPD to show confidently that manual handling training was within his/her scope of practice. Additional insurance cover can be purchased as appropriate.

In any event, the keeping of detailed records should be an integral part of all training strategies.

How is the success of the training evaluated?

In order to evaluate a course successfully, the aims of an evaluations study should be clearly defined. Evaluations can be aimed at:

- measuring the success of the actual teaching skill with reference to style or method
- the content and whether this was appropriate to the trainee
- the effectiveness in that a change in behaviour or work practice will be a result of the training session.

If the individual trainer is designing the evaluation, he/she may choose to ask trainees about their enjoyment of the course and the relevance to their work area, in addition to asking if the teaching approaches are acceptable or if others would be better for some trainees.

If the manager or purchaser of the training is designing the evaluation, it may be more important for him/her to identify problem areas, ask about improvements and length of time of study etc.

Course evaluation traditionally takes place at the end of every session when the trainee fills in a questionnaire.

These can be carefully designed to require a tick in a box of multiple choice questions, eg Did the course meet its desired outcomes? with a choice of "yes" or "no".

- Or it could be more graded, eg Did the course meet its desired outcomes? and giving a scale of one to five, with five being "yes most definitely" and one being "no, not all".
- Or it could be open, eg Did the course meet its desired outcomes? with a text box for a written answer. Although without sufficient explanation, this often still produces a "yes" or "no".

The way in which the results are to be collated and what purpose they will have may determine how the data is best collected.

The trainer must establish at the time of the training needs analysis who will conduct the evaluations, for what purpose and where they will be collated.

The trainer must also make his/her own observations and evaluations to use in regular feedback meetings to the manager or the purchaser of the training or, in the case of a BCP, to the board "champion" or health and safety representative.

Feedback may also be important for the purchaser or manager. Feedback from the delegate directly to the purchaser may be necessary for him/her to evaluate the training provider. This feedback loop should be discussed at regular meetings to attempt to ensure consistency.

This feedback loop may also include clinical governance departments, health and safety departments and equipment provision areas to coordinate the systems approach to moving and handling provision.

How are these results reported, with the aim of influencing the continued development of safety policies?

Training strategies can be designed to meet the needs of a particular organisation, based on the results of an effective training needs analysis but should refer to a series of legal requirements and verified professional guidance as a baseline on which to develop an agreed standard. All feedback from the classroom and the workplace, from both trainers and trainees, should be absorbed by the workforce development departments and fed back into the areas of policy development to maintain the continuum of good practice.

On the job training can give rise to difficulties when trying to work out how the cumulative approach to training can be entered onto a training recording system or database. Workforce development departments are more likely to have systems in place that record more formalised training programmes.

Summary

In summary, training strategies are complex and require commitment from many areas of an organisation, including clinical areas, human resources and governance. These areas ought to have common goals and agreed methods of attempting to achieve those goals. A period of development and planning should lead to agreed protocols for all concerned.

For the employer, this systems approach to training should underpin a culture of change at the point of delivery and aim to improve handler and person safety and care. Employee understanding and compliance in these changes should be observable and measurable and fed back into the continuing loop to modify and refine policy. In addition to care and safety, rehabilitation and enablement strategies should be encouraged by detailed work specific training, which is risk assessment based and dedicated time spent on developing advanced skills with some groups of employees, eg physiotherapists and occupational therapists. It is, typically, these therapists who carry out complex assessments and then delegate care or rehabilitation tasks to other staff groups or prescribe moving and handling equipment.

The training providers involved in developing these strategies, whether they are employed directly by an organisation or whether they are private companies subcontracted for the length of a contract, ought to be very involved in the design and management of the strategy. They should be able to demonstrate flexible working, listening skills and a wide scope of practice to meet the needs of all aspects of the system, including varied areas of work specific training. It would be advisable to involve these trainers in feedback protocols and workplace methods of supervision and monitoring so that

additional training or a change in training content can be identified and implemented. Records of injury or incidents involving moving and handling issues may also be fed into this monitoring system.

In conclusion, for a training strategy to succeed it should ideally be risk assessment based, work specific, and focus on balanced decision making. It should be measured and observed and followed up by evaluation and supervision. The commitment from the most senior staff in the organisation will be the key to the evolution of these strategies and drive change both organisationally and clinically. The experience, expertise and flexibility of the trainer or training company ought to influence the attitude change in individual workers.

References

All Wales Passport (2010), www.wales.nhs.uk/documents/ NHS_manual_handling_passpor.pdf.

Bloom, B (ed) (1956), *Taxonomy of Educational Objectives, the classification of educational goals – Handbook 1: Cognitive Domain*, New York: McKay.

Brichard, E (2010) Teaching methods variety will lead to effective training, *column,* **22.2**.

Chartered Society of Physiotherapy (2008), *Guidance on Manual Handling in Physiotherapy*.

College of Occupational Therapy (2006), *Manual Handling COT Guidance 3*.

Crumpton, E (2003), *Safer staff, better care*, RCN.

Derbyshire Interagency Group (DIAG) (2001), Care Handling for People in Hospitals, Community and Educational Settings. A code of practice.

Fray, M (2005), in Smith, J (ed), *The Guide to The Handling of People*, 5th edition 2005, BackCare.

HSAC (1984), Health Services Advisory Committee, The Lifting of Patients in the Health Services, Health and Safety Commission.

HSAC (1992), Health Services Advisory Committee, Guidance on Manual Handling of Loads in the Health Services, Health and Safety Commission.

HSE (2007), Health and Safety Executive, *Manual handling training, Investigation of current practices and development of guidelines*, A literature review.

Hignett, S & Crumpton, E (2007), Competency-based training for patient handling, *Applied Ergonomics*, Volume **38**, Issue 1, January 2007, p7-17.

Hignett, S, Crumpton, E, Ruszala, S, Alexander, P, Fray, M & Fletcher, B (2003), *Evidence-Based Patient Handling*, p5-7, London: Routledge.

Management of Health and Safety at Work Regulations (1992, 1999).

Manual Handling Operations Regulations (1992) (as amended), HSE Books 2004.

National Back Exchange, Manual Handling Standards (2004), Interim documents for healthcare providers.

Reece, I & Walker, S (2007), *Teaching, Training and Learning: a practical guide*, 6th edition.

Royal College of Nursing (RCN) (1995), *Patient handling standards*, London: RCN.

Ruszala, S, Hall, J & Alexander, P (2010), *Standards in manual handling*, 3rd edition, National Back Exchange.

Skills for Care (2009), www.skillsforcare.org.uk Qualifications and Credit Framework.

The Training Agency (1988), Guidance on National Vocational Qualifications.

6 Training strategies

Equipment strategies

Jean Hutfield MIHM
Chair of the National Association Equipment Providers
Clive Tracey RGN DMS LLB(Hons)
Head of tender and policy management, Eastern and Coastal Kent Community Health NHS Trust

Introduction

Equipment that assists moving and handling is a fundamental element in any risk management strategy. It helps to reduce the burden of potential musculoskeletal injuries to staff while optimising person independence. Having a clear vision for the procurement, supply and maintenance of equipment ensures that adequate resources are available at the point of care delivery.

Equipment that assists moving and handling has two main functions:
- person enablement, sustaining independence as far as possible
- reducing the risk to staff and informal carers.

This chapter recognises the important role that equipment plays in achieving both these functions. It will stress the importance of having in place a strategic approach to moving and handling equipment in the wider health economy, looking at provision within hospitals, community healthcare settings and a person's own home.

Any strategy must address the needs of the local population. The primary starting point for any provision should always be person enablement. This will become paramount given the shift in the average age of the population. In addition, there is an ever increasing insight into the impact of disability and expectation of meeting healthcare needs. There are currently 770,000 disabled children in the UK with the numbers of disabled children increasing by two per cent year on year since 1975. This is against a growing older person population that is expected to increase by 70 per cent by 2036. The greatest growth is in the over 85 year old group by 150 per cent (Department of Health (DH) 2007a).

The Government strategy for independent living for disabled people (DH 2007b) stated that the Government is:

> "committed to delivering a full and equal citizenship for disabled people and sees independent living as being part of the way we advance this".

Independent living enables disabled people to fulfil the roles and responsibilities of citizenship. It is the Government's ambition that by 2013 disabled people will have more choice and control over how their needs for support and/or equipment are met. This is recognised by the Audit Commission in its report that stated:

> "equipment for older or disabled people provides the gateway to their independence, dignity and self esteem. It is central to effective rehabilitation; it improves quality of life; it enhances their life chances through education and employment; and it reduces morbidity at costs that are low compared to other forms of healthcare. It is no exaggeration to say that these services have the potential to make or break the quality of life for many older or disabled people, and of the 1.7 million who provide informal care".
> (Audit Commission National Report, 2000/2002).

The Government's strategy document stated that:

> "disabled people have challenged the meaning of 'independence'. Independent living does not mean doing things for yourself, or living on your own. Instead, it means: *Having choice and control over the assistance and/or equipment needed to go about your daily life*".

One problem however, has been that many healthcare commissioners appear to plan services beginning at the acute hospital's door. They fail to place value on the ability of community support to prevent admissions in the first place or to facilitate prompt and appropriate discharge from hospital. This often leads to isolated planning, creating barriers within treatment and support pathways. It is recognised that the needs of an acute hospital, which is planning to care for Mr A to Z entering its doors, differs from that of community services, which are focusing on individual care packages and maintaining person independence within his/her own home. The challenge for any equipment strategy is to address these differences and optimise benefits where a synergy exists. The community equipment service sits between acute and community service providers. It is ideally placed in facilitating the transition of care and support from secondary to primary care.

Against this backdrop of enablement, we already know that manual handling is the largest single cause of work related injury. It is associated with a high level of work related ill health and sickness absence in the health and social care sectors. It is the responsibility of health and social care organisations to minimise the risk of injury from manual handling. There is a balance to be achieved between person independence, and handler safety; access to the most appropriate equipment will contribute to achieving this balance.

Equipment provision

The NHS often promotes partnership working across health boundaries. Manual handling is one element where this is easily achieved. Joint policies and procedures for the moving and handling of people should be developed and be consistent in defining responsibilities of organisations to meet their statutory duties. Any policy should emphasise the importance of the human rights of those who access the service. The policy should minimise the risk from manual handling operations in all areas of its activity, in particular those activities involving person contact. The policies and procedures should, therefore, set out the framework to manage manual handling operations

as a whole, including the provision of equipment within the respective organisations. It is worth considering however, the different approaches and equipment provision within hospital and community settings. Community may include intermediate care, residential or nursing home or provision within the person's own home. This provision is further compounded within the community through the split of "health" and "social care", albeit most community equipment loan stores are now joint stores providing equipment to meet both "health" and "social care" needs.

Hospitals

In hospitals, equipment is normally funded from a capital budget to meet either a general need or a specific need where assessment has identified a high risk that must be addressed. The original need is often met through the approval of a business case that aims to deliver the most benefit to the most patients and staff, and deliver organisational efficiency. Business cases in the past have often been approved to meet legislative or external factors. They ensure compliance against audit, inspection or validation of service provision and, therefore, often achieve only a minimum standard of equipment provision. However, with the increase of the "internal" market for healthcare provision, the development of foundation trusts and a greater emphasis on client engagement supported through the Care Quality Commission (CQC), business cases are more likely to be approved where they support improvements in clinical outcomes, as opposed to safeguarding staff. Organisation image, reputation, sustainability and the ability to attract business are all current key drivers. Understanding these influences and how suitable equipment can assist in their achievement increases the potential of the funding being released.

There has been a great advance in equipment technology. As a result, many hospitals now have the minimum standard of electric profiling beds, a range of specialist mattresses, hoists, slide sheets, small handling aids and bespoke equipment to assist in rehabilitation or therapeutic interventions. The equipment is usually generic in its application to provide the support on average to the majority of the hospital in-patient population.

Intermediate care

With the increasing demand on hospital throughput, resources and healthcare costs resulting from unplanned hospital admissions, there has been a growth in the provision of intermediate care (DH 2008). Intermediate care is designed to provide the local community with an alternative to hospital admission/long term care where appropriate. It aims to facilitate discharge by providing short term health, social care and/or rehabilitation intervention. Intermediate care teams provide rehabilitation, recuperation and a rapid response service to provide community care, either in the person's own home, where possible, or in an intermediate care bed, usually in a nursing home for a short period.

Services, as outlined in *Our health, our care, our say* (DH 2006a) should adopt a person centred approach in which the individual takes on an active role to achieve maximum independence and quality of life. The intermediate care team provides an intensive package of care and/or rehabilitation over a 24 hour period to meet these care needs. They also support carers experiencing difficulty due to illness.

Persons are encouraged to self care and assisted to be as fully independent with regard to mobility and daily activities of living through the provision of equipment arranged according to need. Equipment, in this instance, is often supplied through the community equipment loan stores, which have a pool of equipment to meet general needs. Where particular short term specialist equipment is required, this may be hired as it may cost less than a hospital admission. Any equipment strategy should consider the potential health needs, costs and benefits to facilitate early discharge and supportive care. For the service to be fully effective with minimal risk to staff, arrangements must be in place to make equipment available promptly.

Different care environments

Nursing homes are funded either privately or through social services to offer people nursing care where this cannot be supported in their own home. The criteria for nursing homes include the facilities, staff and equipment to support long term health needs. Their registration is determined by minimum standards. The provision of equipment, which forms part of these standards, must meet the needs of the majority of the residents and is procured through capital funding.

Paragraph 30 of the Health Service Circular *Guidance on NHS Funded Nursing Care* (NHS 2003) states:

"It is expected that care homes providing nursing care will be fit for purpose, which, in the main, means they will have in place basic handling, mobility, and lifting equipment and adaptations. There may be some situations where they will need to draw on the resources of the local integrated community equipment service. Both health and council services have received additional funding to integrate and enhance these services. Where the NHS has determined that an individual requires a particular piece of equipment, it should ensure either that the care home provides it; or provide it on a temporary basis until the care home is able to provide it; or provide it to the individual for as long as they need it. It would be unreasonable to expect care homes to provide items of equipment that, by the nature of the design, size, and weight requirements, need to be specifically tailored to meet the individual's needs and would not be capable of being utilised by other care home residents."

To facilitate hospital discharge, equipment, such as profiling beds or specialist mattresses, may be provided from the community equipment loan store for a period *up to* six weeks. This, however, is not common in all areas. The provision *normally* will, if provided, be funded through the "health" element of the service. Nursing homes are then expected to fund the equipment long term, with the *maximum* of up to six weeks being a temporary measure. Conversely, residential homes in most cases are deemed to be the person's own home and the six week rule may not apply, dependent on the terms laid down by the registering authority. However, residential homes are reluctant to install fixed equipment, such as ceiling track hoists, thereby limiting the enablement of clients. Small handling aids

such as transfer boards, grab rails and walking aids are often available but privately funded by the person.

Where the residential home feels that it cannot support the health needs of the person, it will give notice, resulting in the person transferring to nursing home care. In some instances, and for short periods, intermediate care can support nursing care within residential homes, thereby supporting the use of more complex manual handling equipment such as hoists.

Equipment is not generally funded by social services as regards social care needs within nursing homes or residential homes unless a joint equipment service budget exists. However, it is important to note that all clients are eligible for a needs assessment through social services. This needs assessment may include an occupational therapy assessment and/or care manager review. The nursing home or residential home is not obliged to address any recommendations from the assessment but should it wish to, the home or the individual may be expected to fund it.

People in their own homes

People within their own homes are free to use and provide any equipment that they can fund. They may or may not be receiving care or support provided through a healthcare team or social services. Care to maintain independence may also be provided through informal carers, including close relatives. However, in all instances they are eligible for a needs assessment through social services, the same as with nursing or residential homes. People may be referred by a healthcare professional or can directly self refer to an OT, social services or their GP. They cannot, however, directly refer to the equipment service. The difference for people in their own homes is that, following the needs assessment, any equipment or support identified would likely be funded through social services. This funding will depend on the internal process and, in some instances, clinical reasoning being accepted.

Depending on the range of moving and handling equipment required, this is either provided through the community equipment loan store, funded as part of a care package or, where provision allows independence, supported by informal carers directly purchased on the person's behalf. The provision of equipment through social services is not always dependent on a care package being required. Justification for purchases of equipment not available through the community equipment loan store and valued over £1,000 often requires a clinical reasoning case to support this.

Housing adaptations, eg floor access showers, ramps etc, are funded as part of a disabled facilities grant that is means tested. In some social service boroughs, the provision of ceiling track hoists also comes under the banner of housing adaptations and is, therefore, means tested. This is not the case throughout the UK. Where a client has a health need that is supported by healthcare professionals attending, then equipment is generally made available through the community equipment loan store.

Clinical reasoning, in place of a business case, often covers elements such as:
• reducing ongoing, or prevention of, complications and progressive ill health

- reducing risk of exacerbation of deformities
- improving quality of care
- dignity
- comfort
- reducing risk to any carer, either formal or informal.

Note: The value threshold for equipment varies from service to service. For some, it may be set lower than £1,000 for the individual clinician to approve and require authorisation through appropriate management levels where higher values can be approved. Some services will have a panel to which the clinician presents a business or clinical reasoning case. Again, the value threshold for this is determined by the individual service.

Clinical appropriateness of medical devices for loan

Medical devices that are made available for loan through the community loan equipment service range from low risk items, such as raised toilet seats and toilet frames, to high risk items, such as dynamic, pressure relieving equipment. As such, all medical devices provided on loan should be issued following either a professional assessment or an assessment carried out by others authorised to do so. The clinical appropriateness of the medical device prescribed to the individual is the responsibility of the prescriber. In addition, any clinical monitoring of the prescribed medical device, as deemed appropriate to the device, and the risk factors associated with that medical device is also the responsibility of the prescriber.

Assessments may be performed by any healthcare professional with suitable training, skills and knowledge. Where an organisation deems the equipment to be high risk for potential injury or misuse, then a competency programme should be established. Competence can be defined as:

> "the state of having the knowledge, judgement, skills, energy, experience and motivation required to respond adequately to the demands of one's professional responsibilities" (Roach 1992).

The Nursing and Midwifery Council (NMC) (2008) states:

> "a registered nurse must have the knowledge and skills for safe and effective practice when working without direct supervision".

Competence is also about empowering staff. It is viewed as a person's ability to perform and their competencies are their total capability, ie, what they can do, not necessarily what they do. Each registered health professional remains personally accountable for his/her own practice and also any delegated practice to the unregistered and professional accountability in line with relevant professional bodies (NMC 2008; Health Professions Council (HPC) 2009). Support workers remain responsible for maintaining and updating their personal competence under the guidance of their line manager.

Training in the use of high risk medical devices, eg mobile hoists, for use directly with the person or his/her family carers is the responsibility of the prescriber. If the prescriber issues the medical device, ie from a buffer store, it is the responsibility of the prescriber to issue user instructions with the device and to fit and/or adjust the device in accordance with the manufacturers' instructions.

For further information on training, refer to chapter 6.

Community equipment services (CES)

CES provide the majority of disability equipment needed by people to support their care within the community. They provide a well informed gateway to other equipment services such as those provided by the NHS, councils and voluntary organisations. In some instances, the service is jointly funded, providing equipment for both social and healthcare needs as the sole equipment provider for social services and the NHS in their area.

CES support disabled people of all ages to maximise independence or meet social and health needs in the community. The equipment that the CES stock can range from simple, low cost aids, eg raised toilet seats, bath boards, extendable hand grabs and transfer boards for daily living, to more complex mechanical and medical equipment such as riser recliner chairs, hoist and slings and profiling electric beds.

Since the Audit Commission Report (*Fully equipped* 2000), there has been a move to integrate both the health and social care equipment loan stores into more comprehensive CES. The vision was that they become more responsive and flexible to meet healthcare demands, while delivering economies of scale from improved logistics and procurement strategies. The range of equipment that they stock, although widespread in range, may be limited in choice. Special equipment for specific people may be considered depending on meeting set criteria. It is this specialist equipment that requires clinical reasoning. CES do not generally become involved in equipment associated with house adaptations or ceiling track hoists. Both remain the sole remit of social services.

Wales
In Wales, the Welsh Assembly has embraced the integration of community equipment services and continues to develop these services. The full integration of community equipment services within Wales is an objective in the strategy *Designed for Life* (Welsh Assembly Government 2005) and the National Service Frameworks for Children and Older People. Their aim is to ensure that:
- formal partnership arrangements are in place
- appropriate storage and decontamination facilities are in place
- appropriate IT systems are in place to ensure equipment is tracked, serviced, recalled, refurbished and recycled as appropriate. Refer to www.wales.gov.uk/topics/health/socialcare/equipment for more information.

Scotland
In Scotland, after consultation with services and service users, the local government developed their *Good Practice Guide for the Provision of Community Equipment Services* (Scottish Government 2009). The guide aims to support local equipment services to develop, deliver, manage and monitor effectively the provision of equipment, and minor adaptations, from the point of assessment through to delivery. It can be used as a quick checklist against which organisations can benchmark and evaluate their equipment service, irrespective of the type of

model adopted. It helps to identify common and key components that should apply to all equipment services and to assist in a systematic approach to service development and delivery across all areas of Scotland.

England: new retail model

Service improvements within England regarding the current provision of community equipment services have been considered over the last few years. The cost versus quality balance is an influencing factor. The original vision of the Government's paper on Transforming Community Equipment and Wheelchair Services (DH 2006b) was that all community equipment would be provided by retailers. It was expected that this would increase innovation, giving greater coverage and choice while driving down cost. However, the risks associated with this model, established through some pilot studies, demonstrated that these were too great and too costly.

The model has since been revised to cover all small aids to daily living, eg toilet raisers, perching stools, four wheeled walkers, chair raisers etc being provided through retail outlets. The vision for complex aids to daily living, eg hoists, slings, beds, dynamic pressure relief mattresses would be provided regionally. The concept gives greater choice and enablement for people requiring smaller aids while, throughout England, the reuse and recycling of more complex equipment that requires more specialist set up, support and maintenance keeps the cost at a minimum. The principle of this new retail model utilises the direct payment scheme, similar to the voucher scheme that has been successfully used in wheelchair and ophthalmic provision.

The transforming community equipment services retail model addresses the new agenda for individual budgets and personalisation through the direct payments route. The personalisation for health is a new concept being piloted throughout England. Retailers are requested, although not mandated at present, to go through an accreditation process to ensure risks through training, including handling of people, are addressed. Information on the national accreditation scheme, training and application can be found at: www.cedonline.org.uk.

The idea is that the person will be provided with a prescription that covers the general cost of equipment provision. Should he/she wish to, he/she can top up to obtain a higher specification or bespoke piece of equipment. The assessment will identify minimum needs. It will be the responsibility of the accredited retail outlet to support the person in the selection of the equipment to fulfil his/her needs and choice. An alternative hybrid to this already exists within some community equipment services regarding items such as riser recliner chairs where they can provide a choice of only one or two colours in a single fabric. In this instance, CES provides the person with a prescription to the value of the riser recliner chair it would provide and allows the person to use this at an established and approved retail outlet (mobility store), affording the person greater choice.

The legal framework

Health and Safety at Work etc Act 1974

The Health and Safety at Work etc Act 1974 is an umbrella Act that puts a range of general responsibilities on both the employer and employee. The Act imposes a duty under section 2.1 that every employer shall ensure, so far as is reasonably practicable, the health, safety and welfare at work of its employees. These duties and those of employees are further defined in the following sections of the Act:

Section 2.2: Employers' duties
- Provision and maintenance of plant and safe systems of work.
- Safety in the connection, use, storage and transport of loads and substances.
- Provide information, instruction, training and supervision of employees.
- Maintain a safe workplace, access and egress.
- Maintain a safe and healthy working environment.

Section 7: Employees' duties
Employees have a general duty to cooperate to ensure their own and others' safety at all times. This includes their acts and omissions at work and willingness to receive training to carry out their work safely.

While health and safety has been taken more seriously in recent years, the Management of Health and Safety at Work Regulations 1992 (replaced in 1999) resulted in a mindset change. Regulation 3(1) requires the employer to make a suitable and sufficient assessment of the risks to his/her employees (and others possibly affected). Employees must be made aware of the risks and appropriate measures implemented to reduce the risk of injury. Where the general assessment under section 3(1) of the regulations indicates the possibility of risks from the manual handling of loads, the requirements of the Manual Handling Operations Regulations 1992 (as amended 2002) should be followed.

The Manual Handling Operations Regulations 1992

The Manual Handling Operations Regulations 1992 came into force on 1 January 1993 to implement European Directive 90/269/EEC. The regulations add to the duties placed on employers by the Health and Safety at Work etc Act 1974. The Manual Handling Operations Regulations 1992 (as amended 2002) establish a clear hierarchy of measures:
- Avoid the need for hazardous manual handling as far as is reasonably practicable. This may be done by redesigning the task to avoid moving the load or by automating or mechanising the process.
- Make a suitable and sufficient assessment of any hazardous manual handling that can't be avoided.
- Remove or reduce the risk of injury from hazardous manual handling to the lowest level reasonably practicable using the assessment as a basis for action. Particular consideration should be given to the provision of mechanical assistance such as hoists but, where this is not practicable, then other improvements to the task, the load and the working environment should be explored.

The extent of the employer's duty to avoid manual handling or to reduce the risk of injury is, therefore, governed by what is "reasonably practicable". This consists of a balance of the cost of avoiding injury compared with the consequences of not avoiding them, and takes into account time, money and effort. When considering the costs, only the magnitude of the risk should be relevant. As such, where staff have no access to equipment, the risk of injury is high and provision is likely to be justified. However, where access to equipment is available, albeit not in the immediate environment or time period, the duty to provide additional equipment to reduce the risk further may not be justified.

The cost benefit/reasonable argument needs to be considered in any equipment strategy as arguments based on safety lines alone may not easily be justified. It may be reasonable to have one hoist available in a three storey nursing home that can be moved around, as opposed to the expenditure for three hoists, one for each floor. This may be because the likelihood of the risk occurring is not an exact science and the costs and consequences of not addressing them cannot be fully evidenced. In addition, the costs and consequence may not be solely borne by the employer, especially where joint care provision is provided by a number of agencies.

It is also worth noting that where employers have provided equipment to reduce the risk to staff, clients and carers, under the Manual Handling Operations Regulations 1992 (as amended 2004) (HSE 2004), employees have the duty to follow appropriate systems of work laid down for their safety. They must make full and proper use of any equipment provided and cooperate with the employer on health and safety matters. The employee must take care to ensure that their activities do not put others at risk, eg if a member of health or social care staff fails to use a hoist that has been provided as the most appropriate form of handling the person, they are putting themselves at risk of injury and the employer is unlikely to be liable.

The reasonable argument can also be justified through benchmarking any organisation or service provider against an organisation of similar size and type. The standard measured would be that of a prudent employer and any strategy and subsequent business case should consider the standards achieved within other organisations, eg if handling aids can easily be delivered to a person's home within 24 hours within one community equipment service, then it would be reasonable to expect that this standard could be achieved in others. This principle has been very effective through the provision of electric profiling beds within hospitals that are now seen as commonplace and a minimum standard.

The Lifting Operations and Lifting Equipment Regulations 1998 (LOLER) and Provision and Use of Work Equipment Regulations 1998 (PUWER)

LOLER aim to reduce risks to staff health and safety from lifting equipment provided for use at work. They place a duty on the employer to ensure that any equipment used to lift/move a person is safe and fit for purpose. There are specific requirements for lifting equipment that is used as work equipment. The term "work equipment" includes hoists, slings and lifting accessories used in health and social care settings, including private homes, by a handler during the course of their employment (whether used exclusively at work or also by others). LOLER does not apply to equipment used only by the person or their unpaid carer. However, service providers still have duties under the Health and Safety at Work etc Act 1974 to ensure the equipment is safe. Responsibility for undertaking the thorough examination required by LOLER should, therefore, be agreed between those parties involved, typically CES, care commissioners and service providers.

LOLER require that equipment be:
- strong and stable enough for the particular use and marked to indicate safe working loads
- positioned and installed to minimise any risks
- used safely, ie the equipment's use should be organised, planned and executed by competent staff
- subject to ongoing thorough examination and, where appropriate, inspection by a competent staff member.

Hoists, bath hoists and slings are covered by the regulations. They state that you should ensure that in using any lifting equipment the requirements of LOLER are met. Where equipment is used for lifting people, it is marked accordingly and it should be safe for such a purpose, eg all necessary precautions have been taken to eliminate or reduce risk. The regulations require that, where appropriate, before lifting equipment, including slings, is used for the first time, that it is thoroughly examined. In addition, lifting equipment must be thoroughly examined in use at periods specified in the regulations – six monthly for hoists, slings and accessories at a minimum and annually for all other equipment. Maintenance should be annual as specified by the manufacturer. Following a thorough examination or inspection of any lifting equipment, a report is submitted by the competent person (staff member or external consultant). For a simple guide to LOLER, go to: www.hse.gov.uk/pubns/indg290.pdf

In addition to the requirements of LOLER, equipment is also subject to the requirements of PUWER. This is because LOLER are specific regulations covering lifting equipment but any other equipment used or issued for work purposes is covered by PUWER, a more general regulation. PUWER state that equipment provided for use at work is:
- Suitable for use and for the purpose and conditions in which it is used.
- Maintained in a safe condition for use so that staff health and safety is not at risk.
- Inspected to ensure that it is, and continues to be, safe for use. Any inspection should be carried out by a competent person (this could be an employee if they have the necessary competence to perform the task) and a record kept until the next inspection.
- Assurance should be written that risks created by the use of the equipment are eliminated where possible or controlled by taking appropriate measures by providing adequate information, instruction and training. For a simple guide to PUWER, go to: www.hse.gov.uk/pubns/indg291.pdf

Equipment provision and design within the UK is well regulated against both British Standards (CE kite mark) and, in some cases, more stringent European standards (TUV in Germany). These standards test against design and intended use measuring standards such as the International Electrotechnical Committee (IEC) standards. For electric hospital beds, the standard is IEC 60601-2-38 "Medical electrical equipment.

Particular requirements for the safety of electrically operated hospital beds". **Note:** there is a proposed new standard, IEC 60601-2-52 "Particular requirements for the basic safety and essential performance of medical beds." Compliance with all these standards affords a sense of security against risk. However, it does not absolve the responsibility to satisfy oneself that the equipment is safe for the intended use. The compatibility of different equipment types must always be considered to ensure that they do not introduce new risks. Adverse incidents involving medical devices and lack of instructions should be reported to the Medicines and Healthcare products Regulatory Agency (MHRA) via the online reporting system at www.mhra.gov.uk (MHRA 2006).

Other legislation and standards

While the Reporting of Injuries, Diseases and Dangerous Occurrences Regulations 1995 (RIDDOR) (HSE 1995) do not specifically relate to equipment or manual handling, being generic to all major injuries, dangerous occurrences and diseases at work, they do require the reporting of:
- over three day injuries
- major injuries that include fracture other than to fingers, thumbs or toes amputation, dislocation of the shoulder, hip, knee or spine
- dangerous occurrences that include collapse, overturning or failure of load bearing parts of lifts and lifting equipment
- diseases, including certain musculoskeletal disorders and upper limb disorders related to manual handling.

Reporting accidents and ill health at work is a legal requirement. The information enables the Health and Safety Executive (HSE) and local authorities to identify where and how risks arise, and to investigate serious accidents. Where incidents involving equipment occur, these should also be reported to the MHRA.

Human rights and dignity

It is often too easy to ignore human rights as they are generally misunderstood due to the legal jargon used or a lack of understanding regarding the impact of not following them. Dignity in Care introduced a simple guide to help people understand the rights that everyone has and therefore ensure that everyone receives the appropriate standards of care that they deserve:

> "Human rights provide a legal framework for service providers to abide by and empower service users to demand that they are treated with dignity."
> Joint Committee on Human Rights

Every person in the UK will come into contact with health and social care services at some point in his/her life, usually when they are at their most vulnerable. Therefore, it is essential that we see human rights as an important consideration for the delivery of quality services. This includes the provision of suitable equipment that respects people's comfort, quality of care and dignity. The dignity that most people wish to enjoy is to maintain their privacy, to be treated equally and enjoy the same values as any human being. Care can be challenging for some disabled people – not being able to escape from conflict means that the disabled person is likely to be the one to build the bridges. Carers have the opportunity to walk out and slam the door, disabled people don't. Many disabled people feel

humbled and grateful for the help they receive. Some have to give up their homes and privacy and do not have a choice about the people they interact with.

Community equipment can help people of all ages and in every walk of life, including those with complex needs. The Social Care Institute for Excellence supports the Dignity Challenge, providing a range of information, including the Dignity Champions Action Pack, to assist in ensuring that organisations put human rights at the heart of the way services are designed and delivered. This can mean a better experience for everyone, with people and staff experiencing the core values of Fairness, Respect, Equality, Dignity and Autonomy (FREDA – Royal College of Psychiatrists 2010). See www.dignityincare.org.uk for further information on the dignity challenge.

Any equipment strategy should aim to ensure that its impact meets the needs of all staff and clients, and that it does not disadvantage any groups or individuals. Equality impact assessments (EIA) provide a systematic way to ensure legal obligations are met and are a practical way of examining new and existing processes to determine what effect they may have on equality for those affected by the outcomes. The duty to undertake an EIA is a legal requirement under race, gender and disability equality legislation. In order to ensure all groups receive equitable attention, the EIA should consider the core values of FREDA during its analysis. It needs to address other factors such as age, sexual orientation, religion and belief and human rights, all being cross referenced to socioeconomic and geographical (deprivation) factors. An illustration of this would be the provision of powered equipment within an Orthodox Jewish family where they would be expected to operate it on the Sabbath. The question regards the use of electricity and any requirement to adjust settings, which would go against Orthodox Jewish law (Steinberg & Rosner). While even the most stringent view may be more lenient in the case of urgent medical need, it may not be in the case of long term needs. In this situation, the provision or availability of hydraulic equipment may be more acceptable.

Enforcement agencies

The MHRA
The MHRA is the executive agency of the DH charged with protecting and promoting public health and client safety by ensuring that medicines, healthcare products and medical equipment meet appropriate standards of safety, quality, performance and effectiveness, and that they are used safely. They achieve this by investigating reports of adverse incidents involving medical devices and, where appropriate, instigating corrective actions to reduce the risk of recurrence. The Adverse Incident Centre (AIC) is the MHRA's focal point for the reporting of adverse incidents involving medical devices. Where the result of investigations of those incident reports (or any other information received) has implications for clients or users, the agency will issue a Medical Device Alert (MDA) advising of hazardous products, potential safety issues or unsafe procedures. Equipment procedures should have systems in place which ensure that any such alert can be addressed and all equipment provided can be traced and dealt with according to the recommendations within the alert. Purchasers should also be familiar with any alerts relating to equipment to ensure that any remedial actions taken by the manufacturer have been implemented.

CQC

From 1 October 2010, all health and adult social care providers are legally responsible for making sure they meet essential standards of quality and safety and must be licensed with the CQC. The CQC is the independent regulator of health and social care in England and will register care services only if they meet essential standards that will be monitored. The essential standards of quality and safety consist of 28 regulations (and associated outcomes) that are set out in two pieces of legislation:

● the Health and Social Care Act 2008 (Regulated Activities) Regulations 2010, and
● the Care Quality Commission (Registration) Regulations 2009.

For each regulation, there is an associated outcome – the experiences the CQC expects people to have as a result of the care they receive. Compliance with the essential standards will be based on the 16 regulations (out of the 28) that come within Part 4 of the Health and Social Care Act 2008 (Regulated Activities) Regulations 2010 – these are those that most directly relate to the quality and safety of care. Providers must have evidence that they meet the outcomes.

TABLE 7.1 KEY REGULATIONS OF PART 4 IN RELATION TO EQUIPMENT OUTCOMES

Regulation	Outcome	Title and summary of outcome
9	4	**Care and welfare of people who use services** People experience effective, safe and appropriate care, treatment and support that meet their needs and protect their rights.
16	11	**Safety, availability and suitability of equipment** Where equipment is used, it is safe, available, comfortable and suitable for people's needs.
21	12	**Requirements relating to workers** People are kept safe and their health and welfare needs are met by staff who are fit for the job and have the right qualifications, skills and experience. Note, this will include training on the use of any medical device/equipment that they use.
23	14	**Supporting workers** People are kept safe and their health and welfare needs are met because staff are competent to carry out their work and are properly trained, supervised and appraised.
24	6	**Cooperating with other providers** People receive safe and coordinated care when they move between providers or receive care from more than one provider.

In addition to registration and enforcement, the CQC will monitor achievement against the Government's *Putting People First* transformation plan (DH 2010). The plan's aim is that people will be able to live their own lives as they wish, confident that services are of high quality, are safe and promote their own individual needs for independence, wellbeing and dignity.

The Government says "personalisation is the process by which services are tailored to the needs and preferences of citizens" and its vision is:

> "the state should empower citizens to shape their own lives and the services they receive. This vision should apply equally to anyone using care and support, whether services are arranged and paid for by the local authority or the individual arranges and funds their own support independently".

To meet this plan, the DH, Association of Directors of Adult Social Services (ADASS) and the Local Government Association (LGA) have established a set of "personalisation milestones" to be achieved by 2011. The CQC will be able to question councils on their progress against these milestones to establish an overall picture of how well the local area is working together in partnership to embrace and implement the personalisation and modernisation of services.

The CQC has claimed that its approach to registration and regulation is well aligned with the reform agenda outlined in *Putting People First* (DH 2010). It plans to continue to encourage and expect councils to perform and deliver on improving the following, for all their local citizens, not just those who are deemed eligible for state arranged and funded services:

● prevention and early intervention
● choice and control
● social capital/"co-production" (redefining the relationship between service professionals and people using services as one of mutuality and collaboration rather than one of dependency).

Key deliverables under the *Putting People First* transformation plan by April 2011 related to equipment strategies include:

● an expectation that 30 per cent of eligible service users/carers have a personal budget (linked to CQC outcome 4, giving increased choice and control)
● evidence that cashable savings have been released as a result of the preventative strategies and that overall social care has delivered a minimum of three per cent cashable savings (linked to outcome 1, improved health and wellbeing).

The CQC, in its evaluation of regulated providers in regards to an equipment strategy, will be looking for support plans and interventions that show evidence of reduced reliance on formal services and wide use of supported accommodation, assistive technology and equipment. Qualitative evidence will include evidence of achieving independence through rehabilitation and/or intermediate care.

NHS Litigation Authority (NHSLA)

As part of the regulatory and governance arrangements under the NHS, joint CES as well as NHS Trusts are also subject to the NHSLA risk pooling schemes. Under these arrangements, organisations are required to measure, monitor and evaluate compliance with the minimum requirements within the NHSLA risk management standards. The NHSLA states:

> "monitoring demonstrates whether or not the process for managing risk, as described in the approved documentation, is working across the entire organisation. Where failings have been identified,

action plans must have been drawn up and changes made to reduce the risks. Monitoring is normally proactive – designed to highlight issues before an incident occurs – and should consider both positive and negative aspects of a process".

The system of internal control is underpinned by compliance with the requirements of the Standards for Better Health which form the basis of the organisation's objectives along with relevant CQC objectives. There are currently five standards, each with 10 criteria, giving a total of 50 to be met.

TABLE 7.2 KEY NHSLA RISK MANAGEMENT STANDARDS RELATING TO EQUIPMENT

Standard	Criterion	Area	Minimum requirements
2	7	Medical devices training	The organisation has an approved documented process for ensuring all permanent staff are trained to use diagnostic and therapeutic equipment safely, appropriate to their role that is implemented and monitored
2	9	Moving and handing training	The organisation has an approved documented process for ensuring the delivery of effective moving and handling training to all permanent staff. This is implemented and monitored
3	4	Moving and handling	The organisation has an approved documented process for managing risks associated with moving and handling that is implemented and monitored
3	7	Maintenance of medical devices and equipment	The organisation has an approved documented process for managing the risks associated with the maintenance of reusable medical devices and equipment that is implemented and monitored

The NHSLA assessment requires organisations to work towards and achieve three levels. Level 1 concerns having the key documents and processes outlined, while levels 2 and 3 review the monitoring and implementation of the processes. Attainment of these levels affords the organisation a reduction in their contribution to the risk pooling scheme of 10, 20, or 30 per cent for each level achieved. For large, acute teaching hospitals whose contributions are several £millions, the financial benefit of achievement of level 3 can be very high. The driving forces, when considering an equipment strategy that aims to meet the NHSLA criteria, are:
● approval of a manual handling policy
● compliance by relevant organisations
● achievement of manual handling standards.

Under standard 1, criterion 1 of the NHSLA risk management standards, health and social care organisations are required to

have a risk management strategy in place. Part of this strategy is the creation of a risk register and is covered under standard 1, criterion 6. In relation to medical devices, the risk register must be kept updated, with written processes in place for monitoring and review in order to comply with MHRA device bulletin DB 2006(05) Managing Medical Devices.

The risk register clarifies the level of risk (consequences) against the chance of the risk occurring (likelihood), based on a 5 x 5 matrix, giving the risk a score ranging from 1 to 25. The higher the score, the more likely action is required to reduce the risk. Although the organisation's Board is responsible for monitoring the risk register, most risk registers are filtered so that the Board only ever views the high risks, eg those scoring 15 or more.

Decontamination of equipment

Staff and persons must be protected against infection by removing pathogenic micro-organisms from potential sources of infection. This can be accomplished by the decontamination of materials, equipment and surfaces. Putting safe systems in place to manage the decontamination of equipment will contribute to meeting the requirements of the Health Act 2009, Hygiene Code and infection control standards. Decontamination should be carried out in accordance with the equipment manufacturer's instructions. If there is no reprocessing information provided with the product, then advice should be available from the manufacturer. If the manufacturer is unable to provide decontamination information, or if it is believed to be inadequate, the MHRA should be notified as all reusable medical devices placed on the UK market after June 1998 must be provided with reprocessing instructions.

Decontamination is a general term used to describe a series of processes to remove or destroy contamination so that infectious agents and other contaminates cannot reach a susceptible site in sufficient quantities to start infection or any other harmful response. The term decontamination includes sterilisation, disinfection and cleaning. Cleaning is an essential prerequisite for disinfection. In some cases, cleaning alone may be sufficient. Although mechanical methods of cleaning are generally preferred, some moving and handling equipment cannot be decontaminated using a mechanical washer disinfector. If, after cleaning, it is necessary to disinfect the item, the chosen method of disinfection must be compatible with the equipment.

All equipment/devices are either "single person use" or reusable. Devices designated for single person use must not be reused under any circumstances as their reuse has legal implications and can affect the safety, performance and effectiveness of the device and expose people and staff to unnecessary risk.

All reusable equipment must be decontaminated before use and between each person's use. Note that any medical or laboratory equipment requiring inspection, service or repair, either inhouse or by a manufacturer/contractor, should be decontaminated to prevent transmission of infection. MHRA DB 2006(05) requires that such equipment should be accompanied by a certificate/statement, which identifies that decontamination has occurred.

Which level and when – decontamination level intended use

TABLE 7.3

Application of item	Area (examples)	Recommendation
Low risk		
• In contact with healthy skin • Not in contact with patient	Mattresses and beds Hoist	Cleaning and drying after PAT test
Medium risk		
• Contaminated with particularly virulent or readily transmissible organism • Heavily contaminated with micro-organisms or blood/body fluids • Before use on immuno-compromised patients	Slide sheets Pressure relief dynamic mattresses	Cleaning followed by sterilisation or disinfection NB: Where sterilisation will damage equipment, cleaning followed by high level disinfection may be an alternative
High risk		
• In close contact with broken skin or broken mucous membrane • Introduced into sterile body area	Surgical instruments	Cleaning followed by sterilisation

When handling used medical devices or equipment staff should assume that it is contaminated and take precautions to reduce the risk to themselves and others. The use of personal protective equipment/clothing should be considered. For a simple guide to personnel protective equipment, go to www.hse.gov.uk/pubns/indg174.pdf

Medical devices/equipment should be decontaminated and stored in accordance with legislative, manufacturers' instructions and best practice requirements. Where appropriate, decontamination should always be carried out in dedicated facilities, eg:
• Community equipment loan stores – dedicated decontamination facility.
• Hospital equipment – on wards for routine cleaning or through either the electrobiomedical engineering or estates department as part of a central equipment library for larger items. Items such as slide sheets go through the laundry process or, as in many hospitals, disposable slide sheets are used for single patients.

Whatever the arrangements, there should be a local policy for the management and transport of medical equipment from the point of use to the decontamination facility. Decontamination requirements should be considered before reusable medical devices and equipment are acquired to ensure they are compatible with the decontamination equipment and process available.

Local protocols for decontamination activities should be written after advice from the following:
• manufacturer of the medical device
• manufacturer of equipment used for decontamination/reprocessing

• infection control staff
• sterile services manager
• consultant microbiologist or consultant in communicable disease control or a public health doctor
• risk assessment officer
• device and equipment users
• advice from appropriate government bodies such as the MHRA and NHS Estates
• advice from appropriate professional bodies such as the Institute of Decontamination Sciences, Infection Control Nurses Association, Hospital Infection Society, National Association of Equipment Providers.

Purchasing decisions have implications throughout the decontamination process and consideration should be given to how equipment will be decontaminated. Any new decontamination equipment must be suitable for the equipment or instruments to be processed.

Training and instruction in relation to medical devices

All organisations must provide adequate arrangements for training in the safe use of medical devices. This also includes agencies providing staff to the care sector. Employers are responsible for ensuring that staff that use medical devices have appropriate training. Equally, all healthcare professionals and support workers have a personal responsibility and accountability to ensure that they are trained in the safe use of the medical devices they need to use (MHRA 2008). The manufacturer is responsible for supplying appropriate instructions, taking into account the knowledge and training of the intended user.

It is recognised by health and social care providers that employers have a duty to ensure that workers using manual handling equipment are given instruction, training and supervision in its use. The duty means that organisations should work together with other employers to provide training where both health and social services, staff are using the same equipment in a person's home or situations where equipment is used by agency care assistants.

Monitoring and enforcement of training is covered by the NHSLA risk management standard 2, criterion 7: Medical Devices Training. It requires that the organisation has approved documentation which describes the process for ensuring that all permanent staff are trained to use diagnostic and therapeutic equipment safely, appropriate to their role. As a minimum, the approved documentation must include a description of the:
• duties
• inventory (or links to an inventory) of diagnostic and therapeutic equipment used within the organisation
• process for identifying which permanent staff are authorised to use the equipment identified on the inventory
• process for determining the training required to use the equipment identified on the inventory and the frequency of updates required
• process for ensuring that the identified training needs of all permanent staff are met
• process for monitoring compliance with all of the above.

MHRA DB 2006(05) states:

> "Training is a key element in medical devices safety. A training policy should be developed by the medical devices management group or equivalent".

Note: Interactive training on the general principles of using medical devices and equipment safety is also available on the MHRA website.

The MHRA stipulates that before a medical device is issued to a person or carer he/she should receive training in how to use the device. This should be supported by written guidance. The manufacturer's instructions should provide some information but this should be tailored to the needs of the individual or carer.

Written guidance should cover the following:
- the name of the device
- the operation and control of the device
- checking of the device while in use
- recognition of a device failure or fault
- action to be taken in the event of a device failure or fault
- individuals to be contacted in an emergency
- specific training for particular devices
- decontamination procedures.

The overall aim of medical device and equipment training is to provide the user of the device with the skills to utilise it safely within their clinical setting, encompassing the practical knowledge and the theory of its functions. It is the responsibility of the ward/unit/team manager to ensure that their area has an up to date inventory of the equipment and devices used within that area. This inventory should be reviewed regularly to ensure it is up to date.

There is a plethora of legislation and quality standards that need to be met. Equipment strategies need to take account of these requirements, ensuring that evidence of compliance can be demonstrated. Key systems and processes for the management, decontamination, tracking, recording and monitoring the use of medical devices are essential parts of this compliance. This includes appropriate levels of training for staff, carers and end users.

Equipment funding considerations

It is clear that the provision of equipment and its funding varies between the different care sectors. In some cases, capital funding is used for generic items or one off bids to support the reduction of risk, and where ongoing needs are not required. The capital is used for the direct purchase. However, maintenance, repair and any consumables would come out of revenue budgets. These are set on an annual basis. CES tend to replace equipment throughout the year and will set an annual revenue budget that would be used for both the procurement and maintenance of equipment. Their budget includes the recycling of more costly equipment when it is no longer required, eg hoists, turning aides, commodes, riser recliner chairs and profiling beds. The third source of funding is through the drive to personal budgets, self directed care or self funding by the individual. All these require a more strategic approach to procurement and management as ever increasing demands are made on budgets.

To optimise value for money, increase purchasing power and economies of scale, several factors must be considered with any longer term strategy. These are:
- VAT requirements
- sustainability
- maintenance costs
- likelihood of breakdown
- consumables
- volume commitment and demand
- standardisation.

The NHS Plan emphasises the importance of closer working between local authorities and the NHS to deliver a range of services, including CES for older and disabled people. These new approaches to partnership working between local authorities, social care and the NHS have established local partnerships which can be structured in a number of ways. They are intended to ensure that services are not duplicated and are delivered in the most efficient and cost effective way.

As a result of the changes, Customs and Excise and the DH provide guidance on the VAT position of the different partnership arrangements. The guidance produced applies specifically to the VAT arrangements for joint NHS/local authority partnership arrangements. It includes within its scope the operation and management of joint stores, including the maintenance and repair of goods, and other shared supplies of services and goods. It is not intended to be used to avoid tax and executive letter (EL) (97)70, which outlaws tax avoidance within the NHS, continues to apply (HMRC 1999).

The VAT guidance is intended to support joint initiatives between the NHS and local authorities, allowing them to be entered into with a broadly neutral impact on VAT arrangements for all parties involved. VAT may apply to an item depending on how it is funded and by whom. Local authorities can reclaim from Customs and Excise most of the VAT they incur in performing their functions, whereas NHS bodies may reclaim VAT incurred on only certain contracted out services. Equipment for individual use may be VAT exempt and require the completion of a VAT exemption form at the time of procurement. Any equipment strategy should consider the most advantageous funding route to reduce, but not avoid, tax payments.

NHS supply chain

The NHS supply chain (formally Purchasing and Supply Agency) has developed a number of framework agreements for the procurement of both medical devices and services. These framework agreements can offer significant savings with some trusts having saved up to 30 per cent on some equipment prices with the average saving being about 12-14 per cent. The advantage being the volume breaks where a commitment to a larger volume affords greater discounts. Use of the framework agreements negate the need for each organisation to undertake an Official Journal of the European Union tender and contract process, saving both time and money.

In order to harness the purchasing power of the NHS, and ensure a strategic approach to the whole health economy, equipment procurement could be driven and coordinated either at regional (collaborative purchasing organisation) or sub regional level, where it is more effective to engage across clinical networks. This approach will enable moving and handling equipment to be standardised across a variety of networks, which will have strategic benefit. The approach will encompass the ability to standardise maintenance, reduce the risks associated with a myriad of equipment being procured and utilised across individual NHS bodies by potentially the same clinicians (therefore providing other efficiency gains), and enable a modern asset base to be developed and supported.

Services hosted by the local authority have the option to use the supply chain, but contracts and prices are often negotiated locally by the relevant council's dedicated or central procurement functions. Significant savings are achieved by this approach with product, costing and performance information shared between the local authorities, to facilitate benchmarking and value for money.

Funding streams for equipment are varied and analysis of all potential income lines needs to be undertaken in order to gain a clear picture of the true spend on equipment. Pooling of budgets may allow greater negotiation ability as more incentive for a supplier.

Making a business case

While a strategy is the overall direction of travel for equipment provision and general demands, individual business cases may be required to fulfil specific needs and gain approval for projects that undertake to evaluate the impact of equipment provision. In project management terminology, the business case is the "driver" of the project. Senior management review the business case before authorising the initiation and at each subsequent stage of the project. The business case is used as a yardstick to measure project progress. Before allowing any change to the project plan, the executive must consider the impact that this change will have on the business case. In other words, without a business case, no project would ever get off the ground. The business case justifies the investment of time, money and resources into a project by outlining the benefits that the project will bring. The principles of defining a business case are similar to that of a strategy as analysis of the current and future provision is required in both.

Understanding equipment needs

Capital budgets are generally decreasing in size despite a greater demand for funding. Equipment strategies need to be creative in how equipment is funded with the potential to use revenue more wisely.

Given the potential funding restraints, regardless of sector, the equipment needs of the population must be considered. An effective equipment strategy for moving and handling outlined to meet these needs must be considered. A range of information is required to help define the framework for the strategy. It has been shown that any strategy should include the potential impact on health needs, quality of care, client enablement, reduction in staff injury and compliance to legal and quality standards. When addressing the wider community, public health statistics can be useful to identify health trends and population groups, eg those with a disability, those who may fall within the category of clinically obese, those over 85 and the likely population over 85 years old within the next five years. These general demographic statistics should be put in context with the hospital information on admissions, average length of stay and performance indicators, eg infection rates, to ensure accurate budget forecasting.

In addition to these background statistics, analysis of service provision will help define more relevant numbers. For example, an audit of the number of patients who require hoisting and their location within a hospital, will give a general picture of the level of patient dependency, and allow for an estimation of the number of hoists required as well as associated equipment needs such as slide sheets. This would be useful if using disposable hoist slings, excluding those used for bathing, as, calculated with the admission rate and average length of stay, the organisation will be able to estimate the number of slings required per annum and negotiate a contract against this demand.

There are no consistent approaches to formal written risk assessment forms which help analyse equipment demand. However, the Royal College of Nursing has published a document *Working Well initiative – Manual Handling Assessments in Hospitals and the Community* (RCN 2003) that has an example risk assessment form that can be adapted for all types of manual handling equipment. In addition, there are self assessment audit tools available from some equipment suppliers that will help establish this data. The tools are designed to assist in the collection of a fast, clear, efficient and reliable overview of the present situation within the care environment in two specific areas: the physical care load and the prevention policy in the unit. The tools will also indicate if there are areas where quality of care can be improved (www.carethermometer.com).

CES should be able to evaluate demand for moving and handling equipment based on the number of referrals, the type of equipment requests, any waiting list and range of equipment required. Evaluation and audit of current service provision and available equipment is required to allow planning for future demand. The audit should cover areas such as average time of use, reassessment process to capture where equipment is no longer required, volume of equipment returns and recycling. The provision of equipment from CES is based on risk assessment, which should be predictable given the caseload of community nursing services, referrals through social services and the number of long term cases. The key to the equipment strategy for a community equipment service is meeting supply and demand. The equipment strategy should address factors that influence this, eg establishing a process for re-assessment of need often increases the return of equipment, thereby lowering the demand for new equipment.

Standardisation and on costs

The standardisation of equipment used for moving and handling, although limiting end user choice, does allow greater opportunity for volume savings. Commitment or call off order agreements for an expected level of expenditure, covering a supplier's complete and comprehensive range where possible, may be an alternative way to achieving the saving and maintain end user choice. Consideration should, therefore, be given to packaging a range of products from one supplier because, as with any commercial organisation, a commitment to volume or spend will allow the opportunity to provide greater incentives. The changing market and acquisition/merging of companies may be an additional opportunity for greater savings for many organisations.

Any equipment strategy or one off business case for procurement should consider not only the initial purchase but also the sustainability, ongoing maintenance, replacement, service and consumable costs. The cost of spares often far outweighs the original purchase price and consideration should, therefore, be given to the volume and cost of spares during the lifetime of the product, eg if an actuator for a hoist or bed on one product is likely to last five years, opposed to the expected 10 year life of the hoist or bed, then the cost of the replacement actuator should be considered in the decision process. In some instances, these costs could be several hundred pounds. The ability to replace parts while the product remains in the care environment can reduce costs considerably, as opposed to those products that require removal from the area which increases down time, unavailability of the product, a substitution product, decontamination and logistic costs.

Equipment that relies on batteries or other regular replaceable spares will require these to be replaced periodically during the product's lifetime. The equipment strategy should consider these costs, the process for ordering/supply and how or who will fit these parts. The establishment of call off orders that cover the annual/predicted demand for consumables can lower costs opposed to individual orders that may be charged at a higher price as seen as a standalone volume. In addition, individual orders increase the administrative burden for both procurement team and finance, each incurring unnecessary cost.

Sustainability

There are now legislative and regulatory requirements for the NHS to reduce both carbon emissions and adapt to climate change. There are also significant financial, health, reputation and environmental reasons for the NHS to become a low carbon, sustainable organisation. Accounting for sustainability – that is, measuring, reporting and managing the social and environmental impacts of doing business is, therefore, a growing agenda within the healthcare arena.

The Foundation Trust Network suggests that

"Accounting for sustainability is essential, not only to meet changing regulatory priorities and the demands of local communities but also to understand and realise financial, reputation and public health gains. It is likely that those healthcare organisations that react strategically to the agenda [of sustainability] will excel as financial and environmental pressures become more acute. Those that react more tactically and do not respond with sufficient vigour will be likely to find themselves struggling to deliver the same high quality of care that they do today with fewer resources" (making sustainability add up – NHS Confederation 2010).

It is evident that service delivery, financial considerations and patient demand will drive sustainability. Sustainability should not, therefore, be pursued as an end in itself but used to deliver the core organisational mission and to connect better with consumers. The prevailing view in the private sector is that

"wherever environmental, social or ethical issues can be addressed, businesses have an opportunity to

innovate, create value and attract more customers" (PricewaterhouseCoopers 2008).

This creates an opportunity for healthcare providers to become innovative and more environmentally engaged during the development of their equipment strategy. The price of waste, water, energy and reputation risks may be seen as potentially crippling threats to an organisation. These factors must be considered as regards equipment provision. The costs may not only be the energy that the equipment uses, but the carbon footprint involved in the logistics of maintenance, servicing and the need to replace spare parts. The higher quality products will inevitably reduce these burdens. In considering equipment options, although carbon will not directly compete with cost or quality, it will help differentiate from two similar products. It is a key deliverable within the life time cost analysis for products and service delivery.

Selection criteria

The selection of moving and handling equipment should always be based on meeting clinical need, enablement, quality of care, effectiveness and ease of use. It should be selected on the grounds of the greatest benefit to the greatest number. While small aids such as slide sheets are simplistic in their design, the provision of handles may make them easier to use and, therefore, more effective. However, more complex equipment such as hoists, slings, standing and raising aids or profiling beds should be considered on the impact they have on the person and his/her clinical ability to use the equipment safely.

A secondary but equally important factor should be contingency planning, especially when dealing with vulnerable people. Powered equipment, for example, is not ideal in areas that are prone to power cuts. The system for addressing breakdowns should ensure that staff and persons have alternative provision or systems of work so that care is not compromised and there is no unnecessary increase in risk. A lot of service providers now work on the basis of equipment swap out rather than repair *in situ* as this is easier to manage. It optimises the technicians' time on repair, opposed to logistics and waiting for parts. The disadvantage is the requirement for additional equipment stocks. Manufacturers tend to accept a failure rate of one to five per cent for medical devices, which means a pool of 100 hoists would require an additional five hoists to cover downtime and associated costs of repair and logistics. It is understood that the automotive industry accepts failure rates of only three parts per million (0.0003 per cent), implying that products such as windscreen wiper motors and powered seats are, theoretically, 1,000 times less likely to break down than, say, an actuator on a profiling bed.

Key stakeholders

When undertaking a business case, project or development of an equipment strategy, it is essential that key stakeholders are involved. The nature of the case will dictate who is required and, therefore, this is not an exhaustive list but one that highlights key players.

If the strategy is ever going to be agreed by the organisation, healthcare trust or social services, it will need a board member sponsor. The board member is essential to be able to present the case addressing any potential objectives. Where the case is repacking the use of existing funding, it is often more advantageous to have the finance director as the sponsor. Quality arguments tend to be led by the clinical or nursing director, while operational efficiency is better supported by the operations director or equivalent.

The caveat to this is that services are set up differently. The clinician with a business case would do well to do his/her homework in relation to his/her particular service, ie finding out what the ideal process is through their line managers, where and who the influencers and decision makers are. There is a variety of funding approval approaches, eg some services have Boards, some have clinical evaluation groups, others have single individuals with clearly delegated budget responsibility.

During the development of the business case or strategy, all key players that may be affected by the proposal or its implementation should be consulted. As such, key members of any working party should include:
- clinical specialists including manual handling, tissue viability, infection control, specialist services, ie continence team and therapists such as occupational and physiotherapists
- clinical managers or hospital matrons
- CES manager
- logistics or portering manager
- estates and/or electromechanical engineering department representation
- driver/fitter
- decontamination operator
- purchasing department and finance representation
- end users, including their representatives.

Once the key stakeholder group is established, the aims and objectives will need to be set.

Business case key elements

Deliverables within a strategy are more generic and aspirational, whereas the business case is more detailed and focused on achieving the identified objectives. The requirement to undertake a business case is more common and discussed further. The business case is made up of key sections depending on the organisation's template but in general should include:

Executive summary

The executive summary is a short, sharp, focused summary of the key elements of the business case. It should provide the reader with a high level overview of vision, headline objective and cover the strategic context of the case. This section should link to the detail within the later sections of the business case.

Reasons

This section of the business case should detail the case for change. The reasons you give must conform to corporate strategy or objectives, linking into key drivers such as compliance with legislation, sustainability, reduction of risk or improving client care. It should lay out the problems that are associated with the identified need and what issues it aims to address. An analysis of existing provision should be included and where improvements can be made these should be highlighted. In developing an understanding of the problem and needs, ensure that any stakeholders are consulted so that

their issues, where possible, may be included. Existing good practice should always be highlighted. Where the provision of equipment addresses an existing risk on the risk register, this must be included.

The needs analysis should be realistic and include the option of milestones, as the provision may not always be able to be achieved in one go. Where provision is phased, alternative measures, such as sharing equipment between two departments or establishing a waiting list, should be incorporated.

Future service requirements

The analysis of service demand, population and any anticipated changes should highlight the impact these changes will have on any options, eg the joint provision of a community equipment service can enhance purchasing power, simplify administration of requests for equipment, improve logistics and potentially increase choice of equipment as more may be held in stock. The outsourcing of logistics, maintenance and decontamination may reduce downtime and the requirement for back-up equipment or the holding of spares. Where a new service, such as introducing bariatric surgery, is likely, the increased demand on specialist equipment must be considered.

External policy and initiatives such as the personalisation agenda, direct payments and self directed care should be considered for the opportunities they bring.

Options

There are always a range of options to be considered. Although it might not appear an option, the "do nothing" option must always be considered. Showing that all the possibilities have seriously been considered will strengthen any business case. The options should provide senior management with all the available information so it can make an informed decision. Canvassing stakeholders can assist in defining options.

Costs

Senior managers need to know the total projected cost before they can authorise the project or approve a strategy. Each area of expenditure should be justified so that nobody is in any doubt that the budget forecast is as accurate as possible.

Reforming the way that moving and handling equipment is acquired, managed and maintained may require both local authority and NHS bodies to be prepared to adopt an innovative and flexible approach to financing, backed by an understanding of the equipment and asset base, long term plans, the range of products and services available and the associated risks and opportunities, including options for effective management of any resulting contracts.

The options for funding must include the requirement for any capital investment and the ongoing dependence on revenue budgets, eg equipment purchase may be from capital but the maintenance and consumables would, in following years, be met from revenue. Existing revenue budgets should be identified. This may be more difficult where combining services or where the options impact on a number of providers who each would be expected to contribute. Existing funding streams may include capital procurement programmes, rental costs, maintenance and service costs, spare parts, staff costs and decontamination. In discussing the costs, it is vital that all funding and any potential hidden costs are identified. Savings which are realistic and achievable should be included. These include those achieved as part of the sustainability agenda.

To demonstrate value for money, and the impact over the term of the moving and handling equipment strategy, costs will need to be projected. In finance terms, the net present value (NPV) is the difference between the present value of cash inflows and the present value of cash outflows. NPV is used in capital budgeting to analyse the profitability of an investment or project, being the standard method for using the time value of money to appraise long term projects. This will include the NHS requirement for a payment or return on capital invested against any capital that is provided by the government.

The publication of the Private Finance Act in 1993 meant NHS bodies could explore alternative finance routes, including leasing. Proposals should consider the use of leasing for large capital intensive requirements. Leasing utilises revenue streams to fund equipment provision over a number of years. The lease provides the capital for the equipment purchase, which is then paid back over the term of the lease with interest. There is, however, a need to understand that opting for leasing solely for the reason of lack of available capital funding may not represent best value for money to the NHS. Lease funding should be a positive decision, based on value for money when fully appraised against other funding routes.

The moving and handling equipment strategy should consider which assets lend themselves to leasing. These are usually those that are hi-tech or likely to benefit from earlier replacement than the working life may suggest. The NHS supply chain framework agreement has now been launched and is available for use by all NHS bodies and third party lease advisors (where operating as agents on behalf of an NHS body). The framework agreement includes 15 leasors, details of which are available on the NHS supply chain website. Using the framework assists both the NHS and industry to procure leases more effectively and cost efficiently and to reduce risk.

The choice of equipment should also consider the ongoing costs for consumables, breakdown and downtime. These should be calculated for the life expectancy of the products so that future impacts on budgets can be established and forecast.

This is crucial when considering two options that may achieve the same outcome. As an illustration (see Table 7.4), the provision of disposable hoist slings (excluding bathing) versus normal slings requiring decontamination after person use can have significant cost implications. This assumes onsite laundry facilities or a contracted provider for decontamination are available. The illustration is based on a 1,000 bed acute hospital for a five year programme and the costs are for illustrative purposes only.

TABLE 7.4 STANDARD SLING VERSUS DISPOSABLE SLING COST ANALYSIS

Issue	Assumption	Quantity	Cost per unit	Standard slings	Disposable sling
Investment in slings	20 per cent of in-patient population requires hoisting at any time	200	£220	£44,000 capital	–
Downtime	Laundry turnaround 10 days	300	£220	£66,000 capital	
Requirement: disposable sling	Two slings per patient during their stay	400	£12		£4,800 revenue
Loss/damage of slings in laundry	Estimated 10 per cent loss	50	£220	£11,000 revenue	
Replacement disposable slings	Average length of stay 10 days thereby 35 new admissions per bed per year	200 x 35 x 2 slings per client stay	£12		£168,000 revenue
Decontamination		200 x 35 x 2 slings per client stay	£3.50	£49,000 revenue	
Year 1 cost				£159,000	£168,000
Year 2 cost				£60,000	£168,000
Year 3 cost				£60,000	£168,000
Year 4 cost	Average life expectancy of sling, three years requiring replacement			£159,000	£168,000
Year 5 cost				£60,000	£168,000
TOTAL COST				£498,000	£840,000

Costs are for illustration only

Capital investment for sling option is £110,000 every three years. Revenue per annum £60,000. Over the five year term, disposable slings would cost an additional £342,000. The illustration takes into account the general statistic of average length of stay and more detailed analysis of the number of clients needing hoisting and the laundry capacity. The sustainability cost savings of decreased manufacturing, delivery and waste would make the case to launder normal slings even more advantageous.

The preferred option

The preferred option should be described in detail, evaluated against the alternative options. The preferred option should be the best choice that maximises the benefits, meets the objectives and enhances efficiency. It may not be the lowest cost, as other deliverables may be more important than purely cost.

Benefits

The benefits section should persuade the target audience that the proposal is worthwhile. Every possible benefit, tangible and intangible, should be considered and justified. If the proposal will increase income or deliver cost savings, then the figures should be presented in detail as evidence. If the primary benefit is improved person care, staff safety or operational efficiency, then how this will be achieved and what the effects will be should be outlined.

The benefits should demonstrate how the proposal/equipment strategy will be achieved and meet the primary objectives outlined in the case. Key drivers for each of the decision makers should be included as understanding their priorities will assist in gaining their commitment.

Key deliverables of an effective equipment strategy or business case may include:
- enhanced image and public perception
- improved quality of care
- improved outcomes, independence or prevention of deterioration
- improved equipment utilisation
- addressing known risks recorded on the risk register
- improved resource management and control
- decreased annual expenditure
- decreased risk to staff and people
- meeting sustainability targets and savings.

Risks analysis and management

The business case must consider the main risks to success. Be frank. Transparency will gain the confidence of senior managers and will demonstrate a foresight, realism and capability to understand the issues.

Risks should cover the impact on stakeholders if the preferred option is not implemented. It should cover the remaining risk to people, staff, carers, organisational efficiency and financial impact. Where options are staged, remaining risks until full implementation should be considered, with possible interim measures to help reduce the risks.

Affordability and investment appraisal

The affordability and investment appraisal should consider the cost and benefits against each option in order to demonstrate once and for all that the proposed option is a worthwhile investment, eg see Table 7.4 as regards the option of standard canvas slings versus disposable slings. The investment appraisal, by detailing the costs and benefits over a fixed period of time, is the most direct way of quantifying value for money.

Here, the attention to detail pays dividends. Understanding the existing status and utilising all influencing factors gained from the initial option appraisal will ensure that all cost impacts have been considered.

The investment appraisal should aim to value the impact of the risk or benefits identified. A reduction of musculoskeletal injuries will save employment costs associated with sick leave, cover, management costs and the potential of a compensation claim. Low standards of decontamination will increase the likelihood of healthcare acquired infections, which are well costed as regards their subsequent treatment, investigation, service disruption and impact on reputation.

Looking at the hoist and sling options, a consideration would be the environmental impact of disposal of the slings. If the sling is classed as clinical waste, it would need to be burnt which is charged by weight. Equally, if not clinical, it would impact on landfill and may not meet external recycling or reduction of waste targets.

It may be difficult to establish the impact that a piece of equipment may have on reducing hospital length of stay, it may be easier to demonstrate equipment that helps prevent admission. However, the cost of delayed discharges is very high and reducing them is a priority for most acute trusts. Where equipment can assist with the facilitation of discharge, then it is often more effective to provide this, instead of the recurring cost and impact of keeping a person in hospital.

Another factor to be considered within the investment appraisal should be the impact on achieving the organisation's key performance or contractual indicators. The achievement of external registration, validation or demonstration of achievement, enhances reputations and the opportunity to be successful in bidding for new business.

Timescale and deliverability

It is important to detail the activities and goals of each stage, explaining why the specified length of time is needed. Elements that impact on the timescale or deliverability should be covered, especially where one element is dependent on the achievement of another.

If operational procedures are changing, consideration must be given to the roll out of these – how they will be communicated, the infrastructure to support them, such as printed referral forms, dedicated telephone numbers and whether a phased introduction is required.

The logistics, commissioning and labelling of new equipment should not be underestimated. If large volumes are being delivered at any one time, consideration should be given to the resources needed to ensure they are safe to use, appropriately tested and entered onto any tracking database. Storage arrangements for bulk purchases of very large items may need to be considered, or the option of staggered deliveries, although this may incur a higher cost.

Staff training and education to ensure competency on the use of the medical devices must be included. If providing new equipment that has never been used by the staff before, then training must be provided before its use. Replacement items or

TABLE 7.5 CRITICAL SUCCESS FACTORS FOR A BUSINESS CASE (ADAPTED FROM WOLVERHAMPTON CITY PRIMARY CARE TRUST, BUSINESS CASE GUIDANCE 2007)

Critical success factors	Potential pitfalls
Agreeing the structure for the business case or strategy early on, and populate it with accepted wisdom and existing knowledge where possible.	Writing the business case "by committee" with not enough central co-ordination.
Key stakeholder "buy in" (management, staff and external stakeholders) – making sure they understand the nature of the process and what the results will be, both for them and for the organisation.	Wasting time and effort by starting to perform detailed analyses before board direction is agreed.
Identifying underlying issues that are driving the need for the development of a strategic plan.	Failure to maintain consistency of assumptions throughout the document.
Identifying the key constraints to the execution of a new strategy (eg infrastructure or capabilities).	Failure to connect healthcare needs explicitly to volumes and activity.
Developing performance goals using the business case as a standard; measuring success at the different levels of the organisation.	Failure to connect volumes and activity to costs and capacity issues.
The business case should be developed to a strict timetable to minimise disruption to day to day business. However, do not assume the business case can be developed alongside everyday commitments.	Delays in engaging internal and external stakeholders in the planning process.
Base the business case or strategy on activity forecasts that are evidenced and that have been discussed with commissioners. Highlight differences where they exist and aim to address them.	Lack of challenge of assumptions.
Base the business case on fact and provide evidence that demonstrates the rationale behind the decisions and future course of action.	Lack of "out of the box" thinking.
Using appendices wherever possible to ensure a clear, concise structure is maintained.	No, or very limited, sensitivity analyses to test the robustness of the options.
Learn from others, site visits and references should be undertaken.	Assuming the plan can be introduced without critical appraisal of current ways of service provision.
Ensure robust and realistic specifications for equipment. Product trials should be controlled and fair.	Lack of discipline in structuring and writing the document, leading to long and wordy passages that very few can or will read.
Learn from suppliers. They have a wealth of experience and information and can help formulate ideas.	Lack of ownership of the plan on the part of those who will be trusted to deliver it.
	Lack of detailed analysis of existing activity data.
	Not "process mapping" the existing system when trying to redesign the service.

increasing the volume of existing equipment will not have such a training burden. Ongoing training or testing of competency needs to be considered as to how this can be achieved.

Evaluation

Consider any business case in an objective light. Analyse the strongest and surest benefits that have been promised, why they are necessary and the best way of achieving them.

Table 7.5 illustrates critical success factors and potential pitfalls. A critical success factor is a term for an element which is necessary for an organisation or plan to achieve its objective. It is not a key performance indicator. Critical success factors are elements that are vital for a strategy to be successful.

Monitoring

CES integration strategies allow for the combining of information technology resources to ensure robust asset management systems are in place. The importance for any service is for reporting on activity, recording provision against demand and key performances, tracking delivery, collection and usage. The system should be able to include monitoring of repairs, maintenance and parts used. A true asset inventory will also assist with planning purchasing based on demand and current age/condition of existing stock. The tracking of

equipment issued to users allows for a regular review to take place to check that it still meets the intended need and avoid harm. Good systems should be able to flag up equipment that has been used for set periods, eg hoists in use for six months so that reminders for maintenance and review can be generated. More complex tools allow for assessments to be completed and recommend equipment measured against clinical need. Recommendation is determined against the healthcare providers' clinical protocols helping to enforce their use.

Any service level agreement or contract with the providers of community equipment to health and social care must include the requirement to have information technology systems that meet the needs of the service to provide commissioners with regular reports. These reports may include, for example, purchasing/prescribing finance update, inventory information, clinical team activity, service and maintenance history, scrap costs, alerts and actions taken, items delivered, items collected, decontamination and complaints and compliments in health and social care to enable them to meet their duty of care.

Tendering

There are strict rules on tendering for the provision of equipment and services within public bodies. The financial standing instructions of the organisation set the first level of authorisation for expenditure. It depends on the value as to whether a number of quotations are required or where a full tender process needs to be undertaken. The European rules apply for the procurement of products valued at more than £101,000 unless procured from a framework agreement or as part of an existing tendered opportunity. The local procurement team will be able to advise and support any process, including the use of mini competition or a restrictive tender process that can simplify and decrease the time required for the process. The rules are complex and information on the UK public body tendering rules are available from www.ogc.gov.uk.

Where the strategy requires tendering, there are some elements that make the process easier and ensure that the end results meet the initial requirements. Remember that suppliers of medical devices are involved in tendering on a regular basis and can be a source of knowledge that can assist in the early stages. The important part is to ensure that any process is transparent and that all suppliers are given equal opportunities and information. The tender should start with a "wish list" which allows for a more detailed specification to be drawn up. It is worth testing the specification with some suppliers as it has been known for specifications to be issued that request product features that together never exist and there is no such product on the market. However, the specification also needs to be general enough so that it does not clearly favour any one company or product. On receipt of supplier submissions, they must be compared and scored against the specifications.

The key stakeholders should be involved in the evaluation of any procurement process. To ensure fairness, evaluation tools should be developed at the start of the process and ideally an indication given within the tender documents as to how the submissions will be evaluated and against what criteria, eg 50 per cent weighting clinical benefit, 20 per cent on product specification and 30 per cent on cost.

Conclusion

The legislation around moving and handling equipment when looked at is basic common sense that has helped us move forward, not only assisting with risk but also the drive for innovation in the supply field, and in the words of Michael Mandelstam (2002):

> "the regulations are a friend rather than an enemy insofar as they set out systematically a general simple framework for safe practice to which professionals can work. Thus, for those working in the field there is a dual incentive to improve safety; namely, the carrot of professional good practice, and the stick of potential legal liability for failure to do so".

Equipment strategies should embrace the requirements of the legislation, using them to assist in ensuring appropriate resources are available to meet the needs of the population. Understanding the needs, potential funding routes and the principles outlined within a structured business case will help to present the argument and secure the additional equipment resources, thereby reducing the risks to staff and informal carers and facilitating the "full and equal citizenship" of people in our society.

References

Audit Commission (2000), Fully equipped: the provision of equipment to older or disabled people by the NHS and social services in England and Wales.

Audit Commission (2002), www.audit-commission.gov.uk/ nationalstudies/health/socialcare/Pages/fullyequipped2002. aspx.

Care Quality Commission (Registration) Regulations (2009), www.cqc.org.uk/_db/_documents/Quick_guide_to_the_ essential_standards.doc.

DH (2006a), *Our health, our care, our say*.

DH (2006b), Transforming Community Equipment and Wheelchair Services (TCES) programme, www.csed.dh.gov. uk/TCES/.

DH (2007a), *Putting people first: a shared commitment to the transformation of adult social care*, www.cqc.org.uk/_db/_ documents/Putting_people_first_briefing[1].pdf.

DH (2007b), Independence, choice and risk.

DH (2008), *High quality care for all: NHS Next Stage Review*.

DH (2010), Prioritising need in the context of Putting People First: A whole system approach to eligibility for social care: guidance on Eligibility.

HMRC (1999), VAT arrangements for joint NHS/local authority initiatives including disability equipment stores and welfare – Health Act 1999 ("SECTION 31"), www.dh.gov.uk/en/Publicationsandstatistics/Publications/ PublicationsPolicyAndGuidance/DH_4076384.

HSE (1974), Health and Safety at Work etc Act 1974. London: HMSO, 1974, ISBN 0105437743.

HSE (1995), Reporting of Diseases and Dangerous Occurrences (RIDDOR) 1995, HMSO London.

HSE (1998), Lifting Operations and Lifting Equipment Regulations 1998, Statutory Instrument 1998 No. 2307, ISBN 0 11 079598 9, www.opsi.gov.uk/si/ si1998/19982307.htm.

HSE (1998), Provision and Use of Work Equipment Regulations 1998, Statutory Instrument 1998 No. 2306, ISBN 0 11 079599 7, www.opsi.gov.uk/SI/si1998/19982306.htm.

HSE (1999), Management of Health and Safety at Work Regulations 1999, Statutory Instrument 1999 No. 3242, ISBN 0 11 085625 2, www.opsi.gov.uk/SI/ si1999/19993242.htm.

HSE (2002), Handling home care: achieving safe, efficient and positive outcomes for care workers and clients.

HSE (2004), Manual handling. Manual Handling Operations Regulations 1992 (as amended). Guidance on Regulations L23, 3rd edition, HSE Books 2004. ISBN 0 7176 2823 X.

Health and Safety Executive (HSE), www.hse.gov.uk/.

Health Professions Council (2009), Continuing professional development and your registration.

HMSO (1993), Private Finance Act 1993.

HMSO (2008), Health and Social Care Act 2008 (Regulated Activities) Regulations 2010, Statutory Instrument 2010/781.

HMSO (2009), Health Act 2009.

Mandelstam, M (2002), Occupational Therapy Legislation and Law, OTdirect Occupational Therapy Study Guide: Moving and Handling, www.otdirect.co.uk/mov_law.html.

MHRA (2008), Medicines and Healthcare products Regulatory Agency, Devices in Practice: A guide for professionals – health and social care, www.mhra.gov.uk.

MHRA, Medical Device Alert MDA/2006/001 "Reporting adverse incidents and disseminating Medical Device Alerts". 2006, www.mhra.gov.uk.

MHRA DB 2006(05) Managing Medical Devices Nov 2006, www.mhra.gov.uk/Publications/Safetyguidance/DeviceBulletins/CON2025142.

NHS (2003), Health Service Circular Guidance on NHS Funded Nursing Care. 2003/006. LAC2003(7). 30.

NHS Confederation (2010), Foundation Trust Network. *Making sustainability add up*. www.nhsconfed.org/Publications/reports/Pages/Making-sustainability-add-up.aspx.

NHS Purchasing and Supply Agency.

NMC (2008), Nursing and Midwifery Council, The Code: Standards of Conduct, performance and ethics for nurses and midwives. www.nmc-uk.org/Nurses-and-midwives/The-code/The-code-in-full/

PricewaterhouseCoopers (2008), The Sustainability Agenda: Industry Perspectives, pp6.

Roach, MS (1992), The Human Act of Caring, Ottawa, Ontario: Canadian Hospital Association.

RCN (2003), Royal College of Nursing, *Working Well Initiative – Manual Handling Assessments in Hospitals and the Community*. www.rcn.org.uk/__data/assets/pdf_file/0008/78488/000605.pdf.

Royal College of Psychiatrists (2010), FREDA – a human rights-based approach to clinical practice, www.psychiatrycpd.co.uk/PDF/FREDA%20human%20rights-based%20approach%20to%20clinical%20practice_THN.pdf.

Scottish Government (2009), *Good Practice Guide for the Provision of Community Equipment Services*, www.scotland.gov.uk/Resource/Doc/924/0089816.doc.

Steinberg, A & Rosner, F. Encyclopaedia of Jewish medical ethics: a compilation of Jewish medical law. http://books.google.co.uk/books?id=aaklGZAID08C&pg=PA880&lpg=PA880&dq=medical+device+use+on+sabbath&source=bl&ots=MM84BOVVRu&sig=2YYw7XsQBZVviHlWCmw9mu6Xu2A&hl=en&ei=qaDWTMu2EZDH4AbJlcTuBw&sa=X&oi=book_result&ct=result&resnum=1&ved=0CBgQ6AEwAA#v=onepage&q=medical%20device%20use%20on%20sabbath&f=false.

Welsh Assembly Government (2005), *Designed for Life, creating world class health and social care for Wales in the 21st century*. www.wales.nhs.uk/documents/designed-for-life-e.pdf.

Wolverhampton City Primary Care Trust, Business case guidance 2007, www.wolverhamptonhealth.nhs.uk/Library/Documents/Corporate/BoardPapers_July2007/pecchairappen.pdf.

Health and wellbeing

Jacqui Smith MSc (Human Factors) MCSP Cert OH
Consultant occupational health physiotherapist, ergonomist and moving and handling practitioner

*Far and away the best prize that life has to offer is
the chance to work hard at work worth doing.*

(Theodore Roosevelt 1903)

Introduction

Historically, there has been a broad acceptance of a direct causal relationship between biomechanical workplace exposures, such as those involved in the moving and handling of human loads, and the prevalence of musculoskeletal disorders in general, and back pain in particular, in health and social care staff. More recently, there has been growing recognition of, and evidence base for, a range of additional risk factors that influence work related ill health, the development of work instability, the risk of chronicity and of work loss.

This chapter will consider the intrinsic and extrinsic factors that may influence the onset, experience and progression of work related ill health; present a conceptual model for understanding the complex relationships between work and health; explore the concepts of work instability and work disability; discuss government strategy in respect of health and wellbeing in the workplace; explore the roles of relevant stakeholders, including occupational health and safety professionals, back care practitioners and line managers, and present strategies focused on improving working lives and job retention relevant to large and small employers in the health, social care and wider sectors.

Definitions and prevalence

Work related

The term work related in the context of altered health status/disability and its impact on work ability has been defined by the World Health Organisation (WHO) as any mental or physical illness or disability that is caused, or made worse, by work and/or that impacts on work ability. More recently, the term work relevant (Burton 2008) has been put forward to describe this wider view that avoids any imputation of cause, since attribution of cause to occupational factors can be problematic. Both musculoskeletal disorders (MSDs) and common mental health problems are increasingly recognised as being multifactorial, with many contributing factors including both work and non work elements. Therefore, if performing any particular task/job leads to an individual experiencing symptoms that impact on work performance and potentially losing time from work as a consequence, then it could be argued that a reasonable employer might wish to implement measures aimed at least to avoid provoking symptoms, thereby supporting retention at work, regardless of aetiology.

The most common health problems that impact on work performance are shown in Table 8.1 below. At least six of these 10 have musculoskeletal components or associations.

TABLE 8.1 THE TOP 10 HEALTH PROBLEMS IMPACTING PRODUCTIVITY IN THE WORKPLACE

Fatigue	Arthritis
Depression	Hypertension
Back/neck pain	Obesity
Sleeping problems	High cholesterol
Other chronic pain	Anxiety

Musculoskeletal disorders

The term musculoskeletal disorder (MSD) is an umbrella label that is used to refer to a range of symptoms and/or medical conditions that affect the soft tissues (muscles, tendons, ligaments, discs, cartilage), bony structures, blood vessels, neural tissue and the skin. MSDs can be caused, contributed to, or made worse, by work, and commonly impact on work performance. The term disorder refers to the clinical effects arising from pathophysiological changes to the affected tissues, the most common being pain and limitation of function. Not all MSDs are work related, but associations between many types of MSDs and work tasks, or specific risk factors to which employees may be exposed when undertaking these tasks, have become established from epidemiological reviews, population surveys, workplace surveys, surveys of profession specific groups such as ultrasonographers, anecdotal reports, clinical case studies and reporting schemes for occupational diseases (see also chapter 4).

Up to 80 per cent of people are affected by an MSD at some time in their life. MSDs are the main reasons for work related consultations in general practice and account for about half of all work related disorders in EU countries, costing between 0.5 per cent and two per cent of GDP. MSDs account for almost 50 per cent of absences from work of three days or more and 60 per cent of permanent work incapacity.

In the NHS alone, MSDs account for around 40 per cent of sickness absence. In social care, handling injuries accounted for over a quarter of all reported injuries to employees in 2009/10 (HSE 2010).

Back pain

Back pain is a symptom not a diagnosis. It is the most common of all MSDs and most adults will experience an episode in their lifetime. In the UK, there is a lifetime prevalence of at least 60 per cent; about 40 per cent of all adults have back pain in a single year, and about 20 per cent have back pain at any one point in time (McKinnon et al 1997; Waxman et al 2000).

Recurrences, relapses and episodes are very common – these occur in over 60 per cent of those who have back pain (Van den Hoogen et al 1998; Linton et al 1998). Traditionally, it was thought that most people experienced brief and transient back pain and that only a minority (seven per cent) had chronic symptoms. Research now shows that 40 per cent of those who experience back pain will have symptoms that persist for several months (Linton et al 1998; Croft et al 1998; Waxman et al 2000).

Research also shows that the majority of people with back pain do not seek any treatment, but cope by themselves (McKinnon et al 1997; Waddell 1994). Evidence indicates that the back pain of individuals who seek care is no different from the back pain of those who do not in terms of severity, accompanying leg symptoms or disability (Croft et al 1998). Thus, these studies provide an interesting insight into the back pain experience that could be summed up as follows:

- back pain is a part of the human experience and should be regarded as normal, and common to the majority of adults
- episodes or recurrences are usual
- symptoms that persist for months are usual
- most individuals cope with back pain without seeking treatment.

It is in the best interest of the employee with back pain to continue with normal activity if possible, including work – and in the best long term interest of both employer and employee for the employer to facilitate retention at work or to promote an early return to work. Once someone goes off work with back pain, their chances of long term disability are:

- 1-10 per cent immediately
- 20 per cent after 4-6 weeks
- 50 per cent after 6 months.

Work related stress

Common mental health problems are the chief health problem of working age and, at any age, mental health problems may compound physical signs/symptoms/disorders and their impacts on performance and participation (see Fig 8.1). The prevalence of mental health conditions requiring treatment increased from 14.1 per cent of the adult population in 1993 to 16.4 per cent in 2007 (ONS survey 2008). Mental health problems were cited by 40 per cent of claimants for incapacity benefit in 2006, compared to 26 per cent in 1996.

HSE (2000) have defined work related stress as:

> "The adverse reaction people have to excessive pressures or other types of demand placed on them at work."

Stress is not an illness – it is a state. However, if stress becomes too excessive and prolonged, mental and even physical illness may ensue, leading to sickness absence, work loss and reduced participation in society.

The incidence of work related stress in recent years is a significant cause for concern, with the cost to British employers estimated at over £500 million per annum. Depression and anxiety are the leading causes of working days lost through injury or ill health. Each incidence of work related stress leads to an average of 30 days lost due to sickness absence.

Relationship between work and health: national strategy

Work is a social determinant of health, and worklessness[1] is a greater risk to health than many "killer" diseases (Black 2008).

---

1 Worklessness describes people of working age who are economically inactive, ie not working, not in full time education or training, not actively seeking work – and it can also include those who are out of work because of illness/disability.

People with long term health problems or disabilities are frequently excluded from work by discrimination, employer's inflexibility and preconceptions, lack of reasonable adjustments (Disability Discrimination Act (DDA) 1995) and other people's low expectations.

TABLE 8.2 FINANCIAL IMPLICATIONS OF WORKING AGE ILL HEALTH

Overall costs of working age ill health in the UK exceed £100 billion per year
Around 172 million working days were lost to sickness absence in 2007, at a cost to the economy of over £13 billion (CBI)
Two thirds of sickness absence and long term incapacity is due to mild and treatable conditions, often with inappropriate "medicalisation".

The Black review

Dame Carol Black, National Director for Health and Work, was commissioned in March 2007 by the then Secretaries of State for Health and for Work and Pensions to undertake a wide ranging review of the health of Britain's working age population. The purpose of this commission was to develop a baseline understanding of the health of working age people in the UK and the impact this has on the economy and society; and to make recommendations to government and wider stakeholders on how to improve the health of the working age population. For most people, their work is a key determinant of self worth, family esteem, identity and standing within the community as well as a means of material progress, social participation and fulfilment, all of which are factors contributing to quality of life. While the economic costs of ill health and its impact on work may be measurable, the human costs are often hidden and privately borne.

At the heart of the Black review (*Working for a healthier tomorrow*, 2008) was a recognition of, and a concern to remedy, the human, social and economic costs of impaired health and wellbeing in relation to working life in Britain. The aim was "to identify the factors that stand in the way of good health and to elicit interventions, including changes in attitudes, behaviours and practices – as well as services – that can help overcome them" (see Table 8.3).

TABLE 8.3 SUMMARY FINDINGS OF THE BLACK REVIEW

Patchy occupational health services access/provision
No national standards available to employers when they purchase occupational health and wellbeing services
Poor understanding of health and wellbeing initiatives by employers
Employers unaware of the business case for investing in health and wellbeing
Sickness absence policies that fail to facilitate early and sustained return to work
Often no policy on mental ill health issues in the workplace
Line managers' behaviour is influential to the quality of working lives. However, there is often little training
Accessible and affordable sources of support and advice are rarely available for small and medium sized companies (SMEs)
Employers inflexible about necessary adjustments for those with chronic disability.

In response to these findings, the Black review set out a vision based on three key principles:
1 prevention of illness and promotion of health and wellbeing
2 early intervention for those who develop a health condition at work
3 an improvement in the health of those not in work.

The review identified the importance of safe and healthy workplaces designed to protect and promote good health and the key role that such workplaces can play in preventing illness from arising in the first place.

The government's response to the Black review, (*Improving health and work: changing lives*) published in November 2008 expressed the desire to create a society where the positive links between work and health are recognised by all, where everyone aspires to a healthy and fulfilling working life, and where health conditions and disabilities are not a bar to enjoying the benefits of work. The seven key indicators identified in the response were:
- knowledge and perceptions about the importance of work to health and health to work
- improving the promotion of health and wellbeing at work
- reducing the incidence of work related ill health and injuries and their causes
- reducing the proportion of people out of work due to ill health
- improving the self reported health status of the working age population
- the experience of working age people in accessing appropriate and timely health service support; and
- improving business productivity and performance.

The Boorman review

An independent review of NHS health and wellbeing was commissioned by the Department of Health (DoH) and led by Dr Steven Boorman to investigate the health and wellbeing of NHS staff. His interim report identified a number of concerns in respect of the health and wellbeing services currently available to NHS staff:
- variations in service standards and specifications
- inconsistency in the range of, and access to, services
- inadequate resourcing
- lack of consultation with staff about the services.

The final report (Boorman 2009) and the response from the DoH were published in November 2009 and state that NHS organisations that prioritise staff health and wellbeing:
- achieve enhanced performance
- improve patient care
- are better at retaining staff
- have lower rates of sickness absence
- reduce agency staff costs
- improve productivity.

Key recommendations from the Boorman Review:
- NHS organisations should have prevention focused health and wellbeing strategies
- senior management of each organisation should be accountable for staff health and wellbeing, measured as part of the annual assessments of NHS performance
- strategies that support early interventions on musculoskeletal and mental health conditions should be implemented to minimise their time impact and support early returns to work.

The success of such strategies in the NHS will be predicated on the commitment of senior managers/board members, the development of, and access to, in-house (and possibly external) expertise, excellent lines of communication and clear triggers and protocols for early intervention. Similar strategies could effectively be applied across a range of sectors.

Risk factors for work related disorders

Work related stress

While work is generally good for people if it is well designed, it can also be a great source of pressure. Work pressure can be positive and a motivating factor, and is often essential in a job. It can help us achieve our goals and perform better. An employee may experience stress when the demands placed on him/her are greater than his/her ability to cope. An employee's ability to cope with work pressure in any given situation is not solely determined by workplace factors.

The experience of stress can be associated with, or bring about, changes in emotional state, behaviour and mental and physiological function. These changes might be benign and transient, or seriously affect an employee's health and performance at work.

There are two different sources of stress at work:
● anxiety about exposure, or threat of exposure, to more tangible and physical hazards of work
● psychosocial and organisational hazards.

Additional factors influencing how well an employee may cope with work pressure include the orange, yellow and blue flag features described later in this chapter, as well as:
● his/her skills and experience
● support networks at work and in his/her private life
● lifestyle
● health status
● other demands both in and outside work (eg health of family members, financial circumstances).

Ideally, line managers would be alert to signs of stress (reduced coping – see Table 8.4) in their team and be aware of relevant health and wellbeing protocols including how to access established internal support services. Early interventions may help the employee to cope and reduce the risk of sickness absence.

TABLE 8.4 INDICATORS THAT AN EMPLOYEE IS EXPERIENCING STRESS

Emotional
● negative or depressive feeling
● self critical
● increased emotional reactions – more tearful or sensitive or aggressive
● withdrawn
● loss of motivation, commitment and confidence
● mood swings (not behavioural).

Mental
● confusion, indecision
● can't concentrate
● poor memory.

Changes from normal behaviour
● changes in eating habits
● increased smoking, drinking or drug taking "to cope"
● mood swings affecting behaviour
● changes in sleep patterns
● twitchy, nervous behaviour
● changes in attendance such as arriving later or taking more time off.

While these are indicators of behaviour related to stress, they may also be indicative of other mental health problems.

Employees experiencing work related stress, or with mental health problems, do not have to be entirely free of symptoms to remain in, or return to work successfully, but there are barriers to be overcome. Evidence on the effectiveness of health and employment interventions is currently weak, and depends on reinforcing accepted best practice to promote mental wellbeing and maintain working life.

Work related musculoskeletal disorders

MSDs are not exclusively a work related phenomenon. However, it is accepted (and there is an evidence base for such a view) that MSDs can be caused, or contributed to, by workplace exposures, usually thought to involve a dose-response relationship where dose relates to patterns of loading/unloading of the relevant tissues. The workplace exposures generally implicated as risk factors for MSDs are well established and include:
● The prolonged maintenance of awkward, static working postures – an awkward posture of a joint occurs when the joint position is maintained beyond its neutral (mid range) position. When awkward postures are maintained, muscles are working at a mechanical disadvantage, often resulting in friction and compression of the soft tissues, blood flow may be significantly reduced, muscles fatigue quickly and there is a build up of metabolites; tendons and ligaments may be stressed – the extent of the risk will relate to the overall duration of maintenance of the posture and the pattern/duration of exposure and recovery.
● The application of force (extent and velocity) relative to the maximum force potential and length of the muscle, which can lead to muscle fatigue, stress and local (anatomical) pressure on tendons and local (external) pressure on tissues, for instance when gripping tools.
● Repetition – if rapid or prolonged may not allow sufficient

recovery time and is often associated with inflammation, degeneration and micro trauma of the affected tissues.
- Duration of exposure – this can be the duration of each task, series of tasks, duration over a working day and the number of days the task is performed over time.
- Certain environmental factors, eg temperature, draughts, lighting etc.

MSD signs and symptoms can include:
- inflammation
- redness
- decreased range of motion
- tingling
- numbness
- stiffness
- pain associated with particular movement(s), variable or sometimes unremitting
- tenderness (local or diffuse, or in combination)
- muscle weakness/decreased grip strength
- fatigue
- limitation in function
- reduced capacity to cope with work demands.

Biopsychosocial models:

Factors influencing health and work ability

Engel (1978) considered that, despite increasingly sophisticated scientific knowledge and technical skills in respect of human anatomy, physiology and disease prevention, diagnosis and management, most health professionals failed to give corresponding attention to the scientific understanding of human behaviour and the psychological and social aspects of illness/disability.

Human beings are complex entities and their responses to, and experience of, illness, disability and pain are necessarily modified and mediated by socio cultural factors, life experience, cognitive and emotional processes, education/knowledge and locus of control[2], all of which can influence health and/or work capability outcomes.

The biopsychosocial model was conceived as a model of clinical care, but it offers a conceptual framework that allows the health professional to take account of the person's subjective experience (person centred health care) by promoting a more participatory (but non dependant) relationship and involvement in clinical decision making and goal setting that can contribute to recovery, rehabilitation and work retention.

In practice, very many healthcare and occupational health professionals remain constrained by mechanistic compliance with the medical model and fail to acknowledge that behavioural elements of presentation may also require investigation and possible modification. Individuals exhibiting behavioural signs have commonly been wrongly labelled as malingerers with consequent loss of rehabilitation opportunity, often leading to work loss/worklessness, and associated socio-economic sequelae.

---

2 Locus of control is a personality construct and describes the extent to which an individual believes that events result primarily from their own behaviour and actions (internal locus) or that powerful others, fate, or chance primarily determine events (external locus).

Occupational flags model

As well as the growing evidence for the involvement of both physical and psychosocial factors in the aetiology and reporting of MSDs (Macfarlane et al 2000; Walker-Bone et al 2004), there is also evidence that physical, psychosocial and organisational/employment factors can act as barriers to recovery and return to work. While much of this evidence comes from the field of back pain research, it is increasingly apparent that similar factors are relevant in the management of wider MSDs (Greening & Lynn 1998; Greening et al 1999). Any management of these patients should focus on reducing obstacles to recovery (Greening et al 2003; Smyth et al 2007).

The corollary of the concept of obstacles to recovery/return to work is that interventions specifically addressing these factors will have a beneficial effect on vocational outcomes (Harris 1999). Guidelines on the management of low back pain (Feuerstein et al 1993) are aimed in part at addressing these obstacles. Many of the principles of these guidelines can be sensibly applied to the worker presenting with MSDs.

Psychosocial factors have the potential to influence an acute musculoskeletal pain problem at three distinct phases:
- the onset of pain
- the seeking and receiving of healthcare
- the development of chronic pain related disability and work loss.

Clinical management that ignores psychosocial factors has done little to stem the flow of individuals from acute to chronic pain and disability, and as such, psychosocial factors should no longer be considered as mere secondary reactions to the pain experience.

Kendall (1999) postulated that the identification of biopsychosocial factors can alert the clinician to a risk of chronicity (the progression of acute symptoms/dysfunction to chronic status) present in workers and non workers alike and there is an increasing body of evidence that psychological parameters can play a significant role in the transition from acute to chronic pain, dysfunction and disability. We now recognise that psychosocial factors are key predictors of chronicity, and that many of the learned behaviours apparent in chronic musculoskeletal pain have their genesis in the first few days and weeks of the problem. Thus, the readily understood concept of "Red Flags" (signs of possible serious pathology) has been extended to the idea of "Yellow Flags" (Linton 2000) (see Table 8.5) that indicate psychosocial barriers to recovery and risk of chronicity. The identification of yellow flags consistently predict poor functional and vocational outcomes, and are arguably more accurate predictors of retention at/return to work potential than an individual's reported symptoms/diagnosis, or their work demands (Crawford & Laiou 2005). The presence of yellow flags does not imply the absence of illness/disability/dysfunction and these approaches are not mutually exclusive with meeting the biomedical needs of patients.

TABLE 8.5 YELLOW FLAGS

Features that are associated with chronicity, disability and poor vocational outcomes
Fear avoidance behaviour (avoiding a movement or activity due to misplaced negative anticipation of the consequences)
Anxiety about pain
Belief that pain is harmful and potentially severely disabling
Belief that pain will have catastrophic repercussions
Depression
Belief in passive coping strategies
Belief that personal health is controlled by others rather than by self (external locus of control)
Low level of belief in one's ability to achieve a particular outcome
Tendency to low mood and withdrawal from social interaction/participation
Expectation that passive treatment rather than active participation will help.

Yellow flags operate alongside a number of associated work related obstacles, so called "Blue Flags" and "Black Flags" that can influence the likelihood of taking time off work and that can prevent workers returning to work following sickness absence. Blue flags describe the perceptions of the worker that can act as a barrier to recovery/return to work (see Table 8.6). Black flags (Table 8.7) are occupational/employer factors that block return to work (Burdorf et al 1998). While not specifically concerned with recovery, these systems obstacles can impede the delivery and success of otherwise appropriate retention at/return to work interventions.

TABLE 8.6 BLUE FLAGS

High job demands/time pressure
Low control/no involvement in decision making
Unhelpful management style
Poor social support
Low job satisfaction
Belief that work is harmful
Work schedules that are imposed
Work that requires high attention
Work that may be inherently upsetting
Not feeling valued
Little opportunity for task variety.

TABLE 8.7 BLACK FLAGS

Employer's sickness policy, for example no phased/supported return to work opportunities
Entitlement to sick leave
"Full fitness" requirement for return to work
Organisational structure and culture
Management style
Ergonomics/biomechanical job demands.

More recently, the term "Orange Flags" has been coined to describe the influence of mental health conditions on impairment and participation, including as a barrier to work.

In light of the above, it is important that effective management of work related ill health addresses the intrinsic physical, psychosocial and extrinsic work factors that can positively or negatively influence outcomes. Such holistic provision inevitably requires a strategic and multidisciplinary approach.

International Classification of Functioning, Disability and Health (ICF)

Disability is an umbrella term, covering impairments, activity limitations, and participation restrictions. An impairment is a problem in body function or structure; an activity limitation is a difficulty encountered by an individual in executing a task or action; while a participation restriction is a problem experienced by an individual in involvement in work and life situations, and which can impact on quality of life.

Thus, disability is a complex phenomenon, reflecting an interaction between features of a person's body and mind, and features of the society in which he or she lives. The way that health professionals think about health and disease determines to a considerable extent what they do and say in their clinical encounters with patients. The World Health Organisation's International Classification of Functioning, Disability and Health (known as ICF, 2001) presents a new way to consider health and disease and thus the ICF offers a promising framework and classification for rehabilitation medicine.

By putting the notions of "health" and "disability" in a new light, the ICF acknowledges that every human being can experience a decrement in health and thereby experience some degree of disability. Disability is not something that only happens to a minority of humanity. The ICF thus "mainstreams" the experience of disability and recognises it as a universal human experience. By shifting the focus from cause to impact, it places all health conditions on an equal footing allowing them to be compared using a common metric – the ruler of health and disability. Furthermore, the ICF takes into account the social aspects of disability and does not see disability only as a "medical" or "biological" dysfunction. By including contextual factors, the ICF acknowledges the impact of the environment, including the workplace, on the person's functioning.

By taking into account the social and environmental aspects of disability, the ICF provides a mechanism to document the impact of the social and physical environment on a person's functioning. For instance, when a person in a wheelchair finds it difficult to enter his or her office building because there are no ramps or elevators, the ICF identifies the needed intervention: it is the building that should be modified, not the person who should adapt. In the UK, there is a legal duty on employers in such circumstances to make the reasonable adjustments necessary to support continued employment (DDA 1995). In clinical settings, the ICF is used for functional status assessment, goal setting and treatment planning and monitoring, as well as outcome measurement.

Fig 8.1 ICF model

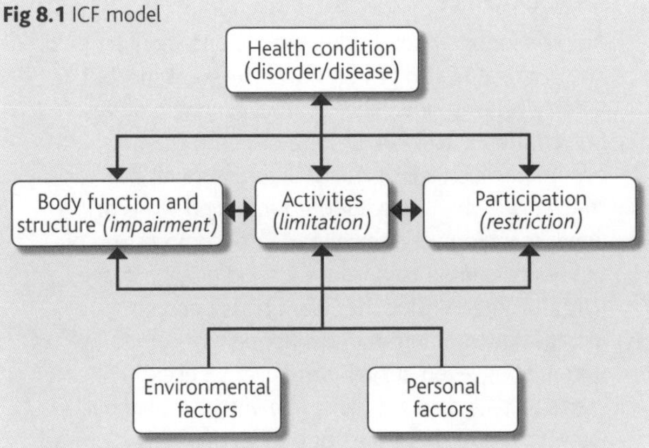

By applying the ICF model shown above, we can explore the impact of a health condition in context. For example, if the health problem is rheumatoid arthritis, the impairment might be pain, reduced grip strength, chronic fatigue. The associated limitation would relate to environment factors such as job demands (hours worked, pattern of work/opportunities for rest/recovery, physical demands of the job, tool design and potentially the blue flags at Table 8.6). Personal factors could include age, gender, anthropometrics, medication, but also include some of the yellow flag features at Table 8.5.

It is only by understanding the limitations imposed by the impairment in context that effective remediation strategies can be implemented:
● personal factors might be addressed through improved drug management, information/advice (diet, activity, sleep...), physiotherapy/rehabilitation, counselling if appropriate)
● environment factors (work related) might be addressed through ergonomics interventions (provision aids/ equipment/work station set up), changes to work organisation (changing shift patterns, agreeing rest breaks, improving task variety, re-allocation of some duties).

Neither of these lists is exclusive.

The ICF does not specifically refer to the flags model but acknowledges the biopsychosocial model and the influence that personal (intrinsic) and environmental (extrinsic) factors can have on the extent that an impairment in body function/structure arising from the health condition (disorder/disease) can give rise to limitation and restrict participation in social and work activities essential to quality of life.

Prevention and management

Primary prevention

The focus of traditional approaches adopted in respect of the prevention and management of MSDs at work has been avoidance or limitation of exposure through risk assessment, and risk management strategies involving ergonomics interventions (see chapter 3), organisational change and technical progress (eg improved equipment/technology). While such approaches may result in "successful" interventions that reduce biomechanical exposure measured by conventional criteria, this does not guarantee symptom resolution or improved health, and data indicates that these approaches

have had relatively little impact on the prevalence of MSDs in the workplace or of MSD related sickness absence.

Despite advances in our understanding of biomechanical exposure-effect associations, we continue to rely on mainly subjective evaluation methods employed, where access to such opportunities are in place, in collaboration between "expert" and worker. This approach to risk analysis may identify critical exposures in a given work situation, but the strategic aim of improved health for workers requires that additional risk factors be considered and addressed, including other work organisation and person based risk factors.

Interestingly, Eriksen et al (2004) looked at the predictors of low back pain in a group of 4,266 Norwegian nurses' aides in a prospective study over 15 months. They found that, after a wide range of adjustments, low back pain symptoms were predicted not only by MSD risk factors (the frequent positioning of patients in bed) but also by perceived lack of support from their immediate superior and perceived lack of a pleasant and relaxing culture in the work unit. Similar findings have been reported across a range of sectors. Thus, organisational culture, line management style and perception about work also have a significant impact on the experience of work and on risk of MSDs and work related stress.

Health promotion

Health promotion has been defined (WHO 2005) as:

> "the process of enabling people to increase control over their health and its determinants, and thereby improve their health".

The primary means of health promotion has historically been applied through the mechanism of public policy that addresses the prerequisites of health such as income, housing, food security, employment, and quality working conditions.

Health promotion programmes typically target exercise/fitness, nutrition/weight management, smoking cessation (and other substance misuse) and stress management. However, given the very high prevalence of MSDs in the workplace, particularly in health and social care, the prevention, early recognition and management of such conditions would be a useful and cost effective target for health promotion activities for employees and their line managers, including encouraging early reporting. However, staff must feel "safe" to report, since, if there is a perception that such reporting might put their job at risk, they will naturally feel reluctant to do so.

Employers must then have a system in place to respond to such reports by establishing clear referral protocols, including access to expert advice/assessment, such as from a back care practitioner/ergonomist, and/or initiating occupational health interventions as appropriate. Such key messages and signposting could also be reinforced during routine mandatory training.

Early intervention

Given the prevalence of MSDs in the population, it is inevitable that, even in well designed work places, employees will develop MSD symptoms that can be made worse by their work, or that impact on work performance. The key to effective, and cost effective, management of these conditions, and to supporting the employee to stay in work is to intervene as early as possible to establish and mediate any work related risk factors and to provide advice to the individual (and the line manager as appropriate) and facilitate appropriate interventions. Similar approaches would be relevant to any health condition that is impacting on work performance.

Work instability

The key to early identification of the risk of an employee's sickness absence – work instability (WI) – was conceived (Smith 1993) to describe a situation in which an employee is experiencing difficulties in coping with the demands of his or her work as a consequence of altered health status/disability/ reduced functional capacity. Thus, the impact on work of any incapacity must relate to the extent of the mismatch between that incapacity and the employee's work demands.

Work instability can be defined as:

> "... a state in which the cognitive and functional impact of a health problem/disability results in a mismatch between work capacity and job demand, and thus can threaten job performance and the ability to sustain work if not mediated".

Proof of concept for WI as a scalable construct on a common metric has previously been explored in a number of long term clinically defined health problems. The first validated clinical or disease specific work instability scale (WIS) to be developed was for rheumatoid arthritis (RA-WIS) (Gilworth *et al* 2003). This scale is now in use in over 40 centres world wide and has been translated into multiple languages. Similar psychometrically robust, validated work instability scales for ankylosing spondylitis (Gilworth *et al* 2005), traumatic brain injury (Gilworth *et al* 2006) and multiple sclerosis and epilepsy have also been developed.

The concept of WI in relation to specific occupational groups has now also been explored, building on previous research and adding to the conceptual framework. The identification of WI in its early stages offers the opportunity of early referral for assessment so that appropriate measures can be implemented at a stage when such measures are most likely to be successful in achieving resolution and sustaining work attendance and job retention.

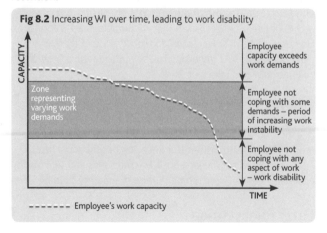

Fig 8.2 Increasing WI over time, leading to work disability

Fig 8.2, above, illustrates a situation in which work performance gradually deteriorates so that the employee is progressively less able to cope with their work demands (increasing WI). Without intervention, eventually the employee is unable to cope with their work at all (work disability).

CASE EXAMPLE

An ultrasonographer gradually develops shoulder pain. The pain eases at night and over the weekend, but quickly returns when she resumes scanning duties. She continues to work despite discomfort, but eventually she cannot maintain pressure on the transducer when carrying out prolonged scans or when scanning very heavy patients (compression of tissue is essential to produce a good quality image). Without intervention, her work tasks become increasingly problematic and her pain becomes unremitting, even at night and over weekends. She starts to take days off work, and even uses annual leave to reduce her hours but on its own this is not an effective strategy and eventually she is unable to cope with scanning at all. Long term sickness absence ensues, placing her at high risk of work loss. Had her state of WI been identified at an early stage, appropriate interventions could have supported retention at work.

The Work Screen concept

Work Screen is the term used to describe work instability scales, developed in association with Department of Rehabilitation Medicine, Faculty of Medicine and Health, University of Leeds. All Work Screens are based on extensive research and meet the robust requirements of modern psychometric measurement. Work Screens are:

- simple, self complete questionnaires that will identify those experiencing WI (see Fig 8.3)
- occupation specific (office, manual and health and social care)
- can be delivered electronically or in hard copy
- focused on looking at the impact of health at work including the impact on work attendance and work performance
- built on a simple scoring system to sort respondents easily on a scale of low, medium and high risk
- comprehensive – physical and related psychosocial components on a common metric in one scale.

It is likely that employers/occupational health advisers (OHAs)/line managers may already be aware of those staff experiencing high levels of WI (frequent/prolonged sickness absence), but they may well not be aware of those employees moving into medium WI, the stage where intervention is most likely to be successful in maintaining work.

Early identification of those experiencing WI and therefore "at risk" has the benefits of:

- ensuring limited occupational health resources are invested in those most in need
- reduced sickness absence via preventative interventions aimed at resolving or reducing the impact of symptoms
- employees being actively encouraged to participate in the management of their symptoms by provision of appropriate advice.

If employees experiencing WI are not identified early and well managed, the consequences are seen in:

- reducing ability to cope with work
- problems in quality control and productivity
- decrease in efficiency
- descent into chronicity
- associated sickness absence

Example results of a Work Screen

ID	Total	Low risk	Medium risk	High risk
1	6		*	
2	11			*
3	4	*		
4	13			*
5	2	*		
6	1	*		
7	4	*		
8	3	*		
9	7		*	
10	6		*	
11	3	*		
12	2	*		
13	4	*		
14	8		*	
15	1	*		
16	2	*		
17	1	*		
18	4	*		
19	3	*		
20	7		*	
21	1	*		
22	0	*		
23	3	*		
24	4	*		
25	5		*	
26	4	*		
27	1	*		

Fig 8.3 Example showing total scores

- negative impact on work colleagues
- costs of staff replacement and training
- the human cost of pain and suffering experienced by employees and their families through ill health

CASE EXAMPLE

A global pharmaceutical company used Work Screens at its UK manufacturing centre to see how its staff was coping at work across different departments.

The WI scores of the 27 workers in a sterile production area are shown in **Fig 8.3**. Of the 27 workers, the scores of two workers demonstrated that they were experiencing high work instability and therefore at high risk of sickness absence, six workers were in the medium risk category and 19 were coping well with their work.

The company's occupational health manager (OHM) was fully involved in the Work Screen process and already aware of the two workers showing high work instability due to frequent episodes of sickness absence. One of these was a newly divorced single parent struggling with childcare. The second had been involved in a road traffic accident and was involved in a compensation claim for whiplash injuries.

The OHM, who had not previously been aware of any problems with the six workers in the medium risk group, held brief triage interviews with them in order to arrange appropriate intervention. Four of these workers were experiencing MSDs, and these were referred for assessment/treatment with the company's occupational health physiotherapy and ergonomics provider. One worker was referred for counselling for reasons unrelated to work, and one worker was worried about a recent diagnosis of diabetes, and the OHM was able to provide helpful advice and information. An ergonomics evaluation was carried out in the production area and some small changes in work organisation were implemented.

The Work Screen was repeated after three months. The "high risk" single parent had transferred to another line when a part time post became available. The "high risk" worker who had been involved in the road traffic accident had improved with NHS treatment and moved into the medium risk category. All four "medium risk" workers who had received physiotherapy advice or treatment, the worker with diabetes and the worker receiving counselling were coping better. Five moved into low risk and one remained in the low end of the medium risk category.

As a result of very early identification of WI and the implementation of appropriate interventions, of the 26 original workers, 24 were now scored as low risk and two as medium risk. There were no workers in the high risk category.

The use of Work Screen facilitated early identification and targeted effective and cost effective management strategies.

Rehabilitation ergonomics

Despite the apparently distinct differences between the disciplines of ergonomics and rehabilitation, they could be described as parallel approaches with identical goals, that is to support employees experiencing WI to sustain work.

Ergonomics aims to enhance the functional capacity of people/workers by optimising the fit between the person/worker and object, equipment, process, task, facility and environment at micro, meso and macro levels (see chapter 3). Therefore, ergonomics can be an enabler that bridges the gap between reduced functional capacity and task demands to help sustain retention at work and/or return to work.

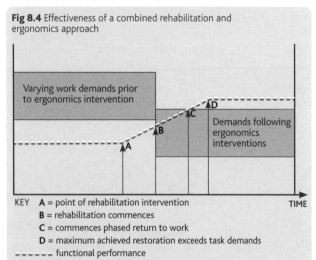

Fig 8.4 Effectiveness of a combined rehabilitation and ergonomics approach

Varying work demands prior to ergonomics intervention

Demands following ergonomics interventions

KEY   A = point of rehabilitation intervention
       B = rehabilitation commences
       C = commences phased return to work
       D = maximum achieved restoration exceeds task demands
       - - - - - functional performance

TIME

Rehabilitation is the art and science of maximising participation (in society/work etc) and enhancing quality of life through mediating the impairment and improving function, and restoring participation insofar as that can be achieved.

Therefore, a blend of these two disciplines can underpin the development of strategies to enhance and optimise the functional and work ability of workers experiencing WI and are, therefore, central to prevention and intervention elements of successful retention at, and return to, work strategies.

Retention strategies

The success of retention at work strategies is predicated on early reporting through objective work screening, or early reporting by individuals/line managers once they become aware of a relevant health problem.

The priority is for an initial assessment (semi-structured triage) to take place so that appropriate expertise can be accessed in early course. Any adequate assessment must take account of both person related factors (taking account of the biopsychosocial model) and workplace factors (physical ergonomics/biomechanical risks, environment, work organisation, workload, management style, relationships etc). Depending on the nature of the problem and the degree of WI, possible retention strategies might include:

- short term restriction of particular duties
- task re-allocation
- task variety
- longer term modification of work practices/work organisation
- refresher training

- occupational health physiotherapy/triage assessment/advice on self management/short term treatment
- ergonomics interventions focused on the individual or on the work system
- access to improved equipment/technology
- access to counselling.

Return to work strategies

Employers concerned for the health and wellbeing of staff should have in place proactive strategies aimed at limiting sickness absence duration. There is good evidence that the longer the absence from work, the less likely it will be that the employee will successfully return to work (see page 108).

Communication between the line manager and employee early on in the period of absence should be encouraged, although it is likely to be most successful when positive relationships are already established. Key elements of the return to work process might involve:

- identifying any barriers to work re-entry
- functional and biopsychosocial evaluation
- developing targeted interventions to reduce their impact
- focusing on functional improvement and work re-entry
- assessment and reduction of ergonomics risks
- implementing reasonable adjustments under the DDA
- signposting to Access to Work.

At present, the assessment of fitness for work remains focused in the biomedical model. A significant percentage of those employed, but who are absent from work due to long term altered health status (reduced participation), are subjected to so called Functional Capacity Evaluations (FCE) designed to "test" functional performance against various population norms. The focus of many FCE models is to identify so-called "behavioural signs" (Main & Waddell 1998) and "inconsistencies in performance" between tests as evidence of malingering and as a means of case closure/termination of employment. Any such evaluation that fails to take proper account of the biopsychosocial model and/or fails to provide evidence based rehabilitation and return to work advice cannot be considered valid.

Workplace health and wellbeing

Great progress has been made in improving health and safety at work but this has resulted in relatively little impact in the prevalence of work related ill health, levels of sickness absence (particularly related to MSDs and common mental health disorders – including work related stress) or of work loss. While the prevention of work related ill health remains paramount, there is increasing recognition of the key role the workplace can play in promoting staff health and wellbeing, and the potential impact that effective health and wellbeing strategy can contribute to improving working lives and reducing sickness absence.

While many employers remain to be convinced of the effectiveness, and cost effectiveness, of such programmes, there is evidence that health and wellbeing programmes produce economic benefits across all sectors and all sizes of business: in other words, that "good health is good business".

A meta evaluation (Chapman 2005) of 56 studies published between 1982-2005 found that worksite health promotion produced on average a decrease of 26.8 per cent in sickness absence, a decrease of 26.1 per cent in health costs, a decrease of 32 per cent in workers' compensation costs and disability management claims costs.

A meta analysis (Kuoppala *et al* 2008) of 46 studies published between 1970-2005 found moderate, statistically significant effects of work health promotion, especially exercise, on "work ability" and "overall wellbeing"; additionally "sickness absence duration seemed to be reduced by activities promoting healthy lifestyle".

The National Institute for Health and Clinical Excellence (NICE) has defined health and wellbeing as:

> "… being emotionally healthy as well as physically healthy. It's feeling able to cope with normal stresses, and living a fulfilled life. It can be affected by things like worries about money, work, your home, the people around you and the environment you live in. Your wellbeing is also affected by whether or not you feel in control of your life, feeling involved with people and communities and feelings of anxiety and isolation."

Key to establishing health and wellbeing strategy and focus is the identification and ongoing monitoring of key threats to staff health and wellbeing through a process of organisation risk assessment and performance monitoring.

Indicators of health and wellbeing status might include:
- sickness absence rate
- working days lost
- percentage of sickness absence by diagnosis (eg MSDs, stress etc)
- workplace accident and near miss rates and trends (by type and location)
- reasons given for leaving in exit interviews
- ill health retirements
- percentage of staff accessing counselling/occupational health physiotherapy services.

In carrying out the assessment, employers must take full account of the range of sometimes specific risks involved in working in their particular sector, eg from exposure to disease, or psychological risks, or physical risks such as manual handling. A participative approach would offer staff the opportunity to influence the strategy and the services to be provided.

Aims of a strategy
- Maintain a safe and healthy working environment.
- Improve physical and emotional wellbeing.
- Educate, encourage and support employees to develop and maintain a healthy lifestyle.
- Support people with manageable health problems or disabilities to sustain work or return to work quickly, thus reducing sickness absence, pressure on colleagues, locum costs etc.
- Improve performance and delivery appropriate to sector, eg care delivery.
- Improve staff satisfaction, recruitment and retention.

The following key components are essential to achieving the aims set out in a health and wellbeing policy:

Primary prevention
- promote a safety culture at work
- have in place effective systems for the management of risk through the mechanism of risk assessment and monitoring
- ensure staff are provided with relevant (to their job role) and up to date risk control training, eg moving and handling training
- empower staff to report unsafe practice and to safeguard health and safety
- ensure managers understand their responsibilities for the health, safety and wellbeing of their staff
- practice good ergonomics
- take advantage of technological/equipment advances
- immunisation programmes.

Health promotion
- raise health awareness
- provide educational resources, eg through the organisation's intranet in relation to specific health issues (cardiovascular health/healthy eating/weight management, dietary advice/diabetes, smoking cessation, substance misuse, women's health, men's health)
- offer lifestyle/health screening
- facilitate fitness for work through schemes such as subsidised gym/sports club membership or cycling to work schemes.

Early reporting
Even in healthy and safe environments, employees will develop health problems that can be made worse by their work and the greatest risk of sickness absence and work loss arises in relation to MSDs and common mental health problems including work related stress. In the case of both MSDs and work related stress, the earlier the intervention, the greater the opportunities for management and for sustaining work.

Currently, reporting is dependent on the employee recognising that he or she has a problem that is impacting on his or her work, and on there being an established system in place so that the employee feels safe to report, and to respond appropriately to any report.

An effective "early warning" system would encompass:
- routine delivery of objective, evidence based and occupation specific Work Screens
- educating staff and line managers regarding symptoms and signs to be aware of in relation to MSDs and work related stress
- having in place a reporting protocol
- having in place an effective response system to support the employee to cope better with his/her work.

Early intervention
- Triage, to establish the nature of the problem and identify challenges to sustaining work.
- Signposting towards established pathways to support staff to cope better with their work through access to relevant expertise/actions such as:
  - risk assessment review
  - workplace ergonomics assessment
  - workload evaluation
  - occupational health advice
  - occupational health physiotherapy/triage/advice/treatment
  - psychological support/counselling/debt advice etc.

Retention

Across all sectors, key strategies focused on MSDs and mental health conditions should be implemented to minimise their time impact and support retention at work.

Neither biomedical treatment nor ergonomics workplace interventions alone offer an optimal solution, rather, multimodal interventions taking account of the biopsychosocial model demonstrate greater effectiveness for occupational outcomes.

- Rehabilitation ergonomics.
- The biopsychosocial approach (screen for yellow and blue flags).
- Person centred support/intervention.

Rehabilitation should address obstacles to recovery and barriers to (return to) work. Rehabilitation should not be a separate, second stage after "treatment" is complete: rehabilitation principles should be integral to clinical and occupational management.

Return to work

Such assessments and interventions are only achievable with the input of a range of professionals outside traditional occupational health provision including ergonomists, back care practitioners, occupational health physiotherapists, occupational therapists, psychologists/counsellors/CBT therapists and others.

The success of health and wellbeing strategy is predicated on an integrated, multidisciplinary systems approach and on the commitment and support of board members, budget holders and senior managers who are accountable for staff health and wellbeing and should be subject to relevant performance targets.

Occupational health services

It is estimated that only in the region of 15 per cent of working people in the UK have access to occupational health services. While the vast majority of health and social care employers in the public sector will have in place direct or indirect access to occupational health, these services are often fragmented, under resourced, under staffed, reactive in approach.

Although studies relating to the beneficial impact of occupational health on productivity and human performance are limited, some occupational health programmes have shown impressive effects, as measured primarily by reduced absenteeism. Although further studies of the mechanisms at work and broader applicability of the findings is needed, the return on investment suggests that the wider adoption of such programmes could prove beneficial for budgets and productivity as well as health outcomes.

Government strategy, the commitment of board (NHS)/ cabinet (local authority) members and adequate investment in health and wellbeing at work offers occupational health professionals opportunities to re-focus towards proactive health promotion, prevention and early intervention to support employees in sustaining work, reducing sickness absence and maximising staff productivity and performance.

Occupational health services must no longer live solely in the clinic investing significant resources in preparing staff for work at the start of employment (eg screening and immunisation) and in supporting sickness absence management. Occupational health practitioners must adopt more proactive approaches, including getting out into the workplace and focusing on those in work, improving health and working lives.

The responsibility for the prevention, and prompt, assertive management, of work related disorders/ill health cannot rest within the occupational health unit alone, but requires the strategic engagement of other key stakeholders such as human resources, the health and safety unit, back care advisory services; on the recruitment or commissioning of specialist services such as occupational health physiotherapy/ergonomics, counselling/cognitive behavioural therapy and other services according to priority; and the establishment of communication and action protocols.

One key challenge for occupational health services as we move further into the 21st century will be an aging workforce and an associated increased prevalence of chronic and lifestyle related disorders including MSDs, cardiovascular and respiratory conditions, obesity, diabetes and treated cancers. None of these should necessarily deny the possibility of fulfilling work or extending working life but will require effective clinical care to minimise ill health, and flexibility and adaptation in the workplace to mitigate the effects of age on function.

Life expectancy is increasing:

- now 77 for men and 81 for women (at birth)
- over 65s will soon outnumber under 16s
- it seems likely that the pension age will be increased to 66 or 67 years within a decade.

An increase in working life expectancy will be difficult to achieve without corresponding improvements in healthy life expectancy. Primary healthcare professionals must understand the relationship between work and health and adapt the advice they give to patients to reflect the importance of remaining in, or returning to, work wherever possible.

Back care/moving and handling practitioner

The role of the back care/moving and handling practitioner has significantly evolved over the 30 years since the first in the series of this publication (1981). We have grown from the often isolated and routine delivery of non evidence based (and sometimes frankly hazardous) techniques in remote training rooms to broad national agreement on evidence based core skills and best practice, to influencing (or writing) policy, contributing to risk management strategy and procurement decisions, supporting generic and complex person specific moving and handling risk assessment and accident/incident investigation (see chapter 5).

Investment by health and social care employers in health and wellbeing strategies offers substantial opportunities for BCPs/MHPs to work with other stakeholders in supporting employees to stay in work at all stages (prevention, health promotion, early intervention) of the process:

- contributing to safety culture
- developing skills and competence through training
- health education – specifically in relation to biomechanics/exposure risk factors
- supporting relevant health promotion activities

- monitoring compliance with safer systems of work
- offering a rapid response risk assessment/workstation ergonomics assessment review service
- advising on work adaptations, reasonable adjustments, ergonomics interventions
- influencing procurement.

The manual handling policy continuum (chapter 6, Fig 6.1) illustrates the key role that BCPs/MHPs have in relation to improved staff safety, health and wellbeing, in addition to quality care, safety and enablement of those in our care.

Line managers

Evidence indicates that line managers have a key role at all stages in the prevention and management of work related ill health and on improving working lives. Employers who are committed to staff health and wellbeing should ensure that managers fully understand their responsibilities for implementing and monitoring healthy and safe working practices in compliance with risk management protocols and for ensuring employees are not injured or made ill by their work.

Relevant information/training programmes for line managers might address:
- the links between work and health
- protocols for accessing relevant advice expertise in relation to risk assessment, ergonomics, occupational health
- the importance of responding positively to reporting and of facilitating early referral
- simple measures that can help prevent and manage ill health at work and promote the benefits of work/healthy lifestyles
- their role and the need for flexibility in supporting employees to stay in work or return to work quickly, such as cooperating in changing working patterns or carrying out/facilitating workplace adaptations
- the organisational and cost benefits of helping employees to stay at work or return to work quickly:

CASE EXAMPLE

A part time community nurse returns to work some weeks after suffering a back injury sustained when single handedly manoeuvring the lymphoedematous legs of an elderly and tall male bariatric patient with poor mobility in order to apply leg ulcer dressings and pressure bandaging.

Occupational health advise a phased return, working alternate days and preferably avoiding weekend shifts. On resuming "normal" hours the nurse is allocated weekend work and consecutive days of working. She finds it increasingly difficult to cope. She formally requests that her contract be reduced by four hours per week so that she need work only on alternate days (Monday, Wednesday, Friday). This is supported by occupational health advice.

The line manager refuses, stating that the nurse would have to move to a different base, even though the current base is already short staffed. Moving base would involve substantially more driving. The nurse cannot sustain her designated work pattern and she goes off sick again. Eventually her employment is terminated. In her 50s and distressed at having lost

her congenial work, and associated loss of income, she successfully pursues a personal injury claim in respect of the back injury she had sustained.

The cost to the employer included the loss of an experienced community nurse, staff replacement and training costs, some elements of the litigation costs (in any event picked up by the NHS) and the loss of reputation since the case was widely reported in local and national media.

Summary

There is a high prevalence of MSDs and common mental health problems in the health and social care sectors, which contributes to high levels of work instability, sickness absence and work loss.

Neither biomedical treatment nor ergonomics workplace interventions alone offer an optimal solution; rather, there is emerging evidence that multimodal interventions based in the biopsychosocial model show considerable promise, particularly for occupational outcomes.

This new approach to workplace health will require a multi disciplinary approach and clear protocols for communication and coordination between key stakeholders and those with relevant expertise.

Effective occupational health and wellbeing strategy must be proactive and focused on prevention, including relevant health promotion activity. Early intervention is predicated on evidence based tools that identify work instability at an early stage or is reliant on self reporting.

Proactive and assertive management of employees' physical and mental health can produce a range of important business benefits including reduction of sickness absence; lost time due to accidents and associated costs; greater staff engagement, wellbeing and productivity; reduced staff turnover and recruitment costs; enhanced performance and improved care delivery.

Key messages

- Good work is good for health and wellbeing.
- Prevention is a priority, but even in safe and healthy workplaces employees will develop health problems that impact on work performance.
- Early identification of work instability is key.
- Early access to assessment/advice/relevant expertise intervention is essential to maintain work capacity and limit sickness absence.
- Effective strategies must address both workplace factors and person specific factors.
- Think beyond physical symptoms – the biopsychosocial model applies.
- Focus on capacity not incapacity.
- Sustaining work, or supporting return to work, may require imaginative and flexible approaches to enable rehabilitation.

8 Health and wellbeing

References

Armstrong, TJ, Buckle, P, Fine, LJ *et al* (1993), A conceptual model for work-related neck and upper limb disorders. *Scandinavian Journal Work Environment Health,* **19**:73-84

Black, C (2008), Review of the health of Britain's working-age population, www.dwp.gov.uk/docs/hwwb-working-for-a-healthier-tomorrow.pdf.

Boorman review (2009), Interim report August 2009, final report November 2009, www.nhshealthandwellbeing.org

Burdorf, A, Naaktgeboren, B & Post, W (1998), Prognostic factors for musculoskeletal sickness absence and return to work among welders and metal workers. Occupational and Environmental Medicine 1998; **55**: 490e495.

Burton, AK, Kendall, NAS, Pearce, BG, Birrell, LN & Bainbridge, LC (2008), Management of work-relevant upper limb disorders: a review. Management of Upper Limb Disorders and the Biopsychosocial Model (2008) London: HSE Books, HSE.

Chapman, LS (2005), Meta-evaluation of worksite health promotion economic return studies: 2005 update. Am J Health Promot 2005 Jul-Aug; **19**(6):1-11.

Crawford, JO & Laiou, E (2005), Effective management of upper limb disorders by general practitioners and trainee occupational physicians. Research Report 380. Sudbury, Sussex: HSE books, 2005. Available at: www.hse.gov.uk/research/rrpdf/rr380.pdf.

Croft, PR, Macfarlane, GJ, Papageoorgiou, AC, Thomas, E & Silman, AJ (1998), Outcome of low back pain in general practice: a prospective study. *BMJ* **316**.1356-1359.

Disability Discrimination Act 1995 – Her Majesty's Stationery Office, www.hmso.gov.uk/acts/acts1995/1995050.htm. From 1 October 2010, the Equality Act replaced most of the Disability Discrimination Act (DDA). However, the Disability Equality Duty in the DDA continues to apply. New guidance is expected to be published in spring 2011.

Engel, GL (1978), The Biopsychosocial Model and the Education of Health Professionals, Annals of the New York Academy of Sciences, interscience.wiley.com.

Eriksen, W, Bruusgaard, D & Knardahl, S (2004), Work factors as predictors of intense or disabling low back pain; a prospective study of nurses' aides, *Occupational and Environmental Medicine*, **61**, 398-404.

Feuerstein, M, Callan-Harris, S, Hickey, P *et al* (1993), Multidisciplinary rehabilitation of chronic upper extremity disorders. Long term effects. Journal of *Occupational and Environmental Medicine* 1993; **35**: 396e403.

Gilworth, G, Chamberlain, MA, Harvey, A, Woodhouse, A, Smith, J, Smyth, MG & Tennant, A (2003), Development of a Work Instability Scale for rheumatoid arthritis. *Arthritis and Research* 2003; 49,3,349-354.

Gilworth, G, Emery, P, Barkham, N, Smyth, MG, Helliwell, P & Tennant, A (2005), Reducing work disability in ankylosing spondylitis: the AS Work Instability Scale (AS-WIS) *Rheumatology*.

Gilworth, G, Carey, A, Eyres, S, Sloan, J, Rainford, B, Bodenham, D, Neumann, V & Tennant, A (2006), Screening for job loss: development of a work instability scale for traumatic brain injury, www.informahealthcare.com.

Greening, J & Lynn, B (1998), Vibration sense in the upper limb in patients with repetitive strain injury and a group of at-risk office workers. International Archives of Occupational and Environmental Health 1998; 71: 29e34.

Greening, J, Smart, S, Leary, R, Hall-Craggs, M, O'Higgins, P & Lynn, B (1999), Reduced movement of the median nerve in carpal tunnel during wrist flexion in patients with non-specific arm pain. *Lancet* 1999; 354: 217e218.

Greening, J, Lynn B & Leary, R (2003), Sensory and autonomic function in the hands of patients with nonspecific arm pain (NSAP) and asymptomatic workers. Pain 2003; 104: 275e281.

Harris, AJ (1999), Cortical origin of pathological pain. Lancet 1999; 354: 1464e1466.

HSE (2010), Health and Safety Executive, Statistics 2009/10, A National Statistics publication. www.hse.gov.uk/statistics/overall/hssh0910.pdf

Kendall (1999) NAS Psychosocial approaches to the prevention of chronic pain: the low back paradigm, *Best Practice & Research Clinical Rheumatology*, Volume **13**, Issue 3, September 1999, pages 545-554.

Kuoppala, J, Lamminpää, A & Husman, P (2008), Work health promotion, job well-being, and sickness absences – a systematic review and meta-analysis, J Occup Environ Med 2008 November; **50**(11):1216-27.

Linton, SJ (2000), Literature Review. A Review of Psychological Risk Factors in Back and Neck Pain, *Spine*: May 2000 Volume **25**, Issue 9, pp1148-1156.

Linton, SJ, Hellsing, AL & Hallden, K (1998), A population-based study of spinal pain among 35-45-year-old individuals. *Spine* 23:1457-1463.

Macfarlane, GJ, Hunt, IM & Silman, AJ (2000), Role of mechanical and psychosocial factors in the onset of forearm pain: prospective population based study. *British Medical Journal* 2000; 321: 676e679.

Main, C & Waddell, G (1998), Behavioral Responses to Examination: A Reappraisal of the Interpretation of "Nonorganic Signs", *Spine*, 1998, http://journals.lww.com.

McKinnon, ME, Vickers, MR, Ruddock, VM, Townsend, J & Meade, TW (1997), Community studies of the health service implications of low back pain. *Spine* 22:2161-2166.

Papageoorgiou, AC, Croft, PR, Ferry, S, Jayson, MIV & Silman, AJ (1995), Estimating the prevalence of low back pain in the general population. *Spine* 20:1889-1894.

Smith, J (1993), Proceedings of ACPOHE Annual Conference.

Smyth, G, Bird, H & MacIver, H (2007), Occupational disorders: non-specific forearm pain, *Clinical Rheumatology* Volume **21**, Issue 2, pages 349-365 (April 2007).

Van den Hoogen, HJM, Koe,s BW, van Eijk, JTM, Bouter, LM & Deville, W (1998), On the course of low back pain in general practice: A one year follow up study. *Ann Rheum Dis* 57:13-19.

Waddell, G (1994), *Epidemiology Review. Annex to CSAG Report on Back Pain*. London: HMSO.

Walker-Bone, KE, Reading, IC, Palmer, KT *et al* (2004), 'Repetitive strain injury' is rare among working-aged adults and is not associated with keyboard use. *Rheumatology* 2004; **43** (supplement 2): S199.

Waxman, R, Tennant, A & Helliwell, P (2000), A prospective follow-up study of low back pain in the community. *Spine* 25:2085-2090.

World Health Organisation (2001), International Classification of Functioning, Disability and Health.

World Health Organisation (2005), Bangkok Charter for Health Promotion in a Globalised World.

Introduction to practical chapters

Mike Fray PhD BSc(Hons) BHSc MCSP
Research fellow, HEPSU, Loughborough University

ADAPTED FROM ORIGINAL TEXT BY
Emma Crumpton MSc (Ergs) BSc MCSP, freelance ergonomist
Sue Hignett PhD MSc MCSP MIEHF Eur Erg, director, HEPSU, Loughborough University
Carole Johnson MCSP Cert Ed, manual handling consultant

Introduction

This chapter contains both an explanation of the reasons and science behind the evidence based approach to healthcare and the evidence collection and analysis delivered in the practical chapters 10 and 11. They were first presented in *The Guide to The Handling of People* 5th edition (Smith (ed) *HOP5* 2005). Full explanations of all the methods and analysis can be found there. This introduction explains why and how the information is laid out, and gives details of a simple evidence gathering exercise that was carried out on each technique presented.

Evidence based practice (EBP)

Increasingly, in the world of healthcare, there is an emphasis on evidence based practice. This section explains what it is and why it is important for professional practice in manual handling. Specifically, it will consider the importance of, and need for, an evidence base for people handling. The following questions will be considered:
● Why have an evidence base?
● What is EBP?
● How is evidence used?

EBP falls within the portfolio of clinical governance, together with risk management, health outcomes, lifelong learning, clinical guidelines and research and development (Wright & Hill 2003). Clinical governance was established in 1998 to provide "a framework through which NHS organisations are accountable for continuously improving the quality of their services and safeguarding high standards of care by creating an environment in which excellence in clinical care will flourish" (Department of Health 1998). It brings together the factors required for organisational (top to bottom) cultural change within a simple concept, which is underpinned by complex components involving patients, health professionals, managers and policymakers.

Most health professionals are altruistic and keen to do their best for patients. One element of being a professional is having a self questioning attitude, with a desire to be self correcting and self regulating. As much of our professional satisfaction derives from being involved, identifying where improvements can be made and taking steps to effect these, EBP provides a framework for questioning our professional practice. The onus for people handling information is often left within the remit of back care practitioners (BCPs), as they are the experts in their organisations. However, people handling is a core skill for all health professionals. Therefore, the information should be of interest to all clinicians.

Why have an evidence base?

An evidence base is the accepted body of knowledge that underpins practice and from which guidelines and professional best practice are derived. The world of healthcare is an environment of increasing information and there is bombardment on a daily basis with guidelines, articles, peer reviewed papers, word of mouth etc, and the quantity of information continues to increase. In 1948, there were about 4,700 scientific journals in publication, by 1990 there were more than 100,000 scientific journals (www.hsl.unc.edu/Services/Tutorials/ebm/whatis.htm). The rapid development of internet search engines and electronically available material have further improved access to all forms of research material and professional guidance.

Gorman *et al* (1994) reported on the use of information from an observational study. Text books were claimed to be used by 39 per cent and were actually used by 12 per cent. Journals were claimed to be consulted by 18 per cent and were observed being used by seven per cent. Human sources of information were claimed by 33 per cent but actually observed by 55 per cent. This would seem to fit with the pattern seen in BCPs as there are no dedicated scientific peer reviewed journals available. To review all the literature would, therefore, necessitate reading many journals. National Back Exchange (NBE) runs an annual conference and local Back Exchange groups convene regular regional meetings. The topics discussed are very varied, based on the "local groups" reports in *column*. However, it does not appear that evidence or practice is systematically critiqued. Therefore, it is suggested that evidence based people handling is needed for the following reasons:
- there are many people handling problems in a wide range of clinical specialities
- there are too many journals to access all the information
- BCPs feel as if they are in information overload
- BCPs have limited time to read
- BCPs read what they are familiar with, eg *column*
- BCPs tend to avoid difficult or complicated papers.

What is EBP?

Firstly, evidence based medicine will be considered, then the way in which this model is being transformed for nursing practice, and, finally, an example of a specific patient handling activity will be given.

Evidence based medicine
The concept of evidence based medicine (EBM) began in the medical profession in the 1970s with Archie Cochrane, who argued that as healthcare resources would always be limited, they should be used to provide services that had been shown to be effective (Reynolds 2000). He drew on his personal experience of applying research results to individual patients, suggesting that the application of scientific principles had been largely absent in the development and evaluation of new treatment methods. He went on to pioneer the use of systematic reviews and meta-analyses in medicine. The development of EBM aimed to help doctors to:
- interpret and use research findings
- use research to inform practice throughout their careers (Reynolds 2000).

The most common definition of EBM is "the conscientious, explicit and judicious use of current best evidence in making decisions about the care of the individual patient. It means integrating individual clinical expertise with the best available external clinical evidence from systematic research" (Sackett *et al* 1997). EBM required that research should be classified into one of the following types of research:
- aetiology
- therapeutics
- diagnosis
- prognosis
- quality improvement, or
- economic evaluation.

Each has specific methodological criteria. This leads to a final hierarchy of evidence, whereby the randomised controlled trial (RCT) is considered to be the best method, followed by controlled trials, cohort studies, case control studies, surveys, qualitative studies and, finally, professional opinions (Hamer & Collinson 1999).

Reynolds (2000) summarised some concerns about EBM, one of which suggests that it presents a distorted and partial view, from a particular viewpoint (or ontology), of the use of science in medicine. This is reflected in the hierarchy of evidence, with RCT gaining a higher ranking than an experimental case study. Another concern was that EBM rejected much that was central to the scientific method by focusing on quantitative research methods, resulting in the values, experiences and preferences of patients being mostly ignored. This trend is reversing with the inclusion of qualitative research (Murphy *et al* 1998; Green & Britten 1998) and a changing attitude within EBM whereby "the principle which determines what kind of research is of value is dictated by the specific clinical question" (Reynolds 2000).

Evidence based nursing (EBN)
EBN is a developing area, so clinical decision making tends to be based on a combination of clinical experience, observation, training, peer group teaching, published articles and personal research (Blomfield & Hardy 2000). DiCenso *et al* (1998) give a pragmatic definition of EBN as "the process by which nurses make clinical decisions using the best available research evidence, their clinical expertise and patient preferences in the context of available resources". The evidence, by itself, does not allow the nurse to make a decision but it does support the process. The integration of the three components into decision making increases the likelihood of successful problem solving, so both patient care and staff health are improved.

The value of EBN is the emphasis it places on rational action through a structured appraisal of empirical evidence rather than the adherence to blind conjecture, dogmatic ritual or personal intuition. However, there are again real concerns about EBN related to the restricted view of nursing and the nurse/patient relationship, which is derived from the concepts developed in EBM. So, nursing is not unquestioningly adopting the medical model definition of EBP. Instead, nurses are setting a broader definition of evidence, which includes a wider range of methodologies, as discussed earlier. This will be helpful when considering how EBP can be used for person handling practice.

EBP in patient handling

BCPs have, perhaps, been more involved with some of the other areas of clinical governance, eg risk management, than EBP. It seems to be the case that some BCPs still work with a paradigm of practice that is based on the following assumptions:

- clinical experience and peer group discussion are a valid way of building and maintaining one's knowledge about the efficacy of manual handling equipment, techniques or interventions
- the study and understanding of basic mechanics, ergonomics principles and musculoskeletal disease is a sufficient guide for practice
- a combination of manual handling training and common sense is sufficient to allow one to evaluate new equipment and techniques
- expertise and experience form a sufficient base from which to generate valid guidelines for clinical practice.

According to this paradigm, BCPs have a number of options for tackling the problems with which they are presented. They can reflect on their own clinical experience, talk to colleagues, reflect on the underlying principles, go to a guidance document, or ask a local expert or expert group such as NBE. This reflects how many BCPs work, using local NBE groups as a support network for peer group discussions and affirmation of practice. As the expert in their workplace, BCPs are usually sought out as a source of information and expertise by staff. According to the new paradigm outlined below, the advice they give should be based on evidence.

The assumptions of the evidence based paradigm (www.cche.net/usersguides/ebm_tips.asp) are:

- Clinical experience and the development of clinical instincts are crucial and necessary parts of becoming competent in manual handling. Many aspects of clinical practice cannot, or will not, ever be adequately tested. Therefore, clinical experience and its lessons are particularly important in these situations. At the same time, systematic attempts to record observations in a reproducible and unbiased way, increase the confidence one can have in knowledge about equipment, techniques and interventions.
- In the absence of systematic observation, one must be cautious in the interpretation of information derived from clinical experience and intuition because it may, at times, be misleading.
- The study and understanding of basic mechanisms of disease, injury, biomechanics and ergonomics are necessary but insufficient guides for practice.
- Understanding certain rules of evidence and its interpretation are necessary to interpret literature correctly.
- It follows that BCPs should regularly consult the original literature (and be able to appraise it critically) in solving problems and providing optimal care. It also follows that BCPs must be ready to accept and live with uncertainty and to acknowledge that management decisions are often made in the face of relative ignorance of their true impact.

This paradigm puts a much lower value on authority as the underlying belief is that BCPs can gain the skills to make independent assessments of evidence and thus evaluate the credibility of opinions being offered by experts.

How is evidence used?

The practice and teaching of EBP require skills that are not traditionally part of healthcare or manual handling training. These include:

- defining a person handling problem
- identifying what information is required to resolve the problem
- conducting a detailed search of the literature
- selecting the best of the relevant studies and applying rules of evidence to determine their validity
- being able to present to colleagues in a succinct way the content of an article, its strengths and weaknesses (critical appraisal), the clinical message and its application to a person handling problem.

These steps will now be described in more detail, using a person handling example.

Defining a person handling problem

The first step involves converting the need for information about prevention, diagnosis, prognosis, therapy, causation, etc into answerable questions. For example:

> We need to do a risk assessment of a very heavy hemiplegic patient who can weight bear and needs to sit out in a chair (from his/her bed) due to a chest infection. It is desirable to promote independence but there is concern about the manual handling risks to staff. So, our question is:

> "What techniques and equipment can be used to achieve this transfer and promote safety for the person and handlers?"

Identifying what information is required to resolve the problem

In order to address this question, the best available evidence needs to be tracked down. Hignett *et al* produced a systematic review of patient handling activities in 2003 and this should be used as the starting point (Hignett *et al* 2003). The evidence was summarised into different sections, so these should be looked at to source the relevant information. Professional guidelines should also be consulted, and the problem discussed with experts and colleagues to ensure that as much information is being accessed as possible.

Conducting an efficient search of the literature and selecting the studies

Traditional reviews of the published evidence have usually relied on experts or researchers in the field to provide the answer. However, this method has two main weaknesses as the reviewer may have a particular prejudice or prior belief and/or the review can miss evidence that can contribute to the answer. So, simply searching, eg Medline, could miss evidence that is published as conference abstracts or research theses (grey literature).

Hamer & Collinson (1999) and Wright & Hill (2003) describe the key components of a systematic review as being:

- definition of the research question with clear and precise objectives
- methods for identifying the research studies with an explicit and rigorous search of published and grey (unpublished) literature

- selection of studies for inclusion with explicit inclusion and exclusion criteria
- quality appraisal of included studies using transparent appraisal processes and consistent data collection
- extraction of the data
- synthesis of the data with clear method of combining results (statistical or narrative).

Hignett et al (2003) described the search strategy for the patient handling systematic review as taking an unusual philosophical stance by appraising studies within a study type rather than comparatively. This means that the previously mentioned hierarchy (with RCTs as the gold standard) was not applied. A string search was run on eight databases (including Medline, CINAHL, EMBASE and Ergonomics Abstracts) and supplemented by searching the grey literature. They give a detailed description of the processes of inclusion, exclusion, appraisal, extraction and synthesis.

In order to select the studies which are relevant to the question, it would be more useful to use Hignett (2003), which focuses on transfers, starting from lying, sitting and standing positions. The number of studies for starting in the sitting position is reduced to 23 and this is further reduced to only 14 papers (listed under Findings, below and right) for our specific question.

Critical appraisal of content of the article and its strengths and weaknesses

Before looking at the evidence from Hignett (2003), a critical appraisal of the review itself should be carried out. The advantage of using Hignett (2003) rather than Hignett et al (2003) is that the former was published in a peer reviewed academic journal, whereas the latter is a book that has not undergone a formal peer review process. Many books suggest critical appraisal questions for different study types. Fig 9.1, below, gives an example of the sort of questions that should be applied in order to increase confidence in the quality of the evidence.

Are the results of the study valid?
- Did the review address a focused clinical question?
- Were the criteria used to select articles for inclusion appropriate?
- Is it unlikely that important, relevant studies were missed?
- Was the validity of the included studies appraised?
- Were assessments of the studies reproduced?
- Were the results similar from study to study?

What are the results?
- What are the overall results of the review?
- How precise were the results?

Will the results help me in caring for my patients?
- Can the results be applied to my patient care?
- Were all clinically important outcomes considered?
- Are the benefits worth the harms and costs?

Fig 9.1 Critical appraisal questions for a review (Wright & Hill 2003)

Findings

The following evidence statements have been selected from Hignett (2003) to address the question:
- Moderate evidence from five studies (Benevolo et al 1993; Garg et al 1991; Garg & Owen 1994; Marras et al 1999;

Zhuang et al 2000) that a walking belt with two carers should be used for weight bearing patients to transfer them from a sitting position to another sitting position.
- Moderate evidence from two studies (Gagnon et al 1986; Marras et al 1999) that a walking belt should not be used with one carer for weight bearing patients. Additional evidence for this statement from two lower-quality studies (Gagnon & Lortie 1987; Pan & Freivalos 2000).
- Moderate evidence from two studies (Roth et al 1993; Zhuang et al 2000) that using a belt lifter (standing hoist) is preferable to manual methods.
- Limited evidence from one study (Owen & Fragala 1999) that sliding between a bed and stretcher chair may be easier than using either a gait belt or hoist.
- Limited evidence from one study (Elford et al 2000) that using one or two handling slings with two carers is preferable to no slings.
- Limited evidence from one study (Gingher et al 1996) that using a gantry hoist is preferable to mobile hoists for bed to chair transfers.

This information should then be integrated with clinical expertise, unique circumstances and the patient assessment. So, the question may become more complex when it is considered whether:
- the recommended equipment is available
- it has been maintained
- the clinician has been trained to use it
- the environment is suitable
- it is suitable for the current condition of the person.

These questions may change the chosen technique and form the wider risk assessment/clinical judgement that needs to be considered with the research evidence. However, by using the evidence available in Hignett et al (2003) it can be said that the preferred equipment and technique for this scenario would be a walking belt with two carers. If this option is not available, then a standing hoist, sliding technique or gantry hoist could be used, although the evidence to support these options is weaker than for the walking belt with two carers.

Conclusion

It can be seen that there are both internal and external drivers for using an evidence base for person handling activities. The external drivers include the framework of clinical governance (and associated audit processes). The internal drivers are related to professional attitudes and behaviour. However, it must be borne in mind that evidence will become out of date and new treatment and technologies will be introduced. So, practitioners should always be seeking new evidence to make sure that they are working with the most relevant information. The availability of evidence for person handling is relatively new, so it is hoped that practitioners and researchers will take the challenge forward to investigate those areas of person handling about which there is currently limited or no evidence available. This presents an opportunity to embrace the new paradigm and learn methods for appraising and interpreting research literature. As part of the process for increasing the evidence available to support person handling, evidence has been collected to identify best practice for a range of situations in the practical chapters (10 and 11).

Using the practical chapters

Introduction

In the five years since *HOP5* was published, there have been developments in the field of manual handling, including research, best practice guidance and legal considerations. This new edition gives a revision of structure and content for the practical chapters. A task based approach has been used, focusing on risk assessment and giving a summary of the available scientific evidence for each task. This has highlighted weaker areas in the evidence base for professional practice in manual handling and shows where further work is needed.

The evidence presented in the *HOP6* practical chapters is an extension of the work presented in *HOP5*. The evidence collected and published in *HOP5* has been reviewed and updated where necessary. Extra information and the evaluation of extra tasks and methods were completed using the same methodology. All relevant best practice guidance has been used to compare the evidence and the methods included in this 6th edition. A full description of the data collection process can be found in *HOP5*.

Interpreting the evidence

Many techniques used and recommended by professional practice do not have a solid evidence base behind them. To assist patient handling practitioners with the selection of the most suitable method for a given situation, evidence is presented for a range of manoeuvres across different handling tasks. The evidence, by itself, does not make a decision for you, but it can help support the process. A detailed risk assessment is essential in all cases as the basis for decision making. The integration of the following three components into manual handling decision making increases the likelihood of successful problem solving, and so care delivery and staff health are both improved:

- clinical expertise
- individual factors
- best evidence.

EBP is the integration of best research evidence with clinical expertise and individual values. This decreased emphasis on authority does not imply a rejection of what can be learnt from colleagues and teachers whose years of experience have provided them with insight into techniques, equipment and intervention strategies which can never be gained from formal scientific investigation. It must be recognised that there is an "art" to people handling and that a great deal of skill and judgement – and success in the field – is gained by experience and professional insight. However, practice must be evidence based as far as possible. Indeed, the professional judgement approach has already led practitioners astray, since the main approach to back pain in healthcare staff has been to provide techniques training and the only strong evidence in this area states very clearly that techniques training in isolation is ineffective (Hignett et al 2003).

Evidence presented

Groups of professional BCPs were used to act as evidence panels. The evidence panels observed the different manoeuvres and collected evidence using the following tools:

- rapid entire body assessment (REBA) to assess the postures of the carers (Hignett & McAtamney 2000)
- 10-point activity scale to describe the effort given by the person being assisted
- 10-point comfort scale reported by the person being moved
- functional independence measure (FIM) for the person requiring assistance (Granger et al 1993)

TABLE 9.1

Measure	Tool	Description of range of measure		Scores
Carer posture	REBA	Risk level 1 = negligible risk 2-3 = low risk 4-7 = medium risk 8-10 = high risk 11-15 = very high risk	Action level 0 = none necessary 1 = may be necessary 2 = necessary 3 = necessary soon 4 = necessary now	1-15
Activity	10-point Likert scale	0 = no patient activity 10 = full patient activity		0-10
Comfort	10-point Likert scale	0 = extreme discomfort 10 = extreme comfort		0-10
Function level of person	FIM	Independent 7 Complete independence 6 Modified independence Dependent 5 Supervision or set up 4 Minimal contact assistance 3 Moderate assistance Complete dependence 2 Maximal assistance 1 Total assistance		7-1
Mobility level of person	Mobility gallery	A = Fully independent E = Fully dependent		A-E
Skill level required for carer	Benner Scale	Novice Advanced beginner Competent Proficient Expert		

- mobility gallery to assess functional ability of person requiring assistance (ArjoHuntleigh ab 2009)
- skill level required for the carers to be able to deliver the method (Benner 1984).

Full details of these tools are given in *HOP5*. Consensus was agreed by the evidence panels as part of the process of analysis. Every effort was taken to ensure accuracy and reliability during the evidence collection process. The evidence presented in each section is presented in the same format table and follows the order and ranges of scores presented in Table 9.1.

Evidence gathering method critique

The methodology is not ideal due to time and resource constraints. The main critical appraisal points are listed briefly below:

- The photographs used for the REBA analysis of techniques were provided by the authors (or were reproduced from *HOP5*) and are the basis for the drawings included in the chapters. They were not standardised, other than they were to be taken at the point of most risk during the manoeuvre. However, the photographs varied in quality and angle as well as the accuracy of the timing.
- Analysis for each technique is based on a single, still photograph.
- Many compromises and assumptions were made in order to complete the assessment. For instance, the position of a hidden wrist or obscure angle of the trunk. These were made by consensus of the experts attending the evidence gathering days.
- The results generated were based on a very small sample of self-selected BCPs with prior knowledge of REBA.
- Models were used, not people with limited mobility.
- The environment on the assessment days was spacious and time and work pressure did not affect handling.

Summary

A larger body of evidence has been presented in this 6th edition than in *HOP5*. It was not possible to present evidence for every possible handling method as the variations are too numerous. The reader may have variations on particular methods discussed and it is hoped that the tools used in this book will aid evaluation of those differences. Some analysis has been given where there is clear indication from the evidence that a certain technique has benefits over others within the section. However, the reader must always ensure that he/she has undertaken his/her own assessment in his/her particular circumstances. The interpretation and use of the evidence reported in the practical chapters must always be used with the knowledge that different assessment tools are regularly developed and new research findings are being published to improve the evidence that supports person handling.

References

ArjoHuntleigh Ab (2009), The Mobility Gallery, Arjo Publication (www.carethermometer.com/mobilitygallery. Accessed August 2009). www.arjohuntleigh.eu/int/Page. asp?PageNumber=2.

Benevolo, E, Sessarego, P, Zelaschi, G & Franchignoni, F (1993), An ergonomic analysis of five techniques for moving patients [Italian]. *Giornale Italiano di Medicina del Lavoro* **15**, 139-44.

Benner, P (1984), *From novice to expert: Excellence and power in clinical nursing practice*, Menlo Park, Addison-Wesley, pp13-34.

Blomfield, R & Hardy, S (2000), Evidence-Based Nursing Practice, in Trinder, L & Reynolds, S (Eds), *Evidence-based practice. A critical appraisal*, Oxford: Blackwell Publishing Ltd, 111-137.

Department of Health (1998), A First Class Service: Quality in the New NHS, Health Service Circular: HSC (98)113, London: Department of Health.

DiCenso, A, Cullum, N & Ciliaska, D (1998), Implementing evidence-based nursing: some misconceptions, *Evidence-based Nursing*, **1**, 38-40.

Elford, W, Straker, L & Strauss, G (2000), Patient handling with and without slings: an analysis of the risk of injury to the lumbar spine, *Applied Ergonomics*, **31**, 185-200.

Gagnon, M, Sicard, C & Sirois, JP (1986), Evaluation of forces on the lumbo-sacral joint and assessment of work and energy transfers in nursing aides lifting patients, *Ergonomics*, **29**, 3, 407-421.

Gagnon, M & Lortie, MA (1987), Biomechanical approach to low-back problems in nursing aides, in Asfour, S (Ed), *Trends in Ergonomics/Human Factors IV*, Elsevier Science Publishers BV, North Holland, 795-802.

Garg, A, Owen, B, Beller, D & Banaag, J (1991), A biochemical and ergonomic evaluation of patient transferring tasks: wheelchair to shower chair and shower chair to wheelchair, *Ergonomics*, **34**, 4, 407-419.

Garg, A & Owen, B (1994), Prevention of back injuries in healthcare workers, *International Journal of Industrial Ergonomics*, **14**, 315-331.

Gingher, MC, Karuza, J, Skulski, MD & Katz, P (1996), Effectiveness of lift systems for long term care residents, *Physical and Occupational Therapy in Geriatrics*, **14**, 2, 1-11.

Gorman, PN, Wykoff, L & Ash, J (1994), Can primary care physicians questions be answered by using the medical journal literature? *Bulletin of the Medical Library Association*, **82**, 2, 140-146.

Granger, CV, Hamilton, BB, Linacre JM, Heinemann, AW & Wright, BD (1993), Performance profiles of the functional independence measure, Am J Phys Med Rehabil; 72:84-9.

Green, J & Britten, N (1998), Qualitative research and evidence based medicine, *BMJ*, **316**, 18 April, 1230-1232.

Hamer, S & Collinson, G (1999), *Achieving Evidence-based Practice*, London: Harcourt Publishers Ltd.

Hignett, S & McAtamney, L (2000), Rapid Entire Body Analysis (REBA), *Applied Ergonomics*, **31**, 201-205.

Hignett, S (2003), Systematic review of patient handling activities starting in lying, sitting and standing positions, *Journal of Advanced Nursing*, **41**, 6, 545-552.

Hignett, S, Crumpton, E, Ruszala, S, Alexander, P, Fray, M & Fletcher, B (2003), *Evidence-Based Patient Handling, Tasks, Equipment and Interventions*, London: Routledge.

Marras, WS, Davis, KG, Kirking, BC & Bertsche, PK (1999), A

comprehensive analysis of low-back disorder risk and spinal loading during the transferring and repositioning of patients using different techniques, *Ergonomics,* **42**, 7, 904-926.

Murphy, E, Dingwall, R, Greatbatch, D, Parker, S & Watson, P (1998), Qualitative research methods in health technology assessment: a review of the literature. *Health Technology Assessment,* **2**, 16, www.hta.ac.uk/fullmono/mon216.pdf

Owen, BD & Fragala, G (1999), Reducing perceived physical stress while transferring residents: An ergonomic approach. *American Association of Occupational Health Nursing Journal,* **47**, 316-323.

Pan, CC & Freivalos, A (2000), Ergonomic Evaluation of a new patient handling device, Proceedings of the IEA2000/HFES 2000 Congress, The Human Factors and Ergonomics Society, Santa Monica, California, **4**, 274.

Reynolds, S (2000), The Anatomy of Evidence-Based Practice: Principles and Methods, in Trinder, L & Reynolds, S (Eds), *Evidence-based practice, A critical appraisal,* Oxford: Blackwell Publishing Ltd,17-34.

Roth, PT, Ciecka, J, Wood, EC & Taylor, R (1993), Evaluation of a unique mechanical client lift, Efficiency and perspectives of nursing staff, *American Association of Occupational Health Nursing Journal,* **41**, 5, 229-234.

Sackett, D, Richardson, WS, Rosenberg, W & Haynes, RB (1997), *Evidence-Based Medicine: How to Teach and Practice EBM* (1st edition), Edinburgh: Churchill Livingstone.

Smith, J (ed), *The Guide to The Handling of People,* 5th edition 2005, BackCare.

Wright, J & Hill, P (2003), *Clinical Governance,* Edinburgh: Churchill Livingstone.

www.cche.net/usersguides/ebm_tips.asp

www.hsl.unc.edu/Services/Tutorials/ebm/whatis.htm

Zhuang, Z, Stobbe, TJ, Collins, JW, Hsiao, H & Hobbs, GR (2000), Psychophysical assessment of assistive devices for transferring patients/residents, *Applied Ergonomics,* **31**, 35-44.

Core person handling skills

April Brooks MCSP PGDip Health Ergonomics
NHS clinical physiotherapy specialist in patient handling
Sheenagh Orchard RGN RNT Cert Ed(FE) DipNurs(Lond)
Registered member of NBE, moving and handling specialist

Introduction

The aim of this chapter is to describe the core elements of safer handling practice from which practitioners and trainers can develop their own practice and manual handling skills. It is impossible for any publication to describe all the variations in manual handling, and so it is important for the practitioner/trainer to be aware of, and understand:

● the core skill that gives the basic framework for the "manoeuvre"
● the principles that must be applied
● the advantages and disadvantages of the adaptations to the core skill that they intend to use (these may be equipment, handler positioning, hold used etc).

The practitioner/trainer is then using their knowledge, skills and experience to identify best practice for their workplace. It also allows for the development of practice that is flexible and relevant but underpinned by evidence and professional opinion.

Over the years, common adaptations of core techniques have developed and have become established as acceptable practice through a process of formal and informal peer review. These are described in many publications including *The Guide to the Handling of People* 5th edition (Smith (ed) 2005), Derbyshire

Interagency Group Code of Practice (2001), Diligent Handbook of Transfers (Knibbe *et al* 2008) and many others. In this practical chapter, only the core skill relating to these techniques is described, not all the options and variations that can be achieved by adapting the core skill. If handlers are unfamiliar with the range of commonly accepted adaptations of practice, they should seek out this additional information. There are other adaptations of practice that are less commonly applied and may retain higher levels of risk, but that does not make them an unacceptable option if assessed and used appropriately and correctly.

Additional considerations

For the core skills described:
● handlers should at all times apply ergonomics and biomechanical principles to reduce the risk of injury
● the person's handling plan must be referred to
● the move must be planned, executed safely for the handler and person and reviewed on completion
● equipment, if used, must have been assessed as suitable, safe and clean to use and the handler trained in its use.

Core skills

The core skills described offer guidance on how people handling manoeuvres can be achieved by applying the principles of good manual handling (Graveling *et al* 2003). The core skills are based on professional guidance on how to interpret the principles of good manual handling in a people handling situation (Chartered Society of Physiotherapy Guidance 2008; College of Occupational Therapists Guidance 2006; Smith (ed), *HOP5* 2005).

Teaching and using core skills has benefits for:
- new handlers
- writing protocols
- generic risk assessment
- consistency of management in a workplace.

Core skills alone will not meet all the handling requirements of people who need assistance. The core skill may need to be adapted in order to do this. The principles must still be applied but can be adapted and applied differently.

For example, if the principle was "appropriate support must be given to assist a person from sitting to standing", potential adaptations could be "support may be given by visual/verbal prompt, a palm to palm hand hold or support at the shoulder".

Each adaptation will result in "different practice", neither of which is "right or wrong" just "different", with different benefits and disadvantages. One handler's approach may well differ from another and, although we often feel most comfortable with what we know, it does not mean the other practice is incorrect. The approach that is appropriate for a particular person must be established through a process of person specific risk assessment.

What is important is that the benefits and disadvantages of the different approaches are recognised and accounted for in the agreed system of work.

Every handling situation will bring with it particular risks – there is no risk free handling of people – and these risks must be recognised and reduced to a reasonable and acceptable level (see chapter 2).

The closer the actual handling activity is to the core skill, the more likely that the risks will be managed to a reasonable level. In some care settings, particularly low dependency settings, it is possible to meet a high percentage of the required handling activities using core skills alone. In other settings where more complex handling is required, adaptations to the core skill will be inevitable, with the result that such handling practice may be of higher risk. Such practice must be assessed carefully, include supporting evidence and demonstrate clinical reasoning on the benefits and disadvantages, and be clearly documented and reviewed. The benefits of using a higher risk practice must outweigh the disadvantages and a team approach is beneficial when undertaking such risk assessments. Risk assessment tools such as Borg Scale of perceived exertion (Borg 1985), Rapid Entire Body Assessment (REBA) (Hignett & McAtamney 2000), Functional Independence Measure (Granger *et al* 1993), The Mobility Gallery (Knibbe & Waaijer 2005) can be used to assist in these complex assessments (Smith (ed), *HOP5* 2005).

As previously stated, the principles must be applied whether the management is a core skill or one that is adapted to manage a complex handling situation.

It is up to the assessor, trainer or organisation to identify the principles that they consider must be applied in their setting. Fig 10.1 illustrates some principles commonly accepted as required for safer handling practice and also how they are used to produce a system of work/instructions for the task.

Risks and controversial techniques

Techniques become controversial when they increase risk of injury to the person or handler(s) beyond acceptable limits. For each manoeuvre, the specific risks and controversial techniques are outlined and additional reference to these techniques can be found in Ruszala (in Smith (ed), *HOP5* 2005).

Manual lifting

Manual lifting techniques of adults, where most or all their body weight is lifted, pose a high risk of injury and are, therefore, considered to be controversial in professional opinion (Ruszala in Smith (ed), *HOP5* 2005). Full body manual lifts of adults can be eliminated in most healthcare situations by the use of hoists and slings (see chapter 11). In some situations, a manual lift is assessed as the only acceptable management, such as within the emergency services, but the justification for retaining this level of risk must be clear and supported by evidence. Additionally, staff involved in this high risk management must be fully aware of the risks, trained to manage the risks to an acceptable level and be empowered to remove themselves from the task if they feel it is beyond their individual capability. This residual high level of risk means that, in most circumstances, manual lifts should be avoided. If a risk assessment identifies that a manual lift is required, then this must be supported by suitable and sufficient documentation detail in the agreed system of work that takes account of the handler's individual capability, management processes, ergonomics interventions, training, supervision and an alternative management if needed (Ruszala in Smith (ed), *HOP5* 2005).

Manual lifts also pose quality of care issues in that they inevitably require close, intimate holds that can be emotionally and psychologically stressful to the person. Additionally, neuromusculoskeletal pain, discomfort or injury can occur as the person's limbs/joints may be used as "handles and levers" and there is a higher likelihood of tissue viability issues such as shear, skin tears and bruising.

The manual lifting of children poses its own risks, not all of which are associated with their weight. Their behaviour and physical status can pose significant issues for manual lifting and must be assessed carefully.

Manual transfer slings are available that resemble a hoist sling but are designed with handles to enable the transfer to be performed as a manual lift. The risk assessment must identify the numbers of handlers to undertake the lift, taking account of their physical suitability, knowledge and skills and their willingness to be involved. Some of the risk of manual lifting for handlers and person can be reduced significantly by using a manual transfer sling. The commonest use would be for one off situations, emergency situations or as a transition towards hoist and sling management, particularly in a paediatric setting.

Risks and hazardous postures

Postural risks

Handlers are also exposed to risks from postural activities
that do not involve a transfer, eg supporting limbs, clinical
procedures, washing, dressing or feeding. These activities also
typically involve components of static muscle work that may
compound the risk (see chapter 4).

Kneeling bases have advantages and disadvantages but all
kneeling is linked with developing knee pain and lower back
pain, especially if for 15 minutes or longer (Dieen *et al* 1997;
Harkness *et al* 2003; Nahit *et al* 2001).

With both knees fully flexed:
- joints at the end of their range with more discomfort
  (Kee & Karwowski 2001; Pheasant 1991)
- centre of gravity low and body relatively stable
- involves flexion of the spine, static muscle contraction,
  increased compression loading with increased intradiscal
  pressure.

High kneeling:
- increased external pressure on the knees and is linked to
  knee pain (Dieen *et al* 1997).

Kneeling on one knee:
- allows movement over a larger base
- can get closer to the load
- found to be more uncomfortable than high kneel
  (Chung *et al* 2003).

Where possible, reduce the time spent in kneeling positions
and consider use of kneeling equipment, such as
ergonomically designed kneelers, to reduce the strain.

The following are examples of hazardous postures:

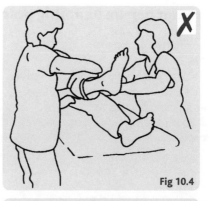

Fig 10.4

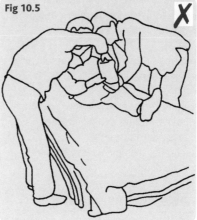

Fig 10.5

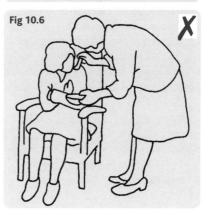

Fig 10.6

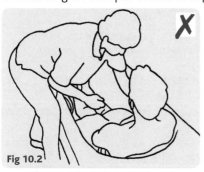

Fig 10.2

Fig 10.3

Framework for safer person handling practice

Justification for moving the person (clinical reasoning)

- The handler(s) are able to justify why the person needs to be moved, and their choice of manoeuvre to meet that need. See examples for care handling and treatment/rehabilitation handling for each manoeuvre throughout the chapter.

Completion of a risk assessment including the TILE format

- Risks associated with the Task itself, the Individual handler(s), the Load (person), the Environment and other relevant factors are recorded, then reduced and/or managed (see chapter 2).
- Knowledge of relevant legislation and Professional Codes of Conduct and Guidance (eg RCN, CSP, COT) are taken into account.
- Handlers refer to relevant records such as any previous risk/handling assessments, profiles and Allied Health Professional (AHP) documentation, eg physiotherapy/occupational therapy assessments in accordance with local guidelines.

Applications of biomechanical and ergonomics principles

- Management of risk always includes the application of biomechanical and ergonomics principles.
- Consideration should be given to reducing unnecessary movement, stooping and task repetition. Knowledge of the base of support, centre of gravity and line of gravity should be used to identify good posture during manoeuvres (see chapter 4).

Optimum start position

- The person places himself/herself (or is facilitated) into the position from which he/she is most likely to succeed in completing the task when given instruction or moved by the handlers.

Hierarchy of approach

The hierarchy follows the Manual Handling Questions (MHQ) hierarchy of approach to encourage the person to do as much for himself/herself as possible (Brooks 2008; Bracher & Brooks 2009). Start with:

- Consider and use normal movement for this person in completing this task: normal movement patterns are those which are optimal, functional, efficient and effective for that person. If the person is asked to move in an alternative way, they will find it more difficult and it will require more effort.
- Teach the person to do this unaided: where possible encourage the person to be able to complete the task himself/herself.
- If the person is unable, identify and provide equipment that would mean the person could then complete the task himself/herself.

- If the person is still unable, one or more handlers should give the minimum assistance possible, with or without handling equipment, to complete the task safely.

Preparation

Preparation of the person

- "Person ability criteria" are the physical and cognitive abilities that a person needs to have in order to complete a manoeuvre or task. Within this chapter, the ability criteria are set out to represent the abilities a person needs to complete the task (a) independently or with supervision (defined as including light touch or verbal prompting) (b) with one handler (c) with more than one handler. Cognitively, the person should be able to consent to carrying out the manoeuvre, be compliant and capable, and be able to follow simple instructions. Assessment of physical ability forms part of the manual handling risk assessment, so these abilities are checked at that time, and monitored for change.

Preparation of handling equipment

- Any person handling equipment to be used is assessed as safe and clean, and meets the requirements of legislation, eg Lifting Operations and Lifting Equipment Regulations 1998.
- The equipment is assessed as suitable for the task, the handler(s), the person, and the environment.
- Handlers are trained in the assessment and use of the handling equipment, according to manufacturers' instructions.
- Handlers can demonstrate competence with the handling equipment within appropriate environments (eg person's home, ward, rehabilitation gym), and with relevant patient/client groups (eg paediatric, bariatric, amputee, stroke).
- Handlers understand the safe system of work in place, including risks involved in performing the task where equipment is used, and know when **not** to proceed.

Preparation for the manoeuvre

To complete the task, the manoeuvre:

- has the desired outcome, eg the person stands from sitting or turns in lying
- encourages the person to do as much for himself/herself as possible (see Hierarchy of approach)
- includes clear and appropriate communication between the handler(s) and person throughout
- comprises appropriate holds that offer the required support without causing physical, psychological or emotional discomfort or harm, eg musculoskeletal pain, discomfort or injury; stress or emotional discomfort, or harmful effects on tissue viability such as shearing, bruising etc
- is controlled and smooth, not jerky or rushed.

On completion

- The person is in a comfortable, safe position.

Fig 10.1 Framework for safer person handling practice

PRACTICAL TECHNIQUES

Task 10.1 Rolling or turning in bed

Example of rolling in bed for care handling
Enables/allows for/promotes ease of nursing care, access to spine, washing, wound dressing, bed linen change.

Example of rolling for treatment/rehabilitation handling
Facilitates head and trunk rotation and toleration of change of centre of gravity and base of support, improves sensory and proprioceptive input, encourages active participation towards a functional goal.

Within treatment handling, it may be that, to begin with, the person can barely tolerate movement of the head. Then, it is likely that two handlers or more will be used at first to obtain and maintain the start position and complete the roll phase. Their hand positions will reflect the person's loss of ability and any missing components of the movement.

Appropriate equipment for rolling
- Bed lever, hoist and turn sling, hoist and repositioning sheet, lateral tilt bed or bed accessory.
- Slide sheets and specialised friction reducing sliding bed systems are used to reposition the person safely in the bed rather than being required to create the roll.

Note: Some equipment, such as a bed lever, will alter the usual pattern of movement for this task: grasping the lever, the person uses a *pulling* (flexion) pattern for their upper body instead of *reaching* (extension) in the direction of motion. However, the benefit of independent movement may override this disadvantage.

Person ability criteria for rolling
For independent movement, the person must be able to:
- tolerate movement from lying to side lying
- initiate the movement from lying into side lying
- maintain stability in side lying, in particular with the reduced base of support.

Assistance from:
- one handler is required if the person:
  - can only give some assistance in the movement, eg turn his/her head and reach across in the direction of movement
- a second handler is usually required if the person:
  - cannot assist in the movement
  - requires support in side lying
  - requires assistance to reposition after rolling – a second handler assists by using a slide sheet to aid the roll and reposition the person central in the bed.

Optimum start position
- The person is lying on his/her back (supine lying) in the middle of a single bed/plinth.
- The handler is standing at the side.

Instructions to enable the person to move independently or assist in the move
- Turn your head towards me.

- Move your near arm away from you, so you won't lie on it when you roll.
- With your far arm, reach across your body towards me.
- Bend your far knee and put that foot flat on the bed.
- When I say "ready, steady, *roll*" I want you to *push* with your foot and *reach* towards me with your arm (indicate arm across body).
- Is that OK? (wait for agreement/consent).
- "Ready, steady, *roll*".

Assistance for rolling
Preparation of the person
- Where possible, use the optimum start position and instructions for assistance (see above).
- The person should be lying flat with no/one pillow.
- Explain the process to the person and the instructions to be given.
- Position the person's near arm away from his/her side.

Preparation of the environment/equipment
- Adjust the bed to an appropriate working height, generally median height in respect of the handlers' waist/pelvic crest height (Orchard in Smith (ed), *HOP5* 2005).
- Ensure brakes are on.
- If placing a knee on the bed, do not exceed the safe working load of the bed.
- If using a slide sheet, check it is the right size, safe, clean to use and inserted under the person's head, hips and shoulders (and feet if he/she cannot move his/her own legs).

Preparation of the handler
- Stand at the side of the bed the person is to face.
- Stand with feet apart and a walk stance, ie one foot in advance of the other (see Task 10.1a) or with one knee on the bed (see Task 10.1b).
- Place a hand on the person's far shoulder blade and another on the far side of the pelvis – do not grip (see Task 10.1c).
- If also repositioning the person into the centre of the bed, the second handler will stand on the opposite side of the bed, with feet apart and a walk stance. Holding the top layer of the slide sheet close to the person's shoulder and hip, transfer weight from front foot to back foot, easing the person across the bed before or as he/she rolls.

Task 10.1a

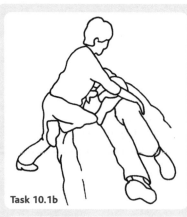

Task 10.1b

Task 10.1c

The manoeuvre
What to do and say:
- give clear instructions, eg "ready, steady, *roll*"
- on "*roll*" transfer body weight from front foot (or knee on the bed) onto the back foot
- assist the person to roll, ideally letting his/her shoulder lead the move
- move back in towards the side of the bed and stand close
- if also repositioning with a slide sheet, on the instruction "*roll*" the second handler will move as described on page 133.

Completion
- Ensure the person is safe, use a correctly fitted bed rail if necessary.
- Ensure the person is comfortable, inserting additional pillows if necessary.

- Remove the slide sheet if used.
- Review the success of the manoeuvre and report/reassess as necessary.

Note: In a very high dependency situation, additional handlers will be required to support at additional points on the person so that the person's whole body is rolled in unison, such as a log roll (see sub-task 10.1.2).

> ### Risks and controversial techniques
> Risk of injury in rolling a person increases when consideration is not given to skin integrity. There must be no gripping of the person. Palms are kept flat.
>
> When a single handler is turning a person, illustrations sometimes show the far bent knee used as a lever, such as for recovery position purposes within first aid. This may increase risk of discomfort or injury at the hip or knee.
>
> Any pulling on the person's arm or shoulder by the handler may also result in injury to his/her own or the person's shoulder/neck.
>
> **Flip turn** (see Task 10.1d)
> This requires the handler to lift the person's hips through and possibly turn at the same time. This presents a risk of back and arm injury to the handler and skin shear on the buttocks of the person (Ruszala in Smith (ed), *HOP5* 2005).
>
>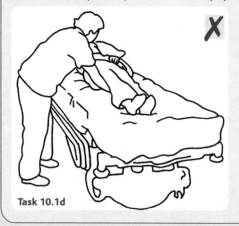
>
> **Task 10.1d**

Evidence review

Technique	REBA	Activity	Comfort	FIM	Mobility gallery	Skill level	Comments
Task 10.1 – Rolling or turning in bed							
Task 10.1a	9	1	7	1	E	Advanced beginner	
Task 10.1b	9	1	7	1	E	Advanced beginner	
Task 10.1c	3	1	7	1	E	Advanced beginner	
Task 10.1d	11 – very high	1	3	1	E		Very high risk, low level of comfort and no activity from the person

Sub-task 10.1.1 Supporting in side lying

When a person cannot maintain his/her own position in side lying, significant issues arise for both the handler and the person.

Issues for the handlers
- The static posture adopted by the handler supporting side lying is often held for a considerable length of time.
- The person is supported close to this handler so the other handler has to reach across the bed to access the person.
- It is difficult to achieve a suitable bed height for both handlers and, if the bed has no high/low facility, the posture of both handlers is compromised.
- The contact can be quite intimate and a close hold which may be emotionally uncomfortable for the handler or person.

Issues for the person
- The person can become anxious as he/she is positioned very close to the edge of the bed and looking at the floor.
- Communication is poor as the person cannot achieve face to face contact with the handler as he/she is under the handler's arm.
- The contact is with a close hold and this can be considered excessively intimate.

All these issues can be addressed by the use of turn slings to support the person in turn rather than being supported by a handler.

There are different styles of turn sling which all address the issue of static posture to support the person. Some, however, turn the person near to the edge of the bed so that the handler still has to reach across the bed to deliver care.

Some allow for good access for hygiene care and also allow the person to be held either central in the bed or to the edge closest to the handler delivering care (see Task 11.5). These are usually used in conjunction with an in-bed sliding repositioning system. In order to assess the right piece of equipment, the assessor must understand the differences in turn slings and what each can achieve.

Sub-task 10.1.2 Log rolling

In an emergency or very high dependency situation, the person may need his/her whole body rolled in unison. Turning or rolling as a core skill should be distinguished from log rolling, which is a specific procedure used to move a person who has potential spinal or pelvic injury onto his/her side.

Log rolling is a specialist manoeuvre requiring a competent and skilled team led by one person who gives clear, pre-designated instructions. More handlers (commonly four to six) will be required to support at additional points on the person's body, such as supporting the head and neck, the upper trunk, the lower trunk, hip, upper thigh, lower leg and foot.

Generally, the handler giving the instruction is the one controlling the head. The next most important handler is the one holding the foot and lower leg to prevent fluctuation of movement (Leigh & Dermott 2010).

There may also be attachments to the person which require the attention of an additional handler, such as intravenous fluids, catheter, drains.

Procedures for log rolling will be specific to each specialist unit and the handlers will need specific training.

Task 10.2 Lying to long sitting

Examples of lying to long sitting for care handling
Enables/allows for/promotes ease of nursing care, dressing, washing, wound dressing, bed linen change, bed adjustment, use of bed pan, eating and ease of digestion and respiration.

Example of lying to long sitting for treatment/rehabilitation handling
Facilitates head control and trunk flexion, toleration of change of centre of gravity and reduced base of support, promotes trunk stability and alignment of lower limbs, trunk alignment over lower limbs and body symmetry, facilitates functional sitting balance, toleration of changes in postural blood pressure, active participation towards a functional goal.

Within treatment handling, it may be that to begin with the person can barely tolerate sitting. Then it is likely that two handlers or more will be used at first within a treatment handling session to obtain and maintain the start position and support the person in sitting – their hand positions will reflect the person's loss of ability and any missing components of the movement.

Appropriate handling equipment for lying to long sitting
Profiling bed, mattress elevator, pillow lifter, bed ladder, bed lever, bed rail.

A profiling bed can be used to promote independence by partially raising the back rest and encouraging the person to use muscle activity to complete the sit.

Some equipment, such as a bed ladder, will alter the usual pattern of movement for this task: grasping the ladder, the person uses a *pulling* (flexion) pattern for his/her upper limbs instead of *pushing* with elbows and then hands (extension) into the mattress. Stability in long sitting is altered while holding the ladder is not as good: it can be difficult to let go of the ladder and maintain sitting without the hands on the mattress behind the trunk. However, the benefit of independence in sitting may override this disadvantage.

Person ability criteria for lying to long sitting
For independent movement, the person must be able to:
- tolerate movement from lying to sitting
- flex forward at the trunk and hips
- lift his/her head

- push up on the bed with elbows, then hands and sit up
- balance in sitting, maintaining trunk control, perhaps using his/her hands on the mattress as a prop.

Assistance from:
- one handler is required if the person:
  - cannot push up on the bed with elbows, then hands and sit up
  - cannot maintain trunk control and sitting balance
- a second handler is usually required if the person:
  - has no or little head control and is not on a profile bed/pillow lifter
  - needs pillows adjusting while he/she is supported in sitting.

Optimum start position
- The person is lying on his/her back (supine lying) in the middle of a single bed/plinth.
- The handler is standing at his/her (weaker) side.

Instructions to enable the person to move independently or assist
- When I give the instruction I want you to:
  - lift your head and put your chin on your chest
  - *push* up on the bed with your elbows, then your hands and sit up.
- "Is that OK?" (wait for agreement/consent).
- Give the instruction, eg "ready, steady, *sit*".
- The person will be more comfortable if he/she now bends one or both knees and puts his/her hands behind on the bed until supported by pillows.

Assistance for lying to long sitting
Preparation of the person
- Where possible, use the optimum start position (see above).
- Ensure the person can raise his/her head off the bed.
- Explain he/she needs to raise his/her head and reach across his/her body and down the bed with the hand furthest from the handler.
- If the person cannot do the above, then a profile bed or pillow lifter should be used.

Preparation of the environment/equipment
- Raise the bed to an appropriate height for the handler – at the end of the move the person's shoulder should not be higher than the handler's shoulder.
- Ensure the brakes are on and the bed rail is lowered on the side of the handler.

Preparation of the handler
- Stand at the side of the bed approximately at the person's waist position.
- Face to face position with the person.
- Adopt a stable base, feet slightly apart and with a walk stance.
- Flex at the hips and knees with weight on the front foot.
- If needed, support the person's far shoulder with the nearside hand, ie right hand to left shoulder or left hand to right shoulder (see Task 10.2a).
- The other hand can rest on the bed.
- Alternatively, a right hand to right shoulder (or left to left) hold can be used but requires a higher skill level as there is more potential for the handler to twist.

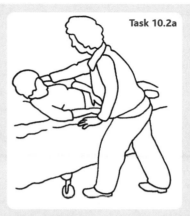

Task 10.2a

The manoeuvre
What to do and say:
- ask the person to raise his/her head and reach across and down with his/her far hand, pushing up with his/her nearside elbow
- give clear instructions such as "ready, raise your head, *reach and push*"
- on "*push*" the handler will transfer body weight from the front foot to the back foot, thus moving out of the person's space (see Task 10.2b)
- guide the shoulder across and down the bed until the person is resting on his/her elbow
- ask the person to push up to a sitting position and support himself/herself by bending one knee and placing his/her hand(s) behind as a prop on the bed (see Task 10.2c).

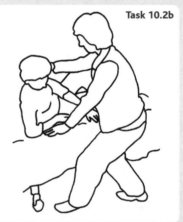

Task 10.2b

Task 10.2c

Completion
- Adjust pillows.
- Ensure person is safe and comfortable – use correctly fitted bed rails if required.

Risks and controversial techniques

Consideration must be given to skin integrity – do not grip, which could cause bruising or tissue damage.

Lifting the weight of the head and trunk of a dependent person can cause injury.

Drag lift

Use of the drag lift, placing the hand or arm under the axilla and using the shoulder as a lever to pull the person up into sitting (see Task 10.2d and e) increases risk of injury to all involved and should be avoided.

Handlers are lifting in an asymmetrical, stooped, twisted and side flexed posture and are prone to moving outside their base of support. Handlers are required to lift over half of the weight of the person who may additionally present with unpredictable movement.

The person's weight is suspended through his/her axilla with the potential for injury or pain. His/her sacrum, buttocks and heels can drag and contribute to pressure sores. The person's head may also need support (Ruszala in Smith (ed), *HOP5* 2005).

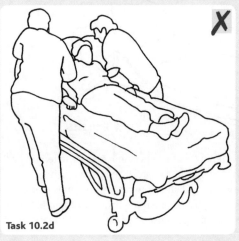

Task 10.2d

Task 10.2e

Evidence review

Technique	REBA	Activity	Comfort	FIM	Mobility gallery	Skill level	Comments
Task 10.2 – Lying to long sitting							
Task 10.2a	9	8	8	5	B	Novice	
Task 10.2c	10	7	4	5	B	Advanced beginner	
Task 10.2d	13 – very high	1	1	2	D		Very high risk to handler, but no activity required from person
Task 10.2e	14 – very high	7	3	2	D		Requires high level of activity from a low ability person. Very high postural risk

Sub-task 10.2.1 Use of a profile bed

There is evidence to support the use of hi/lo profile beds to reduce musculoskeletal strain of handlers (Hignett *et al* 2003). More recently, there is evidence to support their use for the benefit of service users (HSE 2010). All this evidence establishes that profile beds improve independent function, tissue viability and reduce postural strain for the handler and should be considered as soon as a person needs help with bed mobility.

A profile bed with a knee break position reduces slipping down the bed when the person is sitting upright, but the person's head and back must be able to move up the profile section as it is raised (described on page 138).

It is important to recognise certain features of how the person's position changes as the bed is put into profile. If not addressed, the person is left in a poorly supported position and may even slip down the bed, resulting in care staff feeling that such beds are a hindrance rather than a help.

When the back profile is elevated, the bed "bends", creating a shorter edge than when flat. This causes sheeting to bunch at the point of profile which will allow the person to slide down the bed until those creases have been flattened out, usually a distance of 5-7cm (see Task 10.2.1a and b).

Task 10.2.1a

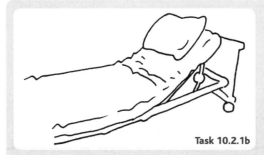

Task 10.2.1b

Task 10.2.1e

The bed is "shortening" but the person is the same length and his/her body has to go somewhere. If the person is not allowed to move up the bed as the profile section is raised, then he/she will be pushed down the bed, with the additional problem of tissue damage caused by friction and shearing.

Raising the knee section helps reduce the movement but, if the back of the person is not also allowed to rise up the bed, he/she will be squeezed into the space between the sections. This creates a poor sitting position with discomfort at the neck and low back, the person will move to try to release this discomfort and move even further down the bed.

To avoid these issues, the person must be able to move his/her back up the bed as it profiles. His/her feet will move closer to the end of the bed (this is not the same as the person moving down the bed as his/her pelvis remains in the same position and when the bed is lowered his/her feet and back will move into the original lying position). This can be achieved by:
- asking the person to move his/her shoulders to release them from the bed as it profiles
- the handler gently easing each shoulder in turn away from the bed as it raises
- using an in situ sliding bed system or inserting a slide sheet between the person's back and the profile section of the bed so his/her back and head can move easily up the bed ensuring his/her bottom is not pushed down the bed (see Task 10.2.1c, d and e).

Sub-task 10.2.2 Manually assisting a dependent person to sit

Sitting a person, who has little or no ability to assist, from lying is a high risk manoeuvre and normally a third handler is needed to pull out the back rest and position pillows. This then becomes a very staff dependent manoeuvre which is not cost effective.

The use of a profile bed, pillow lifter or mattress elevator eliminates the need for handlers to assist a fully dependent person from lying to long sitting.

Where equipment is not available, then two handlers can undertake a manually assisted sit but this should be seen as a short term measure only. The use of a handling strap across the person's shoulders facilitates the manoeuvre and reduces the likelihood of the handlers overreaching or twisting (see Task 10.2.2a and b). The person's head must be supported during this manoeuvre. This may require additional equipment for the handlers to hold, or an additional handler. In either instance, use of a profile bed or pillow lifter would be preferable (Birtles & Williams 2004).

Task 10.2.1c

Task 10.2.1d

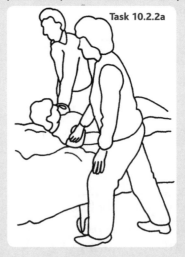

Task 10.2.2a

Task 10.2.2b

To achieve the move:
- assess that the person can bring his/her chin towards his/her chest
- bend the person's knees slightly
- adjust the bed height to an appropriate level – at the end of the move the person's shoulder should not be higher than the handlers' shoulders
- face the head of the bed and adopt a walk stance, with both feet flat on the floor
- hold the handling strap across the person's shoulders (not across his/her neck)
- on the instruction of "ready, steady, sit" move away from the person to raise them into sitting
- ensure the person is positioned comfortably and suitably supported in sitting.

Evidence review

Technique	REBA	Activity	Comfort	FIM	Mobility gallery	Skill level	Comments
Sub-task 10.2.2 – Manually assisting a dependent person to sit							
Task 10.2.2b	5	3	8	3	C	Advanced beginner	This technique slightly increases the postural risk and decreases the activity level of the person when compared to knee on bed. However, it is better for the novice. Scores are the same using strap or netting

Task 10.3 Moving up the bed

Example of moving up the bed for care handling
Enables/allows for/promotes ease of nursing care, dressing, repositioning after sliding down the bed.

Example of moving up the bed for treatment/rehabilitation handling
Promotes improvement in muscle power in limbs, toleration of movement and changes in centre of gravity, active participation towards functional goal.

Appropriate handling equipment for moving up the bed
Bed hand blocks, slide sheet, specialised friction reducing sliding bed systems, hoist and repositioning sheet.

Use principles of independent movement whenever possible, while also using the equipment, eg the person can actively roll for insert of hoist sling, or can assist in inserting and moving using the slide sheet.

Person ability criteria for moving up the bed
For independent movement, the person must be able to:
- in sitting:
  - tolerate movement from lying to sitting
  - flex forward at the trunk and hips
  - maintain sitting using hands on the mattress as a prop
  - transfer weight to each buttock, using hands as a prop
  - bend hips and knees sufficiently to place his/her foot/feet flat on the mattress

  - give assistance with the movement by using his/her foot/feet to push on the mattress
  - lift his/her body weight off the mattress using his/her arms or, sitting on a slide sheet, push with his/her feet to slide up the mattress
- in supine lying:
  - give assistance with the movement by using his/her foot/feet to push on the mattress while lying on a slide sheet.

Assistance from:
- one handler is required if the person:
  - needs his/her feet bracing against the bed to encourage the person to push. However, the handler must be careful not to sustain a hazardous posture in order to achieve this
  - cannot assist as described above but his/her weight and dependency allows a single carer to assist with a slide sheet
- a second handler is usually required if the person:
  - is fully dependent, heavier or has poor compliance. The move is then usually undertaken as a supine slide so that the handlers are not supporting a seated person at the same time as achieving the slide.

Optimum start position
- The person is sitting or lying on his/her back (supine lying) in the middle of a single bed/plinth.
- The handlers are standing at the side of the bed.

Instructions to enable the person to move independently or assist

- Support yourself by placing your hands on the mattress just behind you (sitting move only).
- Bend your knees, and place your feet (or foot for amputee) flat on the mattress.
- When I say "ready, steady, push" I want you to:
  – *push* with your feet, using the mattress.
- "Is that OK?" (wait for agreement/consent).
- "Ready, steady, *push*".
- The person may need to repeat the instructions several times in order to cover the distance.

Assistance for moving up the bed in lying – supine slide

Preparation of the person
- Where possible use the optimum start position.
- The person lies flat with one pillow under his/her head, or no pillow. (A pillow controls the head and neck during the move and can be more comfortable. It also reduces the noise of the slide sheet against the person's head.)
- A slide sheet should be placed under all points of contact between the person and the bed, eg under head, trunk and feet. (Do not place under feet if the person can push with his/her feet to assist.) If a pillow is *in situ*, the slide sheet should be underneath it.
- If it is not suitable for the person to lie flat, he/she can be supported in a semi-recumbent position with three or four pillows on top of the slide sheet but the mattress is flat or virtually flat.
- Explain the process to the person and the instructions to be given.

Preparation of the environment/equipment
- Adjust the bed to an appropriate working height.
- The bed should be flat or not exceeding a 30 degree raise of the profile head section (lowering the head end of the bed, ie reverse Trendelenberg position can be used but there must be no medical contraindications, such as compromising cardiac or respiratory function and the tilt should not exceed 30 degrees).
- Ensure the brakes are on.
- Check the slide sheet is the right size, safe, clean to use.
- Insert under the person (an in-bed sliding and repositioning system can be used and will already be *in situ*).

Preparation of the handlers
- This move generally requires two handlers (assessment can identify, using an adapted manoeuvre, whether one handler can achieve the move as long as his/her individual capability has been assessed and the person is not too heavy).
- Stand on either side of the bed, at the head end (see Task 10.3a).
- Face down the bed or obliquely face the far foot of the bed (the handler(s) can stand behind the pillow at the top of the bed if there is no headboard).
- Adopt a stable base using a walk stance of feet slightly apart and one foot in advance of the other.
- Alternatively, place feet in a stand position, slightly apart, ready to step back.

- Hold the top layer of slide sheet where there is significant weight of the person in contact with the bed, ie shoulder or shoulder and hip.
- The slide sheet can be held with one or two hands depending on the weight of the person on the bed and the individual capability of the handlers (the oblique stand position will prevent twisting if two hands are used).
- Hold your hand(s) in front of you with relaxed shoulder and elbow.
- Ensure the slide sheet is taut preceding the move.
- Identify the handler who will give the commands.

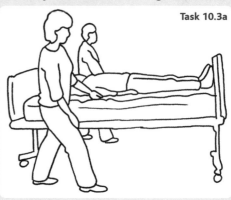

Task 10.3a

The manoeuvre
What to do and say:
- the lead handler gives clear instructions such as "ready, steady, *slide*"
- on "*slide*" the handlers transfer their body weight from front foot to back foot (see Task 10.3a and b) or by stepping back thus easing the person up the bed
- maintain arm length, do not pull, just use the arms with no body weight transfer
- the move should be controlled, smooth and gentle – not jerky and/or fast
- if necessary, repeat the move until the person is in the required position.

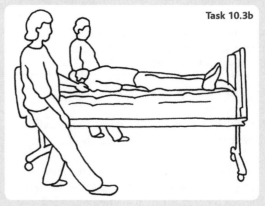

Task 10.3b

Completion
- Ensure the person is safe, use correctly fitted bed rail if necessary.
- Ensure the person is comfortable.
- Remove the slide sheet (a bed system would be left in place) either by rolling the person or removing by passing one corner under the slide sheet and drawing through (see Sub-task 10.3.1f).

Risks and controversial techniques

Risk of injury in moving up the bed increases when consideration is not given to skin integrity, particularly shearing and friction against bed sheets.

For persons with arthritis in the neck or upper limbs, weight bearing through the fists or hands may be painful, even when using bed hand blocks.

Bariatric persons may find it impossible to clear the mattress using the independent method described. It can also be difficult to sit in a long sitting position without a backward lean due to their weight distribution and using a hoist to reposition may be more appropriate.

Supine slide with handlers facing each other across the bed

The risks of this approach are greater than with handlers facing down the bed. There is more likelihood of spinal rotation and lateral flexion when pulling (Hall in Smith (ed), *HOP5* 2005). Pulling by transferring body weight from left to right, or right to left, is less mechanically efficient and the hands tend to come up and lower during the slide creating a lift.

Orthodox lift (see Task 10.3c)

Potential for pain or skin damage to the arms of the handlers. The handlers lift in a stooped posture with arms outstretched and are prone to twisting and moving outside of their base of support.

The person may not be able to lift his/her own head and the buttocks and heels may drag on the bed with resultant tissue damage (Ruszala in Smith (ed), *HOP5* 2005).

Task 10.3c

Two sling lift (see Task 10.3d)

- Handlers are lifting in a stooped or twisted posture with arms outstretched and are prone to twisting and moving outside their base during the move.
- Their arms are exposed to potential pain and skin damage (Ruszala in Smith (ed), *HOP5* 2005).
- Skin shear or bruising of the person may occur as the arms or equipment are introduced.
- Use of equipment, such as handling slings, increases the distance of the load from the handlers' spines and reduces the risk of injury to the lower back.

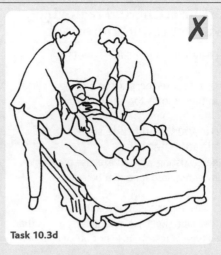

Task 10.3d

Through arm/hammock lift (see Task 10.3e)

- The person's tissue viability could be compromised by shear, bruising, skin tears. The heels and or buttocks may drag on the bed. The person's musculoskeletal health could be compromised by pull under the axilla and/or grasp of the forearm.
- The handlers are prone to twisting in the final stages and side flexing may occur if there is a height difference between handlers and/or the person. The load is taken from outside the handlers' base (Ruszala in Smith (ed), *HOP5* 2005).

Task 10.3e

Shoulder/Australian lift (see Task 10.3f)

Handlers perform an asymmetrical lift on one shoulder and variation in height of the handlers and person will contribute to the postural strain. The position for the person can cause shoulder pain/discomfort/injury (Ruszala in Smith (ed), *HOP5* 2005).

Task 10.3f

Sub-task 10.3.1 Inserting and removing slide sheets without rolling the person

Example of inserting/removing slide sheets for care handling
Enables a hoist sling to be inserted, prior to moving a person who has difficulty in turning or is too heavy to turn.

Example of inserting/removing slide sheets for treatment/rehabilitation handling
Reduces friction when assisting with an exercise programme to regain muscle power required for a manoeuvre.

Appropriate equipment for inserting slide sheets
Roller slide sheets, flat slide sheets, in-bed slide systems that are designed for this type of insertion, ie not bulky or covered in non-slip fabric.

Person ability criteria for inserting and removing slide sheets without rolling
The person must:
- be able to tolerate the feeling of slide sheets inserted this way
- have no tissue viability contraindications.

Assistance from:
- one handler is required if the person:
  - is very small and the handler can reach both sides at the same time without a hazardous posture (usually small children)
- a second handler is usually required if the person:
  - cannot turn to insert/remove slide sheets
  - is of a size, weight or height similar to, or exceeding, that of the handlers (most adult settings)
  - has unpredictable physical or behavioural attributes.

Optimum start position
- The person is lying on his/her back (supine lying) in the middle of a single bed/plinth.
- The handlers are standing on each side of the person.

Assistance for inserting and removing slide sheets without rolling the person
Preparation of the person
- The person should be lying flat (this method can also be achieved for a person who is supported in sitting in a profile bed).

Preparation of the environment/equipment
- Ensure the bed is at an appropriate working height and the brakes applied.
- Check the slide sheets are safe, clean and the correct size and style.
- Fold the slide sheets several times leaving the last part free (see Sub-task 10.3.1a).
- Turn so that the folded panel is next to the bed and pass underneath the pillow and introduced under the person's shoulders (see Sub-task 10.3.1b).
- Alternatively, the panel can be inserted under the feet and legs and the slide sheets inserted from foot to head.

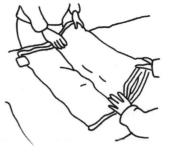

Task 10.3.1a

Task 10.3.1b

Preparation of the handler
- A handler stands on either side of the bed facing the top of the bed (see Sub-task 10.3.1b).
- Create a stable base with a walk stance, feet slightly apart and one foot forward, weight on the forward foot.
- Hold the edge of the panel nearest to the head of the bed, palm up, to be ready to pull the panel back and underneath the person (see Sub-task 10.3.1c).
- Alternatively, hold the corner of the folded panel and be ready to twist back and underneath the person (see Sub-task 10.3.1d and e).
- The other hand can be used for support by placing on the bed.

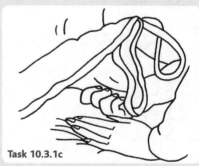

Task 10.3.1c

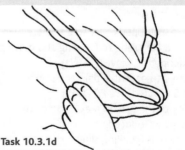

Task 10.3.1d

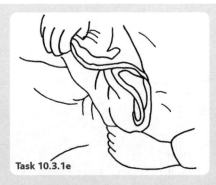

Task 10.3.1e

The manoeuvre
What to do and say:
- give clear instructions, eg "ready, steady, *pull*"
- on the instruction "*pull*" pull the panel back and underneath the person by transferring weight from the front to back foot
- repeat this, moving back down the bed each time, until the sheet is in position
- when the slide sheet gets to the person's hips, it can help for the handler to push the mattress down slightly.

Completion
- If inserting a sling, pass this between the slide sheets or complete the supine slide (see Task 10.3).
- Ensure the person is safe and comfortable.
- Remove the slide sheets by turning one corner underneath the sheet and pass to the opposite side. This corner is then eased up and out. Ensure the sheet is flat and turning on itself at all times (see Sub-task 10.3.1f).

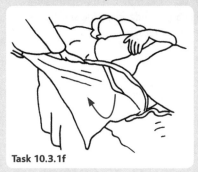

Task 10.3.1f

Sub-task 10.3.2 Undertaking a lateral transfer

Example of undertaking a lateral transfer for care handling
Enables the person to move across a surface or from one surface to another, eg bed to trolley, bed to change table.

Example of rolling for treatment/rehabilitation handling
Enables the person to move across from one surface to another, eg bed to plinth, bed to standing frame.

Appropriate equipment for lateral transfer
There is a wide range of equipment designed specifically to manage this transfer, eg inflatable transfer mattress, roll board, mechanical transfer systems, specific slide sheets with/without extension handles, specialised friction reducing transfer boards, lateral transfer boards for bridging the gaps

and hoists and stretcher slings. All of which will reduce the risks of this transfer in different ways. For specialist areas, such as operating theatres, it is essential to assess which system is most appropriate for the setting/user and then specific training in its use should be given. The system described as a core skill is for less complex settings such as transfer onto a change table trolley or across a double bed.

Person ability criteria for undertaking a lateral transfer
For independent movement, the person must be able to:
- in sitting:
  - tolerate movement from sitting to sitting
  - flex forward at the trunk and hips
  - maintain sitting using hands on the mattress as a prop
  - bend hips and knees sufficiently to place his/her foot/feet flat on the mattress
  - give assistance with the movement by using his/her foot/feet to push on the mattress
  - lift his/her body weight off the mattress using his/her arms and move sideways across the surfaces or, sitting on a slide sheet, push with his/her feet to slide across.

Assistance from:
- two or more handlers (usually three or four) are required if the person:
  - is in supine lying and cannot sit and assist
  - is highly dependent or unconscious.

Optimum start position
- The person is lying on his/her back (supine lying) in the middle of a single bed/plinth.
- The handlers are standing on either side of the bed.

Assistance for undertaking a lateral transfer
Preparation of the person
- In most cases the person is unconscious or highly dependent and should be lying supine.
- If equipment is to be inserted, the person should be rolled as for Task 10.1.
- Place the person's head facing the direction of the transfer – unless assessment identifies that this is contraindicated.

Preparation of the environment/equipment
- Insert any equipment under the person before bringing the two surfaces for transfer together.
- Ensure any gap between the surfaces has been "bridged", eg with a transfer board or the dropped side of the change table.
- If using a transfer board, a third should be placed under the person, a third across the gap and a third onto the receiving surface. Unless it is already integral with the board, a sliding system will also be required over the board.
- Insert a sliding system under the person between all the person's points of contact and the lying surface, ie under head, trunk and feet.
- If a pillow is used, then place the slide system under the pillow so the pillow will move with the person.
- Raise both surfaces to an appropriate working height, at least waist height.
- Bring the two transfer surfaces together.
- Apply the brakes on both the current and receiving surfaces.

Preparation of the handlers

- Identify the number of handlers required – commonly three or four.
- Identify the handler who will give the instructions – commonly the handler at the person's head.
- All handlers create a stable base using a walk stance – standing with their feet apart and one foot in front of the other.
- Handlers who will "push" start with their weight on the back foot and will complete the move by transferring their weight onto the front foot.
- The handler who will push stands by the person and places his/her hands on the person's shoulder and pelvis (see Sub-task 10.3.2a and b).
- If two handlers push, they place one hand on the shoulder or pelvis and the other on the bed or both hands at the shoulder or pelvis.
- Handlers who will "pull" start with their weight on the front foot and will complete the move by transferring their weight onto the back foot (see Sub-task 10.3.2c and d) or by stepping back.
- The handlers who will pull reach to hold the top layer of the slide sheet (reach should be reduced to a reasonable distance, which can be achieved with extension handles if necessary).

Task 10.3.2d

The manoeuvre

What to do and say:

- the lead handler gives clear instruction such as "ready, steady, *slide*"
- on "*slide*" all handlers transfer their body weight in the direction they are to move, ie pull or push
- the move should be controlled, smooth and gentle not jerky and/or fast
- if necessary, repeat the move until the person is across onto the receiving surface.

Completion

- Ensure the person is safe, use correctly fitted bed rails if necessary.
- Ensure the person is comfortable.
- Remove the equipment used, either by rolling the person or removing the transfer board, and then remove the slide sheets by passing one corner under the slide sheet and drawing through (see Task 10.3.1f).

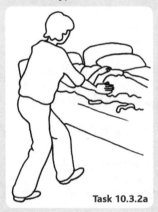

Task 10.3.2a

Task 10.3.2b

Task 10.3.2c

Risks and controversial techniques

Lateral transfers hazardous postures (see Task 10.3.2e, f and g)

If suitable equipment to reduce reach and to allow for variable height and reach is not used as part of the system of work, lateral transfers can lead to a range of hazardous postures and resultant postural strain for the handler (Ruszala in Smith (ed), *HOP5* 2005). The risks can be exacerbated by half kneeling or double kneeling, which affects stability and requires the handlers to change position during the move.

Task 10.3.2e

Task 10.3.2f

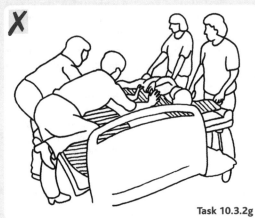

Task 10.3.2g

Two poles and canvas (see Task 10.3.2h)

The arms and shoulders undertake most of the lift as environmental constraints limit the ability to power from the legs. Awkward postures are common with the potential for musculoskeletal strain (Ruszala in Smith (ed), *HOP5* 2005).

Task 10.3.2h

Three person lift (see Task 10.3.2i)

Three or more handlers of compatible height are required and coordination of the move needs to be precise. There is the potential for the person to be dropped or handlers moving awkwardly with resultant strained postures (Ruszala in Smith (ed), *HOP5* 2005).

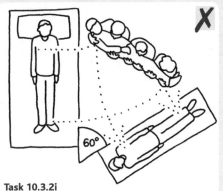

Task 10.3.2i

10 Core person handling skills

Evidence review

Technique	REBA	Activity	Comfort	FIM	Mobility gallery	Skill level	Comments
Task 10.3 – Moving up the bed							
Task 10.3a	4	1	8	2-1	D/E	Advanced beginner	A competent skill level will be needed for sliding people with complex needs. Different slide sheets will have different coupling, eg handles/no handles, and this will affect the REBA score
Task 10.3c	12 – very high	1	1	1	E		High postural risk, very uncomfortable and no activity from the person
Task 10.3d	10 – high	1	4	1	E		Very high risk, low level of comfort and no activity from the person
Task 10.3e	11 – very high	3	3	3	C		Very high risk, very little activity from the person, low level of comfort
Task 10.3f	13 – very high	2	6	3	C		Very high postural risk, low activity and adequate comfort levels
Sub-task 10.3.2 – Undertaking a lateral transfer							
Task 10.3.2a	9	1	8	2-1	D/E	Advanced beginner	In a complex setting or for a person with complex needs, the skill level would need to be competent/proficient
Task 10.3.2c	8	1	8	2-1	D/E	Advanced beginner	
Task 10.3.2e	12	1	7	1	E		A wider sheet would give similar results to using slide sheets with handles
Task 10.3.2f	4	1	7	1	E		A wider sheet would give similar results to using handles
Task 10.3.2g	6	1	7	1	E		Decreased score as not over reaching or kneeling on the trolley
Task 10.3.2h	8 – high	1	7	1	E		A high risk level, but on edge of medium, comfortable for person being moved. No activity from the person

Task 10.4 Side lying to edge sitting

Example of side lying to edge sitting for care handling
Enables/allows for/promotes ease of nursing care, washing, dressing, bed linen change, prepares for transfer stage to standing, to another chair or commode.

Example of side lying to edge sitting for treatment/rehabilitation handling
Encourages active participation towards a functional movement goal. Facilitates trunk control and side flexion. Facilitates weight bearing around the hip. Facilitates trunk and head righting reactions and toleration of rise in centre of gravity and smaller base of support. Encourages stabilisation of blood pressure.

Within treatment handling, it may be that initially the person can barely tolerate sitting. Then it is likely that two handlers or more will be used at first within a treatment handling session to obtain and maintain the start position and support the person in sitting – their hand positions will reflect the person's loss of ability and any missing components of the movement.

Appropriate handling equipment for side lying to edge sitting
Profiling bed, pillow lifter, mattress elevator, leg lifter, bed rail, hoist.

The equipment can be used just for the initial phase or just for the end phase of sitting, encouraging the person to do as much for himself/herself as possible: talking the person through the manoeuvre using the active instructions may motivate and encourage recruitment of muscles.

Note: Consideration must be given to the stability of the mattress, especially where a pressure relieving mattress is in use – follow manufacturers' instructions.

Person ability criteria for side lying to edge sitting
For independent movement, the person must be able to:
- tolerate movement from side lying to sitting
- position himself/herself in side lying
- contribute through his/her own initiated movement, or with mechanical assistance (eg raising head of a profiling bed), to raise the head and trunk
- have sufficient hip and knee function to drop the legs over the side of the bed
- tolerate sitting, in particular to control his/her centre of gravity over the base of support (sitting on edge of surface, feet on floor)
- maintain sitting balance at the edge of bed/plinth, perhaps using hands on the mattress as a prop
- adjust to changes in blood pressure.

Assistance from:
- one handler is required if the person:
  - needs assistance with any or all of the above criteria
  - cannot maintain sitting balance without support
- a second handler is usually required if the person:
  - has unpredictable physical ability or behaviour
  - requires a handler on each side to stabilise sitting.

Optimum start position
- The person is lying on his/her side (side lying) at the side of a bed/plinth.
- The handler is standing at that side of the bed.

Instructions to enable the person to move independently or assist
- Bend your knees up towards your chest, bringing both your feet to the very edge of the bed.
- Bring your top arm forward and put your hand down on the bed in front of you near your underneath elbow.
- When I say "ready, steady, *sit*" on the word "*sit*" I want you to:
  - drop your feet down over the side of the bed
  - *lift* your head
  - *push* down onto the bed with your hand and elbow, and
  - come up into sitting.
  - "is that OK?" (wait for agreement/consent)
  - "ready, steady, *sit*".
- Stand close to the person for a moment – he/she should place his/her feet on the floor. Make sure the person is not feeling dizzy and you have followed advice about what should be on his/her feet before asking him/her to move.

Assistance for side lying to sitting
Preparation of the person
- Where possible, use the optimum start position and instructions for assistance (see above).
- The person should be lying on his/her side (see Task 10.1).

- A slide sheet can be placed on the bed under the feet to aid movement.
- Explain the process and instructions to be used.

Preparation of the environment/equipment
- Adjust the bed to an appropriate working height for the handler. If the person has unsteady sitting balance, it may be better to have the bed height adjusted so that his/her feet will come to the floor without further adjustment. The handler will then need to increase his/her hip flexion to achieve the move.
- Ensure the brakes are on.

Preparation of the handler
- Decide how many handlers will assist.
- Stand at the side of the bed the person is to sit on, facing the person at his/her chest level.
- Stand with feet apart, weight bearing through the foot nearest the head of the bed – weight will be transferred to the other foot as the person comes up into sitting.
- Place a hand under the person's lower shoulder and another on the upper side of the pelvis – do not grip and do not lift the person. The assistance is given by transferring the weight from one foot to the other (see Task 10.4a).
- If the person has more independent function, the handler's hand can be placed on the upper shoulder instead.
- If needed, the second handler adopts the same stable base and rests the person's legs on his/her hands or holds the top layer of the slide sheet.

Task 10.4a

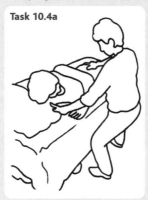

The manoeuvre
What to do and say:
- give clear instructions, eg "when I say ready, steady, *sit*" on the word "*sit*" I want you to drop your feet down over the side of the bed, lift your head, push down on the bed with your hand and elbow and come up onto your elbow or into sitting
- check the person is ready and say "ready, steady, *sit*"
- the handler assists at the shoulder and hip by transferring his/her body weight towards the foot of the bed (see Task 10.4b)
- ideally, the person pushes up until he/she rests on his/her elbow rather than to full sitting as he/she then does not need supporting by a handler
- from this half-way position, the handler again says "*push*"
- the handler assists at the shoulder and pelvis as the person sits – again transferring his/her body weight toward the foot of the bed
- the person slides his/her legs off the bed as he/she sits
- if the person needs assistance with his/her legs, as well as

10 Core person handling skills

assistance to sit, then a second handler will be needed. The second handler will slide the legs off the bed, as the person sits, by transferring his/her body weight from front to back foot and flexing to allow the person's feet down to the floor (see Task 10.4c). Use of a handling strap can extend the reach of the handler and reduce the flexion required (see Task 10.4d)

- alternatively, the handler can assist the person's legs by transferring from a high kneel position to a low kneel to place the person's feet on the floor (see Task 10.4e).

Task 10.4b

Task 10.4c

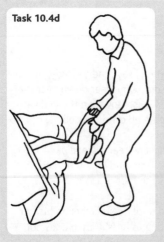

Task 10.4d

Task 10.4e

Completion
- Stand close to the person to ensure the person is stable in sitting.
- Remove the slide sheet, if used, to prevent a slip hazard.
- Ensure person is wearing the correct footwear.
- Lower the bed so that the person's feet can touch the floor.

Alternative methods
The person may be able to sit using a profile bed/pillow lifter and use a leg lifter to assist his/her own legs out of bed (see Task 10.4f).

Task 10.4f

The person may be able to use a bed rail to assist the turn and to stabilise his/her sitting position before standing (see Task 10.4g and h).

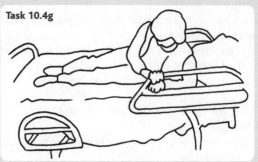

Task 10.4g

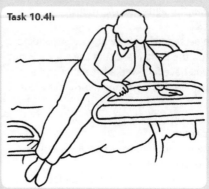

Task 10.4h

Risks and controversial techniques

Risk of injury in lying to sitting a person increases when the person does not meet the ability criteria and the handlers over assist the person up into sitting.

When handlers assist, they must not "lift" at the shoulder or push too hard at the hip in order to help the person sit. If the person requires this level of assistance, then this may not be the most appropriate method and a profile bed should be considered.

This move is less suitable for people who have painful hip joints or have undergone hip surgery.

Hazardous postures can be adopted by handlers when assisting the person to position his/her legs (see Task 10.4i). This can lead to postural strain and cumulative damage of the musculoskeletal system (Ruszala in Smith (ed), *HOP5* 2005).

Use of a drag lift to sitting is not acceptable practice (see Task 10.2).

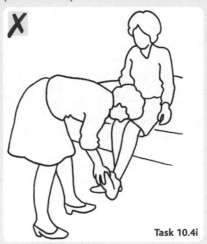

Task 10.4i

Evidence review

Technique	REBA	Activity	Comfort	FIM	Mobility gallery	Skill level	Comments
Task 10.4 – Side lying to edge sitting							
Task 10.4c	8	5	8	4-3	C	Advanced beginner	
Task 10.4c plus strap	3	5	8	3	C	Advanced beginner	Postural risk is less with handling strap (see Task 10.4d)
Task 10.4e	4	5	8	2	D	Advanced beginner	Legs off bed half kneeling

Task 10.5 Edge sitting to side lying

This move is the reverse method of Task 10.4 and has similar requirements.

Example of edge sitting to side lying for care handling
Enables/allows for/promotes ease of return to bed or transfer onto a lying surface.

Example of edge sitting to side lying for treatment/rehabilitation handling
Encourages active participation towards a functional movement goal. Facilitates trunk control and side flexion. Facilitates weight bearing around the hip. Facilitates trunk and head righting reactions and toleration of rise in centre of gravity and smaller base of support etc.

Appropriate handling equipment for edge sitting to side lying
- Profiling bed, pillow lifter, mattress elevator, electric leg lifter, leg lifter, bed rail, hoist.
- The person may be able to lie using a profile bed/pillow lifter and use a leg lifter to assist his/her legs into the bed (see Task 10.4f)
- The person may be able to use a bed rail to assist the turn and to stabilise the sitting position before lying (see Task 10.4g and h)

- Consideration must be given to the stability of the mattress, especially where a pressure relieving mattress is in use – follow manufacturers' instructions.

Note: A profile bed, or pillow lifter can be used, partially raised, so that the person is going from edge sitting to semirecumbent. This encourages the person to do as much for himself/herself as possible, while ensuring he/she does not fall backwards when lying and may motivate and encourage recruitment of muscles.

Person ability criteria for edge sitting to side lying
For independent movement, the person must be able to:
- tolerate and maintain sitting balance, in particular to control the centre of gravity over his/her base of support (sitting on edge of surface, feet on floor)
- adjust to changes in blood pressure
- tolerate movement from sitting to side lying
- position himself/herself in side lying
- contribute through his/her own initiated movement, or with mechanical assistance (eg lowering head of a profiling bed), to lower the head and trunk
- use sufficient hip and knee function to raise the legs over the side of the bed.

Assistance from:
- one handler is required if the person:
  - needs assistance with any or all of the above criteria
  - cannot maintain sitting balance without support
- a second handler is usually required if the person:
  - has unpredictable physical ability or behaviour
  - requires support from both sides to support sitting balance and transfer to lying.

Optimum start position
- The person is sitting on the side of a bed/plinth.
- The person places the hand nearest the head of the bed on the mattress a little away from his/her side.
- If possible, the other hand reaches across his/her lap towards the mattress at the head end of the bed – this is where the hand will be going as the person lowers onto his/her elbow to lie on his/her side.
- If the person is going to lie down straight onto his/her back, this hand reaches behind him/her towards the other side of the bed.
- Handler(s) stand at that side of the bed/plinth.

Instructions to enable the person to move independently or assist
- Place your feet flat on the floor.
- When I say "ready, steady, *lie*, on the word "*lie*" I want you to:
  - lower your shoulder towards the bed, controlling your speed with your elbow and other hand
  - lift your legs onto the bed as your shoulder lowers onto the pillow
  - then turn into the bed.
- "Is that OK?" (wait for agreement/consent).
- "Ready, steady, *lie*".

Assistance for edge sitting to side lying
Preparation of the person
- Where possible, use the optimum start position and instructions for assistance.
- The person should be sitting on the side of the bed in a position where he/she will not have to move up the bed once lying.
- The person should support himself/herself by placing his/her hands behind on the mattress as a prop or against the raised profile section of the bed.

Preparation of the environment/equipment
- Adjust the bed to an appropriate height for the person so that his/her feet are flat on the floor.
- If appropriate, raise or partially raise the profile back of the bed.
- The person may use a leg lifter.
- Use of a handling strap can extend the reach of the handler and reduce the flexion required (see Task 10.4d).
- Ensure brakes are on.

Preparation of the handler
- Decide how many handlers will assist.
- Decide the instructions to be given.
- Stand at the side of the bed where the person is sitting, facing the person.

- Stand with feet apart, weight bearing through both feet – weight will be transferred to the foot nearest the head of the bed as the person lies down.
- Place a hand under the person's shoulder – do not grip and do not support his/her weight. The assistance is given by transferring the weight from both feet onto the foot nearest to the head of the bed.
- If the person has a higher independent function, then the handler will not need to assist with the upper body.
- If a second handler is needed to assist the legs into the bed, he/she adopts the same stable base but facing the foot of the bed.
- The handler can assist the person's legs from a low kneel position, raising up to a high kneel to place the person's feet on the bed (see Task 10.4e).

The manoeuvre
What to do and say:
- the handler gives clear instructions such as "when I say ready, steady, *lie*" on the word "*lie*" I want you to come down onto your elbow and hand, and use them to control your speed
- lift your legs onto the bed as your shoulder lowers onto the pillow
- if you are going to lie on your back, turn into the bed (if necessary, bridge by bending your knees up and using your feet to push, lift your bottom and move across into the bed)
- check the person is ready, and say "ready, steady, *lie*"
- the handler assists at the shoulder by transferring body weight towards the head of the bed
- the person slides his/her legs onto the bed as he/she lies (a slide sheet under his/her legs can aid this movement)
- if a second handler is assisting at the legs, he/she adopts a walk stance facing the foot of the bed, bringing the legs onto the bed as the person sits by transferring his/her own body weight from back to front foot, or using a handling strap or a kneeling position as described above.

Note: It is always preferable for the person to lift his/her own legs into bed or to use a mechanical leg lifter. If assisting the legs, the handler should place the legs onto the edge of the bed only, not lift them into the middle of the bed as this is taking the load away from the handler's body. A slide sheet under the legs can then be used to slide the legs into the middle of the bed and removed before leaving the person.

Completion
- Stand close to the person to ensure the person is in a safe position in the bed.
- Remove the slide sheet if used under the person's legs, to prevent a slip hazard.
- Raise a bed rail if this has been assessed as required.
- Ensure the person has adequate pillows and is comfortable.

Risks and controversial techniques
Risk of injury in sitting to lying increases when the person does not meet the ability criteria and the handlers over assist the person into lying.

Manual assistance of a person's legs into bed must be carefully assessed, particularly if the handler lifts and places the legs into the middle of the bed. Legs can be very heavy, awkward to hold and the load is being taken away from the handler.

Manual assistance of a person's legs can lead to damage to the person's tissue viability, either from over gripping, bruising or skin damage because the person has frail skin or oedema.

Task 10.6 Sitting to sitting transfer using a transfer board

Example of sitting to sitting transfer for care handling
Enables/allows for/promotes ease of nursing care, bed linen change, transfer to an alternate sitting destination, promotes independence.

Example of sitting to sitting transfer for treatment/rehabilitation handling
Encourages active participation in a functional transfer. Facilitates lateral weight transference. Facilitates weight bearing through hip and knee. Facilitates balance reactions and toleration of changes in centre of gravity.

Appropriate handling equipment for sitting to sitting transfer
Straight transfer board, curved transfer board, board with integral slide sheet.

Note:
- Choice of transfer board will be made according to the specific needs of the person and the transfer surfaces.
- Banana boards have a long curved edge at the back and the shorter curve at the front – the person traces a normal pattern of movement along it, back and round. If placed with the person moving along the long curved edge, the person's centre of gravity comes forward over the feet – the person is more likely to fall forwards and the board to tip. Wheelchairs with large rear wheels need positioning at an angle to the transfer surface to allow the person to transfer along the short edge of the board.

Person ability criteria for sitting to sitting transfer (transfer board)
For independent movement, the person must be able to:
- set up the wheelchair (ie position, brakes, arm rests, foot plates), though assistance can be given with this
- place the sliding board, though assistance may be given with this
- flex forward in the trunk
- transfer his/her weight laterally
- place his/her feet (foot if an amputee) on the floor
- sustain functional sitting balance
- place his/her own arm towards the end of the board, and assist with movement across it

- move towards the placed arm, transferring his/her bottom across the board
- remove the sliding board, though assistance may be given with this, and maintain sitting balance.

Assistance from:
- one handler is required if the person:
  - can only partially achieve the criteria above
  - cannot bring his/her feet round to his/her final position (a turntable under his/her feet can assist)
  - is able to transfer his/her weight laterally but requires minimal assistance
- a second handler is usually required if the person:
  - needs assistance with his/her feet and support in sitting (a handling belt may help with this).

Optimum start position
- The person is sitting at the edge of a bed/plinth wearing suitable footwear.
- The handler is standing at the person's side ready to assist with the board if necessary.
- The new sitting surface (chair/wheelchair/commode) is positioned next to the bed (angle is determined by new surface and type of transfer board – see manufacturers' instructions) brakes on, footplates and armrests on near side removed.

Instructions to enable the person to move independently or assist
- Lean away (from the transfer side) so that you can place one third of the board underneath your buttock, one third of the board bridges the gap and one third rests on the bed/chair/commode where you are going – the board should be level.
- Place your hand towards the far end of the board and lean toward it.
- When ready, shuffle across, using your other hand and your feet/foot to *push*.
- Is that OK? (wait for agreement/consent).
- Start when ready.

Assistance for sitting transfer using a transfer board

Note: This move is predominantly an independent transfer, the handler being present for preparation and completion but giving minimal assistance for the actual transfer.

Preparation of the person
- Where possible use the optimum start position and instructions.
- Ensure the person has the cognitive ability to undertake the activity.
- Place the person's feet on a turn disc to facilitate foot movement if he/she has reduced ability to push through his/her legs or to move his/her feet round.

Preparation of the environment/equipment
- Check the transfer board (and turn disc if used) is safe and clean.
- Place turn disc, if used, under the person's feet.
- Ensure a kneeling pad is available if the handler has difficulty kneeling.
- Place the transfer board in position (see instructions on previous page).

Note: If a curved board is used, it is safest to have the short edge next to the person's knees so that the person travels along the short edge. The long edge is thus supported and the board is less likely to tip.

Preparation of the handler
- Identify a stable kneeling base in front of the person.
- Place hand on the person's hip furthest from the receiving destination if the person needs assistance on initiating the move – the person should not be pushed across.

Note: If significant physical effort is required from a handler to assist the person to transfer, an alternative management should be considered, eg hoisting.

The manoeuvre
What to do and say:
- give clear instructions such as "place your hand towards the far end of the board and lean toward it – when ready shuffle across, using your other hand and your feet to *push*". "Is that OK?"
- the person transfers his/her weight in the direction of the move
- the person eases his/her hips across the board
- if the person has difficulty using his/her feet on the floor, a transfer disc under the feet will assist.

Completion
- Ensure the person is safely on the receiving destination.
- The handler removes the board, asking the person to lean/rock away from the board to facilitate removal.
- Remove turn disc from under the feet, if used.
- Replace the arm of the wheelchair if removed before the transfer.
- Ensure person's feet are on the footplates of the wheelchair, if used.

Risks and controversial techniques

Risk of injury in sitting to sitting transfers increases when the person does not meet the ability criteria and the handlers over assist, particularly if the person wears a handling belt.

The risks increase where a person is a bilateral amputee as the centre of gravity very easily comes outside his/her base of support.

Care must be given to skin integrity to avoid entrapment of the person's skin, fingers or genitalia (♂), both during insertion of the board and when shuffling across. Other hazards include:
- movement of the sliding board during the manoeuvre
- shearing forces between the person's gluteal muscles and the board, which compromise tissue viability
- changes in level of cooperation/behaviour of the person
- changes in the physical or medical status of the person
- tonal changes
- the person may lose his/her balance.

For bariatric patients, check the safe working load (SWL) of the sliding board (manufacturer should state on the equipment, or on their web site, and a copy of safety information should be kept).

The use of an additional slide sheet (unless integral with the board) is not recommended because the movement can then become uncontrollable and the person could slide off the board.

Lifting for sitting to sitting transfer
All the illustrated lifts demonstrate postural strain for the handler. The load is held away from the body, much of the effort is taken by the upper body and there is potential strain on back, shoulder and wrist joints.

The person is vulnerable to being dropped, may experience shearing and bruising or soft tissue damage (Ruszala in Smith (ed), *HOP5* 2005).

Examples include:
- leg and arm lift (see Task 10.6a)
- hammock lift (see Task 10.6b)
- through arm lift, two handlers (see Task 10.6c)
- through arm lift, one handler (see Task 10.6d).

Risks and controversial techniques

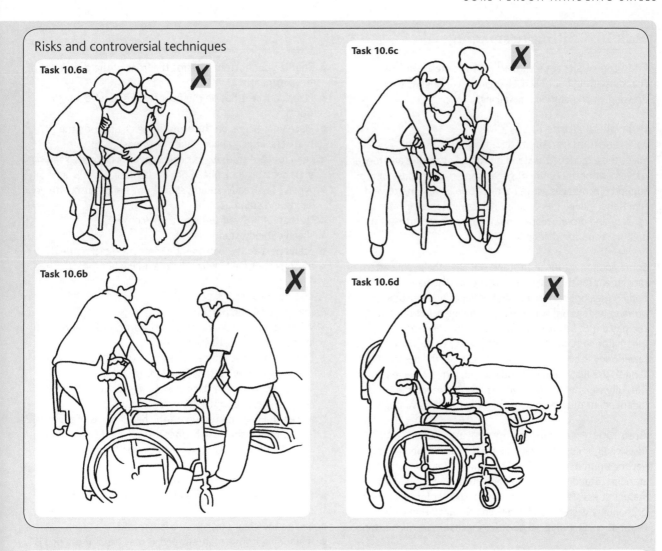

Task 10.6a

Task 10.6c

Task 10.6b

Task 10.6d

Evidence review

Technique	REBA	Activity	Comfort	FIM	Mobility gallery	Skill level	Comments
Task 10.6 – Sitting to sitting transfer using a transfer board							
Task 10.6a	12 – very high	5	1	3-2	C		For more able person, less comfortable but slightly lower risk. Can be performed by a novice
Task 10.6b	12 – very high	3	1	3-2	C		Very high risk, very little activity from the person, very low level of comfort
Task 10.6c	11 – very high	1	4	2	D		Very high risk with negligible activity from the person, low comfort level
Task 10.6d	10 – high	1	1	2	D		High risk with very low comfort and activity levels

1

2

3

10 Core person handling skills

4

Task 10.7 Sitting to standing

Example of sitting to standing for care handling
For transferring out of bed, changing incontinence pads, dressing, in preparation for walking.

Example of sitting to standing for treatment/rehabilitation handling
Gives the experience of standing, including raising and forward movement of the centre of gravity, and reduced base of support. Encourages active participation in working towards functional independence or in maintaining level. Increases sensory and proprioceptive input. Improves recruitment of postural tone. Improves orientation.

Some equipment for sit to stand will alter the usual pattern of movement for this task: grasping the aid, the person uses a *pulling* (flexion) pattern for his/her upper body instead of *pushing* (extension) with the arms. Pulling is not reinforcing the pattern to be encouraged within treatment or rehabilitation handling and is not so easy to do while the lower body is pushing through the feet. So, the person may tend to use just the upper body to pull himself/herself up, and not fully weight bear through the legs. However, the benefit of independent movement may override this disadvantage.

Appropriate handling equipment for sit to stand
Riser chair or cushion, grab rail, hand blocks or bed lever if getting up from a bed. Fixed standing aid for independent standing. Standing aid combined with turner for independent stand but assisted turn. Standing transporter for independent or manual assisted stand and then transportation to destination. Standing aid hoist for mechanical assisted stand.

Person ability criteria for sitting to standing
For independent movement, the person must be able to:
- move from chair sitting to edge sitting (sitting at the front edge of the chair/bed/plinth)
- maintain sitting balance
- place and maintain his/her feet on the floor
- achieve sitting to standing, having the ability to take his/her own weight through his/her legs
- maintain a midline position in standing.

Assistance from:
- one handler is required if the person:
  - can only partially achieve the above criteria
  - cannot maintain standing balance without support
- a second handler is usually required if the person:
  - has unpredictable physical ability or behaviour
  - needs support from both sides to maintain standing balance
  - needs additional support to move from a sitting position.

Optimum start position
- Person is sitting in a chair or at the side of a bed or plinth.
- The handler is standing at his/her (weaker) side.
- The person has appropriate footwear.

Instructions to enable the person to move independently or assist
- Lean forward so that your back is away from the back of the chair.
- Shuffle your bottom towards the front of the chair/edge of the bed/plinth.
- Place your feet flat on the floor (weaker one slightly in front).
- Place your hands on the arms of the chair (or on the mattress, or just above your own knees).
- Lean forward so that your chin is over your knees, keep your head up, look ahead not at the floor.
- When I say "ready, steady, *stand*", on "*stand*" push with your hands and stand up.
- "Is that OK?" (wait for agreement/consent).
- "Ready, steady, *stand*".
- Stand next to the person for a moment – make sure the person is not feeling dizzy before asking him/her to move.

Assistance for sitting to standing
Preparation of the person
- Where possible, use the optimum start position and instructions for assistance.
- Check again that the person can stand and weight bear by assessing his/her current function, eg:
  - is the person able to sit upright unsupported?
  - is he/she able to flex forward?
  - can the person push up off the bed or arms of the chair?
  - can the person raise his/her feet off the floor and place his/her foot forward and back on the floor?

Preparation of the environment/equipment
- Ensure brakes are on if standing from a wheeled item of furniture.
- Ensure the area is free from trip hazards.
- If standing from a high/low bed, it may assist if the bed is raised slightly.

Preparation of the handler
- Stand beside the person facing the direction of movement (see Task 10.7a).
- Adopt a stable base with feet slightly apart and the outer foot ahead.
- Flex hips and knees to lower position.

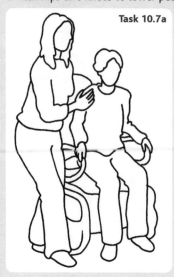

Task 10.7a

For minimal assistance:

- place the inside hand in contact with the person's back to provide touch prompt to stand. The hand can be placed centrally at either shoulder level or lower on the back depending on which prompt assists the person. The prompt must not become a push as this will take the person forward rather than to stand
- support with the outer hand either at the person's shoulder or a palm to palm hold (see Task 10.7b)
- look ahead.

For higher level of assistance:

- place the inside forearm in contact with the person's back – a long arm hold
- support with the outer hand either at the person's shoulder or a palm to palm hold (see Task 10.7b)
- look ahead.

Note: If the person can push from the arms of a chair, this should be encouraged rather than taking his/her hand in a palm to palm hold.

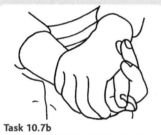

Task 10.7b

The manoeuvre

What to do and say:

- give clear instruction such as "ready, steady, *stand*"
- gentle rocking motion can be used as the instructions "ready, steady" are given
- on the instruction "*stand*" both move together in the direction of movement – first forward and then upwards
- the handler transfers his/her body weight from the back foot to the front foot or steps forward with the back foot (see Task 10.7c and d).

Task 10.7c

Completion

- Stabilise at the end of the move – if the person is unsteady, ask him/her to sit down.
- Continue with a walk or transfer to another sitting destination.

Alternative methods

Two handlers

This move can be undertaken using two handlers, depending on the ability of the person (see Task 10.7d).

Task 10.7d

A handling belt can be considered as long as this is not used to "lift" the person. Handlers often use handling belts incorrectly, leading to their removal from the workplace, but they can be beneficial to extend the handlers' reach in confined spaces, and to stabilise the person on standing without having to grip his/her body (see Task 10.7e).

Task 10.7e

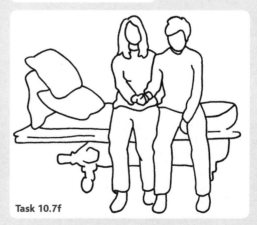

Task 10.7f

Limited access to the side of the person's chair
Consideration must be given to how much assistance a person needs to stand when choosing a type of chair or position of the chair. If a person needs more than touch prompt or verbal prompt, it is not desirable to limit the access to the side of his/her chair as the handler will not be able to assist the stand without increasing the risk of postural strain.

If there is no access to the side of the chair and the person must be assisted, then an adaptation to the core skill will be necessary and should be described in detail on the person's handling plan.

Either:
- ask the person to lean forward from the back of the chair and to one side
- guide one of the person's knees, and the same side hip, forward and across his/her body until they are sitting obliquely across the chair rather than facing straight forward (eg left hip by left back corner of the seat and right hip by right front corner of the seat)
- the handler now has access to the person's back and can assist to a stand as described in assistance to stand
- the person can assist with one hand on the arm of the chair.

Or
- with one or two handlers facing the person, in front of the person and slightly to one side
- adopt a walk stance
- flex down to the person's level
- support with one arm across the person's front from shoulder to opposite hip
- support with the other hand behind the person's shoulder
- ensure the handler's head is aligned and looking over the person's nearside shoulder
- on the command of "*stand*", the handler transfers his/her weight onto the back foot as the person stands.

Note: Consideration must have been given to the additional risks of adopting this position, eg:
- the handler will have to adjust his/her position if the stand is to be followed by walking
- the position puts the handler very close in the person's personal space
- the handler must receive specific training on this technique (Love 2006).

Sitting beside the person on a bed
- Ensure the brakes are on.
- The handler can sit at one side of the person on the bed so he/she is in contact with the person.
- Raise the bed to reduce the vertical distance to travel while standing.
- Face forward with the person.
- Nearest arm across the person's back.
- Encourage the person to take a palm to palm hold with the handler (a shoulder support tends to cause twisting for the handler).
- The handler should place the foot nearest to the person back slightly and the other foot forward so that the handler can transfer his/her weight from back foot to front foot to aid the stand.

- Both flex forward slightly in the trunk.
- On the command "ready, steady, *stand*", both handler and person push up into a standing position and balance in standing before attempting to move (see Task 10.7f).

Note: An assessment must be done to ensure the SWL of the bed can support both individuals.

This is less suitable from a divan bed or low plinth as this creates additional difficulty for both parties to stand, thus the handler can give less support while standing.

Risks and controversial techniques
Risk of injury in standing a person increases when consideration is not given to skin integrity – there must be no gripping of the person which can bruise soft tissue.

Standing a person who is unable to take his/her own weight through his/her legs is highly likely to cause injury to person and handlers: bear hug or pivot transfer stances are not justifiable in this context (see Task 10.7g, h and i).

Task 10.7g

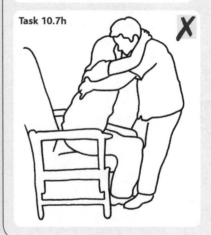

Task 10.7h

Risks and controversial techniques

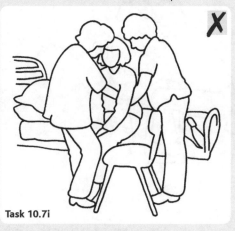

Task 10.7i

Drag lifts (see Task 10.7j, k and l)

As previously described in lying to sitting, this approach poses risks to both handler and person. These risks are considerably raised if such a method is used to assist from sitting on the floor to standing (Ruszala in Smith (ed), *HOP5* 2005).

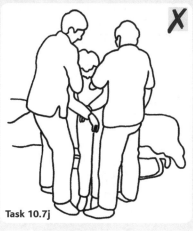

Task 10.7j

Task 10.7k

Task 10.7l

Assistance by pulling on hands (see Task 10.7m)

The person's arms and shoulders are vulnerable to injury and this approach can exacerbate behavioural resistance to stand.

The person is leaning his/her whole body weight against the handler in a "counterbalance".

The handler is blocking the space the person needs to move into, thus restricting the person's independent movement. The person is passive and the handler could lose balance and control of the move if the person was to move in an unpredictable manner (Ruszala in Smith (ed), *HOP5* 2005).

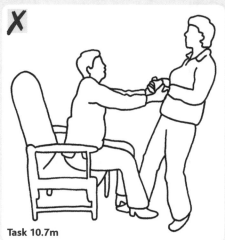

Task 10.7m

Note: This is not the same as standing in front of a person and encouraging him/her to stand by "leading" the person's hands forwards as a visual and touch prompt. This approach is sometimes needed for people with dementia who also benefit from the handler "gap filling" the space in front of them. Risk assessment would identify whether such an approach and position would be acceptable.

Sub-task 10.7.1 Moving forward in the chair

Example of moving forward in the chair for care handling
To prepare for standing or to insert a hoist sling.

Example of moving forward in the chair
for treatment/rehabilitation handling
To practise functional patterns of movement.

Person ability criteria for moving forward in the chair
For independent movement, the person must be able to:
- lean forward in the chair
- lean over to one side, placing his/her weight on one buttock (see Task 10.7.1a)
- lift the other buttock clear of the seat and hitch the hip forward
- repeat with alternate hips.

Note: Some people find it easier if they concentrate on putting one knee over the other as they hitch the hip forward.

Task 10.7.1a

Assistance from:
- one handler is required if the person:
  - can give only some assistance in the movement, eg lean to one side but not hitch his/her hip forward
  - has poor cognition and cannot complete the move without verbal or touch prompt.

Assistance for moving forward in the chair
Preparation of the person
- Explain the process.
- Ask the person to lean forward in the chair.
- Ask the person to lean over to one side, placing his/her weight on one buttock.

Preparation of the environment/equipment
- Ensure brakes on any wheeled item of furniture are applied.
- Ensure a kneeling pad is available if the handler has difficulty kneeling.

Preparation of the handler
- Kneel in front of the person, or at an oblique angle, with one leg raised (half kneeling) to create a stable base.
- Place an open hand on the opposite hip to the buttock the person has leaned on (see Task 10.7.1b).
- Or place the hand on the lower ribs of that side.
- Rest the other hand at the person's knee.
- It may help to change to the other knee and swop sides to ease the other hip forward.

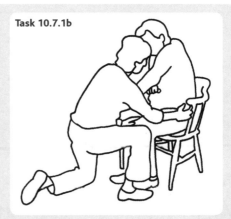

Task 10.7.1b

The manoeuvre
What to do and say:
- give clear instructions such as "when I say *shuffle* – lean forward and to one side, *shuffle* forward by lifting your hip and thigh and bring your knee forward"
- clearly say "is that OK?" and give the instruction "and *shuffle*"
- on the instruction of "*shuffle*", the handler eases the person's hip across and towards the front of the chair, facilitating forward movement of the thigh
- the handler transfers his/her weight back as he/she does this so that he/she does not pull with his/her arms (see Task 10.7.1c)
- repeat this sequence with the other leg.

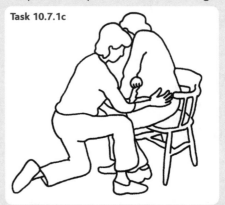

Task 10.7.1c

Completion
- Ensure the person is balanced and safe in the final sitting position.
- Ensure the person's feet are firmly placed on the floor.

Evidence review

Technique	REBA	Activity	Comfort	FIM	Mobility gallery	Skill level	Comments
Task 10.7 – Sitting to standing							
Task 10.7a	4	9	9	5-4	B	Advanced beginner	One handler with one hand on the person's shoulder – this requires skill by the handler and is comfortable for the person.
Task 10.7f	7	9	9	5-4	B	Advanced beginner	From the side of the bed rather than chair appears to increase the postural risk without affecting the person
Task 10.7d	4	9	9	5-4	B	Advanced beginner	Analysis shows a twisted trunk. This can be reduced by altering foot position. Having two handlers does not appear to reduce the postural risk to the handlers in this scenario
Task 10.7h	12 – very high	7	8	4-3	B		Very high risk activity, the person is active, and is comfortable
Task 10.7j	14 – very high	5	4	4-3	C		A harder technique so not for a novice
Task 10.7k	11 – very high	7	5	4-3	B		Able person able to contribute to manoeuvre, but high risk level to handler
Task 10.7l	14 – very high	3	1	2	D		
Task 10.7m	6 – medium			4-3	B		Medium postural risk, can be done by a novice, activity and comfort not scored, but person appears to be active, matching his/her ability
Sub-Task 10.7.1 – Moving forward in the chair							
Task 10.7.1b	9	6-8	8	5-3	B-C	Advanced beginner	Use a kneeling pad to reduce pain/discomfort of the knee

Task 10.8 Standing to sitting

Example of standing to sitting for care handling
Onto a bed, chair, commode or wheelchair.

Example of standing to sitting for treatment/rehabilitation handling
To improve muscle power and promote functional patterns of movement.

Person ability criteria for standing to sitting
For independent movement, the person must be able to:
- maintain standing balance
- move from standing to sitting, having the ability to take his/her own weight through his/her legs.

Assistance from:
- one handler is required if the person:
  - can only partially achieve the criteria
  - cannot maintain standing balance without support
- a second handler is usually required if the person:
  - has unpredictable physical ability or behaviour
  - requires support from both sides for stability.

Optimum start position
- The person is standing in front of a chair or at the side of a bed or plinth, ideally able to feel the sitting surface with the back of his/her legs.
- The person has appropriate footwear.
- The handler is standing at the person's (weaker) side.

10 Core person handling skills

© BackCare

Instructions to enable the person to move independently or assist

- Keep your head up.
- I want you to bend your knees, sticking your bottom right out behind you.
- And reach down for the arms of the chair (or place your hands on the front of your thighs).
- When you're ready, sit down.

Assistance for standing to sitting

Preparation of the person
- Where possible, use the optimum start position and instructions and modify if necessary.
- Ensure the person can feel the seat behind, against his/her legs.

Preparation of the environment/equipment
- Ensure brakes are applied on any wheeled item.
- Ensure it is a suitable sitting destination for the person, eg appropriate size of chair, suitable height of bed etc.

Preparation of the handler
- Be ready to step in the direction of the sit.
- Place one hand on the back of the person's near shoulder to help keep the shoulder forward as the person sits.

The manoeuvre
What to do and say:
- ask the person to look at the seat and then down to his/her feet
- give clear instructions such as "when I say ready and *sit* reach down to the seat or arms of the chair and stick your bottom out" (this ensures the person sits right back in the chair)
- clearly say "ready, and *sit*"
- on the instruction "*sit*", the person leans forward and pushes his/her bottom back into the chair
- on the instruction "*sit*", the handler steps in the direction of the move with the person

Completion
- Ensure the person is safe and comfortable.
- Ensure the person's feet are in contact with the floor.
- Ensure the person is not slipping or slumping in the chair; if that is the case, then re-assess the chair for suitability.
- Slumping in the chair can be an indication that the person has been in a sitting position for too long and his/her body needs to "stretch out". This can best be achieved by the person standing or lying down.

Sub-task 10.8.1 Moving back in the chair

Example of moving back in the chair for care handling
To ensure safety and comfort in the chair, to reposition someone in the chair.

Example of moving back in the chair for treatment/rehabilitation handling
To practise alignment of body segments (head, spine, pelvis) in sitting.

Note: If a person requires repeated repositioning, re-assess the suitability of the chair and ensure the person is not sitting out for too long a period and becoming uncomfortable.

Appropriate equipment for moving back in the chair
One way glide sheet.

Assistance for moving back in the chair

Preparation of the person
If the person can learn to shuffle backwards using the following method, he/she should be encouraged to do this independently:
- the person should lean forward in the chair
- lean over to one side to place the weight on one buttock
- lift the other buttock clear of the seat and hitch the hip backward
- repeat with alternate hips.

Preparation of the environment/equipment
- Ensure brakes are applied on any wheeled item of furniture.
- Ensure a kneeling pad is available if the handler has difficulty kneeling.
- The person can be sitting on a one way glide sheet.
- A pillow used in front of the person's knees can be beneficial to protect from excessive pressure or bruising.

Preparation of the handler
- Kneel in front of the person with one leg raised (half kneeling) to create a stable base.
- Place an open hand at the hip of the person on the side he/she has "lifted" off the seat (see Task 10.7.1c).
- Rest the other hand below the knee.
- If the person is sitting on a one way glide sheet, the handler rests a hand below each knee and can be double kneeling rather than half kneeling (see Task 10.8.1a).
- Transfer your weight forward as also gently pushing the person back in the chair as he/she hitches back.

Task 10.8.1a

The manoeuvre
What to do and say:
- give clear instructions such as "when I say, *shuffle back*, lift your hip and thigh and take your knee back – ready and *shuffle back*"
- on the instruction of "*shuffle*", the handler pushes gently at the knee to ease the leg backwards as the hip is hitched
- the handler transfers his/her weight forward as this is done
- the person then leans over towards alternate sides and the move is repeated.

Completion

- Ensure the person is balanced and safe in the final sitting position.
- Ensure the person's feet are firmly placed on the floor.
- Review the person's assessment and see if he/she is in the right chair and whether he/she is sitting out for an inappropriate length of time.

Evidence review

Technique	REBA	Activity	Comfort	FIM	Mobility gallery	Skill level	Comments
Task 10.8.1 – Moving back in the chair on a glide sheet							
Task 10.8.1a	5	8	9	5-3	B/C	Advanced beginner	One-way glide ensures the person is active and has a medium level of postural risk

Task 10.9 Standing transfer (see also Task 10.7)

Example of standing transfer for care handling
Transfer from bed to chair for wellbeing, from bed to commode, wheelchair to toilet for hygiene.

Example standing transfer for treatment/rehabilitation handling
Encourages active participation in working towards functional independence. Gives the experience of normal movement, of changes in centre of gravity and diminishing base of support. Increases sensory and proprioceptive input. Facilitates weight bearing and weight transference through the legs. Improves orientation.

Appropriate handling equipment for standing transfers through 90 degrees
Use the person's independent ability to assist whenever possible while using the equipment, eg when using a standing aid combined with turner use the same instructions for standing (see Task 10.7) and sitting (Task 10.8) described previously.

Standing aid transporters, framed turning discs, standing aid hoists.

Note: Some equipment, such as a framed turning disc, will alter the usual pattern of movement for this task: grasping the aid, the person uses a *pulling* (flexion) pattern for his/her upper body instead of *pushing* (extension) on the arms of the chair/mattress/own thighs with the arms. Pulling is not reinforcing the pattern to be encouraged within treatment or rehabilitation handling, and is not so easy to do when the lower body is pushing through the feet, so the person may tend to use just the upper body to pull himself/herself up (see Task 10.9a and b). However, the benefit of independent movement may override this disadvantage.

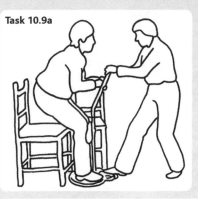

Task 10.9a

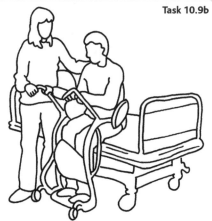

Task 10.9b

Person ability criteria for standing transfer
For independent movement, the person must be able to:
- have functional sitting balance
- place his/her feet on the floor
- move from sitting to standing with verbal and/or light tactile prompting
- maintain standing balance with verbal and/or light tactile prompting
- transfer weight through both legs while standing
- transfer weight to either leg and to release and step with either leg.

10 Core person handling skills

Assistance from:
- one handler is required if the person:
  - has functional sitting balance
  - can place his/her feet on the floor
  - requires assistance to move from sit to stand
  - requires some assistance to maintain standing balance
  - can initiate stepping and transfer weight laterally in standing
- a second handler is usually required if the person:
  - has poor sitting and/or standing balance
  - requires assistance to move from sit to stand
  - can initiate stepping and transfer weight laterally in standing
  - has unpredictable physical or behavioural attributes
  - needs furniture to be repositioned
  - requires support and a second activity at the same time, eg pad change.

Optimum start position
- The person is brought to standing from sitting in a chair or at the side of a bed or plinth.
- The person is wearing appropriate footwear.
- The handler is standing at the person's (weaker) side.

Instructions to enable the person to move independently or assist
- The person is brought to standing (see Task 10.7 for sitting and standing).
- Stand next to the person for a moment – make sure he/she is not feeling dizzy before asking him/her to move. If the person uses a walking aid, put this in place.
- Avoid providing support to a person standing while at the same time helping with washing or adjusting clothing – if the person needs supporting while standing, a rail/prop/additional helper is needed.
- Give clear instructions such as "Take small steps round until you can feel the chair/wheelchair/plinth behind your knees".
- "Keep your head up."
- "I want you to:
  - bend your knees, sticking your bottom right out behind you
  - and reach down for the arms of the chair (or place your hands on the front of your thighs)
  - and when you're ready, sit down."
- "Is that OK?" (wait for agreement/consent) – "Sit when you are ready".
- Check that the person is comfortable. If sitting at the edge of a bed, ensure appropriate support is ready and the person knows what to expect next.

Assistance for standing transfer
Preparation of the person
- Where possible, use the optimum start position and instructions for assistance above.
- Explain the process and instructions to be given.

Preparation of the environment/equipment
- Place the chair or other destination at 90 degrees to the original sitting position.
- Assess the need for equipment, identify the appropriate equipment and bring to the person.
- Check it is safe and clean to use.

- Ensure it can be used freely with the floor surface, eg carpets will affect usage.
- Ensure the manufacturers' instructions of use are available and followed.

Preparation of the handler
- Adopt a stable base.
- Stand on the person's weaker side.
- Try to avoid passing between the person and the chair.
- If using equipment, position and use according to the manufacturers' instructions.

The manoeuvre
What to do and say:
- give clear instruction such as:
  - "put your hand on the arms of the chair" or "put your hands on the handles"
  - "on *stand* look ahead, and push up into standing"
  - "ready, steady, *stand*"
- assist the person to stand and support standing (see Task 10.7)
- assist the person to step round into position (see Task 10.10)
- assist the person to turn to the final destination
- ensure destination point is in the correct position for the person to sit
- give clear instructions such as:
  - "on *sit* bend your knees and stick your bottom right out behind you, and sit down"
  - "ready, steady, *sit*".
- **An alternative approach** would be for an additional handler to remove the seat the person has left and replace it with the new seat (eg standard chair replaced with commode). This would eliminate the need for a 90 degree turn and support through the turn.

Completion
- Ensure the person is sitting correctly, safe and comfortable.
- Review the success of the manoeuvre and report/reassess as necessary.

Risks and controversial techniques

Pulling a person up using the arm or dragging the person with an arm under his/her armpit is highly likely to cause injury to the person and handler (see Task 10.2 Drag lift).

Standing a person who is unable to take his/her own weight through his/her legs is highly likely to cause injury to person and handlers: so called bear hug or pivot transfer stances are not justifiable in this context of handling.

Bear hug or front assisted stand (see Task 10.7g and h)
This position invades the personal space of the person and independent movement is restricted. The passive nature of this approach can lead to the handler taking more control of the full weight of the person and becoming unstable due to the unpredictability of the move and of the amount of effort required (Ruszala in Smith (ed), HOP5 2005).

Rocking lift or belt hold (see Task 10.9c and d)
The same risks occur as for the bear hug, with the additional risks of significant reaching and twisting of both handlers. The use of a handling belt may encourage the handlers to lift and the person to be passive (Ruszala in Smith (ed), HOP5 2005).

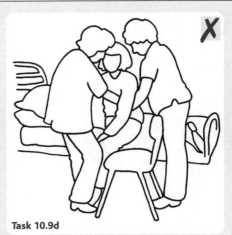

Task 10.9d

Repositioning in chair (see Task 10.9e)
The person is passive and the handler will take the full weight of the person. The handler lifts in a stooped position as the chair restricts knee flexion (Ruszala in Smith (ed), HOP5 2005).

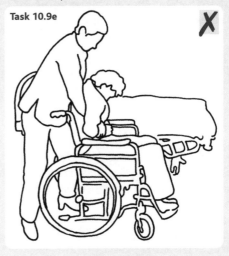

Task 10.9e

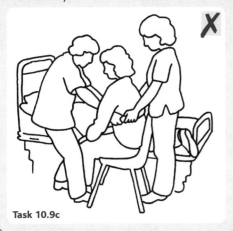

Task 10.9c

Sub-task 10.9.1 Equipment for standing transfers

Standing turners/framed turn disc
Standing turners are suitable for a standing turn through 90 degrees.

Person ability criteria for using a standing/framed turn disc
The person must be able to:
- demonstrate some active hip extension, eg can bridge on the bed
- demonstrate functional sitting balance
- place and maintain aligned feet on the footplate with assistance of one
- place hands on hand grips with assistance of one
- move from sitting to edge sitting to standing independently or with the assistance of one (this handler cannot also counterbalance the standing turn disc)
- stand for sufficient time to allow the standing turn disc to be turned through 90 degrees and will wait to be instructed before sitting
- sit from standing
- follow instructions adequately.

Note: The handler will have to counterbalance this equipment (see Task 10.9a) and his/her individual capability must be taken into account when assessing for this piece of equipment. The handler will not be able to counterbalance a person who is considerably taller or heavier than himself/herself. In this instance, equipment that "self counterbalances" – designed not to have a handler standing on the opposite side to the person – should be used.

The person must stand reliably and not sit before instructed.

Standing transporters
Standing transporters can be used to assist stand and transport a person from one position to another (see Task 10.9b).

They are designed to support the person, after standing, in semisitting while he/she is transferred to the end destination. The person does not need to stand unsupported for any length of time and, therefore, can have less standing function than for a standing framed turn disc, but he/she must have weight bearing ability and upper body control.

Evidence review

Technique	REBA	Activity	Comfort	FIM	Mobility gallery	Skill level	Comments
Task 10.9 – Standing transfer							
Task 10.9a	5	9	9	5	B	Advanced beginner	The stand and turn disc gives a medium level of postural risk and maximises the input from the person
Task 10.9d	12 – very high	7	8	4-3	B		Very high risk activity, the person is active and is comfortable
Task 10.9e	10 – high	8	8	3	B		Very high risk activity, for novice, the person is very active and comfortable

Task 10.10 Walking

Example of assisted walking for care handling
Promotes wellbeing, exercise, enables person to access bathroom and toilet, promotes cardiovascular and lung health, to regain balance and active walking ability as preparation for discharge from hospital, supports a person's desire to remain in his/her own home etc.

Example of assisted walking for treatment/rehabilitation handling
Facilitates normal movement and gait pattern. Encourages righting reactions, postural awareness and ability to cope with instability. Increases sensory and proprioceptive input. Helps maintain joint range of movement. Promotes independence.

Note: Walking a person who barely fulfils the ability criteria is a hazard often undertaken within treatment handling. Two or three handlers may be used at first to achieve and maintain the stand, or support the different phases of the gait, and their hand positions will reflect the person's loss of ability and any missing components of the movement. Risk assessment and management of the risk is paramount, including strategies for any collapse or weakness.

Within treatment handling, the person may require assistance from two plus handlers to:
- transfer weight
- to release leg, then
- to place foot while maintaining the stand.

If this is so, therapeutic input will be required and assisted walking for care handling may be inappropriate and high risk.

Appropriate equipment for assisted walking
Hoist and walking jacket, walking frame, wheeled walkers, elbow crutches, parallel bars, walking stick(s).

Note: Some medical conditions with spinal or abdominal involvement may contraindicate the use of a handling belt.

Note: People must not pull up on walking aids. They should take hold of the aid after standing up. Handlers must not rest their foot on a walking frame.

Person ability criteria for assisted walking
For independent movements, the person must be able to:
- move from sitting to standing
- weight bear in standing
- maintain standing independently
- transfer weight to either leg and step for a period of time.

Assistance from:
- one handler is required if the person:
  - requires assistance to achieve the above criteria
  - requires tactile and/or verbal prompting to weight bear in standing
  - requires assistance to transfer weight and step.

Note: A height difference between handler and person will increase the risks and should be assessed.

- a second handler is usually required if the person:
  - requires support from both sides
  - has unpredictable physical and/or behavioural attributes.

Optimum start position
- Person is standing in front of a chair or at the side of a bed or plinth.
- The handler is standing at the person's (weaker) side.
- The person is wearing appropriate footwear.

Instructions to enable the person to move independently or assist
Ideally, the person will be walking independently or using an aid and the handler will be giving verbal guidance only.

Movement is initiated when the person:
- shifts his/her centre of gravity
- takes his/her weight through one leg
- steps forward with the other.
- give clear instructions such as "*shift*" (meaning shift your weight to the right/left), and "*step*".

Assistance for walking
Risk assessment will identify whether it is suitable to assist a person in walking and this assessment should take account of

any history of falls. The risks to be managed for a care handler assisting the walk should be considerably less than those to be managed in a treatment or rehabilitation setting.

Assessment should identify how many handlers will be required, but if using a walking belt, the evidence suggests, for optimum support when walking a person, two handlers are preferable (Hignett *et al* 2003).

Preparation of the person
- Where possible, use the optimum start position and instructions for assistance.
- Explain the process to the person.
- If the person is known to fall, the assessment and management must enable the handler to detect and prevent, as far as is reasonable, the occurrence of a fall (see chapter 13).
- Assist the person to stand (see Task 10.7) and ensure he/she is stable and not dizzy before walking. If not, sit the person back down.
- If the person uses a walking aid, this should be ready for use, the person taking hold of it once standing. The handler may then walk behind or at the side of the person for encouragement.
- If using a walking belt, then this should be fitted after having been assessed as suitable.

Preparation of the environment/equipment
- Ensure any walking aid is close to avoid stretching or bending.
- If using a walking belt, check that it is safe, clean and assessed as suitable for the person, eg size, and fitted comfortably but firmly at the person's waist. The handler must be trained in its use, taking hold of a loop but **do not put your whole hand through the loop** (see Task 10.10a). **A walking or handling belt must not be used to hold a person up into standing**.
- Check there are no slip, trip hazards.
- Ensure distance to be walked is within the person's capability, have a chair ready or a wheelchair following if they fatigue easily.

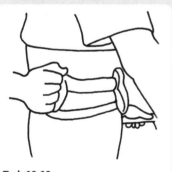

Task 10.10a

Preparation of the handler
- Give assistance based on the risk assessment, ie which side to support from and how many handlers required (see Task 10.10b and c).
- Adopt a stable base with feet slightly apart and the outer foot ahead ready to step with the person.

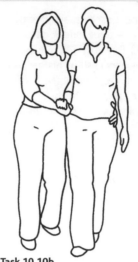

Task 10.10b

Task 10.10c

The manoeuvre
What to do and say:
- clearly say "are you ready and *walk*"
- do not impede the person's natural step or any walking aid
- allow the person to move his/her own feet and in his/her own time
- if the person is using a walking aid such as a stick, this should be held in the opposite hand to any injury, eg right hand following left hip surgery, and the handler should walk on the opposite side
- if the person is using a walking frame, the handler may give confidence and balance by walking behind, but slightly to one side, to ensure clear vision, placing hands just above the person's hips (see Task 10.10d)
- unison walking, ie stepping with the same foot as the person, can be helpful for some people, eg those with dementia

- offer a flat, upturned far hand for the person to place his/her palm onto, **do not link thumbs** (see Task 10.10e). Your joined hands should be at about hip height, and not higher than waist height
- alternatively, if the person only requires guidance and no physical support, a palm and forearm support can be given (see Task 10.10f)
- keep as close to the person as necessary, usually slightly behind with the handler's hip close to or touching the person's pelvis, as you both walk forward
- movement is initiated when the person shifts his/her centre of gravity, takes his/her weight through one leg, and steps forward with the other – this can be given as the instructions: "*shift*" (meaning shift your weight to the right/left), and "*step*".

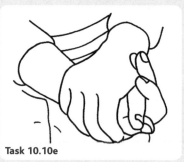

Task 10.10e

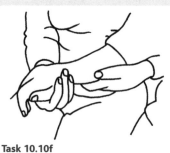

Task 10.10f

Completion
- Accompany the person to his/her destination and assist to sit (see Task 10.8).

Task 10.10d

Risks and controversial techniques

Risk of injury in walking a person increases when there is any foreseen likelihood that the person may fall. This is the case with almost all persons using a walking aid, since it has been given to compensate for poor or compromised balance and effort.

Safety measures *must* be put in place when walking with a person who has a history of falls, eg an additional handler follows with a wheelchair, or a walking jacket and hoist/gantry are used until the person is confident and competent with the aid.

Changes in level of cooperation/behaviour of the person or changes in his/her medical status (eg postural hypotension), or any changes in muscle tone require reporting, vigilance and documented management.

Use of a handling/walking belt

There is some evidence that a handling belt should not be used with one handler. There is evidence that used with two handlers, a handling belt is beneficial (Hignett *et al* 2003). The belt must be assessed as suitable for the person, fit correctly, held in a manner that can be released quickly and not used to hold or lift a person up.

Palm to palm hold with thumb hold (see Task 10.10g)
The handler cannot release the grip quickly. The person may grip tightly causing painful thumb joints (Thomas in Smith (ed), *HOP5* 2005).

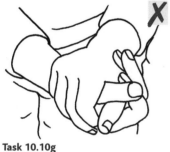

Task 10.10g

Assisted walking supporting at the axilla
(see Task 10.10h)
The handlers' inner arm is raised to support the person which can cause strain to the handlers' arms and shoulders. The handlers may be exposed to holding the person up. The person may be inclined to lean on the handlers (Ruszala in Smith (ed), *HOP5* 2005).

Task 10.10h

Linking arms
Linking arms at the elbow does not give support to the person other than companionship or directional guidance, eg for a person with poor vision. It increases the likelihood of injury to the handlers as they cannot release their hold and risk being pulled away from their stable base.

Evidence review

Technique	REBA	Activity	Comfort	FIM	Mobility gallery	Skill level	Comments
Task 10.10 – Assisted walking							
Task 10.10b	7	9	9	5-4	B	Novice	
Task 10.10c	2	8	8	5-4	B	Advanced beginner	
Task 10.10d	5	9	9	4-3	C	Novice	
Task 10.10h	11 – very high	7	5	4-3	B		Able person able to contribute to manoeuvre, but high risk level to handler

© BackCare

References

Birtles, M & Williams, S (2004), NBE RA HB1 An Ergonomics Evaluation of Hospital Bed Backrests, *column*, **16.2** 18.

Borg, G (1985), *An Introduction to Borg's RPE Scale*, Movement Publications, Ithaca, NY.

Bracher, M & Brooks, A (2009), Moving and Handling Strategies, in M Curtin, (Ed), *Occupational Therapy and Physical Dysfunction* (6th edition), Churchill Livingstone.

Brooks, A (2008), Manual Handling Questions: A tool for training, assessment and decision making in people handling, *column*, **20.1** Spring.

Chartered Society of Physiotherapy (2008), *Guidance on manual handling in physiotherapy*, London.

Chung, MK, Lee, I & Kee, D (2003), Assessment of postural load for the lower limb postures based on perceived discomfort, *International Journal of Industrial Ergonomics*, **31** (1) January 2003, 17-32.

College of Occupational Therapists (2006), Manual Handling (Guidance 3), London.

Derbyshire Interagency Group (2001), Care handling for people in hospital, community and educational settings. A code of practice.

Dieen van, JH, Jansen, SMA & Housheer, AF (1997), differences in low back load between kneeling and seated working at ground level, *Applied Ergonomics*, **28** (5-6) 355-363.

Granger, CV, Hamilton, BB, Linacre, JM, Heinemann, AW & Wright, BD (1993), Performance profiles of functional independence measure. *American Journal of Physical Medicine and Rehabilitation*, **72**: 84-9.

Graveling, RA, Melrose, AS & Hanson, MA (2003), *The Principles of Good Manual Handling: Achieving a Consensus*, HMSO, Norwich.

Harkness, EF, Macfarlane, GJ, Nahit, ES, Silman, AJ & McBeth, J (2003), Risk factors for new-onset low back pain amongst cohorts of newly employed workers, *Rheumatology,* August 2003, **42** (8) 959-968.

HSE (2010), Electric profiling beds in residential and nursing homes – Manual handling and service user benefits, HSE UK.

Hignett, S & McAtamney, L (2000), Rapid Entire Body Assessment. *Applied Ergonomics*, **31**, 201-205.

Hignett, S, Crumpton, E, Ruszala, S, Alexander, P, Fray, M & Fletcher, B (2003), *Evidence-Based Person Handling, Tasks, equipment and interventions*, London: Routledge.

Kee, D & Karwowski, W (2001), The boundaries for joint angles of isocomfort for sitting and standing males based on perceived comfort of static joint postures, *Ergonomics,* 2001, **44** (6) 614-648.

Knibbe, H, Van Panhuys, W, Van Vugt, W, Waaijer, E & Hooghiemstra, F (Thomas, S, UK version) (2008) *The Handbook of Transfers*, Diligent, Gloucester.

Knibbe, JJ & Waaijer, E (2005), Mobility Gallery. A classification and assessment tool for care planning, Arjo, 2005.

Leigh, L & Dermott, L (2010), Log-rolling a patient with a potential spinal/pelvic injury – is it possible to find a method of log-rolling that would suit the generic workplace? *column*, **22.1** 10-12.

Love, S (2006), *column*, **18.4** 11-18.

Nahit, ES, Macfarlane, GJ, Pritchard, CM, Chery, NM & Silman, AJ (2001), Short term influence of mechanical factors on regional musculoskeletal pain: a study of new workers from 12 occupational groups, *Occupational and Environmental Medicine*, June 2001, **58** (6) 374-381.

Pheasant, S (1991), *Ergonomics, Work and Health, Macmillan Academic and Professional Ltd*, London.

Smith, J (ed) (2005), *The Guide to The Handling of People* 5th edition 2005, BackCare.

Core hoisting skills

Julia Love RGN ONC Registered Member NBE
Manual handling adviser, LPS Training & Consultancy Ltd
Ruth Boulton MSc RGN ONC
HM specialist inspector of health and safety (human factors), Health and Safety Executive

Introduction

The use of hoists has become an integral role of handlers over a number of years. It has long been recognised that lifting people is hazardous (Lloyd *et al* 1981; Health Services Advisory Committee 1984). There is also a requirement under more recent legislation – Manual Handling Operations Regulations 1992 (as amended) (HSE 1992) – to avoid hazardous manual handling operations as far as is reasonably practicable, and, where this cannot be achieved, to take steps to reduce the risk. Even when hoists are used, there are still potential risks to the handler. This includes a variety of musculoskeletal disorders attributed to a combination of posture force and effort involved in applying slings and to manipulate and manoeuvre the hoist (see chapter 4).

Recent evidence (Boulton 2009) has brought to light that the person being hoisted is also at risk of injury. Risks to those being hoisted include falls when devices are used incorrectly and injury or discomfort due to incorrect or inappropriate sling choice and fitting.

This chapter will discuss the underlying contributory factors of hoist incidents involving the person being hoisted, outline the types of hoists that are available, the problems that can occur while using them, and the strategies that can be adopted when carrying out basic transfers to increase safety and comfort.

Following this guidance on good practice should help to ensure that the hoisting activities are as comfortable as possible for the person being hoisted and as safe as possible for all personnel involved.

The nature of the problem

Between April 2001 and December 2007, there were 163 incidents reported to the Health and Safety Executive (HSE) (Boulton 2009) in which people have been injured while being moved using hoisting equipment. This is likely to underestimate the problem considerably since anecdotal evidence suggests that only a small proportion of incidents are reported, despite a legal requirement to report major injuries and local policies that require the reporting of near misses.

The outcome of the reported incidents varied, with the degree of injury tending to depend upon with what the falling person made contact. Where the person's head made contact with bathroom fixtures, the hoist frame, bed rails or floor, the outcome was often a severe injury or a fatality.

Why are these incidents occurring?

Most of the incidents reported to the HSE could be linked to human failures, whether intentional or unintentional. However, personnel do not operate in isolation from their surroundings and factors associated with the task, the environment, the equipment and the organisation in which the handlers are working usually play a part (Boulton 2005). Thus, the contributory factors of the incidents will be discussed in two sections. Firstly, the immediate cause, which is typically ascribed to the individual handler(s), and secondly, the root cause(s) arising from background factors that can play a part, and which make it more or less likely that an individual handler will make an error.

Discussion of immediate causes

The immediate ascribed causes of the incidents reported to the HSE have been grouped in Table 11.1 and are discussed in more detail below. By considering the information below, it is possible to reduce the likelihood of persons being injured while they are hoisted by targeting each factor and taking appropriate remedial action.

TABLE 11.1 CAUSES OF HOISTING INCIDENTS

Cause of incident	Number	%
Fall from hoist	99	61
Equipment failure	31	19
Incorrect equipment used	8	5
Left unattended	7	4
Hoist overturn	5	3
Others	13	8
Total	163	100

Fall from hoist

This was the largest grouping, accounting for over 60 per cent of all incidents reported. The most significant identified factor contributing to the fall was the use of the wrong size or type of sling for the person. Commonly, this involved the use of a sling that was too large and thus did not give adequate support, or created a large aperture through which the person could slip. In several incidents, it had been custom and practice to use "toileting" or access slings for all hoisting tasks and the consequent lack of support they afforded was considered a contributing factor. Other factors included failing to attach, or to attach securely, one or more of the sling clips or loops.

For many of the incidents in this group, it was initially unclear why the person had fallen since all sling attachments were still secure. In these cases, contributory factors included an erroneous initial hoist and sling assessment for the individual person or using the wrong configuration of sling attachments. Problems with configuration included the incorrect choice of spreader bar, poor decisions as to how and where the sling was attached to the spreader bar and, finally, problems with the configuration of the sling. This latter group included incidents where the sling had been wrongly positioned for the person being hoisted. For example, use of a "bucket" configuration, use of inappropriate

attachment loop combinations or failing to thread the sling loops through each other properly to secure them.

Equipment failure

This group included slings with damaged stitching, loops and clips and hoists which had received inadequate or no maintenance/inspection. Such problems should be identified during the six-monthly thorough examination required under the Lifting Operations and Lifting Equipment Regulations 1998 (LOLER) (HSE 1998). Advice on medical device management, including hoists and slings, and safety bulletins are issued by the Medicines and Healthcare products Regulatory Agency (MHRA 2006). However, there was also a significant group of incidents that could be attributed to the hoist simply being "worn out". This included damage/breakage of internal bolts, which were discovered when the hoist was dismantled for in depth mechanical inspection as part of the investigation. The equipment failed because it had been used beyond its safe life expectancy. This type of failure is unlikely to be picked up by routine inspection, thorough examination or maintenance. Further information about the life expectancy of the hoist and sling will be available from individual manufacturers.

Incorrect equipment used

There were two main issues in this category. There were instances of use of the wrong size of sling – but, in this group, the handler was aware at the start of the procedure that the sling was inappropriate. A decision to use an inappropriate sling was generally made on the basis of an appropriate sling not being available and the necessity to move the person before a replacement could be obtained. The other issue related to the use of a standing hoist where this was unsuitable for the person being moved because of their physical condition.

Left unattended

In several incidents, people were injured when they were left unattended and in an unsafe position, either just before or just after hoisting. Some occurred when the person had been moved on to the bed and the handler(s) left him/her temporarily unattended as the hoist was moved out of the way. Others occurred in the bathroom when the person was left alone so that the handler could collect bathing materials.

Hoist overturn

There were some instances where people were injured when the hoist, in which they were being moved, overturned. Contributing factors to these incidents included moving the person with the hoist raised to a high level so that its centre of gravity was high, difficulties in manoeuvring the hoist because handlers were working in a confined area, moving the hoist over long distances and/or across difficult surfaces. The latter included across carpets but especially across the junctions (thresholds) between floors covered with carpet and those with smoother surfaces.

Others – bath and pool hoists

The final group included incidents occurring when using bath and pool hoists. The wet and slippery surface of the bath hoist seat contributed to injuries caused by slipping from the seat. This was more prevalent where the hoists were not fitted with safety belts or seat arms, or where the arms were present but not used. Apart from slippage, incidents with pool hoists also included cases of incorrect reassembly. The size of pool hoists means that they are often disassembled between uses. This can then present problems if skilled personnel are not available to reassemble them.

Discussion of root causes

Human failure and rule breaking are inevitable. However, if patterns can be identified and/or are predictable, they are potentially manageable (HSE 1999). By identifying their cause and influencing factors, appropriate risk reduction strategies can be adopted (Kelby 2010). The different human failure types (slips and lapses, mistakes and violations) are discussed below.

Slips and lapses typically occur if very familiar tasks are carried out without much need for conscious attention. They are skills based errors that tend to occur in highly trained individuals. Since they occur in trained personnel, further training is unlikely to prevent them, although minimising distractions and interruptions can help, as will introducing additional checks. Examples of slips and lapses include connecting the wrong sling loop or forgetting to attach one of the loops. Methods of reducing these types of human failure include choosing slings with standardised colour coded loops and implementing checks, preferably by a second person, that slings have been correctly attached and are secure.

Mistakes are a more complex failure where the wrong action is taken but it is believed to be right. Examples include erroneous decisions as to which equipment to use. Many of these can be overcome by providing detailed guidance within the care plan as to which equipment should be used, with details of leg configurations and loop attachments. Photographs showing the configuration of a sling may be beneficial in the care plan, particularly for a person with complex handling needs.

Violations involve the deliberate breaking of rules, policies or procedures. Examples include not using handling equipment that has been prescribed or deliberately using the wrong equipment. However, violations often occur for the best of intentions, eg in order to move a person quickly when the correct equipment is not immediately available. This may be exacerbated by handlers being put under pressure from either the person to be hoisted or their relatives, or from competing work demands.

Human failures are more likely to occur under certain circumstances. Some key factors identified as likely to increase person handling errors are listed below:
- low staffing levels
- high workload
- equipment unavailable, unsuitable or in poor condition
- personnel not competent/confident in use of hoists
- lack of time/pressure from person and/or his/her relatives
- poor communications
- poor working environment (eg limited space)
- culture of poor custom and practice.

Three main areas for concern that can be addressed at a systems level were identified as:
- individual handling/risk assessment
- training of handlers
- equipment provision and maintenance.

Addressing these issues as far as is possible will help to reduce the likelihood of accidents. Each of these issues is discussed

briefly below but for further specific guidance please refer to the chapters on these topics within this publication.

Risk management strategies

Individual handling/risk assessment
Completing risk assessment and care plan documentation requires a competent individual. The person involved in the assessment process needs training and skills in order to make appropriate decisions as to the handling equipment required for each individual (see chapter 1). Mandelstam (2004) reminded us of the judgement in the *East Sussex* case stating that the extent of the competence of the assessor should be in proportion to the degree of complexity in any individual case. The assessor must be familiar with the instructions provided by manufacturers and suppliers on the use, application and limitations of the equipment. Assessments should be routinely reviewed and assessors must also be made aware of any changes in the person's condition so that the assessment can be updated. The person specific risk management plan must be recorded in sufficient detail to enable handlers to use the equipment correctly.

Information provided must specify the hoist, the type and size of the sling, any configurations of loops or legs, the use of any additional safety devices, eg safety belts, and the number of handlers needed to carry out the task. The authors recommend that a photograph in the risk assessment documentation would be of considerable benefit. The risk management plan must be communicated to handlers and kept in a convenient and accessible place for easy reference. Although hoists can be operated by one person, safer systems of work often specify two handlers for hoisting. Whatever the system of work, it should be supported by a sound risk assessment.

Training
Personnel involved in hoisting people require suitable practical training and will require regular refresher training to maintain and update their skills. A training needs analysis should identify the scope of training required and deal with issues such as poor practice, non compliance and infrequent use etc. Training should include the opportunity to use all the different types of hoists and slings within the workplace and the practice of techniques so that skills can be developed. Handlers should be aware of the emergency lowering procedures, the stop systems and the recharging procedures for each hoist. It is important that supervisors and operational managers also receive training so that they are able to monitor, identify and correct poor practice. In addition to the practical elements, training should aim to educate staff about potential risks and aim to influence staff to adopt the safe practices being taught (Ruszala *et al* 2010). Further guidance can be found in chapter 6, and in Derbyshire Interagency Group (DIAG) Code of Practice (DIAG 2001) and the All Wales NHS Manual Handling Training Passport and Information Scheme (2010).

Equipment
In communal settings, sufficient hoists of the appropriate types and slings of the correct size and type must be available and accessible.

There must be sufficient slings to allow for laundering and sufficient hoists or spare batteries to facilitate battery charging. It is essential that a system is in place to ensure that hoists and slings are compatible for use together. This includes a consideration of the type of spreader bar to be used. Following a number of near miss reports, one hospital trust in the North East of England, spread over three sites, decided to use only one type of spreader bar so that it could standardise training and minimise risks arising through the incorrect selection or attachment of slings to spreader bars (see Figs 11.15-11.18 on page 175).

In addition to a thorough examination of hoists and slings required under LOLER – six-monthly or in accordance with a written scheme – systems need to be in place for the maintenance and inspection of both hoists and slings in line with manufacturers' instructions and for pre-use and in-use checks of the equipment. The MHRA device bulletin on managing medical devices (MHRA 2006) gives some guidance on this topic. Guidance is available to determine the number and type of hoists needed in a specific working area through the Hoist Identification Tool (Smith 2005). This tool may help to ensure adequate availability and that hoists do not become overused and worn out. Further details on this topic are in chapter 7.

In summary, while the risk of human error cannot be eliminated entirely, it can be managed more effectively so that the handler is less likely to make errors and the risk of persons being injured during hoisting activities is consequently reduced.

Types of hoist

Hoists are powered by battery or are manually operated (hydraulic).

They can be categorised into the following three groups:
● overhead hoists
● mobile hoists
● fixed hoists.

Overhead hoists

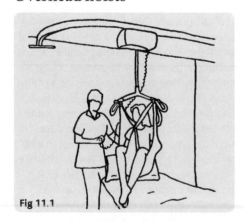

Fig 11.1

Fig 11.2

Overhead hoists are becoming more common as they reduce significantly the musculoskeletal stresses of manoeuvring the hoist, avoid handlers having to spend time finding a mobile hoist and are also available with increased safe working loads for the transfer of bariatric persons. Overhead hoists also address issues such as a lack of space, cluttered environments and inappropriate flooring. They do not require storage space and allow for the possibility of more independent use.
The type of tracking available will depend on the structure of the building and the room coverage required. Tracks can be in a straight line or curved, can transfer through doorways and can cover the entire room, eg X/Y or H framed systems. The controls are usually through an attached cable, but can also be remote. The choice of systems must take into account whether the person transfers independently or with handlers. Systems vary and the movement of the unit can be powered or manual.

Manufacturers have an enormous range of potential fittings and overhead hoists can be fitted even if the ceiling is not suitable. They can be:
● permanently fixed, usually on the ceiling (see Fig 11.1)
● supported by side poles, often attached to the walls
● completely free standing and therefore temporary (see Fig 11.2).

Portable hoist units can also be used where multiple users require hoisting. A strip of track will be permanently fixed in each area and the hoist unit attached where and when it is needed.

Mobile hoists

Mobile hoists come in varying sizes and safe working loads. Generally, the smaller the hoist, the easier it is to manoeuvre, as it will have a smaller turning circle. However, it is important that the hoist is able to fit around chairs and under beds etc. Mobile hoists can be more difficult to manoeuvre if the person is heavier or if the floor surface is uneven. If the person's weight and/or space present difficulties, an overhead hoist may be preferable.

Mobile hoists can be:

Active (standing hoist or stand aid)

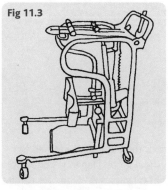

Fig 11.3

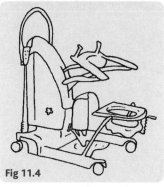

Fig 11.4

Generally, active hoists require the person to be able to bear some weight through their feet (albeit for short periods) and to have sufficient core strength and balance to support themselves in the sling (DIAG 2001). The knee pad necessitates the person to tolerate some pressure on his/her knees or the front of his/her tibia. Anyone with hypersensitive legs may find this uncomfortable. As a rule, it is also necessary for the person to be able to cooperate to an extent (FIM score of 3 or 4).

Often, the person being hoisted prefers an active hoist to a passive hoist as he/she is participating more in the transfer. However, there is a risk of the person falling through the sling if inappropriately assessed. Active hoists can also be used for early rehabilitation to encourage movement, increase strength and confidence (Ruszala 2001).

Passive (sling lifting)

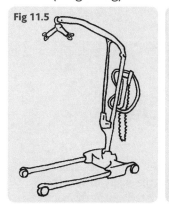

Fig 11.5

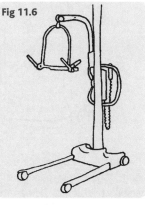

Fig 11.6

This type of hoist lifts all the person's weight. These can be either crane style (Fig 11.5) or column style (Fig 11.6). With crane style hoists, the boom is hinged at the top of the mast. The disadvantage is the boom and the person being hoisted

come closer to the mast when it is lowered, which may cause the person to knock against the hoist.

The alternative is a column style, in which the boom moves up and down the mast so that the "spreader bar to mast" distance remains constant. These hoists tend to be slightly larger and may not be appropriate in small rooms or where space is otherwise limited.

Mobile bathing

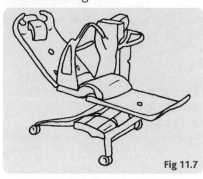

Fig 11.7

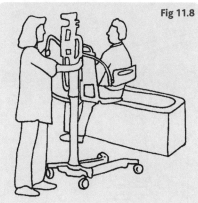

Fig 11.8

Bathing hoists are a specific type of mobile passive hoist that the person is transferred onto and then lowered into the bath. As with any hoist, transport distance should be kept to a minimum.

Fixed floor or wall mounted hoists

Fixed floor and wall mounted hoists include:

Pool

Fig 11.9

Pool hoists may have a sling attachment or a moulded seat, which can often be attached to a wheeled base unit for toileting and personal care.

Bath

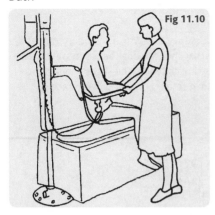

Fig 11.10

Most bath hoists have a moulded plastic seat and drop down arms. The seat rotates around a fixed mast attached to the floor and can be powered by battery or manually (see techniques on page 189). They may have a fixed or removable safety belt or bar.

Wall/floor mounted

Fig 11.11

Wall/floor mounted hoists are usually used in bedrooms or bathrooms. These will normally rotate through approximately 90 degrees and the length of the boom will dictate the range of the lift. They can be used when there is a lack of space for a mobile hoist.

Types of spreader bar

The type of spreader bar – or carry bar – and the attachments found on passive hoists (both mobile and overhead) may differ. Careful consideration as to the compatibility of the sling and spreader bar is essential. Handley (2004) described the risk assessment process recommended if using slings on a different manufacturer's hoist.

There are two main groups of spreader bars:

Rotating

These are sometimes called coathanger style spreader bars. They allow for considerable rotational movement and therefore allow the handler to position the person easily with their legs away from any part of the hoist. However, the hoisted person can swing, which may be disconcerting/disorientating, or may lead to an increased risk of hoist overturn when compounded by other factors (see Hoist overturn on page 170).

Attachment points can be:

Two point

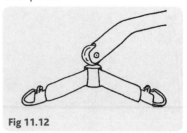

Fig 11.12

There may be a set of one, two or three hooks at each end of the spreader bar and both the shoulder and leg loops hook up to the same or an adjacent point on each side. Side bars can be added to each hook to space the attachment of the shoulder and leg loops for comfort.

Four point – or X shape

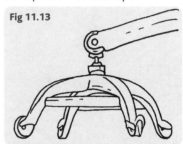

Fig 11.13

This is where the hooks for the shoulder and leg loops are spaced, to avoid the "scrunched" position that some people feel when using the two point spreader bar. This is as much for the comfort of larger or wider people and can facilitate easier positioning.

Tilting

(or three point spreader bar)

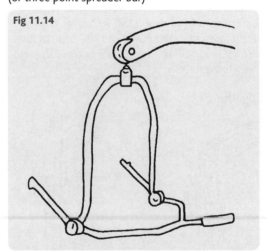

Fig 11.14

The tilting, wishbone, or three point (sometimes called four point, Y shaped) spreader bar has the ability to alter the person's position by being tilted or reclined by the handler using the positional handle. This sometimes necessitates a degree of force exertion by the handler, but this function can also be power assisted, offering potential for independent use. It does have the advantage that it is less liable to swing.

Attachment of sling to spreader bar

Compatibility of sling, hoist and spreader bar is essential to ensure the safety of the person being hoisted (see Figs 11.15 and 11.17). The sling manufacturer will provide information on the compatibility of its slings with other hoists. Any concerns relating to sling/hoist design, supply, manufacturer's instructions or compatibility claims should be referred to the regulator for medical devices – the MHRA.

Sling sizes vary from manufacturer to manufacturer, with no standardisation within the industry. There may then be the risk of an unsuitable sling being used for the person, eg two large slings from different manufacturers may be different sizes, the body of the sling may be a different length, or the number of loop attachments may differ.

At the moment, clip style slings (for wishbone type spreader bars) can never be used on two point (coathanger style) carry bars with hooks for loops (see Fig 11.16). Similarly, loop style slings cannot be used on the wishbone style carry bars (see Fig 11.18).

There are some slings with both clip and loop attachments designed to facilitate a person being moved with their own sling in different establishments, which may have different types of hoists. Before using this type of dual attachment sling, very careful consideration must be given to the competency of the handlers using the equipment, as part of the person's overall risk (or handling) assessment, as the potential for confusion and, thus, unsafe handling is high.

The pictures below illustrate correct and incorrect attachment.

Two point rotating spreader bar

Fig 11.15

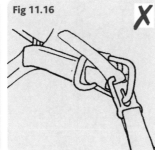
Fig 11.16

Three point tilting spreader bar

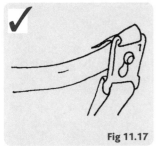

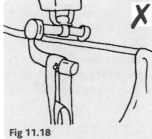
Fig 11.17   Fig 11.18

Sling choice

The style of sling, as well as the fabric of which it is made, will depend on the person's individual risk assessment and consideration should be given to:
- the amount of assistance the person is able to give
- the degree of support needed
- the person's sitting balance, trunk and head control
- the person's skin condition and other vulnerabilities
- the seat or other furniture that the person is being transferred into
- unpredictable movements – restlessness, aggression, spasm or lack of tone
- the task that is to be undertaken and the access required, (eg for personal care)
- necessity for easy removal of the sling
- the position in which the person is comfortable – reclined or sitting
- degree of leg support required
- need for regular laundering (or drying out after bathing or pool use).

Consideration should also be given when deciding whether to leave the sling under the person while he/she is sitting in a chair. Careful risk assessment should include the fabric of the sling, comfort of the person and the risks to the person and carers while inserting/removing the sling.

How to assess the correct size of the sling

Manufacturers will provide guidance for assessing the correct size of sling for an individual person, but the general guidance notes in most sling guides have a considerable range. For example, guidance from one hoist manufacturer states that its medium sling is suitable for people weighing between 57-91kg. Clearly, weight is not the only factor that will influence the appropriate selection. Some manufacturers will ask for an overall height and weight of the person, while others measure around the shoulder or around the chest (for access slings), as well as from nape of the neck to coccyx. Measuring for the correct size is a skilled task and should not be undertaken without adequate training and experience. Most manufacturers offer support for individual sling assessments.

The following is general guidance and should not replace an individual risk assessment and training.

For a general purpose sling, the first measurement would be the length of the back; from the person's coccyx to the shoulder (or nape of neck) (a in Fig 11.19). The sling measurement from the top of the aperture to the top of the sling should match this (a in Fig 11.20). If the sling has integral head support, measure from the person's coccyx to the crown of the head.

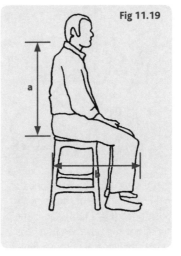
Fig 11.19

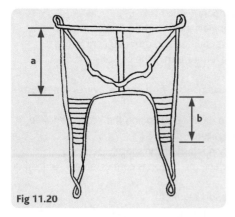

Fig 11.20

Another useful measurement is from the back of the hip to the tip of the knee (b in Fig 11.19). This should match the measurement of the length of the leg piece (b in Fig 11.20).

Consideration must then be given to the width at the person's shoulders and hips and the diameter of the person's thighs. The following are examples of incorrect sling size choice.

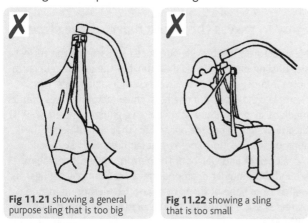

Fig 11.21 showing a general purpose sling that is too big

Fig 11.22 showing a sling that is too small

Types of sling

General purpose universal or universal divided leg sling – which can come with or without head support
It has good support and is generally relatively easy to fit in sitting or lying positions (see Fig 11.23). This sling has a toileting aperture but very limited capability for the handler to assist with adjusting clothing while in the hoist. This type of sling is appropriate for a person with a FIM score of 1 or 2.

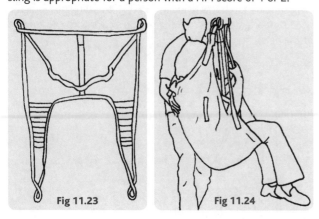

Fig 11.23   **Fig 11.24**

To ensure comfort and safety, the sling must be positioned so that the base of the back panel is at the base of the spine. If the sling has been correctly positioned (Fig 11.24) and is the right size for the person, it should not slip up when he/she is hoisted. The loop configuration on the general purpose sling

(as well as the access sling, right) can vary and will depend on the person's comfort, ability and the task that is to be carried out. A risk assessment must be carried out and details of the leg configuration should be recorded. It may also be useful to use photographs to reinforce this information for handler(s) (see Task 11.2p-r).

Hammock style or quickfit deluxe sling
This sling (Fig 11.25) offers more support, especially to the legs, but is slightly more difficult to fit in a chair. It has a commode aperture but very limited capability for adjusting clothing.

The additional leg loops have a very specific function and handlers need training and therefore a higher degree of competency to fit and attach them. The diagrams (Figs 11.26 and 11.27) show the standard method of loop configurations. Any differences that have been identified must be detailed in the individual care plan and a photograph in the care plan would assist with clarity. This sling is appropriate for a person with a FIM score of 1 or 2.

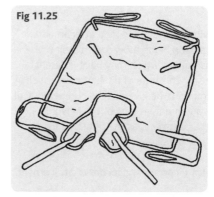

Fig 11.25

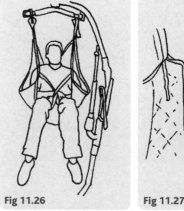

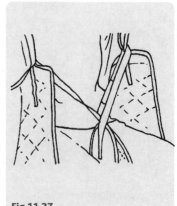

Fig 11.26   **Fig 11.27**

Access or toileting sling
This is one of the easiest slings to fit, but it has significantly less fabric, therefore offering less support to the person. It can come with head support and has good access for clothing adjustment and personal care.

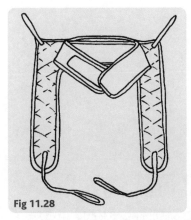

Fig 11.28

The sling (Fig 11.28) should be positioned with the lower edge of the back panel at just below waist level (Fig 11.29). When the waist strap is brought round and fastened, it will be on the waist. If the sling is not positioned low enough, it will slip up slightly, causing discomfort under the axilla. If the sling is slightly too big, it will automatically cause discomfort in the person's axilla and he/she is at great risk of slipping out (Fig 11.30). The sling is appropriate for a person with a FIM score of 2 or 3, following careful assessment of his/her ability.

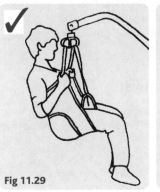

Fig 11.29

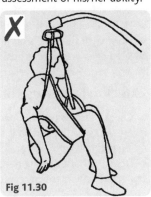

Fig 11.30

A very careful individual assessment must be made when using this type of sling and correct sizing is essential. The person being hoisted must have good upper body tone and sitting balance. He/she should be able to cooperate and understand instructions, such as keeping his/her arms on the outside of the sling (although there are one or two exceptions to this with some individual specialist slings). If he/she is unable to do all the above, he/she is probably unsuitable for this style of sling. This sling should never be used as a general purpose sling and must always be carefully risk assessed.

In seat sling/full body sling

This is usually a sling inserted in bed as it is one piece, often without a commode aperture (see Figs 11.31 and 11.32), and with a variety of loop attachments, including pommels. It is useful to use when inserting and removing a sling is difficult. It remains in the seat once the person is hoisted and can be made in a variety of fabric types depending on the person's individual needs. This type of sling is suitable for a person with a FIM score of 1 or 2.

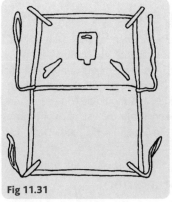

Fig 11.31

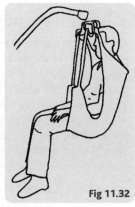

Fig 11.32

Amputee sling

While some general purpose slings may be assessed as appropriate, a specialist sling, which may have divided legs that are brought through additional side loops to ensure security, may meet the person's needs better (see Fig 11.33). Consideration must be made to the person's centre of gravity, balance and muscle tone.

Fig 11.33

Stretcher sling

This is a one piece sling that usually needs its own spreader bar – and careful training is required to ensure correct attachment of the sling (see Fig 11.34). It is used to support/transfer the person in a horizontal position and suitable for a person with a FIM score of 1 or 2, or for any person being hoisted from the floor.

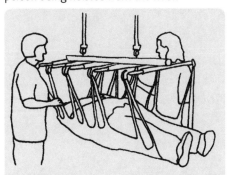

Fig 11.34

1

2

3

11 Core hoisting skills

4

© BackCare

Checking equipment before use

The following checklists are recommendations based on the research carried out on hoist incidents and current best practice and the collective views of members of National Back Exchange, Yorkshire Branch (Yorkshire Back Exchange 2010). The checklist is for the handler and should be considered for every hoisting task undertaken. It may be useful to photocopy and laminate the flow chart in Appendix 11.1 and attach it to each hoist for guidance.

Checklist before using a hoist

- Have you been trained and do you feel confident to use the equipment?
- Does the person's care plan say you should use a hoist? What size and type of sling has been prescribed and what leg/loop configuration has been stated?
- Does the hoist work – does it go up and down, do legs open and close, does it move back and forward (wheels are free running)?
- Do you know how to operate the emergency lowering system?
- Has the hoist been examined in the last six months? Check sticker.
- Is the sling clean and undamaged, and the label readable?
- Does the sling match the hoist?
- Is the sling the right size and type for the person and task? Check label and the person's care plan.
- What is the safe working load (SWL) of the hoist and sling and does the person's weight exceed the SWL?
- Have I told the person what I am about to do and have I got their consent and cooperation?
- Does the current condition of the person to be hoisted present any concerns?

Checklist for during the hoisting task

- Have we got all the equipment needed for the task we are about to do?
- Is the environment as clear as possible (space and clutter, wires on the floor)?
- Is the sling in the right place and smooth under the person's legs?
- Are loops secure and attached appropriately (check care plan) and the same on each side?
- Do a physical tug test to ensure attachments are secure.
- Have the hoist legs been widened?
- Does the person look safe and comfortable?
- Hoist up until the straps are in tension.
- Hoist with the brakes off unless told otherwise (care plan).
- Keep person as low as possible.

Checklist after use of hoist

- Check person's position and comfort before removing sling.
- Are you sure the person is safe before removing equipment (eg bed rails up)?
- Does the hoist or sling need cleaning?
- Return equipment to storage point and recharge if necessary.

PRACTICAL TECHNIQUES

For the remainder of this chapter, it is assumed that an individual risk assessment and handling plan has been undertaken, appropriate equipment has been prescribed and is available for use and that staff have been trained in its safe use.

These are core techniques and there are many other options and variations that could be considered in specialist areas.

Task 11.1 Transfer from chair using active hoist

Person ability criteria
The person needs some weight bearing ability, trunk control and the ability to cooperate, to an extent, with instructions.

Description
Insert sling
- Position sling at the level of the person's waist.
- Secure as appropriate for manufacturer's guidelines (on most slings, the arms should be on the outside).

Hook up and check
- Bring the standing hoist in close enough to the person so that his/her knees are touching the knee pad (adjust the pad if necessary). It may be necessary to open the hoist legs.
- Lower the boom to its lowest setting.
- Ensure the person's feet are on the footplate and he/she is seated to the back of the chair.
- Hook up with the nearest loop that is reachable without pulling the person forward.
- Secure the leg straps if identified as appropriate in risk assessment.
- Check the loops are secure and the person is comfortable.
- Raise the boom to take up the slack (Task 11.1a), check loops remain secure and ask the person to hold on as appropriate.

Task 11.1a

Transfer
- Raise them up sufficiently to meet the needs of the task and the person's comfort and preference (Task 11.1b).

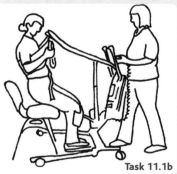

Task 11.1b

Options and variations
- The brakes may be applied if the person has a tendency to push the hoist away with his/her legs. This should be stated in the care plan.
- Some hoists have an arm gutter and handles and this would require the person to be able to hold on.
- Alternative hoists have rope sling attachments which must be secured as per the manufacturers' guidance.
- Alternative slings are also available that offer more support.

Perceived exertion for handler
- There is some low level work while securing the sling and adjusting the knee pad with the potential for stooping. The handler(s) should adjust posture accordingly.

Comfort for person
- Should be comfortable unless the person has knee problems, sensitivity or vulnerable skin on their legs.

Skill level of handler
- The handler needs to be trained and competent to use this specific piece of equipment.
- Two way communication is essential as cooperation is required.

Evidence available
- This equipment was recommended by Busse (2000) for persons able to support a limited part of their weight to reinforce a sit to stand movement.
- Ruszala (2001) showed that this equipment was suitable for early rehabilitation.
- Fragala (1993) showed that use of standing and raising aids reduced occupational injury.
- DIAG (2001) states that the person must have some weight bearing ability, trunk and upper limb control and some ability to cooperate.

Dangers/precautions
- For most active hoists, the person needs to be encouraged to sit back in the sling, otherwise it may ride up.
- Ongoing risk assessment is essential to ensure the equipment remains suitable for use with the person.
- The distance travelled in the hoist must be based on individual risk assessment.

11 Core hoisting skills

Further options

● Active hoists can be used for a transfer from the side of the bed. If the person can sit comfortably and stably on the edge of the bed, this may be suitable (Task 11.1c).

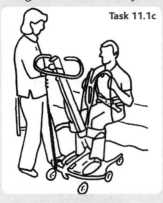

Task 11.1c

Evidence review

Technique	REBA	Activity	Comfort	FIM	Mobility gallery	Skill level	Comments
Task 11.1 – Transfer from chair using active hoist							
Task 11.1a	1	4	7	3	C	Competent	The active hoist has a low postural risk level but that may increase with the fitting of the sling (see Task 11.2)

Task 11.2 Passive hoist transfer from a chair (wheelchair/commode etc)

Person ability criteria

● For the fully dependent person.
● The choice of sling will depend on the person's individual ability and must be based on risk assessment (see section on sling choice on pages 175-177) (Task 11.2a).

Description

● Ensure compatibility of hoist and sling (see previous pages).
● Insert sling (general purpose sling).
● Bring the person forward in the chair and position the bottom edge of the sling in line with the person's coccyx.

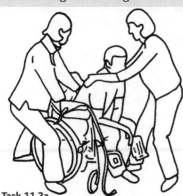

Task 11.2a

● Position the leg pieces to ensure comfort and security (Task 11.2b and c).
● Hook up and check.
● Bring the hoist in and lower the boom over the person's centre of gravity to ensure the attachments reach easily. It may be necessary to open the hoist legs. It is often useful to bring the hoist in at an angle.

Hook up and check

● Hook up with the loops that have been assessed as appropriate for the person's comfort, safety and for the task (see Task 11.2p-r).
● Check the loops are secure and the person is comfortable.
● Raise the boom to take up the tension, check loops remain secure.

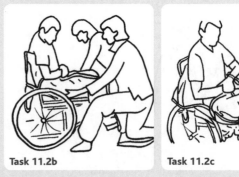

Task 11.2b   Task 11.2c

Transfer

● Raise the person up sufficiently to ensure he/she is clear of the chair and transfer over as short a distance as necessary.
● When manoeuvring the hoist, face the direction of the movement and consider whether it would be appropriate for two handlers to carry out the task (see Task 11.2i).

Positioning into a seat

● Correct positioning can be achieved by the appropriate sling loop configuration. A good sitting position in the chair may also be assisted by one handler gently pushing on the person's legs, the front of the sling (see Task 11.2d) or from the back by a handler drawing the person gently back.

- A wishbone style spreader bar is adjusted by pushing down on the positional handle (Task 11.2e).

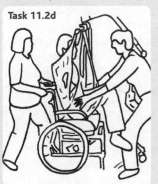

Task 11.2d

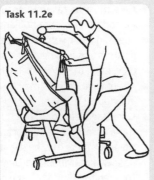

Task 11.2e

Options and variations
Inserting sling
- If the person is unable to sit forward, the sling can be inserted between two flat slide sheets.
- Scrunch up the first slide sheet and place behind the person's shoulders (Task 11.2f). Two handlers to push the slide sheet down.
- Repeat with the second slide sheet.
- Place the hoist sling between the two slide sheets (sling sandwich) and push it down to ensure it is in the correct position (Task 11.2g).
- Bring the leg loops round and place them under the person's legs.

Task 11.2f

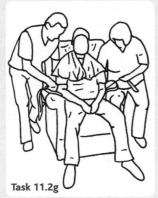

Task 11.2g

- Remove the slide sheet that is lying next to the person before hoisting him/her up (Task 11.2h).

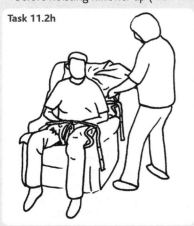

Task 11.2h

Perceived exertion for handler
- Handlers will feel exertion when manoeuvring the hoist, especially on carpeted floors. It may be appropriate to ensure there are two people present, but this will depend

on the individual risk assessment (the weight of the person being hoisted, the flooring etc).

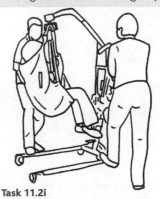

Task 11.2i

Comfort for person
- If the sling is appropriate for the person's ability, body shape and size, it should be comfortable. Comfort may be increased by adjusting the sling loop configuration.
- Adjusting shoulder loops will change the basic position and bring a person forward or reclined which may increase his/her comfort, and will affect the pressure felt on the legs. However, if the shoulder loops are too short, it may bring the person too upright, with the danger of him/her falling forward or banging his/her head on the spreader bar.
- Adjustment of the leg loops may also be necessary to achieve the desired position.

Task 11.2j showing the reclined position achieved by longer shoulder loops

Task 11.2k showing the potential problem of hoisting a person too upright, as he/she could fall forward

Task 11.2l showing the person's head too close to the spreader bar due to the attachment of the short shoulder loop

Skill level of handler
- Handlers need to be trained and competent to use this specific piece of equipment.

Evidence available
- Zhang et al (2000) suggest that as slings/hoists varied in comfort and ease of use, care should be taken in selection/design.
- DIAG (2001) recommends the use of electric hoists over manual, except in certain specified situations, eg as an interim measure, infrequent use, no electric supply, where water may cause problems or difficulty in charging the battery.

11 Core hoisting skills

Dangers/precautions

- Compatibility of hoist and sling (see previous pages).
- Careful attention must be paid to ensure loops are attached correctly and securely.

Task 11.2m showing incorrect hooking up of sling to the spreader bar of the hoist

- Care must be taken when introducing the hoist as the carry bar could swing and may injure the person being hoisted.
- When hoisting on flat surfaces, the brakes should not be applied when lifting/lowering.
- A mobile hoist should be used only to transport a person over a short distance.
- Care should be taken of the person's limbs to avoid contact with the hoist.
- Handlers should NOT use the hand loops to lift the person back into the chair. These are designed to be used to steady the person during the transfer.
- The same length of sling loop must be attached on each side to ensure the person is sitting evenly.

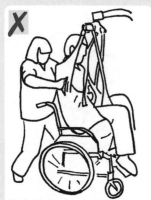

Task 11.2n showing incorrect use of hand loops to lift the person back into the chair

Task 11.2o showing an uneven attachment of the sling loops on each side (longer on one shoulder loop than the other)

Sling size

- Careful assessment must be made to ensure the size of sling is correct for the person. The size must be detailed on the individual's care plan (see section on sling choice on pages 175-177).

Further options

Sling leg configurations

- Care must be taken to ensure the sling is smooth under the person's legs before hooking up.
- The standard method is to cross the leg loops to bring the person's legs into neutral (Task 11.2p). This gives added security, preventing the person being hoisted from falling forward.
- Alternative options may be useful depending on the individual.
- Uncrossed leg loops (Task 11.2q) have the advantage of giving more access for personal care. It can be more comfortable for men, but there may be dignity issues for women. The main danger is that there is an increased risk of the person falling through the sling, if he/she has decreased trunk control.

Task 11.2p   Task 11.2q

- "Bucket" configuration is where each leg loop is passed under both legs (Task 11.2r), which shortens the leg loops and brings the knees higher. This could be more acceptable for some women and may be easier for people with tight adductors, but must be used with care for people with larger or oedematous legs as there is increased pressure from the sling on the outside of the thighs and from the knees being pressed together.

Task 11.2r

Evidence review

Technique	REBA	Activity	Comfort	FIM	Mobility gallery	Skill level	Comments
Task 11.2 – Passive hoist transfer from a chair							
Task 11.2a	4 and 6	2	8	1-2	D	Advanced beginner	Postural risk levels can be high for inserting the sling and manoeuvring the hoist, especially on carpeted flooring.
Task 11.2b	8	2	9	1-2	D	Advanced beginner	
Task 11.2d	4	2	9	1-2	D	Advanced beginner	
Task 11.2e	7	2	9	1-2	D	Advanced beginner	
Task 11.2g	8	1	8	1-2	D	Advanced beginner	
Task 11.2i	9	2	8	1-2	D	Advanced beginner	

Task 11.3 Repositioning a person who has slipped down in a chair

Person ability criteria
- For the fully dependent person who has slipped forward in the chair, and who would fall out of the chair if brought forward to position (or reposition) the sling.

Description
Insert sling
- Place a simple chair with no arms under the person's legs. (see Task 11.3a). One handler to bring the person forward, while a second positions the sling into the correct position (Task 11.3b).

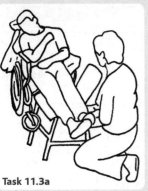

Task 11.3a

Task 11.3b

Hook up and check
- Hoist up as above (Task 11.3c) in Task 11.2 and reposition in the chair in a comfortable position.

Task 11.3c

Evidence review

Technique	REBA	Activity	Comfort	FIM	Mobility gallery	Skill level	Comments
Task 11.3 – Re-positioning a person in a chair if he/she has slipped down							
Task 11.3a	7	2	7	1-3	D	Competent	
Task 11.3b	9	2	7	1-3	D	Competent	

Task 11.4 Passive hoist transfer – from the bed

Person ability criteria
- For the fully dependent person.

Description
Insert sling
- Rolling the person from side to side, ensure the bottom edge of the sling is in line with the base of the spine (coccyx) and the sling is centered behind the person (lining up the central label with the spine) (Task 11.4a).

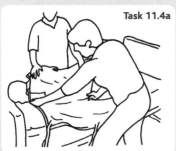

Task 11.4a

- The lower half of the sling is then rolled and tucked under the person (Task 11.4b).
- The person is rolled to the other side and the sling is unfolded (Task 11.4c).

Task 11.4b

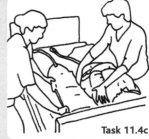

Task 11.4c

Hook up and check
- It may be more comfortable for the person to be placed in a sitting position in the bed before hoisting. Consider which loops are appropriate to ensure comfort and optimum positioning for the task.
- Use the hoist mechanism (as described in Task 11.2) to raise the spreader bar until the loops are under tension, stop and check the loops are secure and the person is comfortable and consider whether additional head support is needed (Task 11.4d).

11 Core hoisting skills

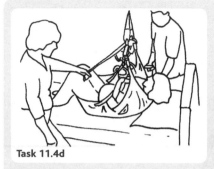

Task 11.4d

Transfer
- Transfer to an appropriate chair and lower as before.

Options and variations
- Inserting a sling by rolling the person onto one side only (sometimes known as the origami technique). This could be useful if the person has one side he/she cannot tolerate being rolled onto, or if he/she is in pain or touch averse and a reduction in general handling would be useful.
- The sling is folded with the handles and labels on the outside. With the person rolled onto one side, lay the sling down on the bed, with the folded edge closest to him/her. Ensure there is a gap of approximately one hand width between the fold and the person (Task 11.4e).
- Bring the leg loop of the top layer only, up, and under the person's neck, or under the pillow (Task 11.4f).
- Roll up the rest of the top layer (Task 11.4g).
- Bring the person back onto his/her back. Gently pull the loop in a downwards direction (Task 11.4h and i).
- Insert sling between two flat slide sheets for the person who cannot be rolled from side to side.
- Roll up a flat slide sheet and bring it under the person's head (or pillow) with the roll facing downwards (Task 11.4j).
- Unroll the slide sheet and repeat with a second flat slide sheet, underneath the first (Task 11.4k).
- Insert the sling between the two flat slide sheets and hold the top slide sheet with one hand and the sling with the other. Gently bring it down into place (Task 11.4l).
- Check the position of the base of the sling is correct and aligned at the level of the sacrum (Task 11.4m).
- Remove the slide sheet next to the person before hoisting (Task 11.4n).

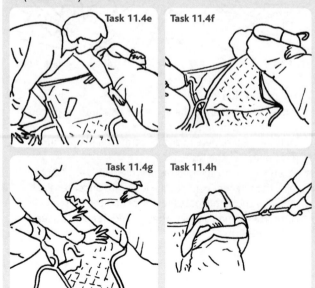

Task 11.4e   Task 11.4f

Task 11.4g   Task 11.4h

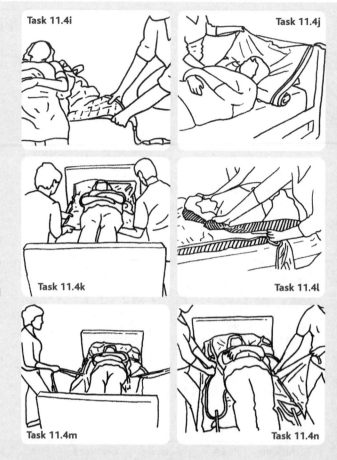

Task 11.4i   Task 11.4j

Task 11.4k   Task 11.4l

Task 11.4m   Task 11.4n

Perceived exertion for handler
- Can be more difficult with the larger person, and may be easier to have the slide sheets in folds rather than a roll.
- Care must be taken to follow basic biomechanical principles when unrolling.
- The use of height adjustable beds will help to reduce the risk to the handlers.

Comfort for person
- The comfort of the person will be determined by the appropriate selection of sling and a sling with head support would be recommended.
- Profiling of the bed will add to the person's comfort.

Skill level of handler
- Competency and practice is essential to ensure the sling is in the right position before hoisting.

Further options
- Use of overhead tracking hoist from the bed. Insert sling as appropriate. Hook up the sling and check as before (Task 11.4o).
- Use of overhead portable tracking. See Dangers/precautions (page 185).

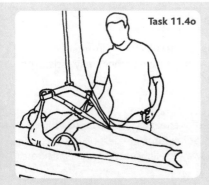

Task 11.4o

- Use of stretcher hoist from the bed.
- Slings vary according to manufacturer and may be fabric or rigid scoops. They maintain the person in a lying position. Attachment of the sling to the hoist is with an appropriate carry bar and should not be attached to a standard coathanger style (Task 11.4p and q).

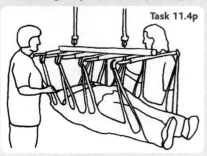

Task 11.4p

Task 11.4q

Dangers/precautions
Use of overhead tracking
- Care must be taken to ensure the hoist unit is directly over the person and the tape is vertical. Failure to do this will lead to the unit cutting out and/or the tape fraying (Task 11.4r).

Use of portable overhead tracking
- Ensure attachment of the unit to the track as per instructions.
- The unit is heavy and should always be placed on a trolley for transportation.
- Do not support the weight of the hoist unit while attaching it. Always lower the unit, so there is plenty of tape available and no need to hold up the unit. Rest the unit on a table or trolley (Task 11.4s).
- Great care must be taken to steady the hoist unit when bringing it in above the person to ensure the unit does not knock into the person.

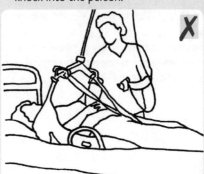

Task 11.4r showing the overhead hoist unit in an inappropriate position with tape NOT vertical

Task 11.4s

Stretcher hoist
- Due to the multiple number of loops, additional checks must be made to ensure that each sling loop is attached to its correct position on the carry bar and that they are all attached securely and symmetrically.

Evidence review

Technique	REBA	Activity	Comfort	FIM	Mobility gallery	Skill level	Comments
Task 11.4 – Passive hoist transfer from the bed							
Task 11.4a	9	1	9	1-2	D	Advanced beginner	
Task 11.4c	7	1	9	1-2	D	Advanced beginner	
Task 11.4k	7	1	7	1-2	D	Advanced beginner	
Task 11.4s	5	n/a	n/a	n/a	n/a	Advanced beginner	

Task 11.5   Using a hoist and turning sheet for personal care in bed

Person ability criteria
- For the fully dependent person.

Description
- There are considerable postural stresses for handlers while initiating a turn and while supporting the position of a person in side lying. This technique may help to address these risks and may reduce the number of handlers needed to carry out the task.
- This technique requires a specialised turning sheet attached to an overhead hoist (Task 11.5b) to facilitate the turning of a person in bed (Task 11.5a).
- Electric profiling beds significantly reduce postural strain and should always be considered in risk assessments of dependent persons requiring care in bed.

Task 11.5a

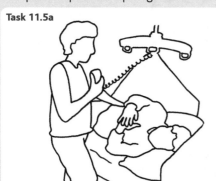

Task 11.5b

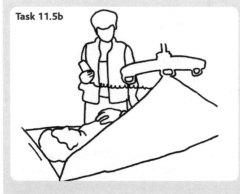

Insert sling
- The person can lie on this sheet permanently.

Hook up and check
- It would be helpful to assist the person into a normal movement pattern, ready for rolling (see chapter 10).

Hook up the sheet as per manufacturer's instructions. A slide sheet underneath the turning sheet may assist with the movement (Task 11.5b).

Transfer
- Bring the hoist up just far enough (Task 11.5a) to achieve the position required. Some turning sheets have a portion that can be brought away to allow access for personal care.

Options and variations
- This can be performed with a mobile hoist and careful consideration must be given to ensure the spreader bar is directly over the attachment loop.

Perceived exertion for handler
- The exertion is reduced considerably by using an overhead hoist.

Comfort for person
- This technique can be used to maximise comfort, especially for people who prefer minimal handling or who are touch averse.
- Care must be taken to ensure the hoist is brought only as high as necessary or the person may feel insecure.

Skill level of handler
- This is an easy technique to learn but handlers must have training to ensure they have the necessary skill to undertake the task (see Dangers/precautions below).

Evidence available
- Smith & Orchard (2009).

Dangers/precautions
- If using a mobile hoist, care must be taken to ensure there is no diagonal pull on the attachment loop and that the hoist legs are opened wide for stability.
- If the handler is working alone, this must be detailed clearly in the care plan and bed rails should be used to ensure safety at the side the handler is not working.

Further options
Other styles of slings, sheets and bed systems are available for use with a hoist (see chapter 10).

Evidence review

Technique	REBA	Activity	Comfort	FIM	Mobility gallery	Skill level	Comments
Task 11.5 – Using a hoist and turning sheet for personal care in bed							
Task 11.5a	4	1	9	1-2	D	Advanced beginner	

Task 11.6 Hoisting from mattress on the floor

Person ability criteria
- If the person is at risk of falling out of bed and bed rails have been assessed as not appropriate, the person may be nursed on a mattress on the floor.
- Ideally, a height adjustable bed with extra low facility should be used.

Description
- If the extra low bed is not available and the person needs hoisting, the following methods could be used:

Using an overhead tracking hoist
- This would be ideal as it would greatly reduce the risk to the person and handlers and is easier.

Insert the sling under the person
- Techniques in Task 11.4.

Hook up and check
- Move the hoisting unit to a position directly over the person who needs hoisting. When raising/lowering, ensure the tape is vertical (see Task 11.6a).

Task 11.6a

Options and variations
- If an overhead hoist is unavailable, a mobile hoist could be used in the following way. This should be a short term measure.

Using a mobile hoist
- Insert sling: roll the person from side to side (see Task 11.6b) to position the sling and place two flat slide sheets underneath the person and the sling.
- With the mobile hoist at right angles to the mattress and the castors up against the mattress, apply the brakes.
- Place a large transfer board just under the person and across the legs of the hoist (Task 11.6b).
- Holding the top flat slide sheet, slide the person across and onto the transfer board (Task 11.6c).
- Hook up the hoist sling, and hoist up (Task 11.6d). Remove

the transfer board and slide sheets, release the brakes and transfer as appropriate.

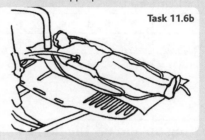

Task 11.6b

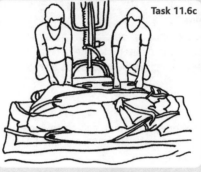

Task 11.6c

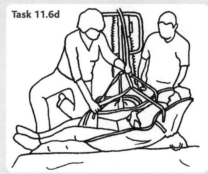

Task 11.6d

Perceived exertion for handler
- This is an awkward working position, as is all personal care taking place at floor level.

Comfort for person
- As with hoisting off the bed.

Skill level of handler
- A high level of skill and practice is essential to ensure the technique is carried out safely.

Dangers/precautions
- As with any hoisting task.
- Any care tasks carried out at floor level will require handlers to adopt compromised positions and care must be taken to optimise good posture.

Evidence review

Technique	REBA	Activity	Comfort	FIM	Mobility gallery	Skill level	Comments
Task 11.6 – Hoisting from a mattress on the floor							
Task 11.6a	9	1	8	1-3	C/D	Advanced beginner	This activity should be considered only in the short term while additional appropriate equipment is sought.
Task 11.6c	10	1	9	1-3	C/D	Competent	
Task 11.6d	10	1	9	1-3	C/D	Competent	

Task 11.7 Hoisting on and off the floor

Person ability criteria
- This might be necessary for physiotherapy and play. The techniques below may also be useful for the person who has fallen onto the floor and has been assessed as safe to move.

Description
- The technique for hoisting a person on and off the floor will depend partly on the hoist available and the ability for the boom to lower to the floor.

Overhead tracking
- This would be the equipment of choice.

Lowering down to the floor
- Insert sling, hook up, check and transfer as previously.
- Loop configuration may be altered to achieve a more semi recumbent position.
- A sling with head support would be preferable, even if person has head control.

Hoisting from the floor
- Roll the person onto the sling (as before), hook up, check and transfer onto the most appropriate furniture, taking care to ensure support of the person's head (by choosing a sling with head support or by offering support as necessary) (see Task 11.7a).

Mobile hoist
- If overhead tracking system is unavailable, the following technique with a mobile hoist may be useful.
- Hoisting from the floor – insert sling by rolling the person from side to side (Task 11.4).

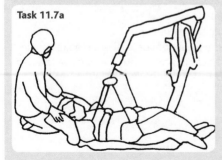

Task 11.7a

Hook up and check
- The angle the hoist is introduced will partly depend on the style, type and dimensions of the hoist. Introducing the hoist diagonally to the person, with one hoist leg under the person's leg and one to the side of the person's head, will

enable the spreader bar to be positioned centrally when the boom is lowered (Task 11.7b).

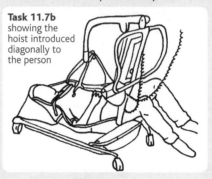

Task 11.7b showing the hoist introduced diagonally to the person

Task 11.7c

Transfer
- Manoeuvre the hoist as short a distance as possible and consider bringing a chair or wheelchair in underneath the person. Lower into the chair (see Task 11.7d).

Options and variations
- It may be necessary to prop the person up against pillows or a chair, if the boom does not lower far enough (Task 11.7c).
- This will also allow for an additional option of bringing the hoist in sideways, with one hoist leg through the upturned chair and the other under the person's flexed knees.
- Some hoist designs allow positioning of the hoist at the person's head
- If major fracture and/or spinal injury is suspected, additional hoist equipment, such as a stretcher attachment, should be used to enable the person to be lifted flat (National Patient Safety Agency 2011).

Task 11.7d showing the person propped on an upturned chair

Perceived exertions for handler
- As with any techniques carried out on the floor.

Comfort for person
- Careful consideration must be made for persons who have spasm, involuntary movements or vulnerable skin. Extra

pillows may be necessary to protect them from any sharp points on the hoist.

Skill level of handler
- A high level of skill is required.

Evidence available
- The Resuscitation Council (UK) (2009) recommends that a hoist should be used to lift a person off the floor post resuscitation.

Dangers/precautions
- Many parts of the hoist are in close proximity to the person being hoisted and great care must be taken to protect the person from injury.

Evidence review

Technique	REBA	Activity	Comfort	FIM	Mobility gallery	Skill level	Comments
Task 11.7 – Hoisting on and off the floor							
Task 11.7a	9	1	5	1-3	C/D	Competent	
Task 11.7c	10	1	5	1-2	D/E	Competent	

Task 11.8 Hoisting into the bath

Person ability criteria
- The person being hoisted must have good sitting balance and be able to maintain a sitting posture if a fixed bath seat is used. If the person has a tendency to go into extension, this type of hoist is not suitable. The person should be cooperative and able to understand instructions.

Description
- The fixed bath seat usually has a moulded plastic seat and seat arms which fold back for easy access. Bath hoists can be electric or manual (Task 11.8a).

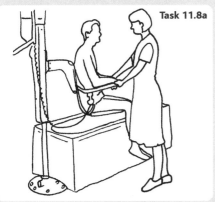

Task 11.8a

Transfer
- It is good practice to drain the water out of the bath before lifting the person out but care must be taken that the person does not get cold.

Perceived exertion for handler
- If the bath hoist has a manual operation, this will require

considerable exertion to operate, especially if repetitive tasks of bathing are necessary during a shift.

Comfort for person
- A hard plastic seat may not be comfortable for all.
- Seat belts are available and many manufacturers now stipulate that they should be used at all times with their equipment. The attachment and the fabric of the belt may be a consideration with regard to infection control.

Dangers/precautions
- All handling in a bathroom will mean an increased risk of slipping. Flooring should be slip resistant and suitable footwear worn by staff.
- The bath seat is usually smooth, and therefore possibly slippery, so there is a risk of the person sliding forward and under the arms of the bath seat. This risk is exacerbated if the arms do not lock down into place.
- If a seat belt is assessed as appropriate, it may be necessary to consider whether this is the safest way to bathe the person, see below. If a seat belt is assessed as not necessary, this should be reflected in the individual risk assessment.
- Before lowering the person into the bath, the water temperature must always be checked. A person must never be left alone in the bath unless risk assessed as appropriate.

Options and variations
- Hoisting directly into the bath with an overhead tracking hoist. This has the advantage that an individually assessed fabric sling can be prescribed to meet the needs of the person better, especially if he/she is more dependent and is not able to sit on a hard seat. The fabric of the sling may

11 Core hoisting skills

need to be considered for personal comfort, to allow water runaway and to ease drying between uses (Task 11.8b).

- Using a mobile hoist and fabric sling into the bath. This may be possible if there is clearance under the bath for the hoist legs. Careful assessment must be made to ensure the sling is appropriate (Task 11.8c).

Task 11.8b

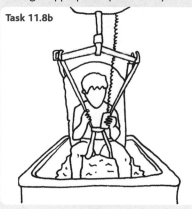

Task 11.8c

Perceived exertions for handler
- As for any hoisting technique. This will depend on the start position of the person, choice of hoist and the method chosen to insert the sling.

Comfort for person
- There is a tendency for slings designed for bathing to be thinner and the padding under the legs may not be adequate for the person's comfort.

Skill level of handler
- As for any hoisting task.

Evidence available
- Boulton (2009) and MHRA (2008).

Dangers/precautions
- The person is wet and slippery and therefore there is an increased risk of slipping off a moulded bath seat.
- As the sling is usually left under the person, they may "float" off the sling, requiring it to be repositioned before he/she is hoisted out.

Evidence review

Technique	REBA	Activity	Comfort	FIM	Mobility gallery	Skill level	Comments
Task 11.8 – Hoisting into the bath							
Task 11.8a	4	5	5	3-4	C	Advanced beginner	

References

All Wales NHS Manual Handling Training Passport and Information Scheme (2010), Swansea.

Boulton, R (2005), Staff perceptions concerning the barriers to safe patient handling in an acute hospital. Unpublished MSc dissertation, University of Cranfield; School of Engineering.

Boulton, R (2009), Human Factors and Ergonomics of patient and client handling incidents. Unpublished Health and Safety Executive report.

Busse, M (2000), Effective rehabilitation and hoisting equipment: a case study. *Nursing & Residential Care*, **2.4**, 168-173.

DIAG (2001), Care Handling of Adults and children in Hospitals and Community Settings – A Code of Practice, Published: Derbyshire Interagency Group.

Fragala, G (1993), Injuries cut with lift use in ergonomics demonstration project. *Provider*, October 29-39.

Handley, R (2004), Sling/Hoist Compatibility, *column,* August 2004.

Health Services Advisory Committee (1984), *The lifting of Patients in the Health Services*, HMSO London.

HSE (1992), *Manual handling. Manual Handling Operations Regulations 1992 (as amended), Guidance on Regulations* L23, (Third edition), HSE Books.

HSE (1998), Safe use of Lifting Equipment. Lifting Operations and Lifting Equipment Regulations (LOLER) ACOP & guidance (L113), HMSO.

HSE (1999), *Reducing error and influencing behaviour* (2nd edition) HSG48, HMSO, Norwich.

Kelby, J (2010), 3 Step Process to Reduce Caregiver Error in the Selection of Safe Patient Handling Equipment, *Ergonomics Today,* April 20, 2010.

Lloyd, P, Osborne, C, Tarling, C & Troup, J (1981), *The Handling of Patients – A Guide for Nurse Managers,* Middlesex: National Back Pain Association.

Mandelstam, M (2004), Casefile: Balanced decision-taking, legal principle, practical implications, *column*, **16** (1), 16-18.

MHRA (2006), Managing Medical Devices (DB2006(05) www.mhra.gov.uk/Publications/Safetyguidance/DeviceBulletins/CON2025142.

MHRA (2008), MDA/2008/010 Ambulift hoist. All models manufactured by Arjo or Mechanaids. (www.mhra.gov.uk/PrintPreview/PublicationSP/CON014121).

National Patient Safety Agency (2011), Rapid Response Report NPSA/2011/RRR001 Essential care after an inpatient fall NHS 2011.

Resuscitation Council (UK) (2009), *Guidance for Safer Handling During Resuscitation in Hospitals,* Resuscitation Council, UK.

Ruszala, S (2001), An evaluation of equipment to assist patient sit to stand activities in physiotherapy. Unpublished MSc dissertation, University of Wales; School of Health Care Studies.

Ruszala, S, Hall, J & Alexander, P (2010), *Standards in manual handling, third edition*, National Back Exchange, January 2010.

Smith, H & Orchard, S (2009), Double Handling within Domiciliary Care: the Potential to Produce Benefits Through Greater Utilisation of Equipment for the Elderly and Those with Physical Disabilities, paper read to the annual National Back Exchange Conference, September, Hinckley.

Smith, J (2005), Hoist Identification Tool, Stourbridge: Sunrise Medical Ltd.

Yorkshire Back Exchange (2010), Checklist for Use of Hoists.

Zhang, Z, Stobve, TJ, Collins, JW, Hsaio, H & Hobbs, GR (2000), Psychophysical assessment of assistive devices for transferring patients/residents. *Applied Ergonomics*, **31** 35-44.

Appendix 11.1

Before use checklist

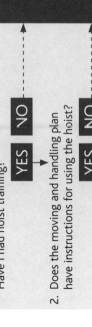

1. Do I feel confident using this hoist? Have I had hoist training?
 — YES → / NO ⇢

2. Does the moving and handling plan have instructions for using the hoist?
 — YES → / NO ⇢

3. Is the hoist working?
 - up and down
 - legs open and close
 - moves back and forward.
 — YES → / NO ⇢

4. Has the hoist been serviced/checked in the last six months (check label)?
 — YES → / NO ⇢

5. Is the sling clean and undamaged?
 — YES → / NO ⇢

6. Is the sling the right size and type for this client (check the label and care plan)?
 — YES → / NO ⇢

7. Does the sling match the hoist?
 — YES → / NO ⇢

8. Have I got consent? Is the person OK to hoist?
 — YES → / NO ⇢

9. Go to next section.

DO NOT USE: Check with my supervisor

During use checklist

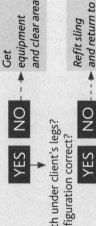

1. Have you got all the equipment needed and is there space to move the hoist?
 — YES → / NO ⇢ *Get equipment and clear area*

2. Is sling smooth under client's legs? Is the leg configuration correct?
 — YES → / NO ⇢ *Refit sling and return to No. 2*

3. Are loops secure, attached same on each side?
 — YES → / NO ⇢ *Re-attach and check. Return to No. 3*

4. Does the person look safe and comfortable?
 — YES → / NO ⇢ *Refit sling*

5. **Tug test:** Hoist up until straps are tight then recheck No. 4.
 — YES → / NO ⇢ *Lower and refit*

6. Hoist with brakes off and hoist legs widened unless told otherwise (in care plan).

After hoisting

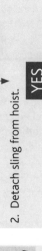

1. Is the person comfortably positioned?
 — YES ↓ / NO ⇢ *Reposition*

2. Detach sling from hoist.
 — YES ↓

3. Make sure the person is safe.
 — YES ↓

4. Put the hoist back and/or recharge.
 — YES ↓

5. Does the sling or hoist need cleaning?

12

People handling for bariatrics, a systems approach

Anita Rush MSc (Health Ergonomics) RGN Dip Health Care Studies
Clinical nurse specialist equipment
Ken Cookson RMN RGN Dip RSA
Manual handling manager/adviser, Aintree Hospitals NHS Foundation Trust

Introduction

The management of people handling for bariatric persons in health and social care presents multiple challenges in terms of communication between agencies, access to, and provision of, equipment, staffing, transport and environmental constraints.

This chapter will address the importance of a systems approach to the issues outlined above and will take account of the needs and dignity of the bariatric person. Factors, including relevant legislation, policy development, communication and strategic planning, will be considered. These, together with the National Health Service Litigation Authority (NHSLA) risk management standards, will form the foundation for the implementation of safer systems of work.

Definition

The origin of the word bariatric comes from the Greek words barys meaning heavy and baros meaning weight. Bariatric medicine is defined as the study of obesity and its causes (Mosby 2006), but the definition of those who may be described as bariatric is less clear. According to Fazel (1997), a bariatric person is anyone weighing 159kg (25st) or more. Cookson (2007) describes a bariatric person as anyone with

morbid obesity as defined by the National Institute for Health and Clinical Excellence (NICE 2006). Persons are defined as being morbidly obese if they have a body mass index (BMI) of $40kg/m^2$ or more, or they have a BMI of between $35kg/m^2$ and $40kg/m^2$ with co-morbidities. There are also some systematic variations in "normal" BMI across ethnic groups (Naylor *et al* 2005). For example, in certain Asian populations a given BMI equates to a higher percentage of body fat than the same BMI in a white European population (World Health Organisation (WHO) expert consultation 2004). In these populations, the risks of type II diabetes and cardiovascular disease increase at a BMI below the standard cut off value of $25kg/m^2$. In some black populations, however, the converse is true and a particular BMI corresponds to a lower percentage of body fat and consequently lower risks of morbidity and mortality than in a white European population. When comparing obesity in different ethnic groups, it can be more useful to use the definition based on waist/hip ratio than the standard BMI classification (Naylor *et al* 2005).

There are other obesity related co-morbidities that can have an affect on a number of bodily systems including respiratory, cardiovascular, musculoskeletal, psychological, reproductive and gastrointestinal. Hypertension, diabetes and ischaemic heart disease are consequences of morbid obesity. Mobility can be affected due to osteoarthritis in the weight bearing joints as a result of increased strain. Some types of cancer are more prevalent in obese subjects, including breast and endometrial cancer in women and colorectal and prostate cancer in men. Obesity can lead to depression and social exclusion or discrimination. It may lead to bullying at school and prejudice in the working environment. A significant consequence of all these co-morbidities is that the mortality rate is increased (Webber 2001). Bushard (2002) suggests that, when dealing with extremely heavy trauma victims, organisations need to take an holistic view and consider several factors in addition to weight, including:

● impact on mobility
● space requirements
● staffing levels.

Having a clear definition of the term bariatric within an organisation's policies, procedures and protocols will influence which control measures will need to be implemented. It will identify roles and responsibilities, bottom up and top down within the organisation, to ensure action is taken in a timely manner. An ambiguous definition may well result in action not being taken at the correct time. Based on single trigger factors, a bariatric policy may state that action must be taken for persons weighing 159kg (approx 25st) or more, but what happens if the person is only 158kg?

The scale of the problem

Bariatric persons are at increased risk of ill health due to the associated co-morbidities and it is therefore foreseeable that this group represents an increased potential for hospital admissions and social care support.

There are estimated annual costs of £4.2 billion linked to the treatment of co-morbidities and this could double by 2050 (NHS Information Centre 2009a). There are one million people in the UK who meet the criteria for bariatric surgery based on NICE guidelines. Despite this, there were less than 4,000 weight loss procedures carried out in 2009. Providing surgery to just five per cent of those eligible would offer savings to the NHS of £382m over a three year period (see Table 12.1). Savings reaching £1.3 billion could occur if surgery was provided to 25 per cent of those eligible (Office of Health Economics 2010a). Some of these benefits occur due to the person having the ability to return to work which can offset the cost of surgery. There may be financial gains due to a reduction in state benefits paid out (see Table 12.2).

It may appear that the solution is to provide better access for NHS patients to have bariatric surgery but, according to the Association for the Study of Obesity (ASO), there is still controversy surrounding bariatric surgery. Improved selection criteria and more long term studies are needed to follow up patients after surgery. Certain procedures may cause additional metabolic and cosmetic problems that may result in additional NHS costs (ASO 2010).

TABLE 12.1 ECONOMIC IMPACT IF FIVE PER CENT OF ELIGIBLE PATIENTS WERE TO RECEIVE BARIATRIC SURGERY

Component	Year 1 £m	Year 2 £m	Year 3 £m	Total year 1 to 3 £m
Paid hours gained	135	135	135	405
NHS costs/savings	−8	56	56	104
Total savings	127	191	191	509
Cost of surgery (excluding aftercare costs)	−127	0	0	−127
Total economic impact	**0**	**191**	**191**	**382**

Source: Office of Health Economics 2010

TABLE 12.2 ECONOMIC IMPACT IF 25 PER CENT OF ELIGIBLE PATIENTS WERE TO RECEIVE BARIATRIC SURGERY

Component	Year 1 £m	Year 2 £m	Year 3 £m	Total year 1 to 3 £m
Paid hours gained	579	579	579	1,737
NHS costs/savings	−8	56	56	104
Total savings	571	635	635	1,841
Cost of surgery (excluding aftercare costs)	−546	0	0	−546
Total economic impact	**25**	**635**	**635**	**1,295**

Source: Office of Health Economics 2010

It is foreseeable that some of these persons will present with mobility problems. The risk must also be addressed for those in primary care who may be seen by their GP or who may be attending specialised weight management facilities. Understanding the scale of the problem is important if proactive measures are to be in place in hospitals or the community. The Health Survey for England 2008 (NHS Information Centre 2009b) was a general population survey of adults and children located at 16,056 addresses and 1,176 randomly selected postcodes.

The United Kingdom combined has the fifth largest rate of obesity in developed countries (Office of Health Economics, 2010b). The 2008 survey revealed that obesity remains a significant public health problem in England, (see Fig 12.1), with 24 per cent of men and 25 per cent of women defined as obese. It also highlighted that most men and women who were overweight or obese also had a high or very high waist circumference. This takes into consideration the issue of fat distribution, which is not always acknowledged in the BMI classification.

The WHO (2000) suggests that waist circumference is defined as the mid point between the lower rib and the upper margin of the iliac crest. The significance of this relates to the impact of a large abdomen on manual handling procedures if mobility is lost, and will be discussed later in this chapter.

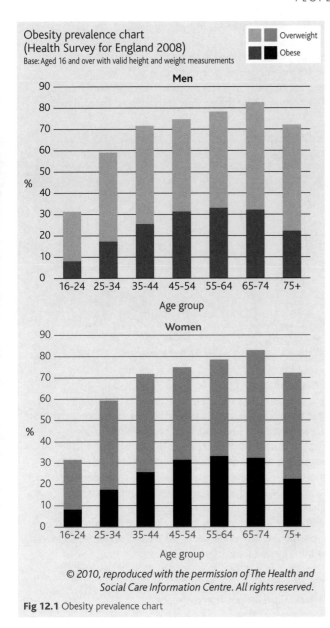

Obesity prevalence chart
(Health Survey for England 2008)
Base: Aged 16 and over with valid height and weight measurements

Overwight
Obese

Men

Women

© 2010, reproduced with the permission of The Health and
Social Care Information Centre. All rights reserved.

Fig 12.1 Obesity prevalence chart

Bariatric body shapes and dynamics

Knowledge of bariatric body shape and dynamics is important as it has an impact on the way a person is able to assist in movement and therefore on the delivery of care. The person's body shape may also have implications when considering environmental constraints and equipment provision to reduce the inherent risks. All these factors combined can have an influence on risk, care provision and, ultimately, the person's dignity.

Understanding the different types of body shape, their clinical implications and potential impact on mobility will enable organisations and practitioners to relate to the individual's associated problems, ie personal care, ambulation, rehabilitation. The excessive weight of bariatric persons will increase joint stress, affect body movement, and decrease lung mobility.

Following long periods of hospitalisation, regaining mobility is critical for bariatric persons. Not only is it challenging for a bariatric person who may be emotionally fragile and fearful of

falling, but also for the handlers who are undertaking the rehabilitation programme. The planning should include a multidisciplinary team that considers the bariatric person's unique ambulation needs such as:

● muscle tone high or low
● trunk stability
● range of movement
● head control.

Manufacturers of equipment specifically used for bariatric persons would benefit from insight into the implications of bariatric body dynamics. The width and depth of chairs is relatively easy to resolve but low height adjustment essential for mobilisation remains a challenge. This can be problematic, especially for those riser recliner chairs that have integrated leg rests. Clothing such as theatre gowns should be sized appropriately to maintain dignity and, in the event of death, it is essential to have access to a concealment bag that is the correct shape and weight capacity. Correctly sized blood pressure cuffs are essential in order to obtain an accurate reading. Cuffs that are too small will create a higher reading compared to the correct sized cuff.

The maximum safe working load of electric profiling beds has increased significantly over the last 10 years but another important feature is the facility to adjust width. Many bariatric persons may weigh less than the maximum weight capacity of the bed but remain uncomfortable due to the standard bed width. Some caution must be exercised when selecting bariatric bed and mattress combinations – the capacity of the mattress may not always be equal to the capacity of the bed frame. An understanding of body dynamics and clinical judgement is beneficial when making this selection.

Observation and practice will assist the practitioners to identify body shapes as follows.

Anasarca
This is severe generalised oedema in which large amounts of body fluid (commonly lymphatic) have leaked into soft tissues and are obstructed from returning to central circulation via the lymphatic vessels.

The impact is:
● markedly reduced range of movement, resulting in inability to flex limbs or whole body segments
● centre of gravity shifting toward knees when person is seated
● diminished ability to flex at the waist, combined with difficulty breathing when reclined
● decreased heat dissipation, resulting in profuse sweating
● increased susceptibility to skin shear and tears
● extreme waste elimination difficulties
● frequent need for mechanical ventilation assistance.

Tissue viability
Maintaining skin integrity is an integral part of bariatric management. Each body shape comes with associated risks of tissue damage.

Bariatric persons are susceptible to friction damage due to increased skin area and diminished energy absorption. For example, a bariatric person reaching for a drink and rotating his/her body can unwittingly create a skin tear. The skin is unable to meet the shear tension loads imposed and simply separates and tears (Dionne 2002).

Atypical pressure ulcers, such as those not located over a bony prominence, can be particularly problematic when associated with obesity. Regular repositioning and continence management may be difficult. The lesions may be exacerbated by local moisture retention that can lead to maceration, infection and delayed healing.

Apple shapes

Apple shaped bariatric persons are at an increased risk of skin breakdown between skin folds due to reduced vascularity of adipose tissue. Pressure ulcers may also develop in unique locations, between and below skin folds, as a result of pressure across the buttocks and other areas of high adipose tissue concentration such as the abdomen/pannus. In these instances, there is a need to offload the pannus or large skin folds to prevent skin on skin pressure. Pressure ulcers can also occur in locations where tubes and other devices have been compressed (European Pressure Ulcer Advisory Panel 2010).

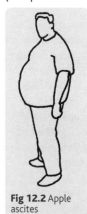

Fig 12.2 Apple ascites

Fig 12.3 Apple pannus

Apple ascites distribution
Dionne (2002) classified apple ascites to enable a clinical description of persons who, like those dominated by right sided heart failure, often demonstrate a rigid abdominal wall. Bariatric persons with this distribution carry weight high, the navel doesn't wander and the abdomen may be rigid in the presence of ascites (fluid collection). Leg size may be relatively normal and there could be limited drifting of the abdomen below the belt line (see Fig 12.2).

The impact is:
● limited trunk flexion
● frequently intact hip and knee flexion
● shortness of breath on exertion
● pillow required for head support when reclined
● poor supine or prone position tolerance
● poor ambulation.

Apple pannus
The person carries weight high but the abdomen is quite mobile. The navel wanders and the abdomen (apron or pannus) hangs toward the floor, although leg size may be relatively normal (see Fig 12.3).

The impact is:
● better ambulation with intact hip and knee flexion
● better supine and prone position tolerance

● pannus fills entire lap, may hang between thighs obstructing lymphatic flow
● susceptible to atypical skin damage between the inner thighs and pannus due to friction and moisture
● susceptible to atypical pressure ulceration and fungal infection under the pannus and between the skin folds.

Pear shapes

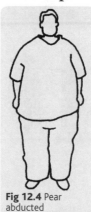

Fig 12.4 Pear abducted

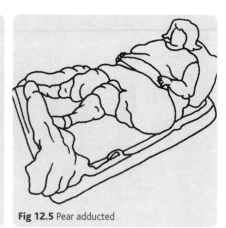

Fig 12.5 Pear adducted

Pear abducted
The person carries weight on the inside of their thighs, with increased adipose tissue around the hips, buttocks and thighs, preventing them from touching or the thighs becoming parallel. Friction and moisture dominate pear abducted body shape, the effects of friction being five times worse where moisture is present. Dionne (2002) states that pericare is a risk factor in pear abducted persons excoriation due to their inability to reach the perianal region effectively. All body shapes are important when planning mobilisation techniques, repositioning and undertaking visual skin inspections especially within the skin folds (see Fig 12.4).

The impact is:
● lack of supine position tolerance
● difficulty rolling
● hip and knee flexion limitations, may often sit with legs fully extended and spread
● groin moisture and urine elimination problems
● susceptible to atypical pressure ulceration between the pannus and inner thighs
● center of gravity toward knees.

Pear adducted
The weight is carried predominantly below the waist, with tissue bulk on the outside of the thighs, allowing the legs to close and the knees to make contact. Dionne (2002) identified that pear adducted persons can fully adduct their knees until the femoral condyles make contact. This pear adducted distribution of adipose tissue allows for log rolling as the tissue bulk is usually mobile. This enables better supine to long or semi-long sitting and short sitting postures and, in addition, is much better for pericare and personal hygiene (see Fig 12.5).

The impact is
● better waste elimination and hygiene
● better rolling ability, supine and prone tolerance
● hip and knee flexion limitations – the person often sits with the knees extended (not spread)
● clear access between legs for leg support placement
● centre of gravity toward knees.

Bulbous gluteal shelf

Excessive buttock tissue creates a posterior protruding shelf that significantly alters seating and supine posture (see Fig 12.6). Bariatric persons may demonstrate a shelf of excessive tissue protruding posteriorly from the plane of their pelvis in sitting positions. However, they may be limited in sitting and supine posture secondary to postural related pain. In supine, excessive tissue bulk on the posterior aspect of the pelvis pushes the person's hips upward relative to the plane of his/her trunk (Dionne 2002).This is then painful for the bariatric person as his/her back arches, therefore reducing trunk support (see Fig 12.6).

The impact is:
- mixed waist to hip ratio
- limited supine tolerance and impaired sitting
- gluteal shelf causes forward seating alteration
- pillow may be required behind shoulders for reclined, supine or even upright sitting.

Fig 12.6 Bulbous gluteal shelf

The size, shape and distribution of body mass and physical ability in each individual always has an effect on the degree and type of assistance that is required during person handling. It follows that a person specific risk assessment must be carried out in order to assist in the management of all relevant risk factors, including anthropometrics and body dynamics. However, in respect of these conditions and situations, there is a clear need to ensure that any organisation and its partners have the capacity to deliver these solutions, and all possible problems should be considered within a strategic systems approach.

A systems approach

The effective management and safer handling of bariatric persons requires a collaborative multidisciplinary and multiagency approach. This should be based on established and effective lines of communication, standardised policies and shared protocols. This will underpin access to relevant expertise, crisis management pathways, shared protocols, complex assessment and equipment prescription and provision in order to ensure that the person's journey is seamless and dignified. This provides cohesion and consistency through the system with the ultimate goal of enabling the integration of the person back into society and, ideally, to their own home. The ideal management of the bariatric person can occur only if there is a full understanding of the needs of that person within his/her home, the community and within an acute hospital environment. The management systems must be designed in a way that directs and supports the handler to select appropriate methods and equipment. Cheung *et al* (2006) states:

"...no one person has the entire picture of the process, especially if it occurs across multiple providers and locations. A multidisciplinary team, consisting of members with different viewpoints of the person care experience, is ideal"

Hignett *et al* (2007), when looking at the bariatric pathway, identified five key areas:
- patient factors
- building/vehicle space and design
- manual handling/clinical equipment and furniture
- communication
- organisational and staff issues.

Cheung *et al* (2006) identified similar factors in which failures and consequences could occur:
- location of equipment for transportation
- door sizes not sufficient for access and egress
- staff not aware of appropriate equipment use
- inadequate medical management of the obese person
- inadequate education of the obese person.

Stubbs (2000) describes a systems approach to ergonomics problems in complex working environments. The concept considers the whole problem and how each component can have an effect on another. This methodology is transferable to the management of bariatric persons in primary and secondary care.

A systems approach would identify and address the main issues that could occur in any part of the bariatric person's journey. This could be related to primary care or the community or extend into secondary care and hospital admission.

For this gold standard to occur, there is a need for the fences to come down and a paradigm shift by the different stakeholders to identify key persons to form an alliance in key areas such as policy making, communication and equipment standardisation. Legislation, risk assessment, training and education and ergonomics are common factors shared by each agency and a common interagency policy can pull together the best solutions from each.

Collaboration, sharing responsibility and pooling resources, despite having a different employer, can be beneficial for a person's care and safer outcomes. This has worked well in areas such as complex admissions and discharges. The use of multidisciplinary and multiagency input has been successful. Acute hospital staff, ambulance trust, social services and fire service staff have all been utilised together with shared reports and solutions being considered.

Complex discharge situations can occur with bariatric persons wanting to be discharged to their own home. Situations may occur when the person's body shape and dynamics may preclude entry back into the home without substantial intervention. Some properties may have door entrances limited to 76cm. If the person is unable to walk through, then it could be difficult or impossible to use the appropriate width wheelchair or trolley (see Figs 12.7 and 12.8). Offering alternative accommodation or nursing home may be a solution but potentially have an impact on human rights (Cookson 2008).

Fig 12.7 Person unable to climb a 19cm step but was able to mobilise on a slight incline.

Fig 12.8 Note that the person's hip width is almost equal to the door width at 76cms (30 inches). In this scenario a wheelchair could not have been used if the person had been unable to weight bear.

Legislation

Health and safety legislation places a responsibility on the employer to provide a safe system of work through the mechanism of identifying, assessing and managing foreseeable and unavoidable risks (see also chapter 2).

In health and social care, a well-defined manual handling of loads policy is essential to address the specific clinical and personal needs of bariatric persons (Hignett et al 2007). The role of policy is to set down the objectives of the organisation and the protocols it will establish in order to meet those objectives. The policy needs to link into individual organisational manual handling policies and across all service providers and address:

- roles and responsibilities
- interdepartmental communication channels
- equipment provision
- resuscitation
- fire evacuation
- interdepartment transfers including radiography, theatres, pathology rehabilitation
- processes in the event of a death
- discharge planning to include transportation home.

It is useful to provide information to support the policy, for example:

- contact names and telephone numbers, including out of hours contacts
- equipment available
- equipment suppliers' telephone numbers (including out of hours)
- information/education on general handling guidelines to include:
  - weighing techniques
  - bed manoeuvres
  - lateral transfers using pat slide
  - transfer from bed to chair
        mobile
        immobile person
  - inserting slings and hoisting
  - mobilising
  - handling heavy limbs
  - personal care
  - toileting.

Policy is the keystone that should support and inform the strategic approaches discussed in section 2 of this publication.

There may be a financial consequence if an organisation does not have systems in place to review and track the efficacy of risk assessments and subsequent controls. The NHSLA Risk Management Standards (2010) provide guidelines for achieving the minimum organisational structures in relation to risk management. These standards are NHS specific but are applicable to independent sector providers of NHS care. Organisations attaining the different levels from one to three will receive significant reduction in insurance premiums if they can demonstrate that they have the relevant structures in place. Failure mode effects analysis (FMEA) is an organisational tool that can be applied to the management of bariatric persons (Cheung et al 2006).

Under health and safety legislation, local authorities have the same responsibilities as health organisations in providing a safer system of work through risk assessment. When conflicts arise, local authorities will refer to their own legal department on a case by case basis for a resolution.

Risk assessment

Generic assessment

Risk assessment underpins all other decisions and actions that may be taken to provide a safer environment. Depending on the complexity of the situation, it may require a single person or a multidisciplinary and collaborative agency approach. It is the first step of the intervention process that identifies goals, care packages, equipment, training and education needs.

It is foreseeable that bariatric persons will, at some time, require intervention within community, primary or secondary services. Ideally, local organisations will have in place interagency protocols, based on proactive generic risk assessment, that identify:

- roles and responsibilities of the individual services personnel
- contact names and telephone numbers
- communication channels.

PEOPLE HANDLING FOR BARIATRICS, A SYSTEMS APPROACH

A proactive approach would ensure that foreseeable activities are considered before the event and not reactively, even during the hours of admission.

The generic risk assessment should consider the tasks, load, environment and individual capability of carers. Bespoke equipment may be needed; there may be environmental and ergonomics concerns or space constraints. It is feasible that there could be an impact on staffing levels, but this may not always be the case. The prompt provision of specific and appropriate equipment can sometimes mitigate the additional risk and need for extra staff.

The Department of Health recommends that the boards of NHS organisations spend proportionate effort and resources on managing their risks (National Patient Safety Agency (NPSA) 2008). The NPSA has developed a risk matrix score that considers consequences to the organisation in addition to injury to staff and patients and which may be seen as helpful to highlight areas that require priority attention. The outcome can be utilised to support a business case, especially where equipment is needed. Lack of equipment and staffing levels can impact on service provision and would therefore attract a higher score, requiring early intervention.

Person specific assessments

Person specific assessments are essential and should form part of the care plan. The design and format of person assessment tools are varied and a balance needs to be attained. A lengthy complex assessment tool is unlikely to promote compliance and a brief, non-specific tool may miss relevant points.

There is a requirement to have some synergy between the organisation's policy and the assessment tool. If the policy states that assessments must be carried out within six hours of admission, be dated and signed by the admitting nurse, then the form must incorporate these fields. If reviews are to be carried out at specific times, then, again, the form design should facilitate this. Consideration should be given as to whether the form content and layout reflects policy requirements and would be robust in the event of a clinical audit. Person assessment tools can be adapted to incorporate the requirements of bariatric persons (see Appendix 12.1). This is an example of a form used in Aintree Hospitals NHS Foundation Trust and has been subject to a pilot study, clinical audit and evaluation.

An example community assessment tool for a bariatric person appears in Appendix 12.4. Written for the London Borough of Sutton (Cassar 2010), it demonstrates how a person assessment tool can be interchanged within organisations to reflect the environment in which it is being used.

Safer systems of work

St John Holt (1999) identifies five basic steps essential for producing a safer system of work that can easily be applied to the management of bariatric persons:

● assessment of the task
● hazard identification and risk assessment
● identification of safer methods
● implementing the system
● monitoring the system.

These basic health and safety principles can be applied to a bariatric person journey throughout an episode of care.

The model shown in Fig 12.9 outlines the five main points to ensure a safer system.

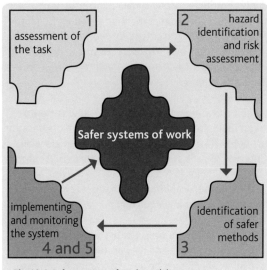

Fig 12.9 Safer systems of work model

Assessment of the tasks
If treatment and care was required for a bariatric person in primary or secondary care today, consider what activities and intervention would be required, eg weighing, lateral transfer, turning and transportation.

Hazard identification and risk assessment
Which of these tasks would prove to be hazardous based on the resources and existing control measures that you have in place? The person may have limited mobility and need to be moved in and out of bed – without a hoist this would be potentially hazardous and a high risk scenario. What is the remaining level of risk?

Define safer methods
The tasks have been identified, those that are hazardous are now highlighted and risk scored. Safer control measures can now be identified and a way to implement them. The chosen solutions should be evidence and research based. The findings at this stage can be used to support a business case and the risk matrix score can be used as supporting evidence and help prioritise.

Implement safer methods
The solutions can now be implemented and supported, if applicable, by the appropriate training.

Monitoring and audit
There is a requirement to monitor any changes that may have been put in place. Introducing changes and potential solutions can sometimes give rise to an additional and previously unforeseen hazard.

National Health Service Litigation Authority (NHSLA)
The NHSLA risk management standards are not statute but a quality assurance scheme that provides an opportunity for Trusts to receive a reduction in premiums relating to Clinical Negligence Scheme for Trusts (CNST) and Risk Pooling Scheme for Trusts (RPST). The standards vary depending on the type of organisation but are applicable to primary and secondary care

12 People handling for bariatrics, a systems approach

and also the independent sector if providing NHS care. The risk management standards have been developed as a result of the clinical, health and safety negligence claims received by the NHSLA.

The standards contribute to, and supplement, a systems approach and, although no direct mention is made of bariatric persons, there are measurable criteria for moving and handling within the different standards. There are moving and handling criteria within Standard 2, ie competent and capable workforce and Standard 3, ie safer environment.

NHSLA Level 1 moving and handling – risk assessments

The minimum requirement here would require the organisation to demonstrate that approved documentation is in place and that the duties of specific staff are outlined. There must be guidance on the techniques to be used for the moving and handling of persons and inanimate loads and this must include instructions on the use of any equipment.

The standard specifically mentions the risk assessment of persons and inanimate loads and how access to specialist advice is provided. There must be an organisational overview and monitoring of compliance with the standards. From this, we can see that compliance with level 1 starts to set the foundation stones for risk assessment documentation and the management of bariatric persons can be integrated into these standards.

NHSLA Level 2 moving and handling – risk assessments

For level 2, the organisation must be able to demonstrate compliance with the objectives set out in level 1. If the documentation specifies that all persons will be risk assessed within six hours of being admitted, then this must be demonstrated. If a policy specifically makes reference to the risk assessment of bariatric persons, then this will be subject to a compliance audit too.

NHSLA Level 3 moving and handling – risk assessments

Compliance at level 3 clearly shows that systems are in place regarding the risk assessment of persons and inanimate loads. There will be approved policies, risk assessment tools and methods to monitor that assessments are taking place. Perhaps one of the main advantages here is that the organisation must demonstrate what it does with the evidence acquired from risk assessments. It is not acceptable to complete risk assessment documentation then fail to act on the findings. The use of risk registers, organisational overviews and risk matrix scoring all form part of a systems approach and these systems can then be used for the benefit of all persons, including bariatric persons (see Appendix 12.2).

Policies

There is a statutory requirement under section 2(3) of the Health and Safety at Work etc Act 1974 for employers to provide systems of work that are safer and supported by policies and procedures (HSE 1974). Policies are therefore required by law. They outline the duties and responsibilities for executives, managers and staff. There will be many different policies within a large organisation and very often some are interlinked. For instance, the manual handling of loads policy may have a link with the falls management policy and the organisational risk management policy.

The management of bariatric persons will be incorporated into the manual handling of loads policy for the organisation, but this raises the question of whether a local policy is sufficient. The admission and discharge process for bariatric persons crosses many boundaries, with the potential for problems at any stage in the journey. A single complex discharge process for a bariatric person may involve a number of internal and external agencies:

- manual handling adviser
- tissue viability nurses
- discharge planners
- ward staff
- occupational therapists and physiotherapists
- ambulance service
- fire service
- social services
- home loan store
- primary care
- housing authorities
- private and local authority nursing care.

The use of multiagency collaborative policies can provide a more seamless approach as outlined by Rush (2006).

Audit

Clinical audit has a pivotal role in any systems approach to the management of bariatric persons in order to ensure that systems are being implemented effectively. Even where appropriate assessment tools may be in place, they cannot be effective if they are either not completed or the findings are not acted upon (see Fig 12.10).

Organisations have a responsibility to implement and monitor a minimal handling culture for the handling of persons and this should logically involve bariatric persons. There must be a system of incident reporting that highlights and provides insight into good and bad practice. The framework should encompass:

- monitoring outcomes so that appropriate corrective action can be taken
- adverse incident reporting/near misses, so that incidents using root cause analysis can be acted upon, and risk reduction actions implemented
- number of persons managed
- frequency and nature of the manual handling injuries recorded
- causation.

Education and training

The development of competency and confidence through education and training is an important element of a systems approach to bariatric management but should never be relied upon as a sole strategy.

There is a statutory requirement to carry out manual handling training for those staff at risk but the legislation is not explicit. No guidance is given regarding duration, frequency and content (HSE 1999).

The education programme should be fit for purpose and designed to enable an organisational approach bottom up and top down. It should provide a personal knowledge base in

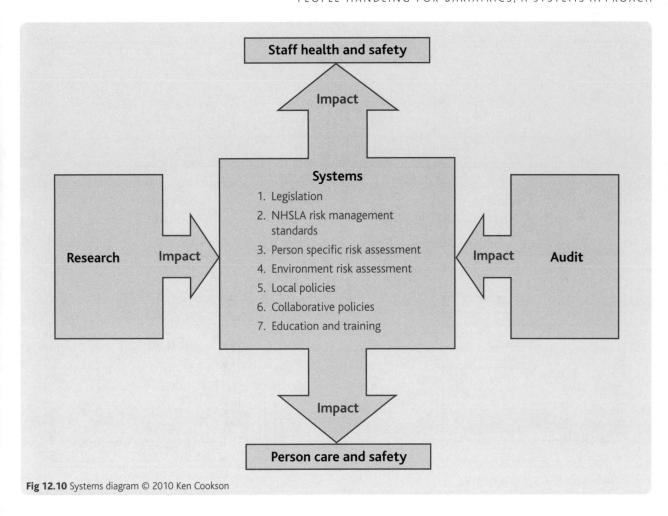

Fig 12.10 Systems diagram © 2010 Ken Cookson

bariatric management that enables staff to be versed in managing the potential risks involved. There is some merit in interagency training schemes, such as the All Wales Passport (2010); this modular approach standardises training across organisations and avoids duplication when employees change employers. (See also chapter 6 for more details regarding training systems.)

If a more specific level of training is required, then modular programmes could be developed addressing the intrinsic and extrinsic factors associated with bariatric management from NVQ to degree level, enabling the emergence of competent practitioners in bariatric management. A suggested outline for such a programme might reasonably cover:
● managing risks and challenges
● physical/physiological aspects
● sociocultural issues
● psychosocial factors
● planned intervention:
 – unexpected
 – unplanned.

Ergonomics systems

There is strong evidence that using an ergonomics approach can be beneficial. Stubbs (2000) outlines an ergonomics model to determine match or mismatch between the individual and the task. Intervention may be training or redesign and requires a multidisciplinary team approach. The use of an ergonomics systems approach acknowledges that changes or problems in one area may have influences on another. A study of current

manual handling training systems (Haslam *et al* 2007) reinforces the advantages of a multidimensional approach and the need for ergonomics intervention and redesign. Therefore, as part of a systems approach, organisations may develop education programmes that take into account the holistic nature of bariatric handling management.

It is important to look at building and equipment design in order to reduce the potential imbalance between the worker and the task. A proactive approach to this will avoid any loss of dignity that can occur, especially when services are provided for the bariatric person. Access and egress into buildings and consulting rooms should not be overlooked. Appropriate seating may be needed and a means to transport the person if he/she has limited mobility.

Implementing safer systems of work

Initial assessment

The person's assessment should start at the initial point of contact, which could either be a planned assessment or an emergency intervention. If planned, the pre-assessment preparation would include evaluation of the medical history and background information as written in the referral documentation. In an emergency intervention, the initial assessment would be based on information gathered at the point of contact, documented and be ongoing throughout the episode. The assessment should be part of the care plan process and involve the multidisciplinary team and the external

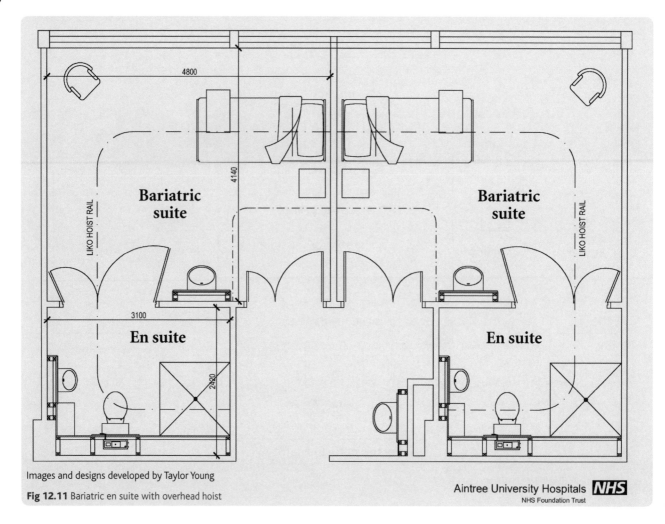

Images and designs developed by Taylor Young

Fig 12.11 Bariatric en suite with overhead hoist

Aintree University Hospitals **NHS**
NHS Foundation Trust

agencies that will be involved throughout the person's journey to ensure dignity and a seamless service.

In order to reduce the risk of injuries to staff and person, it is important that the person's mobility/manual handling and personal needs are risk assessed and documented. This should include:
● the degree of independent mobility
● all predictable handling assistance required
● any handling aids which should be used
● the minimum number of staff required to assist in all handling tasks.

Consideration should also be given to how the person could be handled in the event of a fall, a cardiac arrest or a fire evacuation. Maintaining the correct pace of cardiac compressions to a depth of 5 or 6cm is fatiguing. The problem can be exacerbated if correct posture cannot be attained due to limitations in bed height adjustment. The manual handling of a bariatric person will be beyond the capability of an individual handler. The person's weight and body dynamics will exceed the capability of most carers and a potentially hazardous situation will ensue.

There are contributory and emerging themes that cross all boundaries of health and social care and can make everyday tasks dramatically more hazardous. These themes will be discussed in more detail and in the practical techniques:
● transportation – planned and emergency
● repositioning the person in bed
● lateral transfers

● lifting a limb
● personal care
● rehabilitation
● the falling person.

The person's weight
The weight of the person should be determined and recorded accurately as soon as possible to ensure that the equipment provided is fit for purpose and the maximum capacity is not exceeded.

Weighing should be undertaken in private to preserve dignity. This can be problematic, especially if the person is not mobile. In the community, the local equipment loan store might provide and deliver scales to enable weighing within the home environment. There is a plethora of scales suitable for discreet weighing and should be part of every organisation's equipment provision. These include:
● integral bed scale
● hoist scales
● stand-on scale
● wheelchair/bed scales
● portable load cells for beds and trolleys
● integral floor scales.

Environments
A care environment that is too small to manage bariatric persons increases the risk of musculoskeletal injury to handlers. The area within different community environments or hospitals should have the spatial capacity to enable manoeuvrability of equipment and accommodate the

appropriate number of handlers. There should be sufficient space for equipment to undertake tasks using good body dynamics and posture. Any assessment should also include door widths, ability to manoeuvre in bathrooms, landings and stair widths. Hignett *et al* (2007) carried out functional space experiments to determine the incompressible space required for different tasks associated with bariatric persons. It was concluded that a width of 3.93 metres and length of 4.23 metres was needed. This exceeds the Department of Health Estates and Facilities measurements of 3.6 metres width and 3.7 metres length.

Figs 12.11 to 12.13 illustrate a successful side room design, specifically intended for, but not restricted to, bariatric persons. The design was highly commended for innovation and significantly improved the management of bariatric persons. The installation of an overhead track hoist system facilitates a transfer from the bed to the shower room and any point in between (see Figs 12.14 to 12.16). As a comparison, see Figs 12.25, 12.26, 12.27 and 12.28 where a gantry hoist is being used in an area that has not been designed for the management of bariatric persons. The procedure is not compromised but the temporary erection of the gantry hoist is taking up two bed spaces.

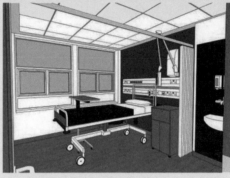

Fig 12.13 Bariatric en suite with overhead hoist

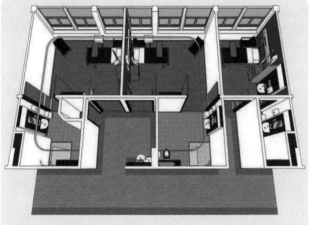

Fig 12.12 Bariatric en suite with overhead hoist

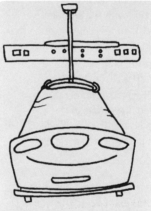

Fig 12.14 Ceiling track route starts above the bed

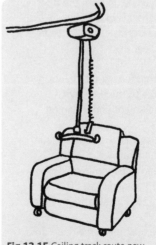

Fig 12.15 Ceiling track route now over the chair

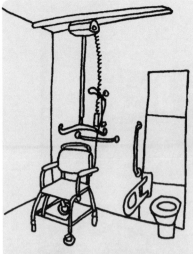

Fig 12.16 Ceiling track route now ends over the toilet and shower area

Community

Access and egress is an important consideration within different environments, whether it be hospital, care home or person's home. Special evacuation and extrication methods may be required for those persons residing at levels above the ground floor, or where the entrance to the home is limited. Where these limitations exist, a comprehensive risk assessment should be completed in conjunction with the ambulance service. If further help is required, then this could include the fire service.

CASE STUDY: SAFE EXTRICATION

A bariatric person (165kg, 26st) fell at home. Due to her limited mobility, she lived downstairs in the lounge/dining room. Two days after the fall, it was agreed that due to the pain in the person's leg, an X-ray was required.

Both the ambulance service and nurse specialist met at the person's house to assess extrication. The side of the house was not wide enough due to an extending chimney breast. It was not possible to use the front door due to the large step leading up from the front path. The incompatible dimensions of the hallway and bariatric stretcher prevented the necessary 90 degree turn required for access and egress.

The assessment identified that further intervention was required. A call was made to the fire service which assisted with the assessment and a plan of action was agreed.
- Using the back entrance and alleyway, the person could be moved into the ambulance.
- The back fence would need to be removed.
- A steel ramp would need to be built over the garden from the alleyway to the patio door of the house.
- A ramp would need to be built up to the patio door height.
- Using bariatric slide sheets, a lateral transfer onto the bariatric trolley would be carried out.
- The person would need to be transported out on the bariatric trolley, through the patio door, across the ramps onto the concrete pathway and into the ambulance.

The person was successfully moved to the acute trust, which had been informed of the person's impending arrival. The ramp has been left in place for the person's return home.

Access and egress is an important consideration when assessing the person within the home and any other relevant care environments. Special evacuation and extrication methods may be required for those persons residing at levels above the ground floor. Plans should be in place to cover adverse incidents and hospital admissions, either planned or unplanned. The relevant person within the local fire and ambulance service should be aware of the situation and involved in any planning.

Before installing any equipment, it is necessary to consider the load bearing capacity of floors and ceilings. The advice of a competent person, ie a structural engineer, should be sought in all cases. As a general rule of thumb, a solid ground floor can sustain a load of 2,000kg (315st), based on a 3x3 metre square room with a solid concrete floor. The first and upper floor rooms will accommodate less weight bearing because of the structure of most buildings. If the ground floor is not solid, then a competent person will need to advise on the suitability of joists and types of floor in conjunction with room size.

Hospital

Planners and practitioners should look carefully at access and egress and consider where the person is going to be cared for. The outcomes will be dependent on the person's capability. If the person is fully dependent, it might be necessary to adapt the environment at each stage of the person's journey through the hospital system. These areas may include radiology, theatres, lifts, corridors and bathrooms. Nilsson (2006) suggests the recommended bathroom dimensions are 4,000mm x 2,300mm. The toilet/shower room, ideally, should be 2,700mm x 4,600mm, with at least 800mm on either side of a floor mounted toilet, and the toilet placed 200mm from the wall.
- A traditional floor mounted ceramic pan will take a load of about 20 stone. The maximum weight capacity of a lavatory seat will vary and is dependent on the model and manufacturer.
- Cantilever style wall mounted toilets may be less suitable for bariatric persons and the handlers will need to refer to the manufacturers' specifications.
- If it is not possible to ascertain the weight capacity of the toilet, a solution would be to purchase a height adjustable heavy duty toilet surround.

Controllers of care environments should seek the guidance of an expert planner or practitioner if planning for a bariatric person admission. The expert planner or practitioners will understand the relationship between the person's body dynamics, dependency, staffing numbers, equipment manoeuvrability and spatial needs. Muir (2009) studied the space within critical care areas which were spatially limited, particularly where a person was totally dependent. Insufficient space would restrict nursing activities from six practitioners working from all four sides of the bed. There was restricted space for lateral transfers and manoeuvrability of a hoist. Muir recommends the critical care environment be at least 3,780mm long and 4,000mm wide, with the acute environment extending to 8,200mm.

Hignett *et al* (2007), on behalf of the HSE, produced a research document that looked at the risk assessment and planning process for bariatric persons. The research explored the functional space to determine the spatial requirements for the safer care of bariatric persons. This study identified a functional spatial requirement of 16.61m^2, but, if lateral transfers were included, it required extending to 17.54m^2.

The community or hospital environment may be the pivotal point of the bariatric person's lifestyle transformation. Planning the environment should be holistic, evidence based and person centred. Kilpatrick *et al* (2009) discuss an optimal caring and healing environment that consists of five equal components. These five components can be transferred into any health and social care setting (see Fig 12.17):

● an attitude and consistent behaviour of caring
● a person centred approach
● culturally competent health, social care provider
● safety, cleanliness
● integration of the ARTS (A ¼ aesthetics, R ¼ recreational movement, T ¼ therapeutic and S ¼ spiritual).

These essential elements promote caring and healing to nurture, educate and serve bariatric persons to assist in their transition, transformation and transcendence in healing and lifestyle transformation.

Fig 12.17 Caring and healing environment model (Kilpatrick *et al* 2009)

A person centred approach enables bariatric persons to be viewed as a whole, including advocacy, empowerment and respecting autonomy, voice, self determination and participation in decision making.

Quality of care and retention of dignity can be delivered and enhanced by the provision of equipment fit for purpose within an appropriate environment. This standard, together with increased staff numbers, will not only ensure quality management in a dignified manner but is more likely to encourage enablement rather than disablement.

Equipment for bariatric persons

All the necessary and appropriate equipment must be provided, ensuring the safe working load is appropriate so that activities of daily living can be facilitated. There is also a requirement for improved ergonomic conditions as the equipment is likely to be heavier and wider than standard.

There is a common misconception that bariatric persons can be accommodated by simply asking for equipment designed for a "large size". Most of the attention focuses on a bed and hoist to accommodate the person. These items are only part of the overall needs and practitioners need to analyse tasks and consider other handling aids that can be used to facilitate these tasks.

All equipment used by the bariatric person must be fit for purpose, supporting their body dynamics and anthropometrics. Standard items of equipment all have relatively low weight limits, **which must not be exceeded under any circumstances**. See Fig 12.18.

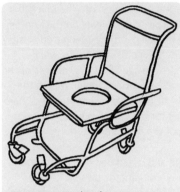

Fig 12.18 114kg (18st) capacity commode, buckled frame left front due to overload by 267kg (40st) person

Organisations will need to consider the implications of renting or buying and should bear in mind the following questions:
● Is the equipment needed available from one company or several?
● Is the equipment compatible with other equipment used?
● What are the timescales from ordering to delivery?
● Does the rental cost exceed the buying cost?
● Will the company convert the rented item to a purchase?
● If purchasing, where is it going to be stored when not in use?
● Who will assemble, maintain and service the equipment?
● Will warranty issues be addressed in the contractual agreement from the outset?
● What is the manoeuvrability of the bed through the hospital environment, including lifts?

For community based services, additional considerations may include:
● Will the community equipment loan store be able to provide and deliver from a standard list of bariatric resources?
● Will the equipment needed come direct from a specialist manufacturer?
● Will the equipment break down into component parts for ease of delivery and assembly in the person's home?

Responsibility for maintaining equipment under the LOLER and PUWER would depend on the following:
● if a capital purchase, then the purchasing organisation would transfer responsibility to their medical engineering department
● if the equipment is leased, then, as part of the leasing agreement, the supplier would be responsible for service/maintenance of the equipment.

Certificates of compliance must be issued. In all cases, the certificates should be easily accessible and recorded for audit purposes.

Beds

Bariatric beds should fit the person from the time of provision. The bed should have efficient profiling functions, including low height, and be width adjustable. Access and egress via the foot end is desirable and if scales are fitted they should conform to class 3 standards. Grade 3 non-automatic weighing instrument (NAWI) scales (NWML 2008) should be used in healthcare premises for the calculation of medication, treatment and monitoring (Medical Device Equipment Alert 2008). A NAWI requires the intervention of an operator during weighing. For example, to deposit on, or remove from, the load receptor the load to be measured and also to obtain the result.

Class 4 (less accurate domestic type scales) may be in use but only for monitoring/recording persons' weights on their notes in GP consulting rooms, community settings (peripatetic visits), nursing homes, and when there is no risk the scales will be used to weigh someone under the age of 18 – regardless of the clinical environment. The mattress surface should match the weight capacity of the bed, but there are inconsistencies. There has been a gap in the market for the ideal product, with beds having some, but rarely all, of the required features.

Some insight into the design and use of bed rails is important, especially when beds are used for bariatric persons. Bed rail design is a complex matter with the horizontal and vertical rail gap dimensions being determined by anthropometric data. The gaps are spaced and sited to minimise the risk of entrapment should the person attempt to climb out. The decision to use bed rails for any person regardless of size should always be based on a risk assessment.

In addition to the increased risk of entrapment, there is a further potential hazard that can occur due to the relative height of the bed rails in relation the person's body. The rail height may be less effective with bariatric persons and can be made worse if incompatible frame and mattresses are used. There may be slight variations in bed frame length and width and this can impact on the efficacy of dynamic and static mattress surfaces if not selected carefully.

When the person's mobility is compromised, then handling should be kept to an absolute minimum. This can be facilitated by using electrically operated profiling beds fitted with a suitable pressure relieving mattress to reduce the risk of tissue damage. Points to consider when choosing a bed are:
● Safe working load of the bed in all profiling states.
● The width of the bed to ensure the handlers do not overreach while carrying out care tasks. A wide bed is more comfortable for the person but increases biomechanical risk for the carers. A narrow bed reduces reach for the carers but can restrict movement for the person (see Fig 12.19).

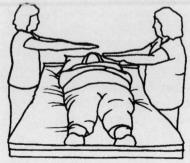
Fig 12.19 Measuring correct bed size

● Compatibility of the mattress and bed – the bed frame and mattress capacities may not be equal.
● Bed and hoist compatibility – does the bed go low enough and the hoist high enough to ensure smooth transfers on and off the bed to avoid any potential tissue damage through shear or friction?
● Interaction of the bed within the care environment – is there sufficient space for the equipment and handlers to move as the equipment will be wider than the norm, and the number of handlers will exceed three? The design of the bed should offer sufficient low height adjustment to encourage independent movement into bed.
● Positioning the person at a 45-degree angle allows apple shaped persons an easier breathing position without slipping down.
● Does the bed rail have a gap in the down position? Ideally, this should be minimal to facilitate transfers and limit obstruction for the handlers.
● The handlers' weight should also be taken into account as, in some instances, one or more handlers may need to get on the bed to undertake a task.
● Consider how the person gets on and off the bed, in some circumstances they will fall into bed, and use a rocking motion to get out.

Lateral rotational therapy

The use of positioning therapy for the management of respiratory conditions in critically ill persons has long been recognised. An additional feature of beds fitted with lateral tilt profiling is that the person respositioning can be facilitated and pressure relief improved.

Goldhill et al (2007) suggested that persons with a high BMI benefited more than others – recognising that these persons may be more likely to have respiratory compromise and because of their body stature they might receive less manual handling repositioning and turning.

Consideration should be given to:
● Lateral rotation therapy can be used for persons with or without tissue damage. It improves pressure redistribution, reduces shear and microclimate control benefits when there is evidence of shear injury. Lateral rotation therapy offloads the pressure.
● Lateral rotation surfaces can be used to help turn the person, making it easier and safer to perform linen changes, examinations and other routine tasks.
● Where maximum inflation can be used, it will provide a firmer surface, making it easier for the handlers to reposition persons in bed, perform procedures or transfer them to another surface.
● Maintenance of skin integrity.
● Manual handling techniques.
● The high/low function of the bed, with regard to handlers' posture.
● Person dignity.

Lateral rotation therapy reduces cost, the length of stay for high risk persons in critical care environments, improves persons' outcomes and provides safer systems of work.

Turning mattress

The purpose of the pressure redistributing turning mattress system is to provide therapeutic benefits through continuous low pressure and low air loss and aid person management. European Pressure Ulcer Advisory Panel (EPUAP) and National Pressure Ulcer Advisory Panel (NPUAP) (2010) Pressure Ulcer Prevention and Treatment Guidelines (1,2) place a strong emphasis on pressure redistribution immersion and envelopment in order to minimise tissue interface pressure.

CASE STUDY: CHOICE OF APPROPRIATE BED

A bariatric person weighing 254kg (40st) was being cared for in the community in a two storey house. She had been known to the community nursing team for many years for management of her lymphoedematous legs.

This person had previous episodes of cellulitis, which were usually managed at home with appropriate antibiotic therapy. However, during one episode, she became unwell and her mobility decreased. This resulted in long periods sitting in the riser recliner chair as she was unable to get into bed due to the weight of her legs. She then had a fall, was unable to get up herself and was on the floor for three hours.

Pressure damage was discovered when the district nurse visited the following day and it was decided that care was unable to continue at home. An admission to a community hospital in-patient unit was arranged.

Unfortunately, the hospital was not informed of the person's weight and on arrival no suitable equipment was available. The time delay to source equipment meant the person having to wait several hours. Once the equipment was in place, the senior back care practitioner educated the staff on its use and safer handling techniques.

The person's height restricted independent access in and out of bed due to the combined height of the bed and mattress. This resulted in the person having to be hoisted for all transfers. Over a period of time, the person's mobilising capability became diminished and her fear of falling increased.

The goal of the multidisciplinary team was to increase the person's mobility to enable discharge. Unfortunately, the bed and mattress were too high, and the chair provided was too low.

A multidisciplinary case conference was arranged to include the person and her family. It was decided that other equipment options were to be sourced as the person was keen to go home without a hoisting system in place.

The chosen bed facilitated the person's independence; it provided the high/low functionality necessary to reduce the manual handling risks for personal care and treatment tasks.

Once the bed was supplied, lift pants in conjunction with a hoist were used to start mobilising the person who had been bed bound for a significant time. The lift pants supported the whole body and gave the person the confidence to take those first steps. They provided freedom of movement, while relieving some or the entire burden of body weight. They lifted safely, allowing the person to move on his/her own without the risk of falling. Six months after being admitted to hospital, the person was able to return home independently with the bed used in hospital.

A bariatric bed was sourced that enabled the person access and egress from the foot of the bed see Figs 12.20 and 12.21 showing the lying to sitting features of the bed that facilitated the person's independence etc.

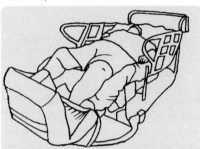

Fig 12.20 Profiling to supine position

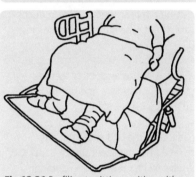

Fig 12.21 Profiling to sitting position with foot access and egress

Consideration must be given to the width of the bed required for community use as well as to the person's access and egress. It is rare for a bariatric person to sit on the edge of the bed and lift his/her legs up into the bed. When prescribing the bed, it is essential to observe the person's activity to ensure that he/she is able to get in and out of bed, and therefore remain independent.

Slide sheets

Low friction slide sheets can be a useful item to facilitate safer handling manoeuvres but clinical factors and the risk assessment need to be taken into account.

Moving bariatric persons around the bed is a challenging task, often requiring three or more handlers. When carrying out this task, it is important to minimise friction and shear when positioning the person correctly (Mastrogiovanni *et al* 2003). Bariatric persons can be positioned using different types of equipment, including slide sheets, which may decrease the risk, but carers should be aware and trained in their use.

The shape, size and style of slide sheets vary enormously and the choice should consider the following:
● the task being undertaken
● the dependency level of the person and whether they can assist in the task
● the number of handlers available
● reach and stretch for the handlers to undertake the task.

If the slide sheet is too big, this may be hazardous as too much material interferes with the smooth low friction action. If too small, the slide sheets may be difficult to insert and cause the handler to reach and stretch to find the material under the person to move them.

To assess for a suitable size, the person should be measured at his/her widest point while lying down to determine the maximum width, ie abdomen, hips, upper body, thighs, legs. Flat slide sheets are preferable if hoist slings are to be inserted between the two flat sheets (see chapter 11, Task 11.4k-n). Consider also:
● the width of the bed
● the type of mattress being used, eg static or dynamic, and can the dynamic mattress be programmed to a firm static mode?

Repositioning sheet

A repositioning sheet is a useful aid when used with a hoist, ideally an overhead gantry or ceiling mounted type. This is preferable to using a mobile hoist as it reduces the number of care staff required and enables position changes while reducing the risk of friction injuries. Kirton (2008) identified that the repositioning of persons using a repositioning sheet reduces the risk of the person sustaining tissue damage and nursing staff sustaining injury.

Used with an overhead hoist, it is also a tool that can reduce the pushing and pulling forces for handlers and potentially their risk and exposure to musculoskeletal injury.

The repositioning sheet becomes the bed sheet but the requirement to leave the repositioning sheet under the person should be considered, based on clinical factors, including:
● the person's tissue viability
● the breathability of the fabric
● any rough or uneven edges to the sheet
● the compatibility with the prescribed pressure reducing systems.

Fig 12.22 and Fig 12.23 show how the repositioning sheet is attached to the hoist to lift the person off the bed for repositioning. The loops are placed on the sling bar from the head to calves. It is not essential to connect all loops.

Fig 12.24 shows the sling bar parallel to the person. The person's body weight will stop the sheet from being pulled out from underneath. Using the hoist, slowly turn the person. If the person has a large pannus, pillows will need to be positioned appropriately on the support surface to protect the pannus. Also, correct positioning of the head, arms and legs will need to be done before the roll is started. The handler, with the control, must be facing the person in order to monitor the turn.

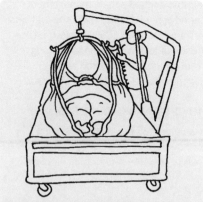

Fig 12.22 Repositioning sheet vertical lift strap attachment configuration

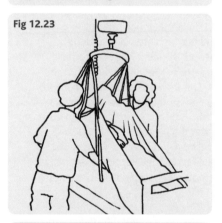

Fig 12.23

Fig 12.24 Final stage of turning process using a repositioning sheet. Handlers in control, facing the bariatric person

Hoists

Hoists are essential pieces of equipment in bariatric person management for dependent person transfers as well as potential retrieval from the floor after falls. If they are not fit for purpose, they will increase the risk of musculoskeletal injury to both handlers and persons. The risk assessment process should consider whether a floor based mobile hoist or overhead ceiling and gantry type is more suitable. More information on this subject can be found in chapter 11.

Mobile hoists

The following should be considered for the use of a mobile hoist:
● Any environmental constraints? There needs to be enough circulation space for hoist and chair manoeuvrability.
● The potential spinal forces on the carers when manoeuvring the mobile hoists will increase significantly when hoisting bariatric persons as compared to overhead systems. This will be increased on a carpeted floor. The number of staff needed to use a mobile hoist for a bariatric person needs to be considered.

- Motorised wheels and spreader bars may decrease or eliminate the pulling/pushing risk.
- Hoists are generally used indoors but in extreme circumstances and complex discharge cases for bariatric persons there may be a requirement to hoist outdoors. Consideration of slopes, gradients and rough ground should be made.
- The width of sling bar may need to expand with the sling width.
- Mobile hoists may be more suitable for lifting persons from the floor, but the environmental constraints and the amount of exertion required to manoeuvre the hoist with a bariatric person should be considered.
- Are weighing scales attached? The lift height can be reduced with certain hoist scales fitted above the spreader bar.
- Is the hoist to be used for more than one person?

Overhead hoists

It is often considered a better solution to have an integral ceiling track system or an overhead gantry hoist. Environmental constraints will need to be considered as the gantry needs to fit over a wider bed, chair and/or a commode, often taking up two bed spaces. This will also apply to the community environment.

Overhead gantry hoists travel on a load bearing beam and this can either be performed as a manual action or can be powered, further reducing the forces required. Depending on the design, the hoist may be sited head to foot or side to side and therefore provides a means to move the person up the bed or in and out of bed, for transfers and rehabilitation.

The following should be considered if a gantry hoist is to be used:
- Gantry hoists come either static or on wheels. The wheeled gantries may be more suitable for rehabilitation.
- A ceiling track "H" or traverse system enables more flexibility of movement and provides increased lift height when weighing the person.
- The design of sling bar may need to be different according to the body dynamics of the person. Many bariatric persons find the four point spreader bar (see chapter 11) creates a more comfortable lifting position than a traditional "coathanger" style.

A number of factors will need to be considered before placing a hoist in any environment within a hospital or community setting. The hoist will need to be ergonomically compatible within the allotted space. Is the height adjustment range appropriate for the person in order to facilitate a smooth transfer and mobilisation? Other factors to consider within the community setting will relate to the position and location of power sockets, along with the load bearing capacity of the floor structures.

CASE STUDY: BED TO CHAIR HOISTING PROCEDURE

A 53 year old male bariatric person weighing 222kg (35st) suffered a stroke following significant abdominal surgery. He was initially nursed in critical care and required a specific bariatric bed with a dynamic mattress surface to minimise risk of pressure ulcers.

The person was mobile prior to being admitted but the extent of the surgery and minor stroke had contributed to some weakness to one side and rendered him immobile.

The person had no cognitive impairment and was able to cooperate with moving and handling tasks within the bed. As the surgical condition improved, the next step was to provide intensive stroke rehabilitation and he was transferred from critical care to the appropriate ward.

The bed was designed with foot egress and an integral dynamic mattress surface. The hoist was a mobile gantry design fitted with twin motors. The bedside chair was appropriate for the weight and dimensions of the person. The standard ward side rooms did not have the spatial requirements to accommodate all the equipment. The hoist was therefore assembled in a ward bay area and occupied two bed spaces.

The bed was wide enough to allow the person to move freely and, because he could cooperate, it was relatively easy to insert the sling. Transfer from bed to chair was possible and from here he made good progress with the rehabilitation programme and was discharged home fully mobile within a few weeks (see Figs 12.20, 12.25-12.29).

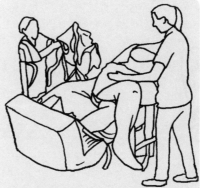

Fig 12.25 Person able to roll and raise leg to assist with sling insertion

Fig 12.26 Appropriate width bed and bed rails facilitate sling insertion

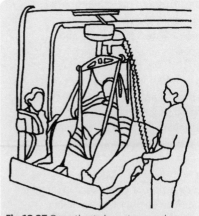

Fig 12.27 Operating twin motors requires synchronisation and maybe one or two handset controls

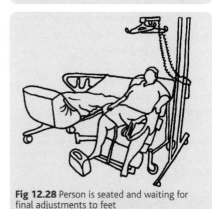

Fig 12.28 Person is seated and waiting for final adjustments to feet

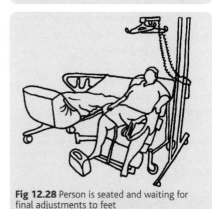

Fig 12.29 Final adjustment to leave in a comfortable position

Seating

Chairs can be static but are also available with a range of powered functions, including rise and recline.

There are four main types of bariatric seating.

Chairs can be:
- static, with optional drop down arms
- powered riser recliner style, with either two or four motors fitted
- specialised electric, height adjustable type that tilt in space, adjust from a chair to stretcher position to facilitate a lateral transfer
- tilt in space chairs.

Bariatric persons often sleep in powered reclining chairs as they can be used to enable their mobilisation. Static chairs should be height adjustable and a drop down arm may be useful to facilitate lateral transfers. It is advisable that chairs used within care organisations, where possible, have a castor brake facility

on the chair. However, this has a contraindication, as it will raise the height of the chair and impact on independent transfers. The risk assessment will need to identify which is the priority – either braked castors or enabling independent transfer.

To date, there remains a lack of anthropometric data to aid the design of bariatric chairs. A chair width in excess of 76cm is often required and capacities up to 381kg (60st) are available.

Riser recliner chairs aid bariatric rehabilitation and independence. They can be used in cases where the person's legs are too heavy to lift into bed. They also reduce the amount of exertion required by the person to achieve sit to stand activities. When prescribing chairs, consider the following:
- The height, depth, seat width and safer working load.
- The pressure relieving properties of the chair.
- Does the leg rest of the chair have a safer working load that accommodates the weight of the person's legs and pannus?
- Does the chair provide a comprehensive range of independent adjustments that enables cardiac management, effective pulmonary function and lymphatic drainage and secretion?
- Does the chair enable supine positioning of the person without flexing or extending? This can be useful for persons with apple shapes. It enables reduced flexion at the waist/hips and also causes minimal arterial blood pressure changes and improves oxygenation (Perilli *et al* 2000).
- Functional spatial requirements for the person.
- When procuring a chair consider the fabric option, especially if the chair is to be part of a bariatric resource from local community equipment stores. Will the fabric be suitable for decontamination/cleaning processes?
- Does the surface texture of the chair fabric facilitate the insertion of slide sheets or slings? Inserting slide sheets behind the person can be more difficult if there is friction and resistance due to incompatible surfaces.

Transportation

The bariatic person's journey, in essence, can begin within any environment(s). The service provider attending to transport a bariatric person, whether on a planned or emergency basis, will require the knowledge and experience of established protocols and lines of communication. This will establish integrated professional interventions throughout the person's journey(s).

The assessor needs to consider:
- how it will begin
- evacuation from the person's home
- transportation to and from hospital, clinics etc
- access and egress.

Bariatric persons are often independently mobile but there may be some limitations regarding the ability to walk a long distance or negotiate an incline. For this reason, there is often a need to plan and procure appropriate and timely transportation. It comes under two categories:

Planned transportation
Planned extrication should be proactive, with communication between all service providers. A multi service risk assessment process should be undertaken to ensure the person journey is seamless and may include:
- ambulance and fire services (non-emergency)

- a taxi service
- the person's own transport via relatives.

Emergency transportation

In an emergency, the delay in extrication impacts on person outcomes, especially if associated with trauma. Possible scenarios may include:

- emergency services fire and ambulance triggered by 999 call
- team in attendance may be multidisciplinary and multiagency, with specialists from the community and/or acute trust if collaborative policies are in place.

Transportation trolley

Ideally, this should have a capacity of at least 250kg (39st) and needs to be wider than the standard 65 or 70cm wide trolley – a width of 75cm is more suitable. A backrest adjustment should be powered or gas assisted to reduce the pushing/pulling forces required to adjust the backrest. An understanding of the bariatric body dynamics is needed as apple shaped persons cannot lie flat on their back. It is advantageous for the trolley to have adjustable back and knee break profiling to reduce the risk of the person sliding down the trolley. This also minimises the risk of shear and friction.

Wheelchairs

Bariatric wheelchairs need to accommodate more than just the weight of the person. The width, length, depth and body dynamics would need to be considered. A person that has pear shaped characteristics will require wider leg rests.

When prescribing or procuring a wheelchair, the following further considerations may need to be factored into the provision:

- Availability of wheelchair design.
- Is a ramp needed when entering a building?
- The compatibility of the wheelchair with thresholds and ramps (see Fig 12.30).
- The width of doorways.
- Turning circle required for manoeuvring the wheelchair – which will need to be in excess of the usual 1,200mm.
- Number of persons required/available to manoeuvre the wheelchair.
- Is there a need to transfer the wheelchair into a vehicle? What is the weight?
- The distance the wheelchair needs to be pushed, and any slopes.
- Is there a removable motor available to eliminate the pushing/pulling forces?
- What weight does a hospital lift take?

If a self propelled wheelchair is used, the individual will require sufficient upper body strength to mobilise physically and all the above considerations would need to be assessed.

CASE STUDY: TRANSPORTING A PERSON TO HOSPITAL

A person weighing 191kg (30st) needed to see a urologist. He had problems with a catheter, which could not be solved by the district nurse or GP. The person lived in a small extension to his elderly parents' home.

The person was refusing to go to hospital as his previous experience had been terrifying. He had sustained pressure damage from lying on an inappropriate couch until a suitable bed arrived.

A multi service risk assessment took place, involving the person's parents. The room size and front door width were measured and an emergency protocol planned:

- the front door required removal to enable trolley access and egress
- manoeuvrability within the room would just about facilitate the bed and trolley being side by side
- a bariatric trolley with the foot end entering first into the environment would enable a hoist lateral transfer utilising the fixed track already in place.

The access route to the house was a long, steep slope and consideration was given to the pushing and pulling forces as outlined in the Manual Handling Operations Regulations 1992 (as amended 2002). Concerns related to person dignity as the long slope did not allow privacy. The home was near a school so it was essential that the task be carried out in the early morning to minimise interest from the public.

The tailgate capacity of the ambulance was assessed to ensure that it would not be exceeded with the total weight of the person and trolley. Having undertaken these precautions and communicated results to the receiving hospital enabled the person to be admitted and treated with an overnight stay before returning home next day.

It is important to undertake a risk assessment to assess the pushing/pulling forces for all mobile transportation. Where possible, the transportation should be motorised to reduce these forces.

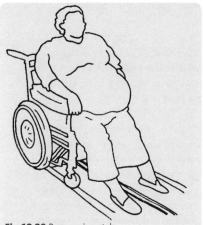

Fig 12.30 Ramp mismatch

Specific areas for concern

The previous sections provide a range of information that supports the systems approach within health and social care organisations. There needs to be proactive risk assessment on an individual and organisational basis and clear policies, procedures and processes identified to deliver the environments, skills and equipment to control the risks of moving very heavy persons effectively. The systems in place in various health and social care locations are improving and guidance for some specific locations and functions is described in this section.

Independent living

Wherever possible, bariatric person care and social care delivery should be focused on independent living. In the event of a medical deterioration that is not life threatening, wherever possible, care delivery should be maintained within the person's home.

CASE STUDY

A person weighing 286kg (45st), living in a terraced house, slept and sat in a riser recliner chair. The chair broke, so the person reverted to his only supporting surface, which was his divan bed and mattress. The GP was called out because the person had developed a pressure sore on his abdomen due to long periods of lying on the mattress.

The district nurse visited to dress the wound and found the person cyanosed and breathless. The person refused hospital admission and was referred to intermediate care for ongoing care provision.

The intermediate care sister undertook a risk assessment, which identified that immediate equipment provision was required to enable the service to provide a safer system of work for the staff and to address the person's breathing problems.

Equipment provided:
- bariatric bed and mattress
- riser recliner chair
- bariatric commode.

The rental equipment was delivered within 24 hours.

The care staff were trained in using this equipment and visited the person twice a day to undertake personal care, dress the abdominal wound and clean under the person's large pannus. The training was cascaded to all care staff in the service.

Social services were involved in regards to providing a wet room. All this was discussed at a multidisciplinary meeting held at the person's home to explore all the options available for keeping the person at home. At this meeting, the person agreed that the emergency services could be informed of his circumstances. Once this had been agreed, the ambulance service visited and undertook an evacuation risk assessment.

With the above systems in place, the person remained at home for six weeks after the initial intervention processes had been implemented. Unfortunately, he had a fall in the bathroom and required hospital admission, which was undertaken seamlessly due to recent risk assessments and service implementation.

Complex admission/discharges

The complexity of hospital admission and discharge is a worrying experience for most bariatric persons and professionals trying to organise the transfer. Timing the transfer with the ambulance service's specialist vehicle and staffing availability can delay the person's admission to hospital or discharge home. Organisations should have bariatric care pathways in place that have been developed by multidisciplinary teams and services that enable the bariatric person's seamless transfer. The pathway should identify specific communication channels, cross boundaries information sharing and equipment provision in a timely manner. All service providers should educate staff members on how to implement the care pathway. This multidisciplinary input should include:

- social services
- emergency services
- community care
- primary care trusts
- acute/secondary care.

Hignett & Griffiths (2009) identified the need for a pathway approach to the management of bariatric persons. This approach is guided by legislation and must be supported strategically and supplemented with policies, procedures and protocols.

These will include:
- risk management processes
- policies and procedures
- safer systems of work
- quality assurance standards
- audit
- education and training
- access to competent persons.

Investigative procedures – CT, MRI, fluoroscopy scanners

Extreme obesity and body mass may sometimes preclude the person from routine investigations or require a transfer to another hospital. The limitations stem from the table capacity or the diameter of the tube and, while some persons may not exceed the table weight capacity, their body dimensions exceed the diameter of the tube. Typical tube dimensions can be 50 or 60cm. Some fluoroscopy systems may have high load capacity tables but these are compromised by being fixed height and necessitating a step up.

Standard high load capacity steps may not be wide enough for the bariatric person so it is important to source a wide step, ideally with a supporting handle. The table is fixed height due to the position of the X-ray tube below the table.

It can be difficult to insert the plate beneath the person when a chest X-ray is required. Low friction slide sheet pockets can help with this task. There could be technical difficulties with the movement of adipose tissue when the scanner table moves. Air assisted devices can facilitate lateral transfers onto the examining table. The air assisted mats are radiolucent and extension hoses are available to permit use in MRI scanners.

Some risk reduction features are designed into the items of equipment used in the radiography department. A range of tables is available, offering variable adjustment and some can profile vertically. Floating tables, based on using "hovercraft" technology, are also available. An important point to note is that the maximum safe working load will vary depending on the type and design of the equipment. These same principles also apply to operating tables.

Resuscitation

The revised algorithms provided in the Resuscitation Council (UK) 2010 guidelines apply to bariatric persons as the physiological principles of resuscitation are unchanged. However, there is a recognised poor outcome due to morbid obesity, body shape and mass. This results in a mentally challenging and more complex scenario for the physician or rescuer (Eadie 2004).

Some guidance relating to the manual handling and practical aspects of resuscitation and bariatric persons is mentioned in the *Guidance for safer handling during resuscitation in healthcare settings*, Resuscitation Council (2009). Undertaking cardiopulmonary resuscitation will require practical amendments to the organisation's locally agreed resuscitation policies and procedures to ensure the wellbeing of staff and good clinical outcomes, where reasonably practicable, for the person.

The Resuscitation Council guidelines recommend that fit for purpose equipment is used to transfer bariatric persons, that they should not be lifted and electric profiling beds should be used to enable appropriate care. The beds should have good height range adjustment and ideally be width adjustable. The criteria for carrying out cardiac compressions with the person in a profiling stretcher/chair would be determined by the degree of stability, firmness and manufacturers' guidelines. Recovery from floor level may require the use of an air assisted lifting device as illustrated in Task 12.6.2b. This device provides a stable base and is firm enough to continue cardiac compressions, if required.

A concealment trolley of appropriate size and weight capacity may be needed if the resuscitation attempt is unsuccessful. Market choice is limited for this item of equipment but an alternative is to modify an existing high load capacity trolley. It is possible to have bespoke stainless steel frames and shroud covers fabricated to fit existing trolleys. These can be made without impacting on the integrity of the trolley structure and made to a height that will encompass a very large abdomen.

Mortuary

The handling of deceased bariatric persons within a mortuary environment can be complex and will impact on medical staff, porters, undertakers, scientific and technical staff. The ergonomic design of the building and integrated equipment is an important aspect that plays a part in determining safer systems of work.

Mortuaries in older establishments may have restricted space, making it difficult to improve the ergonomic design. In addition, there are Department of Health guidelines that must be adhered to, ie HBN 20 Facilities for mortuaries and post mortem room services (NHS Estates 2005).

The systems and equipment in place will vary depending on the organisation, and some mortuaries may not be attached to a hospital. The range of manual handling activities will be very similar and fall within the following categories:
- receipt of the body – may be internally via a concealment trolley or from an external source by ambulance
- transfer from trolley into the fridge

- transfer from fridge to the post mortem area
- transfer from trolley to the post mortem table
- preparing the chest, abdominal and skull cavities for post mortem
- transfer from fridge to the relatives' viewing room
- transfer from trolley to the undertakers' coffin.

Each category must be risk assessed and the appropriate control measures applied. In some cases, the same equipment and methods used for a living person would be appropriate. These would include hoists with horizontal stretcher attachments, lateral transfer boards and variable height trolleys.

Other control measures will be specific to the mortuary environment and should not be overlooked, especially during major refurbishments and new builds. This will include:
- multifunctional combined concealment, transportation and stacking trolley
- extra wide fridges and appropriately spaced stacking shelves
- double ended fridges that link the body receipt area and the post mortem room
- motorised and height adjustable body stacking trolleys
- variable height and tilting post mortem tables
- variable height dissecting tables
- extra wide high capacity post mortem tables
- overhead hoisting systems, post mortem and collection areas.

Safer policies and protocols are still needed within a new and ergonomically designed mortuary. The fridges may be wider but stacking bariatric bodies on high shelves can be difficult even when using a motorised trolley with powered rollers. Systems should be in place to stack bariatric bodies in the lower section of the shelving area. This will be easier biomechanically if no motorised trolley is available.

Conclusion

Evidence that the bariatric population is increasing creates the need for a proactive rather than reactive approach to caring for this population. Organisations must ensure that processes are in place to facilitate a person's journey through an episode of care that benefits both handlers and the person. This should include equipment provision, education and providing environments that promote person dignity.

Equipment provision for bariatric persons is not straightforward and bespoke equipment will predominantly be required to meet individual need. Organisations must have in place a clear policy statement, identified competent assessors who can risk assess environments, provide equipment information, accessibility and train formal/informal carers.

Nursing staff may be apprehensive and may have an inherent anxiety about being injured when caring for bariatric persons. It is possible to allay these anxieties by educating the workforce and providing specific facts regarding bariatric persons that will enhance safety and promote high quality care. Providing bariatric care with dignity for the person is important and an understanding of the different body shapes and dynamics will contribute to this decision making process.

The installation of equipment and the provision of training are not sufficient to improve quality of care and reduce manual handling risks to staff and persons. Evidence based practice and robust management systems are essential for progress to be made. The systems should incorporate statutory requirements, policies, protocols, risk assessment and quality assurance standards as a minimum requirement. Compliance is essential and, therefore, any systems implemented must be tested and formally audited. The risk management of bariatric persons is not a one-off process. It should remain high profile and be continually active to promote high quality care for persons and a safer environment for staff.

The previous pages have outlined the statutory, quality assurance and local organisational systems that are essential to facilitate the safer handling and management of bariatric persons within hospital or the community. The following pages will address a range of core practical techniques and illustrate the type of equipment that can be used. The techniques may be transferable into a variety of different scenarios within hospital or the community and the decision to use them should be based on a suitable and sufficient risk assessment that takes account of the person's clinical condition and all other relevant person specific and environmental risk factors.

PRACTICAL TECHNIQUES

Task 12.1 Repositioning a person in bed

The risks associated with this task increase significantly in bariatric management and risk reduction plans need to be implemented. The following equipment should be considered in terms of short, medium and long term control measures:
- the bed
- turning mattress/turning beds (see Task 12.1b)
- slide sheets
- repositioning sheets.

See Task 10.1 in chapter 10.

Options for moving the bariatric person up the bed, include:
- asking the person to move themself
- moving up with slide sheets
- using a repositioning sheet (see page 208) plus hoist
- using a hoist and appropriate sling.

Note: Before turning or rolling, consider sliding the person to the edge of the bed away from the direction of the roll to accommodate the abdominal pannus. If the starting position is incorrect, the person may be too far over with the abdominal pannus close to the edge. See Task 12.1a.

Turning in bed
This can also be achieved using the repositioning sheet or slide sheets.

Consider the person's body dynamics, especially if the person is an apple pannus. The width of the bed will need to be

sufficient to ensure that the pannus is supported and is not overhanging. Before undertaking the task, pillows should be positioned on the bed to support the turning pannus.

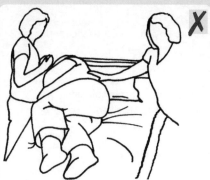

Task 12.1a Person too near the edge due to incorrect starting position

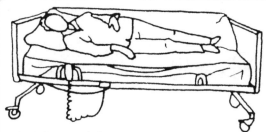

Task 12.1b Turning bed

Task 12.2 Personal care

Accessing under the pannus to the perineal area for hygiene care or to wash and dry the person within the skin folds requires caregiver exertion and is potentially a high risk task. One possible solution is a combined hoist and multistraps that can move the pannus upwards, but this is not an option in all cases. Points for consideration:
- can the person assist by moving or holding the pannus
- whether the pannus is pliable
- the risk of the multistrap slipping during the task
- how long the person can tolerate the pannus being supported by the multistraps.

Possible alternatives if this combination doesn't work, would be:
- strategically positioning slide sheets or towel fitted as follows
  - Recline the back rest down as far as possible, reverse tilt the bed for gravity assist and then move the pannus towards the patient's chest by walking up the pannus. Insert the towel or sliding sheet with the handlers holding the sliding sheet or towel at an angle to give access under the pannus.
  - Position person correctly by rolling him/her to one side, position another sliding sheet on the flat of the bed with the pannus positioned on it. Position your hands on the pannus and, using the combination of the sliding sheet

and a massage movement, manoeuvre upwards. Proceed to clean as required. Repeat for the other side.

For the bariatric person in end stage heart and lung failure and not able to lay flat, this may prove a more comfortable and dignified method.

Note: Rest breaks should be mutually agreed between handlers as these tasks might require more exertion.

Sub-task 12.2.1 Positioning limbs

The manual lifting and supporting of limbs can be a high risk scenario with risk of musculoskeletal injury to the handler and also the person. Chaffin *et al* (1999) and Pheasant (1992) refer to the weight of limbs and associated calculations. Chaffin identifies that a leg will be 15.7 per cent of the total body mass and an arm 5.1 per cent. For example, if a person weighs 200kg (31st) the leg weight would be 200 x 15.7 per cent = 31.4kg. This does not take account of the additional weight occurring due to conditions such as lymphodema.

Positioning limbs for personal care and dressing changes is, therefore, a potentially hazardous and difficult task when it involves bariatric persons. This task can be made easier by the use of limb supports of various designs (see Task 12.2.1a).

There are different sized limb lifters available and some can be used with a hoist. Consideration needs to be given to:
- the safety and comfort of the person who may need to have his/her limb held in a potentially awkward position for a long period of time
- neurovascular issues
- joint problems
- potential tissue damage from the sustained pressure on the skin
- the momentum required by the carers to secure the bandages.

Equipment options:
- leg lifters attached to the bed or free standing
- slide sheets to position limbs in the bed
- mobile/gantry hoist with limb slings
- mobile limb lifter
- limb attachment for theatre tables.

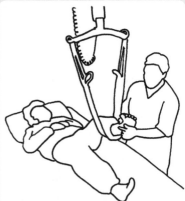

Task 12.2.1a Lifting a limb using mechanical aid

Sub-task 12.2.2 Managing leg ulcer dressings in the community

Managing bariatric heavy limbs is a constant problem for nurses in all settings. The postural positioning for nurses when attempting to apply dressings and bandages does not allow for best practice and most nurses will agree that they experience discomfort/low back pain during such tasks.

Task 12.3 Hoist transfer from bed to chair

See chapter 11, Task 11.4 and notes starting on page 205 on equipment and suitable hoists.

Task 12.3a Lateral hoist, bed to chair transfer, three staff – person able to assist

Undertaking leg ulcer dressings does have musculoskeletal risk factors for the nurses – individual to each nurse – often related to the difficulty of some nurses with kneeling.

Managing the task of leg ulcers is not one single task but a combination of tasks identified below:

Task 1
- prepare the clean dressings
- prepare the environment
- obtain a bowl of warm water
- move the bowl to the person's side.

Task 2
- remove the contaminated dressings
- disposal.

Task 3
- wash and inspect the leg(s)
- dry.

Task 4
- apply dressing
- apply bandaging.

Task 5
- clear up
- wash hands
- write the notes.

The above tasks can vary from 30 minutes to two hours and may need the attendance of more than one nurse. The nurses can work together or one visits early to undertake tasks 1-3, and 5, the second nurse arriving later to complete task 4.

In most instances, the nurses will use the person's own stool, a garden kneeling pad, or develop a technique which is most comfortable to them. Sitting on the flooring with legs spread, or kneeling, is not comfortable, especially if the nurse is having to support the limb. Most nurses will identify the inspection of the leg as the most difficult, due to the positions they are required to maintain while looking at the back of the legs.

- The number of staff required will be determined by the level of risk, including the person's clinical condition and ability to assist (see Task 12.3a).
- Twin motors and spreader bars will facilitate a better range of movement by moving shoulders or legs independently.
- When using twin motors, the lift must be synchronised to prevent overloading of one motor.
- A single motor can be used but it may require a more appropriate design of spreader bar for the bariatric person.

Task 12.4 Lateral transfer from bed to bed/trolley

See chapter 10, Task 10.9

Points to consider for lateral transfer of bariatric persons:
- use only equipment designed for the purpose
- slide sheets should be the correct width – too narrow and too large may cause problems
- extension straps fitted to slide sheets may improve the handlers' posture and facilitate the move
- any gaps should be minimal or bridged with an appropriate transfer board
- hoist systems with a stretcher sling attachment may be appropriate.

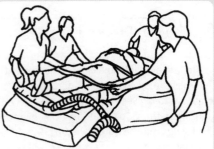

Task 12.4.1a Air assisted hover system – bed to trolley

Sub-task 12.4.1 Air assisted lateral transfers – hover systems

These devices use the hovercraft principle to move the person on a cushion of air and are commonly used to slide persons laterally from bed to trolley or trolley to operating table as recommended by Baptiste *et al* (2006) (see Task 12.4.1a and b).

The original use was for the management of extremely heavy persons but the versatile nature enhances any lateral transfer, regardless of the person's weight. The hover devices do not generally have a restricting upper weight limit. The mat width tends to be the limiting factor but a range of widths are available. The fabric make up of the mat is designed to be laundered if required and single person use mats are an option.

Extension straps can be fitted to air transfer devices but caution must be exercised as control can be lost if excessive effort is applied.

Task 12.4.1b Air assisted hover system – operating table to trolley

Task 12.5 Assisted walking

Assisting a patient to stand has been identified as a major cause of back pain (Ruszala & Musa 2005). When rehabilitating bariatric persons, we need to consider equipment that facilitates best practice and the person's mobility.

Understanding the diversity of bariatric body shape and movement patterns is extremely important in the rehabilitation programme in order to treat specific persons safely and effectively. Dionne (2002) suggests that bariatric people move in a wide variety of ways. The body shape determines the bariatric persons' limitations in postural control and the way they stand and learn how to maintain their centre of gravity. Daus (2002) suggests they usually avoid standing by pulling themselves forward because of the fear of falling and Dionne (1997) says they may develop compensatory activities. Bariatric people, therefore, will often require specific mobilisation techniques.

Dionne's egress test (DET) is a useful method for assessing the ability to mobilise from a sitting to a standing position including weight bearing and taking steps. The process involves three repetitions to rise from the bed starting with just one or two inches. Once standing, the person is then

asked to step in place by raising a foot completely clear of the ground. This, too, must be repeated three times. The final test is to step forward and return. The heel of the stepping foot must move forward to at least the toe level of the static foot. The DET is considered a success if the person can complete the tasks with only minimal tactile intervention from the assessor. Smith (2008) carried out a study to compare therapists trained in DET methods and nurses untrained in the technique. The result showed a high level of reliability and agreement with the trained staff and newly instructed personnel (Smith 2008).

When rehabilitating a bariatric person, the following needs to be considered:
- a careful assessment needs to be undertaken of the person's ability to weight bear and/or assist, especially when he/she has been in bed for a considerable time
- a bed that converts to a chair is often useful, as well as a riser recliner chair
- the width of the walking frames may need to encompass the excess adipose tissue
- the types of sling that will be appropriate for rehabilitation, as bariatric persons may have breathing difficulties and often cannot tolerate constriction around their chest

- are there adequate numbers of staff with appropriate skill and training to undertake the task?

Persons would require some weight bearing capacity, cognitive response and compliance in the task.

Sub-task 12.5.1 Hoist slings for assisted walking

A number of sling styles are available and careful assessment of the person's needs must be taken into consideration. If he/she cannot tolerate a walking vest/harness, then alternative designs incorporating a "pant" design may be more appropriate. Choice of slings may be determined by:
- the person's tissue viability status
- any wound healing issues
- potential rib injuries
- environmental constraints and the type of equipment available
- staff competency.

Task 12.5.1a Hoist slings for assisted walking

Task 12.5.1b Hoist sling for unaided walking

Task 12.6 Retrieving a person off the floor

Assisting a fallen person off the floor is another challenging task for handlers and is described in more detail in chapter 13 (Tasks 13.4-13.10). Depending on the injuries incurred and the dependency level of the person, three options are open to handlers:
- Encourage the person to get up slowly by themself using normal body movement.
- Use an inflatable device that can be positioned under the person and raise him/her up. This can be a seated device or a supine device.
- Hoist system.

Sub-task 12.6.1 Inflatable lifting chair – fully inflated position

The seated device has been designed to assist the heavier person into sitting and lift him/her from the floor, either independently or with assistance. It offers a comfortable and dignified solution and can be used anywhere, indoors or outside. The clinical condition of the fallen person and lifting capacity of the device should always be considered before proceeding to raise from the floor. See chapter 13 (Task 13.10)

Task 12.6.1b Rolling to insert deflated, lifting cushion

Task 12.6.1c Re-adjusting the lifting cushion

Task 12.6.1a Positioning the lifting cushion

Task 12.6.1d Rolling the person back onto the lifting cushion

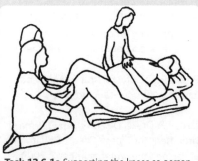

Task 12.6.1e Supporting the knees so person doesn't slide

Task 12.6.1f Inflating the lifting cushion

Task 12.6.1g Three chambers inflated

Task 12.6.1h All chambers inflated

Task 12.6.1i Rising from the lifting cushion

Sub-task 12.6.2 Inflatable lifting device – supine position

If the person's clinical condition precludes sitting and the use of a hoist or inflatable seat to assist him/her is not appropriate, another option is to use an air assisted lift device that allows the person to remain in a supine position. The device is placed under the person by log rolling him/her onto it and has four chambers which are inflated independently and sequentially, starting from the bottom. The person is then raised to a level that will facilitate a lateral transfer onto a stretcher, bed or trolley. The extremely high load capacity makes this device particularly useful for bariatric persons and can be used together with the air assisted lateral transfer device to recover the person from the floor.

Task 12.6.2a Air inflated lifting device

Task 12.6.2b Rescue from floor and transfer to trolley (300kg, 47st)

Sub-task 12.6.3 Hoist off the floor

See Task 11.7 in chapter 11.

- An overhead system is preferred and more stable.
- Bariatric persons can be hoisted from floor level using a mobile hoist but the procedure can be complex.
- Hoisting bariatric persons from floor level is not condemned but safer options are available, including the use of air assisted devices (see Task 12.6.2b).
- Some hoists may have horizontal attachments for supine lifting, which may reduce the maximum lift capacity as the wide load can make the hoist unstable.
- Lifting from floor level is one occasion when the use of hoist brakes may be indicated.
- A diagonal approach is usually the most practical when using a mobile hoist
- An alternative flat lift method must be used if major fracture and/or spinal injury suspected (NPSA 2011).

1

2

3

4

References

All Wales NHS Manual Handling Training Passport and Information Scheme (2007), Swansea. www.wales.nhs.uk/documents/All%2DWales%2DNHS%2DManual%2DHandling%2DTraining%2DPassport%2Dand%2DInformation%2DScheme%2DV2%2Dfinal%2Epdf Accessed 1 November 2010.

Association for the Study of Obesity (2010), Press release Access to NHS Weight Loss Surgery, www.aso.org.uk/wp-content/uploads/downloads/2010/09/100121-Press-Release-Bariatric-Surgery.pdf accessed 7 October 2010.

Baptiste, A, Boda, SV, Nelson, AL, Lloyd, JD & Lee, WE, III (2006), Friction-Reducing Devices for Lateral Person Transfers: A Clinical Evaluation, *AAOHN Journal*; Apr 2006; **54**, 4; pg 173.

Bushard, S (2002), Trauma in Persons who are Morbidly Obese *Cardiometabolic risk and weight management*, Vol **2** No 1, p14-16, January 2007.

Cassar, S (2010), Manual Handling Protocol for People who are Bariatric or have exceptional needs. The London Borough of Sutton.

Chaffin, D, Anderson, G & Martin, B (1999), *Occupational biomechanics* (3rd ed), New York: Wiley.

Cheung, DS, Maygers, J, Khouri-Stevens, Z, De Grouchy, L & Magnuson, T (2006), Failure Modes and Effects Analysis: Minimizing Harm to Our Bariatric Patients. *Bariatric Nursing and Surgical Patient Care*, Volume **1**, Number 2, 2006 p107-114.

Cookson, K (2007), *Large but unseen: bariatric persons and manual handling*.

Cookson, K (2008), Complex admission and discharge situations – bariatric patients, *column*, **20.3** Winter 2008 pages 8-11, ISBN1461-0922.

Daus, C (2002), Rehab and the Bariatric Person Rehab Management. *The Interdisciplinary Journal of Rehabilitation* January:14(9) **42**, 44-45.

Dionne, M (1997), *Treating the Bariatric Patient*, PT & OT, January 1997.

Dionne, M (2002), One Size Does Not Fit All *Rehab Management*, March 2002, Vol **15**; No 2. Accessed 25 November 2010 www.rehabpub.com/features/32002/1.asp.

Eadie, R (2004), Resuscitative challenges in the obese patient. Obesity. *NAASO's newsletter*, Vol **2** No 8.

European Pressure Ulcer Advisory Panel & US National Pressure Ulcer Advisory Panel (2010), International Pressure Ulcer Guidelines for Prevention and Treatment Quick Reference Guide accessed via: www.epuap.org/guidelines.html.

Fazel, E (1997), Handling of Extremely Heavy Persons, *column*, Vol **9.2**, Apr 97, p13-16, National Back Exchange, Towcester 1997.

Goldhill, D, Imhoff, M, McLean, B & Waldmann, C (2007), Rotational bed therapy to prevent and treat respiratory complications a review and meta-analysis, *American Journal of Critical Care*, January 1007.

Haslam, C, Clemes, S, McDermott, H, Shaw, K, Williams, C & Haslam, R (2007), *Manual Handling Training – Investigation of current practices and development of guidelines*, Health and Safety Executive Research Report RR583.

HSE (1974), Health and Safety at Work etc Act 1974.

HSE (1992), Health and Safety Executive, The Manual Handling Operations Regulations 1992 (as amended), Her Majesty's Stationery Office.

HSE (1999), The Management of Health and Safety at Work Regulations 1999, Her Majesty's Stationery Office.

Hignett, S, Chipchase, S, Tetley, A & Giffiths, P (2007), *Risk assessment and process planning for bariatric person handling pathways*, Health and Safety Executive Research report RR573.

Hignett, S & Griffiths, P (2009), Risk factors for moving and handling bariatric persons. *Nursing Standard*, **24**, 11, p40-48.

Kilpatrick, MK, Esterhuizen, P & Drake, D (2009), An Optimal Caring/Healing Environment for Obese Clients *Bariatric Nursing and Surgical Person Care*, Vol **4**, number 2 2009 Mary Ann Liebert Inc.

Kirton, H (2008), Helping make 1:1 care mean 1:1 care! 8th Annual Safe Patient Handling and Movement Conference, Poster presentation, 11-15 March, 2008. Tampa, Florida.

Mastrogiovanni, D, Phillips, EM & Fine, CK (2003), The bariatric spinal cord-injured person: challenges in preventing and healing skin problems, *Topics in Spinal Cord Injury Rehabilitation*, **9** (2): 38-44.

Medical Device Equipment Alert (2008), Alert MDEA (NI2008/036) issued 23 May 2008.

Mosby's Medical Dictionary, 7th edition 2006. Mosby Elsevier.

Muir, M (2009), Clinical Developments and Metabolic insights in Total Bariatric Person Care, *Bariatric Times* March 2009.

Naylor, P, Raynsford, H, Kurowski, P, Demis, J & Goodwin, A (2005), Choosing Health in the South East: Obesity, South East England Public Health Observatory, www.sepho.org.uk/Download/Public/9783/1/SEPHO%20obesity%20report%20Nov%2005.pdf.

NHS Estates (2005), HBN 20 Facilities for mortuaries and post mortem room services. Department of Health ISBN 0113227159, Crown copyright.

NHS Information Centre (2009a), *Health Survey for England* (2008), Physical Activity and fitness – Summary of key findings, p12, ISBN 978-1-84636-371-9, www.ic.nhs.uk/webfiles/publications/HSE/HSE08/HSE_08_Summary_of_key_findings.pdf accessed 14 January 2011.

NHS Information Centre (2009b), *Health Survey for England* (2008), Physical Activity and fitness – Summary of key findings, p3, ISBN 978-1-84636-371-9. www.ic.nhs.uk/webfiles/publications/HSE/HSE08/HSE_08_Summary_of_key_findings.pdf accessed 14 January 2011.

NHSLA (2010), National Health Service Litigation Authority. Risk Management Standards for Acute Trusts and Primary Care Trusts and Independent Sector Providers of NHS Care. Website www.nhsla.com/RiskManagement/accessed 19 July 2010.

NICE (2006), Obesity Guidance on the presentation, identification, assessment and management of overweight and obesity in adults and children. National Institute for Health and Clinical Excellence Document, CG43, http://guidance.nice.org.uk/CG43/Guidance/Section.

Nilsson, B (2006), Bariatric person handling joined up Management Development Diversity Delivery Institute of Healthcare Management Annual Conference & Exhibition Manchester 2005 *N Journal*; March 2006; **54**, 3; pg 113.

NPSA (2008), A risk matrix for risk managers National Patient Safety Agency www.npsa.nhs.uk accessed 19 July 2010.

NPSA (2011), Rapid Response Report NPSA/2011/RRR001, Essential care after an inpatient fall NHS 2011 www.codp.org.uk/documents/Essential%20care%20after%20an%20inpatient%20fall%20supporting%20information.pdf.

NWML (2008), Guidance to the Non-Weighing Instruments

Regulations 2000 as mended by the 2008 NAWI (amendment) Regulations 2008.

Office of Health Economics (2010a), Shedding the Pounds, Obesity Management, NICE Guidance and bariatric surgery in England, p4 ,The Office of Health Economics, Whitehall, London, September 2010.

Office of Health Economics (2010b), Shedding the Pounds, Obesity Management, NICE Guidance and bariatric surgery in England, p5 ,The Office of Health Economics, Whitehall, London, September 2010.

Perilli, V, Sollazzi, L, Bozza, P, Modesti, C, Chierichini, A, Tacchino, RM & Ranieri, R (2000), The Effects of the Reverse Trendelenburg Position on Respiratory Mechanics and Blood Gases in Morbidly Obese Persons during Bariatric Surgery. *Anaesthesia and Management*, December 2000, Vol **91**, No 6, 1520-1525.

Pheasant, S (1992), *Bodyspace*, London: Taylor & Francis Ltd.

Resuscitation Council (UK) (2009), *Guidance for safer handling during resuscitation in healthcare settings*, Working group of the Resuscitation Council (UK), London, November 2009, pages 28-29.

Resuscitation Council (UK) (2010), *Resuscitation Guidelines 2010*. ISBN 978-1-903812-21-1, Resuscitation Council (UK), London, October 2010.

Rush, A (2006), An Overview of Bariatric Management, www.dlf.org.uk/factsheets/Overview%20of%20 Bariatric%20Management.pdf, Disabled Living Foundation Accessed 29 August 2010.

Ruszala, S & Musa, I (2005), An evaluation of equipment to assist person sit-to-stand activities in physiotherapy, *Physiotherapy*, **91**(1), 35-41, March 2005.

Smith, BK (2008), A pilot study evaluating physical therapist-nurse inter-rater reliability of Dionne's egress test™ in morbidly obese patients. www.thefreelibrary.com/A+pilot+study+evaluating+physical+therapist-nurse+inter-rater...-a0200409972 accessed 9 November 2010.

St John Holt, A (1999), *Principles of Health and Safety at Work* 5th edition, p105, IOSH Services 1999, Wigston Leicestershire, ISBN 0901357243.

Stubbs, DA (2000), Ergonomics and Occupational Medicine: future challenges. *Occupational Medicine*, Vol **50**, No 4 pp277-282.

Webber, J (2001), The co-morbities of obesity, *Practical Diabetes*, Int 2001, **18**(8), 293-296.

WHO (2000), Obesity: Preventing and Managing the Global Epidemic WHO Technical report Series 894, WHO Geneva 2000 http://whqlibdoc.who.int/trs/who_trs_894.pdf.

WHO expert consultation (2004), Appropriate body mass index for Asian populations and its implications for policy and intervention strategies, *The Lancet*, 2004; 157-163.

Appendix 12.1 Person assessment tool

Manual handling risk assessment for persons

NB: All persons must undergo an assessment:
- within six hours of admission · · · · · (Assessment Code 1)
- on transfer from another ward · · · · · (Assessment Code 2)
- if there is a change in the person's general condition · · · · · (Assessment Code 3)
- weekly review from date of most recent assessment · · · · · (Assessment Code 4)

Person ID label		Ward:	Date of admission: - - / - - / - -	Time of admission: (24-hour clock): - - / - -	Grade of admitting nurse
		Admitting nurse name:			
		Admitting nurse signature:			
Assessment date		- - / - - / - -	- - / - - / - -	- - / - - / - -	- - / - - / - -
Assessment time (24-hour clock)		- - / - -	- - / - -	- - / - -	- - / - -
Reason for assessment (code: top of page)		1 2 3 4	1 2 3 4	1 2 3 4	1 2 3 4
For verification of assessment as per policy	RGN Signature				
	RGN Name				
Re-assessment done by: (Signature)					
Re-assessment done by: (Name)					
Re-assessment done by: (Grade)					
MOBILITY Does the person have any mobility problems? NB: mobility may deteriorate at different times of the day due to medication, fatigue etc.		Y N	Y N	Y N	Y N
COMMUNICATION DEFICIT Does the person have any communication deficit, eg can't respond to simple commands?		Y N	Y N	Y N	Y N
SPECIAL RISKS Is the person at special risk, eg recent CVA, post operative, amputee, neurological deficit, pressure ulcers, wounds, infections, external lines, alcohol, new fall etc?		Y N	Y N	Y N	Y N
WEIGHT Does the person's weight impact on mobility, available space, transferring, staffing levels or necessitate special bariatric equipment?		Y N	Y N	Y N	Y N
FALLS HISTORY Is there any known history of falls within the home or hospital environment?		Y N	Y N	Y N	Y N

If the answer to ANY question is YES, please see Care Plan Guidelines (overleaf)

If the answer to any question is NO, then reassess if the person's condition changes OR weekly.

Appendix 12.2 Example of organisational overview

Organisational overview – manual handling risks – progress and relevant costs

	Risk + Matrix score	Source of risk	Action	Responsibility	Timeframe	Progress of action
1	Manual handling bariatric persons	Insufficient riser recliner chairs. **Identified by review**	Purchase additional riser recliner chairs x 4 **Cost £13,719.00**	All directorates Trust wide	March 2009 Review April 2010	Purchased chairs x2 September 2009 Trust H&S budget
	Matrix score 12 Also impacts on quality of care					
2	Manual handling bariatric persons	Insufficient bariatric commodes **Identified by risk assessment 2008 MH Advisor**	Purchase additional more robust high load capacity commodes x 10 **Cost £5,911.00**	All directorates Trust wide	March 2009 Review April 2010	Purchased commodes x5 September 2009 Trust H&S budget
	Matrix score 12 Also impacts on quality of care					
3	Manual handling stroke persons	Postural and musculoskeletal hazard during acute stage and rehabilitation of stroke persons. Risk assessment by physio staff. **Identified by review physio staff**	Replace inadequate and 10-year old-stand aid hoist with more appropriate therapeutic hoist, ie Sara Plus Hoist **Cost £8,409.00**	Clinical business manager	March 2010	Capital expenditure April 2010 Action complete
	Matrix score 12 Also impacts on quality of care					
4	Manual handling cardiac persons from seated to standing	Bedside chairs too low – a variety of sizes needed. **Identified by risk assessment at ward level, ie cascade trainer**	Partially resolved – six chairs purchased 2008. An additional six chairs are required **Cost £1,800**	Ward manager	March 2010	Funding not identified
	Matrix score 6 Also impacts on quality of care					
5	Hydrotherapy person hoist improvements Overhead tracking hoist required to extend service provision and improve access and egress to pool for morbidly obese persons	Potential for staff and person injury during access and egress to pool including emergency extrication	Install overhead tracking hoist to permit horizontal and seated access and egress and increased weight capacity from 160kg (25st) to 200kg (31st) **Cost Total £7,972.95**	Physiotherapy manager		Project funded and hoist ordered – for completion August 2010
	Matrix score 9					

Appendix 12.3 Record of service users who are bariatric or who have exceptional needs

Please record information about those service users for whom there has been a need for specialist equipment due to their size, shape or weight. Please note this includes all service users even if there is no manual handling involved.

Service user name:	Weight:	Height:
Address:		
Phone number:	Paris number:	

Outline the main reason for the need for specialist equipment:

List the items of equipment you got from the ICES stores and list any items you needed to order externally and state from where you sourced these items.

List below any additional costs for these items.

Did you need the services of an external professional/expert, if so whom?

Did you use the bariatric protocol to help manage the service user?

How did the person's size impact on the number of carers you recommended?

Did you weigh the person in their home, if so how?

What problems or difficulties did you have when managing this service user?

Please email this form to the Manual Handling Advisor and retain a copy in the service user's case notes.

This must be completed by the home care provider as a means to ensure equipment in the home will be suitable.

Appendix 12.4 Bariatric moving and handling assessment checklist for home use

Please complete if the person's weight is suspected to be in excess of 18 stones/114kg or if their body dynamics and shape exceed the dimensions of the supporting surface

Name:			Date of assessment:
Contact details:		Name and contact details of assessor:	
Date of moving and handling full assessment:	What is the service user's current weight?	Where and when was the last weight taken?	
Is the weight likely to change?– give details:			

This form is a checklist to ensure the service user has equipment with an adequate Safe Working Load (SWL).

What equipment is required?	If on site, name the equipment and note the Safe Working Load?	If to be ordered, name equipment. What is the minimum SWL required?	Follow up action and by whom. (If none required, put NR)	Date when correct equipment is in place and add signature
Profiling bed				
Mattress				
Commode				
Shower chair				
Toilet surround Raised toilet seat Bath seat Bath hoist				
Armchair or riser chair				
Dining room chair				
Mobile hoist and sling Overhead hoist				
Standing hoist and sling				
Slide sheets (check dimensions and purpose of use)				
Other small handling aids				
Wheelchair				
Walking aids				
Any other equipment				

Training needs: Please check all current carers are familiar with the use of the above equipment and adequate instructions are on site and necessary training is arranged. Please record training provided in the use of any specialist equipment.

Please check if person is to use transport or leave the premises that preparations are made to ensure the journey will be safe and the destination has appropriate systems of work in place.

Contact Occupational Therapy or the Manual Handling Co-ordinator for advice or refer to the LBS bariatric protocol. Do not use equipment with an inadequate Safe Working Load

Assessor's signature: _____ Date: _____

Manager's signature: _____ Date: _____

© BackCare

Personal moving and handling profile and risk assessment

Service user's name:	Assessor:
Date of birth:	Organisation:
Address:	Contact details:
	Date of initial assessment:
	Re-assessment suggested date:
Computer number:	Date re-assessed:

a)   Summary of service user's physical conditions and any relevant diagnosis:
Complete level of mobility and identified risk factors following assessment. _____

_____

b)   Approximate height, weight and build of service user: _____

When was the person last weighed? _____

If weight possibly over 18 stones/114 kilos, please also complete a bariatric checklist

c)   Does this service user have a recent history of falling? If yes, give details. YES/NO
NB Follow your service procedure and refer to London Borough of Sutton Safer Manual Handling Policy for falls protocol

_____

_____

d)   Action to be taken following a fall:

_____

e)   Does this service user require any assistance with moving and handling? YES/NO
If the answer is *no* you *do not need* to complete the rest of this form, but ensure you have a summary of the service user's ability in (a) above.

_____

f)   Is the assistance required *only* verbal encouragement? YES/NO
If the answer is yes, please summarise in (g) below the verbal prompts that are necessary.

_____

g)   List the moving and handling tasks that need to be done (eg chair to commode transfers etc) and state current method being used.
If only verbal prompting is necessary, please write the prompts required ensuring re-ablement goals are met.

Task 1   _____

Task 2   _____

Task 3   _____

Assessor signature _____
Service user has received and understood the factsheet and accepts the care

Manager signature _____

Manager name _____

Service user/advocate signature _____

Risk factors

Risk factors – the service user/load
Note any factors that may affect the handling of this service user.

Does the service user have any of the following problems? (Put an X in the relevant boxes.)

Please indicate how the service user or carer is affected in the comments box below.

- ☐ Pain
- ☐ Osteoporosis
- ☐ Weakness (site)
- ☐ Poor balance (sit/stand)

- ☐ Impaired mobility
- ☐ Difficulty weight-bearing

- ☐ Incontinence catheter/bowels
- ☐ Inability to co-operate
- ☐ Loss of co-ordination
- ☐ Loss of feeling (site)

- ☐ Pressure sores/broken skin
- ☐ Anxiety/depression

- ☐ Attachments, eg syringe driver/colostomy
- ☐ Involuntary movements (eg tremor/spasms)
- ☐ Unpredictable behaviour
- ☐ Comprehension and cognitive problems/memory loss/learning impairment
- ☐ Visual/hearing/speech impairment
- ☐ Cultural issues – service user family preferences

Comments:

_____

_____

Is this service user able to assist physically with any of the transfer? If yes, give details. YES/NO

_____

_____

_____

Risk factors – the staff
Would any specific staff group be more at risk handling this service user?
For example, very tall or short, history of knee or back problems, inexperienced, pregnant?   YES/NO

Do the tasks require any special knowledge or skills?   YES/NO

Have all the team got the knowledge and skills required?   YES/NO

Is there any follow up action required? If yes, detail here: YES/NO

_____

How many staff are required? _____

Risk factors – the task

Do the manual handling tasks referred to in (g) on the front page involve any of the following? (Put an X in the relevant boxes.)

	Task 1	Task 2	Task 3			Task 1	Task 2	Task 3
Awkward position	☐	☐	☐		Lifting a dependent weight	☐	☐	☐
Stooping	☐	☐	☐		Holding load away from body	☐	☐	☐
Reaching	☐	☐	☐		Is the task repetitive?	☐	☐	☐
Twisting	☐	☐	☐		Lifting weight from below knees or	☐	☐	☐
Pushing/pulling	☐	☐	☐		above shoulders			

Additional comments/summary of risk factors above (relate to tasks). How do these things affect risk to service user or carer?

_____

_____

_____

Risk factors – the environment

Locations in which the tasks are completed

	Location 1	Location 2	Location 3
	_____	_____	_____

Do any of the above have the following risk factors? (Put an X in the relevant boxes.)

	Location 1	Location 2	Location 3			Location 1	Location 2	Location 3
Limited space	☐	☐	☐		Uncontrolled pets	☐	☐	☐
Stairs/slopes	☐	☐	☐		Electrical hazards	☐	☐	☐
Poor lighting	☐	☐	☐		Excessive furniture	☐	☐	☐
Clutter	☐	☐	☐		Difference in furniture height	☐	☐	☐
Hazardous flooring	☐	☐	☐		Lack of space under bed	☐	☐	☐
Trip/slip hazards	☐	☐	☐		Low working surface	☐	☐	☐

Additional comments /summary of risk factors above and how they affect risks to service user or carer:

_____

_____

List current manual handling equipment in use

Equipment name:				
	YES/NO	YES/NO	YES/NO	YES/NO
Is the service in date?	☐	☐	☐	☐
Is it in good condition?	☐	☐	☐	☐
Does it belong to service user?	☐	☐	☐	☐
Does it belong to ICES?	☐	☐	☐	☐

Are there disposable slides?   YES/NO

If so, are they labelled as disposable?   YES/NO

Is the Safe Working Load of all equipment appropriate for the service user?   YES/NO

Is there any other equipment required to perform safely any of the tasks or any follow up work required? Give details and order from OT/ICES store now (date equipment requested and by whom).

_____

_____

Control measures

Give details below as to moving and handling techniques to be used to complete each task with minimal risk.

State any short-term action if equipment is to be supplied and is not yet available.

If using equipment, eg sliding sheet, specify size, name and technique to be used.

Ensure that if there is a hoist in place there is a detailed hoist plan.

Include a description of what the service user is able to do for themselves during the manoeuvre and how carers can promote service user participation. You may also refer to Sutton locality manual handling procedures to help you.

Task number and description	Details of method to be used including equipment and technique	Date of changes

© BackCare

Risk evaluation matrix

Step 1 – Likelihood (frequency or probability)	
Score	Description
1 RARE	Do not believe will happen, one off. Exceptional circumstances
2 UNLIKELY	Not expected but possible. Could occur at some time
3 POSSIBLE	May occur at some time
4 LIKELY	Will probably occur
5 ALMOST CERTAIN	Likely to occur on many occasions. A persistent issue

Step 2 – Severity (consequence)		
Score	Impact on individual	Impact on organisation
1 INSIGNIFICANT	No injury No apparent injury	No risk to the organisation No impact on service No impact on environment
2 MINOR	First Aid Minor injury or minor illness up to one month	Minimal risk to organisation Slight impact on service Slight impact on environment
3 MODERATE	Temporary incapacity. Short term monitoring. Additional medical treatment required up to one year	Some service disruption Potential for adverse publicity, avoidable with careful handling Moderate impact on environment
4 MAJOR	Major injury (reportable) Major clinical intervention Permanent incapacity	Service restriction Adverse publicity Impact of reputation Major impact on environment
5 CATASTROPHIC	Death	National media interest Severe loss of confidence in organisation

Likelihood (frequency)	Step 3 – Risk matrix likelihood x severity				
	1 INSIGNIFICANT	2 MINOR	3 MODERATE	4 MAJOR	5 CATASTROPHIC
5 CERTAIN	5 L	10 M	15 H	20 H	25 H
4 LIKELY	4 L	8 M	12 H	16 H	20 H
3 POSSIBLE	3 L	6 M	9 M	12 H	15 H
2 UNLIKELY	2 L	4 L	6 M	8 M	10 H
1 RARE	1 L	2 L	3 L	4 M	5 H

KEY:
H High risk. Urgent action required. **SEEK EXPERT ADVICE NOW**
M Medium risk, senior manager attention required. Be alert.
L Low risk, local manager responsibility, manage by routine procedures

RISK LEVEL

	Task 1	Task 2	Task 3
Service user	☐	☐	☐
Staff	☐	☐	☐

PLEASE CHECK THAT YOU HAVE GIVEN DETAILS OF ACTION REQUIRED IN ABSENCE OF EQUIPMENT. ORGANISE ANY FOLLOW UP ACTION NOW!

ANY CHANGES MUST BE CONTINUED ON THE REVIEW SHEET AND THE DATE OF THE CHANGES/RE-ASSESSMENT ENTERED ON THE FIRST PAGE

Assessor's signature: _____ Date: _____

Team manager's signature: _____ Date: _____

Personal moving and handling profile and risk assessment – review sheet

Service user's name:	Assessor:
Date of birth:	Organisation:
Address:	Contact details:
	Date re-assessed:
	Date re-assessed:
Computer number:	Date re-assessed:

Task number and description	Details of *updated* method to be used including equipment and technique. Please ensure counter signature for any changes	Print name, sign and date

13

A systems approach to the prevention and management of falls

Melanie Sturman MSc RGN

Moving and handling adviser, Norfolk County Council, Adult Care Community Services

Introduction

Evidence indicates that falls are a common occurrence in health and social care. Falls can occur in residential care homes, nursing homes, hospitals and individuals' own homes. Evidence from the Department of Trade and Industry (2007) found that, in each year in Britain, a third of the population aged over 65 has a fall. The Health and Safety Executive (HSE) Shattered Lives Campaign (2010) identified that falls can occur at any age. The Royal Society for the Prevention of Accidents (2007) found the majority of accidents occurring in the home were related to slips, trips and falls. Falls have become one of the most serious problems that face those aged over 65 years (Department of Health 2001, 2007). Gillespie *et al* (2001 and 2010) and Help the Aged (2006) found that older people living in residential and nursing homes are three times more likely to fall compared to older people living in their own homes. The HSE (2006a) found incidences such as falls account for one third of patient injuries in the NHS. In-patient falls are the most frequently reported incident for acute facilities (National Patient Safety Agency (NPSA) 2007b).

Definitions of falls

There are numerous definitions of falls. Masud & Morris (2001) define a fall as an untoward event that results in a person coming to rest unintentionally on the ground or lower surface. Morse (1997) describes an accidental fall as an event, such as

slipping, tripping or other mishap generally related to environmental factors. Morse describes an anticipated physiological fall as an event that occurs with people who are identified at risk of falling. Unanticipated physiological falls are described as falls that cannot be predicted (Morse 1997).

Consequences of falling

Impact on organisations

There are personal, social and financial costs associated with falls. The Royal College of Physicians (2005) estimates that falls associated costs to the NHS and social care providers are in the region of £1.7 billion each year. Falls related injuries are a leading cause of mortality in people aged 75 and over (Cameron *et al* 2009), with at least 647,721 people attending Accident and Emergency Departments each year as a result of a fall (National Institute for Health and Clinical Excellence 2004). Help the Aged (2004) found that 25 per cent of older people who fall in care homes suffer serious injury, and that 40 per cent of all hospital admissions of the over 65s were as a consequence of a person falling. Tinetti *et al* (1998) found that at least five per cent of falls result in fractures. Injuries arising from falls, and their sequelae, are a leading cause of death (Help the Aged 2006). Sterling *et al* (2001) found that falls related injuries can increase disability and can lead to premature death.

Falls and the impact on employees

The HSE (2002) found that 50 per cent of accidents reported in the healthcare sector are attributed to assisting people whose mobility is reduced by disease or chronic illness. In 2005, the HSE found manual handling to be a major source of non-compliance in care homes, where staff were not following best practice techniques. Poor manual handling practices, including assisting people who were falling or had fallen, resulted in 5,000 injuries a year. Manual handling risk increases when people fall because a handler may attempt to catch, support or intervene with a falling person, or because they attempt to retrieve the fallen person manually.

During 2008-2009, there were 131 RIDDOR (2005) reports of injuries to care staff working in care homes that involved supporting, catching, intervening incorrectly or being grabbed by a falling person (HSE 2010b). The majority of these incidents occurred when care staff were assisting the person to transfer between surfaces, eg chair to toilet, bed to chair, etc. This evidence is supported by Hignett & Sands (2009) who identified a relationship between manual handling and falls, in finding that 20 per cent of patient falls are likely to occur during a moving and handling activity, eg transferring from a bed to chair. Nevertheless, the majority of falls are not witnessed and the falling person is found lying on the floor (Hignett & Sands 2009; Sturman 2008).

Biomechanics of catching a falling person
Work undertaken by Fray (2003) calculated forces on the spine, when catching a person, will exceed safe levels, eg a handler catching a person weighing 53kg is likely to experience a force in the region of 5,250 Newtons in the lower back. Fray in Smith (Smith (ed), *HOP5* 2005) identified that catching a falling person is likely to put the employee at risk of musculoskeletal injury.

Biomechanics of supporting or "holding up" a falling person
The calculation set out below shows the compression forces at the level of the 5th lumbar/1 at sacral joint (L5/S1) of the spine experienced when a handler attempts to support a falling person. Kroemer & Grandjean (2003) recommend the use of free body diagrams to add the force of the falling person with the forces already acting upon the handler. Fig 13.1 from Fray (2003) provides an example of a free body diagram that can be used to calculate the turning moments around L5 and S1. Kroemer & Grandjean (2003) and Fray (2003) suggest that the weight of the body trunk should be calculated as two thirds of the body weight.

Assume body weight as 97kg
Two thirds of 97kg =
        65kg or 650N (lever 0.2m)
Weight of falling body =
        69kg or 690N (lever arm 0.5m)
The force to overcome the fall =
        2,415N (lever arm 0.5m)
Calculating the turning moments at the level of L5 and S1
Muscle x 0.05 = (650 x 0.2m) + (690 x 0.5) + (2415 x 0.5)
Muscle x 0.05 = 130 + 345 + 1207.50
Muscle force = 1,682.50/0.05 = 33,650 Newtons

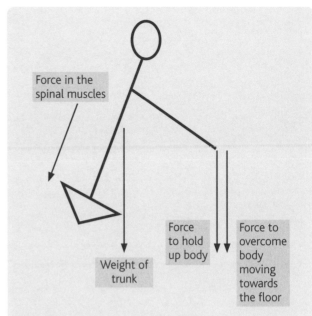

Fig 13.1 Free body diagram from Fray (2003)

Labels in figure: Force in the spinal muscles; Weight of trunk; Force to hold up body; Force to overcome body moving towards the floor

Contributory person related risk factors

There is an abundance of literature exploring factors contributing to falls in specific age groups and within a range of environments (domestic, social care, NHS etc). The College of Occupational Therapists (2006) and Royal Society for the Prevention of Accidents (2007) conclude that falls generally occur as a result of an interaction between different potential risk factors. The reasons why people fall are complex and influenced by contributing factors such as illness, mental health, medication, age and environmental factors. Masud & Morris (2001) and Steinhoef *et al* (2002) break down the risk factors into three groups:
- intrinsic
- extrinsic
- behavioural.

Intrinsic risk factors include the medical, physical and functional ability of the person, extrinsic risk factors are concerned with the environment, and behavioural risk factors are concerned with the mental health and cognitive level of the person.

TABLE 13.1 INTRINSIC

Risk factor	Reference
Medical conditions, such as Parkinson's Disease, arthritis, cardiac problems, cerebral vascular accident	College of Occupational Therapists (2006); Help the Aged (2004)
Changes in mobility, balance, postural stability, gait and reduced muscle strength	Jensen et al (2002); Lord et al (2000); Covinsky et al (2001)
Polypharmacy – taking three or more medications or over use of sedation	Lord et al (2000); Kalin et al (2002)
Syncope or loss of consciousness	Department of Trade and Industry (2007); Rubenstein & Josephson (2002)
Dizziness and postural hypotension	Tinetti & Williams (2000); Kario et al (2001)
Continence – the need to get to the toilet or regular trips to the toilet can cause some people to fall because they are in a hurry and can trip or fall	Tromp et al (2001); National Patient Safety Agency (NPSA) (2007a and 2007b)
Widespread pain	Leveille et al (2002)
Decreased vision, including a reduction in visual acuity, contrast sensitivity, dark adaptation, accommodation and depth perception, increase the risk of falls	Lord & Dayhew (2001); Lord et al (2000)
Foot and ankle problems, eg ankle flexibility, sensation and strength or toe muscles can increase falls risk	Menz et al (2006)
Reduced mobility, eg difficulty walking 400m can increase the risk of falling	Cryer & Patel (2001)
Acute illnesses, eg urinary tract infections	Cryer & Patel (2001)

TABLE 13.2 EXTRINSIC

Risk factor	Reference
Hazards in the environment, eg rugs, flexes etc	Day et al (2002); HSE (2007)
Uneven flooring and floor coverings can increase the risk of falling. Friction between the floor and shoe worn. Degree of toe clearance during gait cycle. One example as a rough guide, when an object is 10mm or more in height it can become a trip hazard. The level of toe clearance is reduced significantly in older people or people with disabilities	HSE (2010)
People who are unable to use the stairs independently are at increased risk of falling on stairs	Kalin et al (2002)
Lack of appropriate adaptations, walking aids, stair rails and grab rails can increase the risk of falling	Bateni et al (2004)
Inappropriate furniture height	Oliver et al (2004); NPSA (2005)
Space and adaptations in the home	Cryer & Patel (2001)
Reduced lighting can impede transfers and cause some people to fall	Jensen et al (2002)

TABLE 13.3 BEHAVIOURAL

Risk factor	Reference
Fear of falling and lack of confidence. Someone who has had three falls or more in the last year or has been injured as a result of a fall may develop more psychological problems	Fisher et al (2000); Zijlstra et al (2007)
Person's perception that they may not be at risk of falling	Ballinger & Payne (2002); Yardley et al (2006)
People with cognitive impairment can increase the risk of falls	Brennan et al (2005)
Certain mental health conditions can increase the risk of falls, eg dementia	Help the Aged (2004)
A person admitted to a new environment is at increased risk of falls	Tinetti (2003)
A person prescribed an ambulatory aid, eg a frame, may not be aware how to use the frame correctly and subsequently increase their risk of falling	Bateni et al (2004)
The level of exercise is linked to falls. Organisations that encourage their occupants to take part in activities and exercise can increase their co-ordination, muscle strength and flexibility – a low level of exercise is linked to a higher risk of falls	Day et al (2002)
Wearing inappropriate footwear can increase the risk of falls, eg slippers, ill fitting shoes or shoes without fixation	Sherrington et al (2003)

The prevention and management of falls

The prevention and management of falls, particularly in older people, is a key government priority. Given that falls can usually be considered a foreseeable event, and given the costs potentially associated with falls, the key priority must be the development and implementation of falls prevention strategies informed through appropriate generic and person specific multifactorial risk assessment (Department of Health (DH) 2001, 2007).

Organisations should start by investigating their falls management systems. Sturman & Hancock (2009) investigated falls management systems using a failure mode effects analysis (FMEA). This is a process designed to identify potential problems before they actually occur and action points to manage any risks identified.

Organisations should ensure they have a falls strategy or policy to manage falls risks and interventions (DH 2001, 2007). The policy should be balanced and acknowledge the duty of care workers have in protecting both themselves and the recipient of care from injury.

Organisations should refrain from blanket "no intervention" systems and should focus on risk management strategies to reduce the risk of falls in the first place. Strategies should focus on multifactorial risk assessment (Cochrane Review 2010), the use of assistive technology, eg use of low-level beds, caring for people on a mattress on the floor, use of wrist or necklace pendant alarms, mattress or seating alarms and tumble/crash mats to reduce the impact of falls.

A person specific risk assessment should be carried out in respect of persons potentially at risk of falls that takes account of the intrinsic, extrinsic and behavioural risk factors detailed above, which may place the person at higher risk of falls. Falls risk assessments and falls scores have been the subject of systematic literature reviews (Oliver et al 2004). Tools by Morse (1997) and Stratify (Smith, Forster & Young 2006) have been validated for use outside of their original study. Organisations should defer away from numerical score assessments and follow an assessment of risks and action plans to reduce identified risks (Sturman 2008).

The aim of the risk assessment is to identify the risks and implement reasonably practicable control measures aimed at reducing the risk of the person falling in the first place, thus reducing the risk that handlers will be involved in a situation that might involve intervening in a falls situation. Organisations should address falls management issues within their moving and handling training or as a separate course. Training and risk management strategies should include the following (Cochrane Review 2010; Sturman 2008):

- Use of assistive technology to reduce falls, eg use of low-level profiling beds, tumble or crash mats, mattress, seating alarms and different methods of person alarms.
- Implementation of activity and exercise-based programmes in long term care environments.
- Encourage the person being assisted to be as independent as possible but have a chair half way down the corridor so they can rest rather than attempt to walk the entire length of the corridor.

- Consideration should be given to the height of the furniture, eg falls are likely to increase if the bed or chair is too high.
- Consider the person may have a variable level of mobility, eg in the morning may be able to stand and transfer with the help of one handler but in the evening, when fatigued or in more pain, may require assistance from two handlers.
- Consider the person may require a flexible risk assessment of their moving and handling transfers, eg may be able to stand and transfer with walking frame in the morning but may require assistance with a stand aid and transferring sling in the evening.
- The person with mental health diagnosis may require a handler to support them verbally on how to use their ambulatory aid.
- A person who may fatigue quickly may require a handler to follow behind with a wheelchair.
- A person who has a period of bed rest may require physical therapy interventions to increase their muscle power and strength.
- A person who experiences dizzy spells may require the handler to assist them from a sitting to standing position slowly and to allow a few seconds to stand, before proceeding into walking. This gives the person being assisted the opportunity to sit down while they are near the chair rather than during walking.
- Insertion of a pacemaker can reduce falls in people with frequent falls associated with carotid sinus hypersensitivity, a condition which may result in changes in blood pressure or heart rate.
- How carers can support people with the use of their ambulatory aid.
- Supporting and assisting a person with gait or balance problems.
- Exercise programmes may target strength, balance, flexibility, or endurance. Programmes that contain two or more of these components reduce rate of falls and number of people falling.
- Some medications increase the risk of falling. Ensuring that medications are reviewed and adjusted may be effective in reducing falls.
- Gradual withdrawal from some types of drugs for improving sleep, reducing anxiety and treating depression has been shown to reduce falls.
- Cataract surgery reduces falls in people having the operation on the first affected eye.
- Strategies and techniques to manage a falling and fallen person.

Case law

In *Brown v East Midlothian NHS Trust (2000)*, an auxiliary nurse working on a rehabilitation ward for older people sought damages for a back injury when she tried to stop a patient falling. The court was satisfied that the trust had provided appropriate training, which included discussions on how to manage a falling person. The court accepted that practical demonstrations of manoeuvres to manage a falling person were not essential because of the difficulties of recreating a true falling scenario. The court acknowledged that theoretical and pictorial discussions regarding systems to manage the falling person were sufficient for organisations and felt it was not practical to practise techniques of how to assist a falling person to the floor.

In the case of *Fleming v Stirling City Council (2000)*, a care assistant working in a residential home sought damages for a back injury after trying to stop a person falling. The person had attempted to stand and fell sideways. The court found the employer to be in breach of the *Manual Handling Operations Regulations 1992* because they had failed to assess people who were at risk of falls. The court concluded that the defendant should have undertaken an assessment of falls risk because it is a foreseeable event. The court also recommended the implementation of safe systems of work to reduce injury to employees.

In *Dockerty v Stockton-on-Tees Borough Council (2006)*, a home care assistant sought damages after an elderly person, being assisted by her son, relaxed and fell onto the carer. The court found the employer had a defective policy because it stated employees should allow a person to fall. The court felt that the organisation's policy and training failed to recognise the human desire of employees wanting to assist people in receipt of care. The court emphasised that neither training nor policies should be aimed at eliminating the desire to care.

A case in 2008 found Suffolk Coastal PCT (Thompsons 2008) had failed to provide appropriate training for an employee who had been injured while assisting a colleague to transfer an elderly person with dementia. The claimant and her colleague were using a handling belt to transfer the patient from a bed to chair. During the transfer, the patient fell on top of the claimant, causing her to suffer a back injury. The court felt the incident could have been avoided through identifying the risks and appropriate moving and handling training.

In all four cases above, the court acknowledged that it is not appropriate for organisations to adopt a no-intervention policy and to advise employees not to intervene and simply do nothing. The judgements acknowledged the importance to organisations of having a falling intervention policy or guidance that acknowledges the human nature to prevent harm to people in receipt of care. They all recommended organisations should include training on how to manage falls risks through risk assessment and employees should be instructed on how to assist a falling person as safely as reasonably practicable (Task 13.1). Including pictures of poor practices was also recommended because they will clearly explain the consequences of using the wrong practices. Figs 13.2-13.5 are examples of high risk practices.

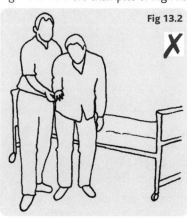

Fig 13.2

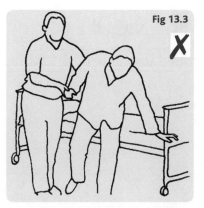

Fig 13.3

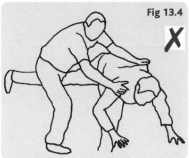

Fig 13.4

Fig 13.5

Conclusion

This chapter has identified falls have significant social and financial costs to health and social organisations. There is evidence that falls can contribute to increased mortality and morbidity and a consequence of not managing falls can have serious injury risks to individuals. Without appropriate management and risk assessment strategies, employees are also at risk of musculoskeletal injuries.

Organisations have a duty of care and health and safety responsibility to reduce the risk of injury to both employees and to those receiving care and treatment. This chapter recommends organisations undertake a multifactorial risk assessment for people at risk of falls. The emphasis of the risk assessment is to identify potential contributory factors and actions to reduce the person from falling.

The chapter also has tried to acknowledge the moral duty organisations and employees have in reducing the risk of injuries to the people in their care. There is still no definitive answer as to whether you should or should not intervene with a falling person. However, there is much evidence to support that there are more serious consequences to the person sustained by not managing falls risks, compared to the number of employee injuries. It is time organisations and individuals considered morally the real risks to people in their care and implement strategies to reduce the risk of falls.

PRACTICAL TECHNIQUES

Task 13.1 Controlled lowering of the falling person

Person ability criteria
The person should at least be either fully able to weight bear or partially weight bear.

Description
- Release the hold of the person and move behind the person (Task 13.1a).
- Once behind the person, have one foot in front of the other and form a stable base with the front knee bent more than the back knee (Task 13.1b and c).
- With both hands open, grasp the person by holding onto their trunk, near their hips.
- Allow the person to slide down the front leg until they are lowered safely to the floor (Task 13.1d).
- Handler should avoid flexing their back too much and end up kneeling behind the person (Task 13.1e and f).

Perceived exertion for the handler
- As the handler bends their knee, the person may put all of their weight onto the handler's leg, causing a risk of musculoskeletal injury.
- During the move, the handler will be taking the majority of the person's weight.

Comfort for the person
- Should be comfortable for the person.
- A manual handling risk assessment must be completed that is specific to the person and handlers.

Skill level of handler
- High level of skill and fitness is required.
- Staff should receive theoretical training on when it is appropriate to intervene.

Evidence
- Sturman (2008) recommends robust risk assessment, training and technique will only work in a minority of situations.
- Betts & Mowbray in Smith (2005) found the technique to be high risk and recommends risk assessment specific to person and handler.
- Derbyshire Interagency Group (DIAG) (2001) recommends handlers bend their knees for technique and to grasp the person by their trunk.

Dangers/precautions
- Many authors believe this is an unsafe practice due to the risk of catching a falling person, (DIAG 2001; Betts & Mowbray in Smith 2005; Sturman 2008). This technique focuses on a controlled descent to the floor rather than catching the falling person.
- The risk of injury will increase with the weight of the falling person.
- Sturman (2008) argued that if you have your hands on the falling person at the time of the fall that the handler has contact and therefore would not be catching the person.
- This technique is likely to be used only on rare occasions and does require robust risk assessment of the person's level of dependency and the handler's level of fitness.

- There is risk the handler will be taking the majority of the person's weight during the move.
- There is a risk the person may grab the handler's arms.

Task 13.1a

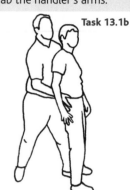

Task 13.1b

Task 13.1c

Task 13.1d

Task 13.1e

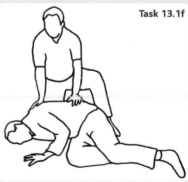

Task 13.1f

- There is a risk the handler may lose their balance.
- Before undertaking the task, it is recommended that organisations consider the following:
  - Does the person have a similar stature to the handler?
  - Is the person smaller than the handler?

A SYSTEMS APPROACH TO THE PREVENTION AND MANAGEMENT OF FALLS   239

- Does the handler have a hold of the person that can easily be released so they can move behind?
- Is the person falling towards the handler?
- Is the handler able to slide the person towards the floor?

- Consider whether the handler has any current or previous history of musculoskeletal disorders.
- Consider whether the handler is likely to be pregnant.

Evidence review

Technique	REBA	Activity	Comfort	FIM	Mobility gallery	Skill level	Comments
Task 13.1 – Controlled lowering of the falling person							
Task 13.1d	9	1		6-7	A/B	Expert	

Task 13.2 Allowing a person to fall – redirecting the fall

Person ability criteria
The person may be partially or fully weight bearing. The person may have some mental health problems, eg not aware of immediate dangers and require redirection to reduce risk of harm.

Description
- This technique would be used when the handler is in close proximity to the person and has physical contact or no contact at the time of the fall and when the person is falling away from the handler (DIAG 2001).
- As the person falls, if the handler has contact at the time of the fall, the handler would immediately release their grasp and move away from the falling person to allow them to fall towards the floor.
- If the person is falling towards a dangerous situation, eg onto a busy road, the handler should attempt to redirect the fall away from the road.

- If the person is transferring between surfaces, eg chair to bed and chair to chair and their legs give way, it may be possible for the handler to redirect the fall by gently pushing the person onto the bed or the chair.
- The handler must try to move obstacles out of the way of the falling person.

Perceived exertion for the handler
- Little physical effort is required to redirect the fall.

Comfort for the person
- The handler needs to be aware of the consequence of injury risk, allowing a person to fall onto furniture or a busy road.
- Injuries to the falling person are likely (*The Guide to The Handling of People* 5th edition (Smith (ed), *HOP5* 2005).
- A manual handling risk assessment must be completed that is specific to the person and handlers.

Task 13.3 Redirecting a falling person on the stairs

Person ability criteria
The person should be able to weight bear and would usually be undertaking stair activity through a rehabilitation programme with therapeutic support. Some recipients of personal budgets may ask their personal assistant to escort them to ascend and descend stairs.

Description
- There may be some occasions where a handler is expected to assist or support a person undertaking an ambulatory assessment on the stairs.
- If the person falls on the stairs or steps, it may be possible for the handler to redirect the person's fall towards the higher stair/step (Task 13.3b and c). **In Task 13.3b and c the handler is in front of the person being assisted.**
- If the handler is following the person up the stairs, the handler may be able to use their body weight to push the person down a wall or onto the banister (Task 13.3a). If there is a second banister on the left side, it would be preferable for the handler to hold onto it for support.
- The handler would not be standing directly behind the person (Task 13.3a).
- If the handler was in front of the person assisting a descent and the person fell towards the handler, the handler could stretch out an arm and use their body to lean forward, pushing the person back onto the step (Task 13.3b and c).

Comfort for the person
- Injuries to the person are likely.
- Severity of injury risk is significantly reduced through intervention.
- A manual handling risk assessment must be completed that is specific to the person and handlers.

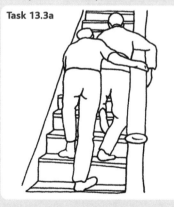

Task 13.3a

13 A systems approach to the prevention and management of falls

© BackCare

Task 13.3b

Task 13.3c

Skill level of the handler
- The handler needs to assess the situation quickly.
- The handler should be skilled and an expert in assisting ambulant person to ascend and descend the stairs.

Evidence available
Smith (Smith (ed), *HOP5* 2005) identified that it may be possible to redirect falls on stairs and steps.

Dangers/precautions
- The banister or wall will need to be of solid construction otherwise the person's weight could break the banister/wall.
- There is a risk the person could fall onto the handler.
- The handler would need to ascertain there is sufficient space for both people to use the stairs.
- Standing immediately in front of or behind the person could increase the risk of musculoskeletal injury.

Evidence review

Technique	REBA	Activity	Comfort	FIM	Mobility gallery	Skill level	Comments
Task 13.3 – Redirecting a falling person on the stairs							
Task 13.3c	12	1	5	6/7	A/B	Competent	

Task 13.4 Assisting people who have fallen

When a person has fallen the handler should always check for the following:
- Airway, breathing and circulation.
- Check for injuries, bruising, possible fractures, pain and behaviour. If handlers are not competent in checking for fractures and injuries, they should always ask for medical assistance.
- If there was an obvious reason for the fall.
- If there is any doubt, the person should be left safe on the floor and handlers should request medical assistance.

- The environment for obstacles and space.
- The number of handlers required for the task.
- If the handler has been trained to undertake the task. Many of these tasks are high risk procedures and should not be undertaken without training.

The employer has a responsibility to ensure the health and safety of their employees. All of these tasks should be assessed and procedures implemented to reduce the risk of injury to all employees.

Task 13.5 Instructing a person to get up from the floor, using minimal supervision (backward chaining)

Person ability criteria
- Person being verbally instructed should have the physical ability to be able to roll onto their side and be able to kneel.
- The person should also be compliant and be able to follow instructions.
- This task is scored FIM 7.

Description
- Position a chair at the head end of the fallen person.

- Verbally support the person to bend their knees up and to bring one arm across their chest (Task 13.5a).
- Ask the person to move the other arm away from the body (Task 13.5b).
- Ask the person to roll onto their side into side lying (Task 13.5c).
- Once on the side, ask the person to bring their arm over their body until the hand is flat on the floor (Task 13.5c).
- Support the person to push up on their hand and at the same time push up on their forearm that is resting on the

floor until they are in half sitting (Task 13.5d).
- Support the person to keep pushing up until they end up on all fours until they are facing the chair (Task 13.5e).

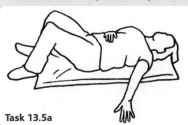

Task 13.5a

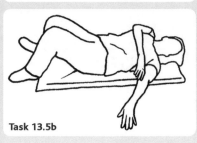

Task 13.5b

Task 13.5c

Task 13.5d

Task 13.5e

Task 13.5f

- Ask the person to position lower arms onto the chair and ask them to lean onto the seat of the chair (Task 13.5f).
- Ask the person to raise their stronger leg and place the foot flat onto the floor (Task 13.5g).

- Push up to straighten legs and turn to sit onto the chair (Task 13.5h).

Perceived exertion for the handler
- There would be little exertion for the handler.

Comfort for the person
- People with knee and hip problems may find the task difficult and uncomfortable.
- A manual handling risk assessment must be completed that is specific to the person and handlers.

Skill level of handler
- The handler needs to be able to instruct the person confidently.

Task 13.5g 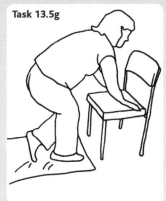 Task 13.5h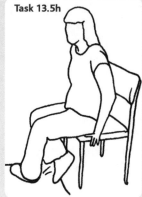

Evidence
- Smith (Smith (ed), *HOP5* 2005) identifies the use of one chair to assist a fallen person up from the floor.

Dangers
- If assessed inappropriately, the person may lose their balance.

Further options
Option 1
- For a taller person, the handler could position the chair to the side of the kneeling person (Task 13.5i).
- The person holds the arm or seat with their nearest hand (Task 13.5j).
- The person raises their nearest leg so that their foot is flat on the floor (Task 13.5k).
- The person slides their bottom onto the chair (Task 13.5l).

Task 13.5i  Task 13.5j

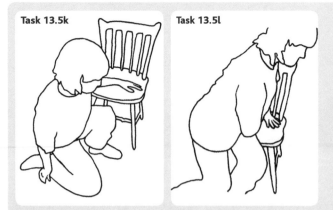

Task 13.5k   Task 13.5l

Task 13.6 Instructing a person to get up from the floor, using minimal supervision and two chairs

Person ability criteria
The person should be able to follow instructions and do the majority of the task without physical intervention from handlers.

Description
- Position a chair at the head end of the fallen person. Ask the person to bend their knees and to roll into side lying (Task 13.6a).
- Ask the person to bring one arm over the chest until hand is flat on the floor.
- Push up with one hand and lower arm into side sitting, as in task 13.5.
- Face the chair and position forearms onto the chair (Task 13.6b).
- Ask the person to bend one knee and place a foot flat onto the floor (Task 13.6c).
- At the same time, ask the person to push up on their forearms and hands.
- The handler can assist by placing a second chair behind the person, under their hips (Task 13.6d).
- The person should be encouraged to sit backwards in the chair.

Perceived exertion for the handler
- There is no physical exertion for the handler.

Comfort for the person
- This task is recommended for people who are unable to kneel (Smith (ed), *HOP5* 2005).
- A manual handling risk assessment must be completed that is specific to the person and handlers.

Skill level of handler
- The handler needs to be able to instruct the person confidently.

Evidence available
- Smith (Smith (ed), *HOP5* 2005) recommends this task when people are unable to kneel or turn around to sit on one chair.

Dangers/precautions
- If inappropriately assessed, the client could lose their balance.

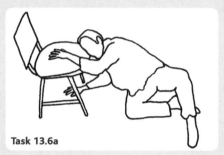

Task 13.6a

Task 13.6b

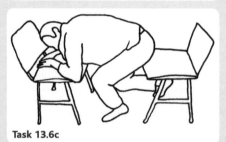

Task 13.6c

Task 13.6d

Evidence review

Technique	REBA	Activity	Comfort	FIM	Mobility gallery	Skill level	Comments
Task 13.6 – Instructing a person to get up from the floor, using minimal supervision and two chairs							
Task 13.6a			8	5	B	Advanced beginner	No REBA no assistance

Task 13.7 Rolling a person on the floor to position handling equipment

Person ability criteria
- The person may be able to assist with the transfer, eg assist with turning.
- The person may not be able to assist with the transfer and require full assistance from handlers.

Description
- Ask or assist the person to position the furthest arm across the chest.
- At the same time ask or assist the person to bend one or both knees, ensuring the feet are flat on the floor.
- Bring the nearest arm away from the body and leave flat on the floor, to prevent the person from rolling onto their arm or hand.
- Ask the person to turn their head and face the direction of the turn.
- One handler kneels down on both knees and starts off with their heels off the buttocks, high kneeling (Task 13.7a).
- At the same time, the handler holds the person's hip and shoulder (Task 13.7a).
- The handler brings the hips and shoulders over as they sit back onto their heels, low kneeling (Task 13.7b).
- Once the equipment, ie sling has been fitted, roll the person onto their back and repeat on the other side (Task 13.7c and d).

Perceived exertion for the handler
- The handler should be fit and able to work in low-level and high-level kneeling.

Comfort for the person
- The person will require a pillow or cushion to protect their head.
- If the person has fallen on a hard surface, they will find the transfer uncomfortable.
- A manual handling risk assessment must be completed that is specific to the person and handlers.

Skill level of handler
- The handler should be physically fit and must be able to work in high and low kneeling positions.
- Some handlers with high body mass index may not be able to reach the person's hip and shoulder and transfer their weight from high kneeling to low kneeling.

Evidence
- Smith (Smith (ed), *HOP5* 2005).

Dangers/precautions
- This method of rolling should not be used for people with spinal problems.
- Some people who are confused and/or resist movement will not suit this technique.

- If the person has a large body mass index, it may be difficult for the handler to reach the hip and shoulder.
- The person should always be rolled towards the handler and not pushed away from the handler.

Task 13.7a

Task 13.7b

Task 13.7c

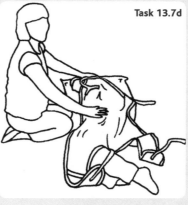

Task 13.7d

Task 13.8 Management of a person who has fallen in a confined space

Person ability criteria
- The person may be able to assist with transfer.
- The person may not be able to assist with the transfer.
- Useful technique where there is insufficient space for the person to roll over and get up onto all fours, for tasks 13.5 and 13.6.

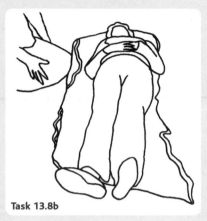

Task 13.8b

Description
- After completing an assessment of the person and the environment, the handler should assist the person to position furthest arm across the chest and bring the nearest arm away from the body, to prevent entrapment during turning.
- The handler starts in high kneeling and supports the fallen person's hip and shoulder.
- The person should be rolled onto their side until the handler ends in low kneeling.
- Once the person is on their side the second handler should roll two full length slide sheets or a tubular slide sheet and position it lengthways and half under the rolled person (Task 13.8a).
- Lower the person and repeat on other side (Task 13.8b).
- One handler may be required to support the person's head.
- Depending on the assessment, one or two handlers should kneel in high kneeling at one end of the fallen person, nearest the open space (Task 13.8c and d).
- One handler should be responsible for co-ordinating the move.
- The handlers should hold the top layer of the slide sheet and transfer their weight until they end up in low sitting (Task 13.8e).
- This should be repeated in small movements until the person has been slid into a larger space.
- One handler should support the person's head for the duration of transfer, or protect the head with a pillow on top of the slide sheet (Task 13.8f).
- Once the person has been transferred to the open area, the handlers should assess whether the person can get up independently, or requires assistance with an inflatable cushion or hoist.

Task 13.8c

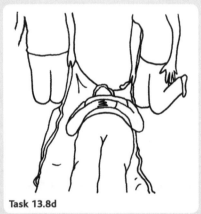

Task 13.8d

Task 13.8e

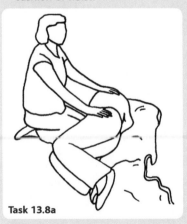

Task 13.8a

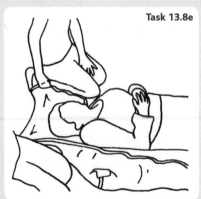

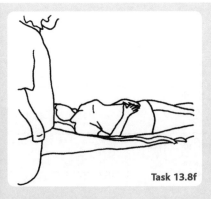

Task 13.8f

Further options

Option 1

- Alternatively, the handlers can use extension handles attached to the top slide sheet.
- One person should be responsible for co-ordinating the move.
- The handlers start in walking stance position with all their weight on the front leg (Task 13.8g).
- On a given signal, the handlers should transfer their weight to the back leg (Task 13.8h).
- As the weight is transferred, the slide sheet will move.
- The technique is repeated until the person has been moved to a larger area.

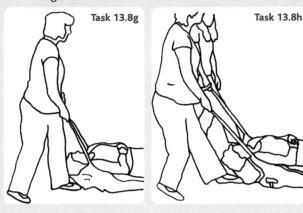

Task 13.8g   Task 13.8h

Option 2

- Alternatively, handlers can fold two full length slide sheets and position these under the head end or foot end of the person (Task 13.8i).
- Handlers grasp the roll of slide sheet and start in high kneeling position (Task 13.8i).
- The handlers transfer their weight into low kneeling and at the same time the slide sheets unravel down the person's body (Task 13.8j and k).
- This is repeated until the slide sheets are flat under the person.

Task 13.8i

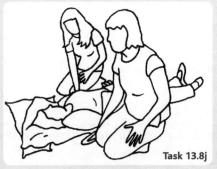

Task 13.8j

Task 13.8k

Perceived exertion for the handler

- Some people may fall in a confined area, eg adjacent to a toilet. This may result in handlers working in compromised postures.
- The person may require head support and the handler may be required to sit on furniture, bath or toilet lid, which could cause some flexion or rotation of the lumbar spine.

Comfort for the person

- Use option 2 if the person is unable to turn from side to side.
- A manual handling risk assessment must be completed that is specific to the person and handlers.

Skill level of handler

- The handlers should be fit to undertake task and be able to work in confined areas.
- The handlers should be able to work in low level and high level kneeling.
- The handlers should receive instruction on how to undertake task safely.

Evidence available

- Smith (Smith (ed), *HOP5* 2005).
- Resuscitation Council (UK) (2009).

Dangers/precautions

- Sometimes people fall in a confined space and are unable to get up independently or with verbal prompting.
- People are likely to fall adjacent to a bed, in a small room, eg within a residential home environment or become wedged by a toilet or bath.
- The handlers using option 2 may require larger working space because they would be kneeling either side of the person during the positioning of the slide sheets.

Evidence review

Technique	REBA	Activity	Comfort	FIM	Mobility gallery	Skill level	Comments
Task 13.8 – Management of a person who has fallen in a confined space							
Task 13.8d	8	1	6	1-2	C-E	Advanced beginner	

Task 13.9 Use of the inflatable cushion without back rest to assist a person up from the floor

Person ability criteria
- This technique is useful when a person is unable to roll onto their knees for tasks 13.5 and 13.6.
- The person should be compliant and able partly to assist with the transfer, eg by shuffling onto cushion, rolling onto cushion or bridging.
- When using the cushion without a back rest the person should have sitting balance and good trunk control.

Description
- The handlers should undertake a risk assessment of the person and the environment.
- Ask the person if they are able to shuffle their hips onto the cushion or lift their bottom up for the cushion to be positioned under the bottom (Task 13.9a and b).
- If the person is unable to assist, one handler should roll the person onto their side while the second handler rolls the pipe free side of cushion and positions it under the person's bottom (Task 13.9b).
- Repeat on other side and ensure the pipes are not entrapped under the person (Task 13.9c).
- Ask the person if they are able to sit themselves up.
- Alternatively, both handlers should assist the person from supine to sitting.
- Handlers should kneel on either side of the person and use their inside arm to grasp the person's elbow.
- The person should also have a secure hold of the handler's elbow.
- On a given signal, the handlers should transfer their weight from high kneeling into low kneeling until the person is in a sitting position (Task 13.9d and e).
- One person should support the sitting person by low kneeling behind the person and placing their hands onto the person's shoulders (Task 13.9f).
- The second handler should secure the pipes, according to manufacturer's instructions, to the battery pack.
- Inflate the cushion until the person is in a position to stand or transfer safely (Task 13.9g).

Task 13.9b

Task 13.9c

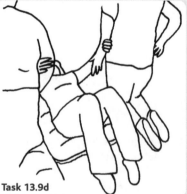

Task 13.9d

Task 13.9a

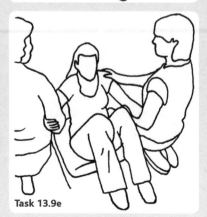

Task 13.9e

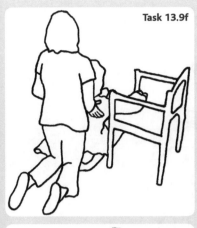

Task 13.9f

Task 13.9i

Task 13.9g

Further options
Option 1
- If the person resists rolling to position the cushion, a folded flat or small tubular slide sheet should be positioned half under the person's bottom and half on top of the cushion (Task 13.9h).
- The person should be encouraged to slide themselves onto the cushion (Task 13.9i).
- The slide sheet must be removed before the cushion is inflated.
- The person may find the task easier if they are assisted into sitting before sliding their bottom onto the cushion.

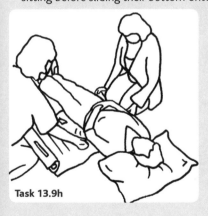

Task 13.9h

Perceived exertion for the handler
- The handlers should be of good fitness and be able to kneel in high and low kneeling positions.

Comfort for the person
- During the transfer, the person's head should be protected with either a pillow or cushion.
- During cushion inflation, the person should be supported by 1-2 handlers to ensure they do not fall off the cushion.
- A manual handling risk assessment must be completed that is specific to the person and handlers.

Skill level of handler
- The handler should be fit and able to work in kneeling positions.
- The handler should receive training on equipment use.

Evidence
Smith (Smith (ed), *HOP5* 2005) has guidance on how to use cushion without integral back rest.

Dangers/precautions
- The handlers may be tempted to pull the person into a sitting position.
- The person being assisted may also pull on the handlers.
- If the handlers find the level of assistance physically overloading they should stop the task immediately and decide if transfer with a hoist is more appropriate.
- Some people may find the cushion inflation frightening.
- Requires individual risk assessment to identify suitability of person that could use the equipment.
- If the person is not supported during the cushion inflation they could fall off.

Evidence review

Technique	REBA	Activity	Comfort	FIM	Mobility gallery	Skill level	Comments
Task 13.9 – Use of the inflatable cushion without back rest to assist a person up from the floor							
Task 13.9e	10	1	7	4	B	Competent	

Task 13.10 Use of an inflatable cushion (with integral back rest) to assist a person up from the floor

Person ability criteria

- The inflatable cushion with integral back rest is very useful for people who have behavioural problems and may not be fully compliant.
- The cushion would also support people who may have reduced sitting balance.

Description

- Wherever possible ask the person to shuffle onto the cushion.
- There are two other alternatives that can be used to assist the person onto the cushion. In Task 13.10a, the handler has positioned a tubular slide sheet under the person and is gently pushing the person onto the cushion. This can be completed by one or two handlers, as in Task 13.10b.
- Alternatively, the handlers could fit two flat, long slide sheets under the person (Task 13.10c).
- The handlers can position extension handles on the top sheet and one person can co-ordinate the move.
- Both handlers should start off with one foot in front and the knee bent (Task 13.10d).
- The handlers should transfer their weight so their weight ends up on the back leg (Task 13.10e).
- At the same time the person will slide.
- The technique should be repeated until the person is flat on the cushion.
- Once the person is safely onto the cushion, the slide sheets must be removed before inflating the cushion.
- The handler should inflate part of the back rest first (Task 13.10f).
- The handler should continue to support the person until the cushion is fully inflated.
- Once the cushion is at the desired height, the back rest can be fully inflated (Task 13.10g).
- Once the cushion is fully inflated, the handlers can stand either side of the cushion and assist the person to transfer onto a seat or into a standing position.

Task 13.10b

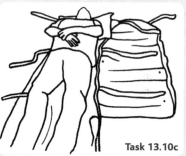

Task 13.10c

Task 13.10d

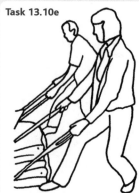

Task 13.10e

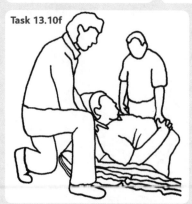

Task 13.10f

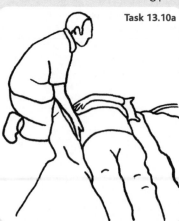

Task 13.10a

Task 13.10g

Perceived exertion for the handler
- The handlers should be of good fitness and be able to kneel in high and low kneeling positions.

Comfort for the person
- During the transfer, the person's head should be protected with either a pillow or cushion.
- During cushion inflation, the person should be supported by 1-2 handlers to ensure they do not fall off the cushion.

- A manual handling risk assessment must be completed that is specific to the person and handlers.

Skill level of handler
- The handlers should be of good fitness and be able to kneel in high and low kneeling positions.
- The handler should be fit and able to work in kneeling positions.
- The handler should receive training on equipment use.

Evidence
- Smith (Smith (ed), *HOP5* 2005) has guidance on how to use cushion with integral back rest.

Dangers/precautions
- Some people may find the cushion inflation frightening.
- Requires individual risk assessment to identify suitability of person who could use the equipment.
- If the person is not supported during the cushion inflation they could fall off.
- Equipment is bulky and may not fit in confined areas.

Evidence review

Technique	REBA	Activity	Comfort	FIM	Mobility gallery	Skill level	Comments
Task 13.10 – Use of an inflatable cushion (with integral back rest) to assist a person up from the floor							
Task 13.10e	4	0	6	3	D	Competent	

Task 13.11 Hoisting from the floor

If a fallen person is unable to get up independently or with the aid of an inflatable cushion, it may be necessary to use a hoist to lift from the floor (see chapter 11).

References

Ballinger, C & Payne, S (2002), The construction of the risk of falling among and by older people. *Ageing & Society*, **22**, 305-324.

Bateni, H, Heung, E, Zettel, J, Mcllory, W & Maki, B (2004), Can use of walkers or canes impede lateral compensatory stepping movements? *Gait & Posture*, **20**, 74-83.

Betts, M & Mowbray, C, in Smith, J (ed) (2005), *The Guide to The Handling of People* 5th edition 2005, BackCare.

Brennan, M, Horowitz, A & Ya-Ping, S (2005), Dual Sensory Loss and its impact on everyday competence. *The Gerontologist*, **45**, 337-346.

Brown v East Midlothian NHS Trust (2000), SLT 342, Outer House, Court of Session, Scotland.

Cameron, ID, Murray, GR, Gillespie, LD, Robertson, MC, Hill, KD, Cumming, RG & Kerse, N (2009), *Interventions for preventing falls in older people in nursing care facilities and hospitals* (Review), The Cochrane Collaboration.

Cochrane Review (2010), Interventions for preventing falls in older people living in the community. *Cochrane Database of Systematic Reviews 2009*, Issue **2**. Art. No: CD007146. DOI: 10.1002/14651858.CD007146.pub2

College of Occupational Therapists (2006), *Falls Management Guidance*. London. ISBN 0-9546491-8-4.

Covinsky, K, Kahana, E, Kahana, B, Kercher, K, Schumacher, J & Justice, A (2001), History and mobility exam index to identify community-dwelling elderly persons at risk of falling. *Journal of Gerontology and Biological Medical Science*, **56**. 253-259.

Cryer, C & Patel, S (2001), Falls, fragility and fractures. The case for and strategies to implement a joint health improvement and modernisation plan for falls and osteoporosis. *National Service Framework for Older People*. Available at www.unicef-icdc.org/publications/pdf/repcard2e.pdf. Viewed 20 June 2007.

Day, L, Fildes, B, Gordon, I, Fitzharri, M, Flamer, H & Lord, S (2002), Randomised factorial trial of falls prevention among older people living in their own homes. *British Medical Journal*, **325**, 128.

Department of Health (2001, amended 2007), *National Service Framework for Older People*. Available from www.dh.gov.uk/en/Publicationsandstatistics/Publications/PublicationsPolicyAndGuidance/DH_4003066

Department of Trade and Industry (2007), *Research on the pattern and trends in home accidents*. Government consumer safety research. www.berr.gov.uk/files/file21453.pdf

Derbyshire Interagency Group (DIAG) (2001), Care Handling for People in Hospitals, Community and Educational Settings. A code of practice.

Dockerty v Stockton-on-Tees Borough Council (2006). Available from Thompson Solicitors www.thompson.co.uk Viewed 08/01/2007, Fisher *et al* 2000. www.thompsons.law.co.uk/ltext/lb0506-catching-falling-patient.htm

Fisher, A, Davies, M, McLean, A & Le-Couter, D (2005), Epidemiology of falls in elderly semi-independent residents in residential care. *Australasian journal on Ageing*, **24** (2), 98-102.

Fleming v Stirling City Council (2000), GWD 13-499. Outer House, Court of Session. Scotland.

Fray, M (2003), Worked example for catching a falling body. Course work, Module 4. Postgraduate Diploma in Back Care Management, Loughborough University.

Gillespie, L, Gillespie, W, Robertson, M, Lamb, S, Cumming, R & Rowe, B (2001), *Interventions for preventing falls in elderly people* (Review). The Cochrane Collaboration. Available from www.thecochranelibrary.com. Viewed 1 June 2007.

Gillespie, LD, Robertson, MC, Gillespie, WJ, Lamb, SE, Gates, S, Cumming, RG & Rowe, BH (2010), Interventions for preventing falls in older people living in the community. *Cochrane Database of Systematic Reviews 2009*, Issue **2**. Art. No.: CD007146. DOI: 10.1002/14651858.CD007146.pub2

Help the Aged (2004), *Preventing Falls. Don't mention the f-word*.

Help the Aged (2006), *Preventing falls: Managing the risk and effect of falls among older people in care homes*.

HSE (2002), HSE Press release E043:02. www.hse.gov.uk/press/2002/e02043.htm

HSE (2006a), Patient safety and health: Two sides of the same coin. Health and Safety Minister addresses patient safety 2006. www.hse.gov.uk/press/2006/e06011.htm

HSE (2006b), Public sector programme 2006/07 musculoskeletal disorders (MSD) in the health services, SIM 07/2006/05

HSE (2007), What causes slips and trips?

HSE (2010), Shattered Lives Campaign

HSE (2010b), RIDDOR injuries in care homes 2008-2009. Unpublished statistics.

Hignett, S & Sands, G (2009), Patient safety in moving and handling activities. Proceedings of the 17th Triennial Congress of the International Ergonomics Association Beijing, China, 9-14 August 2009.

Jensen, J, Lundin-Olsson, L, Nyberg, L & Gustafson, Y (2002), Falls among frail older people in residential care. *Scandinavian Journal of Public Health*, **30** (1), 54-61.

Kalin, K, Jensen, J, Lundin-Ollson, L, Nyberg, L & Gustafson, Y (2002), Predisposing and precipitating factors for falls among older people in residential care homes. *Public Health*, **116** (5), 263-271.

Kario, K, Tobin, J, Wolfson, L, Whipple, R, Derby, C, Singh, D, Marantz, P & Wassertheil-Smoller, S (2001), Lower standing systolic blood pressure as a predictor of falls in the elderly: A community prospective study. *Journal of the American College of Cardiology*, **38**, 246-252.

Kroemer, K & Grandjean, E (2003), *Fitting the task to the human: A textbook of occupational ergonomics* (5th edition). Taylor and Francis, London.

Leveille, S, Bena, J, Bandeen-Roche, K, Jones, R, Hochberg, M & Guralnik, J (2002), Musculoskeletal pain and risk for falls in older disabled women living in the community. *Journals of the American Geriatrics Society*, **50** (4), 671-678.

Lord, S, Sherrington, C & Menz, H (2000), *Falls in older people. Risk factors and strategies for prevention*. Cambridge University Press. ISBN 0521589649.

Lord, S & Dayhew, J (2001), Visual risk factors for falls in older people. *Journal of the American Geriatric Society*, **49** (5), 508-515.

Manual Handling Operations Regulations, L23. Health and Safety Executive.

Masud, T & Morris, R (2001), Epidemiology of falls. Age and Ageing, 30-S4: 3-7.

Menz, H, Morris, M & Lord, S (2006), Foot and ankle risk factors in older people: A prospective study. *The Journal of Gerontology Series A: Biological Sciences and Medical Sciences*, **61** (8): 866-870.

Morse, J (1997), *Preventing patient falls*, Thousand Oaks, Sage.

National Institute for Health and Clinical Excellence (2004),

The assessment and prevention of falls in older people. Understanding NICE guidance – information for older people, their families and carers and the public.

National Patient Safety Agency (2005), Bedrails reviewing the evidence. A systematic literature review.

National Patient Safety Agency (2007a), NPSA launches most comprehensive report yet on patient falls in hospitals.

National Patient Safety Agency (2007b), The third report from the patient safety observatory. Slips, trips and falls in hospitals. London.

Oliver, D, Daly, F & Martin, FC (2004), Risk factors and risk assessment tools for falls in hospital in-patients: a systematic review *Age and Ageing*, **33**, 2. 122-30.

Reporting of Injuries, Diseases and Dangerous Occurrences Regulations (RIDDOR) (2005), Health and Safety Executive.

Resuscitation Council (UK) (2009), Guidance for the safer handling during resuscitation in healthcare settings.

Royal College of Physicians (2005), Falls and bone health in older people.

Royal Society for the Prevention of Accidents (2007), Home Safety: Advice and Information: Preventing Accidents.

Rubenstein, L & Josephson, K (2002), The epidemiology of falls and syncope. *Clinical Geriatric Medicine*, **2**, 141-158.

Sherrington, C, Lord, S, Latt, M, Mun-San Kwan, M, Tiedemann, A & Hylton, B (2003), Reliability of Clinical tests of foot and ankle characteristics in older people. *Journal of the American Podiatric Medical Association*, **93** (5), 380-387.

Smith, J (ed) (2005), *The Guide to The Handling of People* 5th edition 2005, BackCare.

Smith, J, Forster, A & Young, J (2006), Use of "Stratify" fall risk assessment in patients recovering from acute stroke. *Age and Ageing*, **35** (2): 138-143.

Steinhoef, P, Diederiks, J, Knottnerus, J, Kester, A & Crebolder, H (2002), A risk model for the prediction of recurrent falls in community-dwelling elderly: A prospective cohort study. *Journal of Clinical Epidemiology*, **55**, 1088-1094.

Sterling, D, O'Connor, J & Bonadies, J (2001), Geriatric falls. Injury severity is high and disproportionate to mechanism. *Journal of Trauma injury, Infection and Critical Care*, **50** (1), 116-119.

Sturman, M (2008), Are falls a problem for local authorities? MSc dissertation, unpublished, Loughborough University.

Sturman, M & Hancock, CP (2009), Analysing falls management using failure mode effect analysis. *Health Care Risk Report*, February 2009, pp17-19.

Thompsons (2008), *Thompsons v Suffolk Coastal PCT*. Available from www.thompsons.law.co.uk/ntext/back-injury-better-training.htm

Tinetti, M, Speechley, M & Ginter, S (1998), Risk factors for falls among elderly persons living in the community. *New England Journal of Medicine*, **319**, 1701-1707.

Tinetti, M & Williams, C (2000), Health, functional, and psychological outcomes among older people with dizziness. *Journal of the American Geriatric Society*, **48** (4), 417-421.

Tinetti, M (2003), Preventing falls in elderly persons. *New England Journal of Medicine*, **348**, 42-49.

Tromp, A, Pluijm, S, Smit, J, Deeg, D, Bouter, L & Lips, P (2001), Falls-risk screening test. A prospective study on predictors for falls in the community-dwelling elderly. *Journal of Clinical Epidemiology*, **54** (8), 837-844.

Yardley, L, Bishop, F, Beyer, N, Hauer, K, Kempen, G, Piot-Zieger, C, Todd, C, Cuttlelod, T, Horne, M, Lanta, K & Holt, A (2006), Older people's views of falls-prevention interventions in six European countries, *The Gerontologist*, **46**, 650-660.

Zijilstra, G, Van-Haastregt, G, Eijk, J, Van Rossum, E, Stalenhoef, P & Kempen, G (2007), Prevalence and correlates of fear of falling and associated avoidance activity in the general population of community-living older people. *Age and Ageing*, **36** (3), 304-309.

1

2

3

4

13 A systems approach to the prevention and management of falls

Index